RUNAWAY AMERICA

BENJAMIN FRANKLIN.

Né à Boston, dans la nouvelle Angleterre le 17 Janvier 1706.

RUNAWAY AMERICA

Benjamin Franklin, Slavery, and

the American Revolution

———◆◆◆———

DAVID WALDSTREICHER

〽 HILL AND WANG

A division of Farrar, Straus and Giroux

New York

Hill and Wang
A division of Farrar, Straus and Giroux
19 Union Square West, New York 10003

Copyright © 2004 by David Waldstreicher
All rights reserved
Distributed in Canada by Douglas & McIntyre Ltd.
Printed in the United States of America
First edition, 2004

Library of Congress Cataloging-in-Publication Data
Waldstreicher, David.
    Runaway America : Benjamin Franklin, slavery, and the American Revolution / by
David Waldstreicher.
        p.   cm.
    Includes bibliographical references and index.
    ISBN-13: 978-0-8090-8314-5
    ISBN-10: 0-8090-8314-0 (hc : alk. paper)
    1. Franklin, Benjamin, 1706–1790.   2. Franklin, Benjamin, 1706–1790—
Views on slavery.   3. Slavery—Political aspects—United States—History—
18th century.   4. United States—Politics and government—1775–1783.
5. United States—Politics and government—1783–1789.   6. Liberty—Political
aspects—United States—History—18th century.   7. Statesmen—United States—
Biography.   8. Printers—United States—Biography.   9. Indentured servants—
United States—Biography.   10. Slaveholders—United States—Biography.   I. Title.

E302.6.F8W25 2004
973.3'092—dc22

                                                            2003027916

Designed by Jonathan D. Lippincott

www.fsgbooks.com

1   3   5   7   9   10   8   6   4   2

Frontispiece: Benjamin Franklin, circa 1777. Engraving by Augustin de Saint-Aubin. (Benjamin Franklin Collection, Yale University)

To J.R.
Wherever we run to is home

Contents

claffes, *gentlemen*, *traders*, and *good livers*;
the latter cultivating a fmall eftate of their
own, with their own hands, and the affift-
ance of three or four negroes, and the
former, owners of a large territory, with
three or four or five hundred negroes. Such
poffeffors cannot certainly be deemed indi-
gent; and how greatly would the burdens
of the inhabitants of this ifland be lighten-
ed, were there no parifh-poor nor common beggars to be found in Great-Britain.
The produce of the planters purchafes for
them what others buy with gold and filver;
but even feveral of the colonifts of the rank
of *good livers* have often been feen to pay the
price of a negro with gold. As inftances of
Virginian luxury, I have been affured, that
there are few families there without fome
plate; and that at fome entertainments, the
attendants have appeared almoft as numerous as the guefts. ✱

But we may form a judgement of the general wealth of the colonies from their im-
portations, which from Great-Britain alone,
by their own account, amount to full three
millions *per annum*. If we add another
5   million

The true constitutional means for putting an end to the disputes between Great-Britain and the American colonies (1769), with marginal notes on slaves by Benjamin Franklin. (Rare Books Division, The New York Public Library, Astor, Lenox, and Tilden Foundations)

Preface: Inheritances, or Slavery and the Founders

When Americans think of Benjamin Franklin, they think about freedom. They think of the Founding Fathers and the forging of a nation in which all men are created equal. But when Americans think about their country's eighteenth-century origins, they also, and rightly, think about slavery.

This book tells the story of slavery and freedom's meeting in the life, thought, and politics of the best-known colonist and revolutionary, the "first American." Benjamin Franklin's life, the story goes, shows how in America ordinary persons can rise above their humble origins. Franklin not only did so and wrote about it in his widely read memoir, he helped lead a political revolution that has been credited with making such opportunities possible for later generations. He epitomizes freedom and equality.[1]

I do not come to bury this story, this Benjamin Franklin, so much as to show how it became *the* story, and how the story Franklin told about himself and the Revolution he led made it difficult to see how much American freedom depended on American slavery.

In the wake of the civil rights movement, some of the best scholarship on U.S. history has plumbed the "paradox" of slavery's existence in a nation "conceived in liberty." Historians have rediscovered some of the revolutionaries' own qualms about decrying their own oppression, which they often termed "slavery," at the hands of the British while themselves holding Africans and their descendants in bondage. Winthrop D. Jordan, David Brion Davis, Edmund S. Morgan, and others have depicted how the Revolution emboldened opponents of slavery yet also permitted slaveowners to consolidate their position in the republic with new laws and new justifications—especially, though not for the first or the last time, with racism.[2]

This interpretation has proven as unstable as the paradox it so richly describes. For other tales have needed telling. An emboldened tradition of African American history has pointed out that slaves and free blacks served on both sides of the revolutionary cause. This history certainly fit the paradox of slavery and revolution, but it also made clear that African Americans fought for one kind of freedom, while diverse white colonists fought for a rather different, less inclusive kind of liberty. The rise of antislavery itself may have had less to do with the Founding Fathers' ideals of liberty than with the actions of African Americans as a fifth column, as fugitives, and as crafty negotiators of their own freedom, for during the long revolutionary period America faced as never before the reality of Africans as free Americans. Other scholars have reconsidered the evidence attesting to the postrevolutionary spread of slavery and concluded that the American revolutionaries at best maintained slavery; at worst, the founders hypocritically perpetuated the institution. According to this view, slavery itself, far more than antislavery, became foundational to the American republic.[3]

In response to the foundational slavery argument, we have seen a resurgent defense of the Founding Fathers and their Revolution, a defense that draws selectively on post–civil rights scholarship to make the case for what might be called foundational antislavery, or the idea that the American revolutionaries mainly deserve credit for the beginning of the end of slavery. In Gordon S. Wood's influential and often quoted formulation, the founders are responsible "for all our current egalitarian thinking." Their failures were born more of context than conviction. Old-fashioned in their racism but modern in their denunciations of slavery, the founders deserve our appreciation, not our censure. They anticipated what is best in us; we must not blame them for the sins of an earlier world they did so much to transform.[4]

It has been easier to stress the impact of the Revolution on antislavery than to grapple with the importance of slavery *to* the Revolution.[5] Easier still has been the recent tendency to concede the hypocrisy of certain founders on the slavery question in order to salvage the reputation of others. With the polarization of the debate over slavery and the founders, we have seen the reemergence of Benjamin Franklin,

champion of freedom and opponent of all forms of slavery—a view
first advanced by the aging Franklin himself, then spread vigorously
by nineteenth-century abolitionists eager to ennoble their struggle by
associating it with the Revolution, and kept alive by progressive and
African American scholars, such as W.E.B. Du Bois, in the early
twentieth century. Oddly enough, the antislavery Franklin is claimed
not only by both sides of the "slavery and the founders" debate but also
by those who, wisely enough, try to mediate between them. Joseph J.
Ellis, for example, has emphasized the bad faith of Thomas Jefferson
and James Madison on slavery, only to hold up Franklin's antislavery
credentials—his presidency of the Pennsylvania Abolition Society in
1787 and his prominent signature on a petition presented to the first
federal Congress—as the jewel in the founders' crown. Meanwhile, the
most forthright recent critic of the founders on the slavery question justified his harsh judgment of Jefferson in light of the fact that Franklin
"believed in racial equality." A prominent scholar of race and the law in
U.S. history argued, in an op-ed piece, against the erasure of history involved in a New Orleans school's decision to give up the name of George
Washington because he owned slaves. It is important to remember,
she wrote, that Washington had a better record on slavery than Jefferson, adding that "some contemporaries of Washington like Benjamin
Franklin and John Quincy Adams were against slavery and did not own
slaves."[6]

When Franklin of the 1780s, Washington of the 1790s, and John
Quincy Adams of the 1830s are all conflated to oppose a timeless Jefferson, the notion of founders and foundings departs history and enters the
realm of myth. Certainly the notion of a founding "generation" means
very little if it stretches the entire fifty-nine years from the Declaration of
Independence to the *Amistad* case and if, in what seems a curious sort of
Founding Grandfather complex, what matters most is what great men did
in their old age when they were already known to be great. Avoid both
mythologizing traps, and assumptions can be reversed. For example, one
could argue that Jefferson did more to undermine slavery during the era
of the American Revolution than did Franklin. While the Pennsylvanian
was busy blaming the British for slavery, the Virginian pushed for the
end of the slave trade and gradual emancipation in Virginia and almost
succeeded in closing the Northwest Territories to slaveowners. Insofar as
they acted as contemporaries, Franklin and Jefferson converged in the

writing of the original draft Declaration, with its simultaneous indictment of slavery, blame of England, and outrage at the king's enlistment
of slaves. Historical reality, it seems, is more complicated than any good
founder–bad founder morality play.

Events after 1776, of course, do matter, as do the final acts of great
lives. Franklin lived just long enough for his slaves to run away and die
off, and for antislavery to become politically safe in his home state. Perhaps he was less hypocritical than fortunate, or more skilled at shaping
his own image. If so, that too should be part of the story. Jefferson lived
still longer—more than long enough for slavery to be put on the road to
extinction in half the country and for his relationship with his slaves to
become a partisan issue and, a quarter-century before his death, a national scandal.

History is often remembered backward. The stress on postrevolutionary antislavery developments is reassuring in retrospect and important
for understanding the broadest sweep of U.S. history, but it all too com-
fortably neglects what happened before and during the colonists' struggle for power, independence, and nationhood. Antislavery gained real, if
minority, support long before the Declaration of Independence or even
the Stamp Act protests. In the colonies it became a public issue during
Franklin's youth in Boston and during his young adulthood in Philadelphia. By the 1760s, Franklin's contemporaries at home and in England
and France were well aware of the similarities between colonists' claims
to liberty and those made by and on behalf of slaves. The slavery issue
itself became inseparable from the debate over the governance, and liberties, of the American colonists. The American revolutionists and their
leaders—most notably Benjamin Franklin—often worked to stave off
criticisms of the institution, for they rightly perceived criticism of slavery as attacks on themselves, their way of life, and their campaigns for
freedom.

Franklin's antislavery credentials have been greatly exaggerated. His
debt to slavery, and his early, persistent engagement with controversies
surrounding slaves, have been largely ignored. He profited from the
domestic and international slave trade, complained about the ease
with which slaves and servants ran off to the British army during the
colonial wars of the 1740s and 1750s, and staunchly defended slaveholding rebels during the Revolution. He owned a series of slaves between about 1735 and 1781 and never systematically divested himself of

them. After 1731 he wrote publicly and regularly on the topics of slavery and racial identity but almost never in a straightforwardly antislavery or antiracist fashion. He declined to bring the matter of slavery to the Constitutional Convention of 1787 when asked to do so by the abolition society that he served as president. There are enough smoking guns, to be sure, to condemn Franklin as a hypocrite, Jefferson-style, if one wishes to do so.

But would another round of condemnation tell us what we need to know about the relationship of slavery to this country's founding? Do these debates about the relative virtues of the founders do anything besides increase our obsession with the founders and their personal traits? The very question has its biases toward smoking guns, moral judgments, individuals and their last words. "Character" is said to explain Jefferson's flaws, the fact that his deeds did not match up to his words; we can proceed by celebrating Washington instead, even though Washington the politician did far less to challenge slavery than Jefferson. The problem, in other words, is as much in how we approach the past as in the facts themselves.

Neither defending, condemning, nor rating different founders according to their "character" gets us very far in understanding the paradox of liberty and slavery in America. The most telling aspect of Franklin's engagement with the problem of slavery is its continuous presence in his life, thought, and politics. This was inevitable given slavery's importance in his world. Franklin was too much of an entrepreneur, too interested in his changing society, and too much of a statesman not to repeatedly deal with the problem of slavery. Franklin's remarkable creativity, and his central role in crafting the stories that explained America and Americans, also made a tremendous difference. He had a talent for being present at precisely those moments when slavery was being challenged—and a knack for eloquently finessing the issue.

Franklin's importance to the history of slavery may lie less in his contribution to antislavery after 1787 than in his earlier mediation of slavery, freedom, and revolution. It took a Pennsylvanian, a printer, a cosmopolitan, a slaveholder with doubts about slavery, to explain the paradox of American slavery and American freedom to a skeptical world—and to America itself. The American Revolution may have pushed some Americans, like Franklin, toward a more explicit opposition to slavery. But it did so only after giving Americans the cultural

tools of denial and forgetting, as well as the political wherewithal to resist a national and international attack on the institution. Franklin, in
other words, was a champion of freedom but also the author of our greatest myths. We need to remember what he helped Americans to forget,
how he did so, and why.

This book paints a picture of American slavery and of the American
Revolution that is not only multicolored—to use our great American
racial trope—but also contains shades of gray. It is simultaneously a
study of Franklin's life and a recovery of some of the other self-made
men and women who were forgotten so that the Revolution and Franklin
could be remembered in nation-making ways. Franklin's life serves as a
central connecting thread tying the social history of unfree labor to the
political history of nation-making. The fact that Franklin was the only
one of the great Founding Fathers to have almost been "taken up" as a
runaway in his youth suggests that he understood viscerally some hard
truths about his world.

Franklin repeatedly failed to redress the oppressions that his close
associates and family members faced, in part because those relationships helped make him free. His own rise depended on the labors and
sometimes the misfortunes of others. The details of those relationships
help to clarify why he tended to avoid acknowledging slavery and why he
preferred to imagine and describe a free, white America. In a highly
politicized environment, doing so might have been the only way to make
it someday prove true, or true enough for certain purposes. Nations are
not made without a good deal of forgetting.[7]

Nor are lives. Franklin's history as a worker and employer, as a
printer who became an important commentator on economic as well as
political matters, puts us in a better position to understand him and his
generation. Through his life, a Revolution that seems at times to have
been about rather abstract matters of rights, or a peculiar hatred of taxes,
turns out to have also revolved around everyday matters: work, status,
power, and identity.

Does such treatment knock Franklin off his deserved pedestal? Or
does it rather restore some measure of reality, not to mention humanity,
to his fascinating and important life? The problem of slavery touched
Franklin to such an extent that its investigation actually permits, rather

than prevents, a deeper appreciation of the man and the Revolution he helped lead.

We should begin as Franklin began, in the company of some of the more ordinary Americans who confronted freedom, unfreedom, and revolution. They too fled their masters and changed their identities, hoping to invent themselves anew, and free.

PART ONE

Origins: Slavery, Religion, and Family

1735	Benj.ᵃ Franklin Dʳ			
Aug 20	To a pʳ for his Son — Lᵒ	0	2	6
	To a pʳ for Ditto — —	0	2	9
oct 4	To a pʳ for parchment maker	0	5	6
Dec 16	To a pʳ for Negro boy Left unpaid	0	3	6
Jan 10 1736	To a pʳ for frank —	0	2	6
mar 24	To Make his Wifes Shoes —	0	5	0
Apr 12	To a pʳ for frankey —	0	2	6
19	To a pʳ for old Lewes —	0	7	0
24	To make a pʳ for the maid —	0	5	0
may 19	To a pʳ for his Son —	0	8	0
19	To a pʳ for his Son —	0	2	6
Aug 3	To a pʳ for Ditto —	0	8	3
no 27	To a pʳ for his Son Wᵐ	0	3	0
feb 20	To a pʳ for his Son Wᵐ	0	3	0
mar 5	To a pʳ for his maid Sull	0	5	6
Jane 30	To a pʳ for his maid —	0	5	6
Jaly 16	To a pʳ for Biley —	0	8	3
		£3	5	3

E E H S Warner

Bill from a shoemaker named Warner to Benjamin Franklin, 1737. (Courtesy of the American Philosophical Society)

ONE

Runaways and Self-Made Men

In 1723 Benjamin Franklin was a seventeen-year-old apprentice printer and the servant of a master in serious trouble. James Franklin, who was also his brother, had printed sharp criticisms of the Massachusetts authorities in Boston and had twice been taken to jail. The General Court decreed that he "should no longer print the paper called the *New England Courant.*" The elder Franklin brother escaped worse punishment in part because of the laws of servitude. His inquisitors chose not to badger young Benjamin for information about who had written the offensive articles, reasoning that the younger Franklin was bound to do the bidding of his master and remain silent.

The magistrates of Boston valued their domination of public institutions, but they also valued the rights of masters. To them, the two were inseparable—so inseparable, in fact, that they missed the loophole that James Franklin would seize to keep his paper afloat and himself out of the hands of the law. He signed the back of the old indenture, or servant contract, that Ben had signed binding himself until the age of twenty-one, with a "full discharge." This seemed to free Ben, but meanwhile James had him sign "new Indentures for the remainder of the Term," another four years. These were kept secret, to be produced if necessary—that is, in the event that Ben decided that, as a servant no longer, he could do what he pleased. The *Courant* appeared to adhere with the letter of the decree: the name of Benjamin Franklin, not James, now graced the masthead as printer. At seventeen, Benjamin Franklin appeared to the public as what he was not—a free man—to serve his brother's dreams of success.

Almost fifty years later Franklin remembered James's "harsh and tyrannical treatment," his grasping at every advantage he could get. "Tho' a Brother, he considered himself as my Master, & me as his Apprentice; and accordingly expected the same Services from me as he would from Another." Hoping for "more indulgence," Benjamin complained to his father—a tactic that succeeded, for a time. When Josiah Franklin turned arbitrator, his youngest son came out ahead, perhaps because James had "often beaten" his brother-servant. But now another kind of authority, the General Court, in the very act of putting a rebellious printer in his place, had affirmed James's power over his brother. Even under threat of incarceration, he was a master. The collective power of masters, in the end, trumped even the authority of Josiah Franklin over his sons.

Benjamin edited the paper while James remained incarcerated for libel and contempt. As printer, Benjamin got credit for what he had begun to do without even his brother's knowledge: writing pseudonymous articles for the paper, exercising his considerable intellectual talents and his "Turn for Satyr." For the first of many times, he invented personae and set them to speak and act in the marketplace. The experience emboldened him. The next time he and his brother argued, perhaps the next time he received blows, he proclaimed himself free, daring James to admit publicly that he had shown false indentures.[1]

By speaking to his fellow master printers—men with whom he otherwise competed—James saw to it that Benjamin could not find printing work in Boston. And father Josiah sided, this time, with his elder son. So Benjamin Franklin, free or not (or free *and* not), did what unfree people did at last resort. He made up stories. He ran away.

A master in jail. A servant playing master. Both playing author—anonymously. An artisan manipulating the letter of the law, trying to keep his business going. A talented young apprentice, knowing he was being exploited, telling a succession of tales to serve his master, to gain advantage with reigning patriarchs, to preserve himself, and finally to escape. A friend helped him concoct a likely story to tell the ship captain, about getting a "naughty girl" pregnant and needing to escape a marriage forced by "her friends." He sailed to New York. Only after failing to find work there did he turn to Philadelphia.

Writing the first part of his *Autobiography* in 1771, Franklin took great pleasure in narrating the moment when, after various nautical mishaps, he finally strolled off Philadelphia's Market Street wharf in his sodden, filthy clothes. Stopping at inns, he was "suspected to be some runaway Servant, and in danger of being taken up on that Suspicion."[2] The humor in such scenes derives from what we, and Franklin, know happened afterward.

Benjamin Franklin quickly impressed some important Philadelphians with his hard work and his skills as a printer. He went to England to learn the trade, as his brother had done, and returned with a Quaker merchant who taught him business skills. Within a few years he had his own printing operation. He survived a number of competitors, and potentially ruinous debts, by making his newspaper and general store efficient operations that well served the larger community in a region that, just at that moment, was experiencing its first major growth spurt. He made friends, married the hardworking Deborah Read, founded a series of mutual improvement societies and public works projects, and by his thirtieth birthday in 1736 could consider himself a prosperous artisan.

Franklin sent his own former apprentice to open the first printing operation in Charleston, South Carolina, to be followed by others up and down the coast. He cultivated the patronage of great men, observed their doings as clerk of the colony's General Assembly, and subtly commented on public affairs in his *Pennsylvania Gazette*. In 1740 he risked his good relations with the pacifist Quakers and exhorted the citizens to defend themselves against a possible Spanish attack. He invented a stove and founded America's first scientific society. By the age of forty he was experimenting with electricity and could afford to devote more and more time to such projects. He had made enough money to hand over the day-to-day operations of his printing shop to a partner in exchange for half of the profits. In twenty-five years he had turned himself from a servant into a gentleman, a learned man, a statesman.

Franklin worked for himself and yet had time to work for the public good. He was nobody's servant; nobody was his. Imagine Benjamin Franklin being mistaken for "some runaway Servant"! It is enough to make one forget that he *was* a runaway servant, at least as far as his master was concerned. He could well have been arrested, had James Franklin decided that his claim to four more years of Ben's labor was important enough to risk exposure of the fraudulent indentures and his own manuevers. And then Ben's life story might have turned out quite differently.

How did Benjamin Franklin become free? Through ingenuity, by seizing opportunities. But also by trickery. By lying. By taking advantage of distance, of the newness of the seaboard colonies and their lack of legal comity or economic integration. Out of Boston, out of Massachusetts, young Franklin could rely on appearances and on skill—not on what was already known, already said about him on the streets of Boston. It took a real crime, the stealing of his own labor, to make the self-made man.

In the nineteenth century Benjamin Franklin's *Autobiography*, and his life, were read as a story about how in America ingenuity, virtue, and hard work were rewarded. But when we see only that part of Benjamin Franklin's America, the rise of a self-made man and a nation of strivers, we miss the other side of the story, that of the runaway Benjamin Franklin, the unfree Benjamin Franklin. America is also the story of the James Franklins, the not-so-fortunate sons who tried to become self-sufficient and found that other people's unfreedom was one of the few resources at their disposal.

In so many ways, American freedom often depended on running away and on keeping others from running away. The flip side of the self-made man in eighteenth-century America was the servant and the slave. In some cases they were the same people. In others, one person might play different roles in an ongoing drama of personal liberation and subjugation, freedom and unfreedom. But even those who never served or ran away were touched by the remarkable extremes of freedom and unfreedom that characterized the Atlantic littoral.[3] When Franklin fled to New York and Philadelphia, he entered a changing social world. It was a world of new opportunity that depended on the unfreedom of a great many people, people just as mobile, and often just as creative and skilled, as Franklin. Some were able to use those skills to reinvent themselves. Others found that masters got the best of them.

Franklin's *Autobiography* is the culmination of the self-inventions that he began when he wrote anonymously for his brother's newspaper and that continued when he ran away. The book, in turn, inspired many self-made men of the nineteenth century and the development of the secular memoir as a popular genre—how-to books for the making of self-made men.

For the other runaways of eighteenth-century America, though, we have few memoirs.[4] Rather, we have other kinds of printed stories about the daring fugitives: the advertisements that their masters published in newspapers like the one Franklin printed, the *Pennsylvania Gazette*. The ads from the mid-Atlantic region show us a world of remarkable freedom and unfreedom. In brief but revealing fashion, they tell the stories of self-transforming Franklinian characters, and in doing so they give the lie to stereotypes about white and black, slave and free, in early northern America.[5]

Consider the advertisement Nicholas Everson placed in 1751, ten months after the disappearance of his slave, Tom:

> Run away in July last, from Nicholas Everson, living in East-New-Jersey, two miles from Perth-Amboy ferry, a mulatto Negroe, named Tom, about 37 years of age, short, well-set, thick lips, flat nose, black curled hair, and can play well upon the fiddle: Had on when he went away, a red-colored watch-coat, without a cape, a brown coloured leather jacket, a hat, blue and white twisted yarn leggins; speaks good English, and Low Dutch, and is a good Shoemaker; his said master has been informed that he intends to cut his watchcoat, to make him Indian stockings, and to cut off his hair, and get a blanket, to pass for an Indian; that he inquired for one John and Thomas Nutus, Indians at Susquehanna, and about the Moravians, and the way there. Whoever secures him in the nearest goal or otherwise, so that his master may have him again, shall have Forty Shillings reward, and reasonable charges, paid by
>
> NICHOLAS EVERSON.[6]

Who was Tom? We like to think that the early American past was composed of discrete groups of people who largely hewed to their communities, who belonged to one culture. But Everson's ad paints a portrait of someone very much aware of the diversity and complexity of his world, a diversity that was reflected in his own background as a mulatto and, more important, evident in the path he took to liberty. Somehow Everson learned that Tom planned to pass for Indian, possibly among the Moravians, which must have made sense to someone as multilingual and multiracial as Tom.

Tom's savvy use of clothing is also typical of successful runaways. Slaves and servants themselves owned few changes of clothes, and those they wore, though of low quality, might be so distinctively combined or patched as to render them easily identifiable. Slaves who stole their masters' clothes, to which they often had access because of their household duties, might more easily evade capture—or if they sold the clothing on the ubiquitous informal market, they might provide themselves with needed capital. Tom's particular use of clothing to aid his racial camouflage was only one variant on the ways runaways used popular stereotypes about color and deportment to their advantage. A man who made shoes, Tom probably knew exactly how to dress to avoid suspicion.

Tom was more, even, than a "good shoemaker": he had multiple skills. Like many other runaways, he could fiddle—a talent that could bring in surplus income and, like other learned skills, made him more valuable. If Tom made the most of his rural existence, urban slaves took advantage of the city's more market-oriented opportunities to stretch the bounds of servitude. Evan Powel, a Philadelphia master, found it necessary to place an ad to prevent "Molatto Bess, who used to go about selling Cakes," from "borrowing of and taking up Goods upon Trust in her Master's Name, and unknown either to her Master or Mistress."[7] Powel's moneymaking scheme—to turn a domestic into a freelance baker, a hawker of pastries, or both—had backfired, because Bess was at least as (and possibly more) aware of the possibilities of the marketplace as her owners.

Runaways, whose descriptions at times took up several columns of newspaper space, were adept at role-playing. Many had traveled or worked at different tasks or jobs. These characteristics were not limited to urban slaves like Bess. One Kent County, Maryland, mulatto had "worked some Time in a Mill, in a Tan-Yard, and on a Plantation." A Virginia slave advertised in a Pennsylvania paper could "turn his hand to many sorts of trades, and particularly that of a Carpenter." Benjamin Hill, a master from North Carolina, thought enough of the skills of Virginia-born Tony, a "good sawyer," that he sought to track him as far as Pennsylvania two years after he absconded.

Hill underlined the fact that Tony also "pretends to making and burning Bricks." Why is this detail important? Had Tony been seen at a brickyard? Slaves who ran and sought to use their skills mirrored the efforts of runaway apprentices and indentured servants escaping a system that squeezed profit out of scarce labor. Remembering his own efforts to stay in the class of independent artisans, Benjamin Franklin described how, in order to appear industrious, he theatrically wheeled his purchases of paper back to his shop. People who worked with their hands had to prove their value in public demonstrations. The more one could pretend to do, the greater one's chances of employment or status.

These skills and experiences made slaves and servants valuable and gave masters an incentive to rent them out and sometimes to overwork them. The irony, for the masters, is that these skills also made it easier, and more attractive, for their laborers to run away. As a result, masters were reluctant to admit that their fugitives filled the ranks of the skilled—or aspired to do so. Disinclined to grant servants and slaves the status of artisan, they would say that a runaway "pass[es] for a currier," "pretends to be a Tanner," "pretends to be a Black-Smith," "professes to be a Barber, Cook and Sailor."[8]

Even when masters had to admit to such skills and aspirations in a runaway (for mentioning them increased the chances that readers would recognize the person), they still disparaged the fugitive. A rhetoric of pretense suffuses the ads: as Simon, for one, "talks good *English*, can read and write, is very slow in his Speech, can bleed and draw Teeth, Pretending to be a great Doctor and very religious and says he is a Churchman." The "famous infamous" Tom Bell, the best-known confidence man of the day, pretended to gentility, traveling up and down the seaboard in the guise of various gentlemen of note. The unfree most often pretended to the freedom associated with having a trade and owning it—while sometimes developing less common skills on the side, like Simon the practicing doctor or a well-known fugitive from Philadelphia named Preaching Dick.

Another master insisted on describing how his "very talkative" slave Anthony "pretends to be a preacher," even while acknowledging that Anthony "sometimes officiates in that capacity among the Blacks." These accusations of false piety epitomize the masters' desire to strip the runaways of their hard work and skill, their respectability and successes as self-made men and women. Christianity, after all, was a source of strength and self-determination for many poor people, black and white, in the eighteenth-century Atlantic world. And Christian piety shown by some people of African descent had already become an argument against slavery. The very markers of slaves' assimilation and acculturation had to be denied lest their cultural as well as economic creativity imply, where it did not create, the possibility of freedom.[9]

Like the slave preachers who were already appearing in Philadelphia during the 1740s, many runaways were as adept in the use of their mouths as in the use of their hands. They had experienced travel and often knew more languages and dialects than their masters. Hailing from all over the Atlantic world, the slaves and mixed-race servants of the mid-Atlantic were remarkably cosmopolitan; like other commodities, they were forced to move in the commercial circuits of the maritime empires. Like the produce they grew, the goods they shipped and cared for, and the clothes they wore, unfree laborers moved among colonies regularly. As a result, there were "French negroes," "Spanish negroes," "country born" English speakers who were fluent in Dutch or German, and West Indian–born slaves who knew the pidgins of trade as well as distinct local lingos. These multilingual slaves had long greased the wheel of maritime commerce.[10]

There were distinctly African-tinged and discernibly Caribbean ways of speaking in the mid-Atlantic. Later in America's history of slavery and race, whites would seize on such a dialect as a sign of black inferiority common to both slaves in the South and freedmen in the North. The runaway ads of the colonial era tell a different story. Advertisers for runaways commented on language proficiency, or lack thereof, without ascribing it to a racial essence. Masters had not yet developed reasons to pretend they did not know that everyday encounters in the colonies were meetings of tongues, or at least of accents.[11]

Generally, masters valued their slaves' and servants' multilingualism, finding it a potential problem only when they ran away. Runaways who spoke multiple languages, or could write, had the most success. Advertising masters hoped that fugitives could be marked by their very proficiency in language, as in the case of Jamaican Cato—who "speaks English as if country born"—or of George, whose Staten Island master believed that his tendency to "tal[k] a good deal upon the New-England Accent" would make him conspicuous. If George was in fact a spectacle when he spoke Yankee, the Chester County, Pennsylvania, slave who "speaks Swede and Mulatto well" certainly had more options. Richard Swan of Philadelphia did succeed in recapturing his stereotypically named Cuffy after describing him in print as "a Creole, born at Montserrat, and speaks good English and French." This slave (or indentured servant—the ad, like many, does not say) was marked by a scar and slowed down by "sore feet." Yet these handicaps did not keep him from running away again, two months later, under the almost comically Anglo-Irish sounding name of Billy Farrell.[12]

Like fast-talking confidence men, linguistically proficient slaves and servants could make a mockery of attempts to fix accents on them or even to define their fluency or lack thereof. Heterogeneity, as elsewhere in the slave societies of the Americas, divided the slaves; it also meant that masters did not hold all the cards. A 1726 advertisement described a New York slave who "talks no English or feigns that he cannot." This owner, himself probably a Dutch speaker, associated the uncertainty of his slave's language skills with the runaway's insistence on "calling himself Popaw," his African name.

The advertisements often catalog the known aliases of runaways with a sense of injury and outrage. Masters wished to reserve the privilege of naming property: "He always changes his name, and denies his master." One particular slave, an "excellent hammerman" from an iron forge who had run before and would later be rented out only to run again, was known to his master by the rather generic moniker of Cuff Dix. But the jailer who advertised having him in custody six weeks later noted that "he says his name is *Willis Brown.*" When arrested, he carried a bolt of striped linen, presumably to sell or to make into clothing for disguise. The jailer associated both the cloth and his acts of speech with his transformation into "a preacher, as he says, among the Indians."[13]

Likewise Robbin, a fifteen-year-old belonging to Noah Marsh of Westfield, New Jersey, chose the right nickname in "call[ing] himself Levi alias Leave." In the master's mind, at least as revealed in the ad he wrote, there was some relationship between this insistence on self-naming and Levi's ability to "frame a smooth story from rough materials." The ability to change names, and thus identities, seemed of a piece with other feats of speech—skills that masters admired and desired in their chattel even as they posed a capital risk. Even though he "stammers in his speech," Robert Freeland's slave would probably "change his name [and be] at no loss for a plausible story." A "Guinea Negroe" accent was no obstacle to Cuff, a Dutchess County, New York, slave whose master described him as "very flippant; he is a plausible smooth Tongue Fellow." In calling their runaways smooth talkers, some owners tried to capture their mixed feelings about their human property. The master of Buck lurched between seemingly contradictory descriptions of Buck's personal and linguistic abilities, trying and failing to separate valuable skills from their use by one who seemed "sensible, artful, and deceptive in conversation, firm and daring in his efforts to perpetrate villainy, though of mild temper, and plausible in speech." More often masters veered between narrating the runaways' daring speech acts and cursing them for an increasingly racial propensity to lie and steal, a proof of their dishonor and servile status.[14]

In Franklin's world, these contests between masters and servants marked slavery and indentured servitude alike. The permeable boundaries of freedom, of servitude, and even of slavery could work to the advantage of canny masters. Their stories about runaways could help their own prospects—especially when they had something of their own to hide. Who was the rogue, the confidence man, and who the follower of law, the teller of harsh truths? For both masters and bondsmen, freedom turned on the answer.

The best example of all ran straight across Franklin's path in the person of one of his later printer protégés. John Holt eventually became an important patriot printer in New York City. He began his career not as an apprentice or artisan, however, but as a Virginia gentleman. By the late 1740s Holt had established himself as a merchant operating in the English trade. He must have acquired some significant patronage and trust, because in 1752, at the young age of thirty, he was elected mayor of Williamsburg, the colony's most important city. He married the sister of William Hunter, the Virginia printer who, with Franklin, shared oversight of the postal system in the mainland colonies.[15]

Yet all was not right with John Holt. Like many in the speculative shipping and consignment businesses of the tobacco economy, he got himself into serious financial trouble. In one near scandal, he accused a shopkeeper of selling alcohol to slaves, only to have the accusation turned onto him. A few weeks later the shopkeeper found his house and store on fire, and Holt, as mayor, not only refused to provide him with aid but ordered slaves to tear the burning building down immediately as a public hazard.[16]

The perquisites of office and family did not keep Holt solvent. In the spring of 1754 he went bankrupt and fled to escape legal proceedings and perhaps jail. In these straits Holt, a sometime author of essays for the *Virginia Gazette*, asked his brother-in-law William Hunter to appeal to Franklin, his co–postmaster general for the colonies, on his behalf. As it happened, Franklin was looking for someone to take on the new postmastership in New Haven and perhaps edit a newspaper there. Franklin's longtime partner and protégé in New York, James Parker, agreed to do so. Holt, upon contributing a bond, cosigned by Hunter, for his part of the investment, came on as a junior partner. After a few months setting up the New Haven establishment, Parker returned to New York. Holt was left in charge.[17]

The Virginia merchant seemed to have transformed himself into a New England printer-editor—two different breeds, according to our standard images of the past; yet his financial problems and his means of evading them remained strikingly consistent. On June 21, 1757, someone broke into the New Haven post office and stole a pocketbook containing £260 of lottery tickets, along with "a considerable sum of Connecticut paper money" collected for paid tickets already sold. Holt placed an ad in his paper offering a reward for the tickets. Fifteen months later, on September 27, 1758, he formally accused his mulatto servant, Charles Roberts, and George, a slave belonging to Yale College president Thomas Clap, of the theft.[18]

From here the story becomes worthy of a detective novel.

The family of Humphrey Avery, New Yorkers who legally owned the tickets because their land (Fisher's Island) was the prize in the state-commissioned lottery, did not believe that Roberts or George had acted alone. Suspecting that Holt had framed Roberts even to the point of forging documents, or had put him up to it and profited from the scam, they refused to prosecute the servant. So Holt prosecuted George and Charles Roberts himself.

George pleaded guilty—as a slave, he had little to lose. But his would-be accomplice, Roberts, pleaded innocent. Despite their mixed pleas, George and Charles broke out of jail together a few days later. Holt, in an advertisement for their recapture, described Charles as "a Molato about 25 years of Age, pitted pretty much with the small-pox, well set, talks good English, and is a smooth tongued Fellow." That description must have been sufficient, for the prisoners were back in custody a month later to stand trial.

The court records do not tell us much about the trial itself besides the pleas. But a brief filed fourteen years later by the Avery heirs, at a time when Holt had become a very successful printer in New York, accused Holt of forging documents relating to the tickets and Roberts's involvement. In response Holt maintained that Roberts was "a great dealer in lottery tickets," but he could never explain why, if Roberts stole the tickets, he had not produced a winning ticket and collected a prize, when he had months to do so before he was accused.

Roberts was either framed or outmaneuvered. Avery's brief existed only because Holt won his case against Roberts, who—because he was a servant and not a slave—bore the full weight of Holt's alleged financial loss. (Holt actually withdrew his case against the slave George.) Having no funds to offset the £240 judgment plus court costs, Roberts was sentenced on November 18, 1758, to have his indenture extended from its remaining three years to forty, in effect a term of enslavement to his nemesis, John Holt. He also received ten stripes across his bare back.[19]

Holt took Roberts with him when he moved to New York in 1760 to run Parker's newspaper there. Less than two years later, in April 1762, Charles Roberts, who would have just about then become free by the terms of his original indenture, ran away. John Holt immediately published a combined legal warning and runaway advertisement:

WHEREAS My Servant *Charles Roberts*, alias *German*, a Mulatto, has villainously abused the liberty I allowed, and the Trust I placed in him [upon a Supposition that the frequent Punishments his Crimes has brought upon him having several Times been Whipped at the public Whipping Post, and the narrow Escapes he has had from the Gallows, would have made him act Honestly from a sense of his own Interest] and has embezzled Money sent by him to pay for Goods, leaving them charg'd to me, borrow'd Money, and taken up Goods in my Name unknown to me, and also borrow'd Money and taken up Goods on his own Account, pretending to be a Free Man. All persons are here forewarned, not to have any dealings with the said Servant, not to trust, harbour, or entertain him on any Account whatever without a Note from me. And whereas he has frequently absented himself on various plausible Pretences, which I have since discover'd to be absolute Falsities, all persons who see him abroad without a Note from me, shewing his Business, or the Reasons for his being from home, are desired to take him up and send him to me as a Runaway, for which they shall be well and thankfully paid. He is a likely, well set fellow, about 5 feet and a half high, 30 years of Age, and has had the Small Pox. He has a Variety of Clothes, some of them very good, and generally wears a wigg. He is excessively complaisant, speaks good English, smoothly and plausible, and generally with a smile, is extremely artful and ready at inventing a specious Pretence to conceal a villainous Action or Design. He plays on the Fiddle, can read and write tolerably, and understands a little of Arithmetick and Accounts.

RUN AWAY, on Monday last,

The above Servant. Whoever brings him home shall be handsomely rewarded. All Masters of Vessels and others are warn'd not to entertain, conceal, or carry him out of the Province, as they will answer it at their Peril. JOHN HOLT.

Holt paints a dark picture of the runaway as a knave and confidence man. Yet if Roberts was such a criminal, a deadbeat, and a headache, why did Holt want him back? Why indeed, again and again?

This was the question the Averys asked in their 1772 lawsuit, in which they still sought to get some money back on the lost lottery tickets. They maintained that they were entitled to some if not all of Holt's award against Roberts—the award being, of course, a cash estimate of Roberts's value. To make the case that Holt owed them money, they had to prove that Roberts was worth something. In his own brief, Holt maintained that Roberts was worth little. But the Averys gathered impressive testimony that Roberts was not only skilled but literate, the backbone of Holt's printing operation: he "worked at the press, wrote on the papers, etc." Holt's former partner and employees maintained that Roberts's labor was worth eighty pounds a year. One even said that he would have been glad to have Roberts himself as a partner.

Holt had in fact admitted as much himself. Shortly before the lottery theft in New Haven, and perhaps not at all coincidentally, Charles Roberts had apparently tried to buy his remaining time with money he had earned fiddling, only to have Holt demand £200 for his three remaining years. Other witnesses held that Charles, contra Holt, had never wronged his master before his alleged theft of the tickets: a direct rebuttal of Holt's testimony in the New Haven court and in print when Roberts ran off five years later. Roberts certainly had motive to steal from Holt and to run away. But apparently Holt had motive to implicate Roberts in crime.[20]

Perhaps by telling this other side of the story, Roberts gained allies; he remained at large, despite Holt's placement of similar advertisements in other New York papers. Holt then responded by running an even longer advertisement denying Roberts's story about being or deserving to be free. This notice goes even further in trying to fit Roberts into the already well-known stereotypes of the black slave and the runaway confidence man. Charles "effects to dress very neat and genteel," yet his style is "obsequious and insinuating": he not only smiles but speaks "with a cringe." The ad also implicates Roberts in a Gotham crime wave that Holt himself had blamed just two weeks earlier, in his paper, on black chimney sweeps. Holt depicts himself as a virtuous, innocent, wronged patriarch. "Deceived by [Charles's] seeming Reformation," he "took him into my family on trial" in New Haven, even after "he was guilty of various Crimes and Felonies." Holt describes Roberts's life as the pathetic history of a bad former slave, with a series of near escapes from the gallows, or from shipment to the West Indies. The lottery ticket affair is not mentioned, and neither is the location of Roberts's quite profitable labor: the print shop. The ad transforms Roberts into an unskilled domestic who holds no rights and deserves no sympathy. At great length, Holt sought to turn "one of the most artful of Villains" back into a slave whose value he denied even as he made his claim.[21]

Holt had placed "amasing confidence" in Roberts, as the Averys asserted and as Holt actually admitted in his second advertisement, because Roberts had earned that confidence. Perhaps Holt had little choice: he was a struggling printer with debts; he needed Roberts's cheap, and apparently remarkably useful, labor. The situation placed him in a bind that in 1757, in 1762, and again in 1772 became public and controversial. Each time he resolved the problem—in his published portraits, and courtroom performances—by reenacting the well-worn contemporary drama of the runaway servant as a villainous confidence man.

For in the end it was not only Roberts's status but Holt's own that was tied up in their struggle. By the time Holt moved to New York in 1760, his own failings, his flights, and his reputation as a debtor, a liar, and even a drunk had caught up with him. In New Haven he had taken money from the postmaster's fund and the printing business to erect an expensive house—debts he never paid after moving to New York, presumably with Roberts, to run James Parker's newspaper. In April 1762—at the very moment when Roberts ran away—Parker was desperately seeking to get a settlement out of Holt and end their partnership, which he did upon getting a promise of more cash, most of which Holt never remitted. By the mid-1760s, Parker and others described Holt in the same terms—"Smooth tongued," a "deceitful knave and Villain"—that Holt had used to describe Roberts.[22]

Holt recognized no kinship with Charles Roberts, although there are good reasons to believe that Roberts was far less the knave than Holt. That Charles Roberts was a mulatto made it easier for Holt to argue, and for a time to see to it, that he be treated like a slave. One thing is certain: we cannot understand the one without the other. Who was the real printer, the self-made man, and who the runaway, the confidence man? Charles Roberts is lost to history after 1762—probably the better for his sake. The qualities that made him valuable made it easier for him to disappear. Holt's quest for freedom and even gentility went on, a quest that continued to depend on his mastery of the very skills, and crimes, he sought to pin on Roberts.

The newspapers of provincial Philadelphia and New York, supported in part by the cash generated by advertisements for runaways, connect John Holt, Charles Roberts, and Benjamin Franklin in far fewer than six degrees of separation. Franklin especially had much in common with the slaves and servants whose descriptions ultimately filled the advertising columns in his newspaper. Later, he was one of the reasons why John Holt was in New Haven and New York in the first place. And yet it goes deeper still. When we suspend for a moment the old, legally true story of the master's property rights, or the newer, morally true drama of the servant's trampled-on human rights, we can see that in many cases like that of James and Benjamin Franklin, master and servant mirrored each other in acts of resourcefulness and guile. One's freedom was, after all, another's misfortune, even ruin.

The enduring image of colonial Pennsylvania, like our picture of Franklin's early life, belies this simple truth. In part because of Franklin's own autobiography, we think of a thriving region of agriculture and trade, a "best poor man's country," where immigrants might begin as indentured servants for seven years but most if not all people became self-sufficient, land-owning men, like Franklin.[23] Recent research suggests that this rosy image has been exaggerated. Pennsylvania and the adjacent colonies of New York and New Jersey were exceptional only in having large numbers of *both* servants and slaves. This trend, along with the region's economic role in the larger Atlantic economy, actually set the stage for Franklin's own emergence as a master printer, a facilitator of the trade in persons, and before long, a slaveholder.

Slavery and servitude came over with some of the first ships to the new world: they were present at or soon after the creation of each North American colony. Yet in Pennsylvania and New York as much as in Virginia and South Carolina, the enduring pattern of labor relations did not emerge until significantly later, when the colonies became more prosperous and populated.[24] Because of still later developments—the rise of antislavery in the North, and the decline of indentured servitude in the years following the American Revolution—we associate slavery with a colonial, preindustrial, even precapitalist past. Like antebellum southern slavery, northern slavery is seen as distinctly premodern, even antimodern.

It helps to remember that slave societies like the Caribbean sugar islands and the Deep South came to appear premodern only after slavery declined in other parts of North America. During the seventeenth and eighteenth centuries, the presence of slaves signified healthy, wealthy empires and viable colonies. The planter aristocracy of early-nineteenth-century South Carolina defined itself as modern, even scientific in its use of up-to-date agricultural techniques. It was the abolitionists of the early nineteenth century who first began to argue that slavery was a relic of a barbarous past and unworthy of a modern capitalist America. In defense, southerners began to develop the proslavery image of their pastoral America as an alternative to a rapacious northern and British industrial capitalism.[25]

To see eighteenth-century America through the necessarily biased eyes of the nineteenth century and its struggles of North versus South and free (wage) labor versus slavery is to miss the meanings of distinctively early modern—yet still modern—imperial and colonial struggles for prosperity and freedom. If only those content to be self-sufficient had settled in the colonies, the North American mainland colonies would have remained fairly small and economically insignificant, as they did in fact remain in comparison to the West Indies during the seventeenth century. The development of staple crops on the mainland, however, changed all that. Virginia led the way with tobacco, followed closely by the South Carolina low country with rice and later indigo. New England entered the booming Atlantic trade with fish and timber and ships to carry everyone's goods. The mid-Atlantic lagged behind until its farmers and merchants discovered the market potential of the colonies to their south, so busily growing their sugar and tobacco that they found it unprofitable to even try to feed themselves and their increasing numbers of slaves.[26]

As a result, New York's first big boom occurred in the 1720s, and Pennsylvania's in the 1730s. Philadelphia and Manhattan soon rivaled and then surpassed Boston as seaboard entrepôts, thanks to their ability to bring cheaper grain to their nearer neighbors in the empire. During the years that followed, the mid-Atlantic region turned decisively from a frontier backwater into a dynamic partner in production and trade, a sterling example of a "golden age" of prosperity for white men and women in colonial America. The free inhabitants of the mid-Atlantic enjoyed the "best-balanced" economy anywhere; they probably also began to experience the highest standard of living in the Western world, as economists measure such things. The 1740s saw a remarkable increase in the amount of imported exotic produce (including sugar and its by-products) as well as manufactured items, many of them previously considered luxuries available only to the most wealthy. The ever-lengthening lists of goods advertised in Franklin's *Pennsylvania Gazette* tell the story eloquently.[27]

Some of those lists of goods included slaves. The first noticeable leap in the mid-Atlantic's slave population occurred in New York during the 1720s and in Philadelphia during the 1730s—the first decades of the trade boom. Initially the introduction of more slaves may have been a side effect of increased trade, as enterprising shippers looked for any commodity that would bring a good price. Slaves themselves, in other words, constituted "part of the larger system of exchange." But both slave and servant imports increased rapidly afterward in response to a very real and widely perceived labor shortage.[28]

The most fundamental difference between the colonies and the mother country, after all, lay in the relative shortage of labor in the new world, a shortage that spelled opportunity for some and bondage for many. The enclosure of British estates and England's recovery in population growth created an increasingly footloose, "strolling" poorer class in the newly united United Kingdom. Yet freeborn Englishmen did not choose to emigrate in large numbers, especially when times were better. As a result, over the course of the eighteenth century immigrants tended to come from the provinces—Ireland, Scotland, the Continent—and more and more of them came as indentured servants bound for five to seven years.[29]

In the longer run, because of its fertile hinterland less encumbered by granted estates, Pennsylvania drew unusually large numbers of these "redemptioners," often whole families who sold themselves to raise the price of their passage but hoped eventually to own their own farms. The existence of these people underwrites the image of the "best poor man's country": that was the way things looked from the perspective of those able to procure some land on the frontiers of settlement. William Moraley, an indentured servant, saw it differently. He wrote that former servants had been made landholders "to encourage them to continue there; but [they] were likewise obliged to purchase Multitudes of Negro Slaves from *Africa*, by which Means they are become the richest Farmers in the World, paying no Rent, nor giving Wages either to purchased Servants or Negro Slaves; so that instead of finding the Planter Rack-rented, as the *English* Farmer, you will taste of their Liberality, they living in Affluence and Plenty."[30] Pennsylvania, in other words, was only the "best poor man's country" because of the labor of unfree people.

Every servant turned freeman, moreover, was one less in the labor pool. Even as Pennsylvanians freed themselves, they turned to indentured servants and slaves. During Benjamin Franklin's years in Pennsylvania, servants and slaves became more and more "interchangeable." Masters learned to rely on an incredibly broad variety of servants—apprentices, those bound to servitude for debt, and imported convicts as well as slaves. Their relative numbers in the labor pool waxed and waned according to supply and prices, a trend that repeated itself across the colonial North. When Spain revoked the *asiento*, the exclusive contract allowing England to supply its colonies with slaves, the price of Africans already on the market plummeted, and New Yorkers gladly bought large numbers. Indentured servants became cheaper in the 1750s, until the disruption of shipping and the empire's increased manpower needs during the Seven Years' War—a war provoked, it might be added, by the pressure of land-hungry immigrants on the frontier—when masters turned to African slaves again.[31]

The entire system, in other words, was predicated upon the continued flow of unfree labor and the master's ease in switching between one supply and the other. The interchangeability of slaves and servants in Benjamin Franklin's America made good economic sense. Colonial farmers, artisans, and merchants could not control the flow of scarce labor from abroad as easily as they could minimize the risks of their investment in relatively expensive workers. The great opportunity of bound labor, of course, was that the investment is guaranteed, which seemingly limited turnover cost—the expense of replacing workers. The problem was that capital investment in bound labor could make turnover costs all the higher. Turnover costs might seem to favor indentured servants—who cost less than slaves—but in some areas it favored slaves, who after all never became free and were less likely to run away because, as racially marked individuals, they were more likely to be caught. As a result, in places like rural Monmouth County, New Jersey, slaves became a "core labor force." Even as slaves remained a significant percentage of the urban population (6 to 10 percent in Philadelphia, 15 to 20 percent in Manhattan), slavery became a rural, even more than an urban, institution.[32]

The ruralization of slavery in the North should not be mistaken for its premodernity. The mid-Atlantic labor market showed remarkable efficiency and resiliency precisely because of the ways it made slaves and servants into performers of every kind of toil. Recall the sheer number of occupations runaway slaves could "pretend." Mid-Atlantic masters turned the scarcity of skilled laborers to their advantage by setting different kinds of workers against one another. Slaves and servants drove down wages, as free artisans often complained. At least some colonial American masters proved quintessentially capitalist in segmenting the working classes to their great advantage. The owners and managers of the most industrial American enterprise—the burgeoning mid-Atlantic iron industry—systematically introduced slaves to their forges in order to undercut the independence of forgemasters and the demands of their skilled free workers.[33]

Perhaps more innovatively, masters developed a remarkably fluid internal market for bound workers. The striking mobility of runaway slaves reflects their experience of often having served several masters, for slaves and servants alike were regularly sold and rented. In a booming economy, strikingly modern mixes of bondage and wage labor emerged. Slaves sought to rent themselves out on behalf of their masters, often gaining some real autonomy in the process. A slave could rent for half the cost of a free wage laborer and still bring in a 10 to 30 percent annual return on the master's investment. The tendency for masters to treat their slaves as well as their servants as "short-term speculation" led to some remarkably modern innovations. In 1764 a convicted, transported felon and lawyer named John Coghill Knapp opened a "Scrivener's office" on the Manhattan dockside and advertised in the local newspapers. His main service, it seems, was to register servants, and especially slaves, for sale and rental. Putting himself forward as a neutral market agent matching up buyers and sellers of laborers, Knapp prospered for at least six years—even after his own criminal past as a convicted "cheat" and "fraud" saw print in the same paper in which he placed his ads. In America, Knapp's past mattered less than his canny ability to rationalize the market in the unfreedom of others.[34]

The results were as contradictory as the realities described in the runaway ads. The seemingly unslavelike mobility of unfree laborers created more profit for the masters and at the same time posed an ever greater capital risk. It is tempting to stress the very liberating potential in the market-driven lives of these people. Certainly the market for workers helped runaways: employers looking for casual, cheap help regularly looked the other way when hiring fugitives. Yet much available evidence suggests that the risks to and possibilities for profit drove masters to treat their bondsmen with a cruelty and lack of care more often associated with the slave societies of the Caribbean and early South.[35]

The interest of the master class in keeping slaves and servants "footloose" helps account for their ubiquity and, at the same time, their historical invisibility. Moreover, it was no merely local phenomenon. The proper context for gauging the nature of slavery and servitude in Benjamin Franklin's America is the larger British Empire in the late seventeenth and early eighteenth centuries. There "liberty came to be associated with private property; and private property came to be concentrated in the hands of fewer people." Those people increasingly had capital to invest in overseas ventures, and they found the nonpropertied to be an ever greater threat to their orderly acquisition of more property. In early-eighteenth-century England the laws of vagrancy and impressment turned an increasingly picaresque working class into an increasingly mobile unfree population, who could look forward to a life of servitude in households or on the high seas. In the broadest perspective, this "picaresque proletariat" was an international phenomenon comprised of numerous races and nationalities. The slaves and servants of the mid-Atlantic were part of this depressed class, a group of people who paid the price of British imperial glory, drive for profits, and capital formation on the eve of the industrial revolution.[36] Indentured servants expressed the truth of their situation by repeatedly calling themselves "white slaves" and describing that phenomenon as a departure from traditional liberties. It may be unwise to conflate the fate of indentured servants in Western history with that of slaves: servants were not as often chattel but rather household dependents. Yet it would be equally inappropriate to ignore the chorus of voices who noticed that servants and slaves *during this period, in many places,* had a great deal in common, even as the law distinguished between them.[37]

If mid-Atlantic masters did not always or even often act as a class, they did share the techniques of their peers among the "better sorts" in England who sought to contain an increasingly footloose poor population during the same period. The laws they fashioned worked to their advantage in numerous ways: servants who ran away, for example, had to serve from two to five days for every day they missed. Masters could also rely on the powers of the state to enforce not only their ownership but their specific commands. In light of the slave revolts that rocked the Atlantic world in the 1710s and 1730s, special laws prevented blacks from gathering together. Free people of color were targeted for special surveillance. Many were driven back into servitude or slavery. William Moraley blamed "the Severity of the Laws, there being no Laws made in Favour of these unhap[p]y wretches" for the "very bad" state of Africans in Pennsylvania: "For the least Trespass, they undergo the severest Punishment."[38] One can read in the sources contrary trends: resistance and punishment, fleeings and beatings. As masters sought to control their increasingly sophisticated and market-oriented charges, they relied all the more on every means available to them.

These means included the ads themselves. The proliferating advertisements for the sale and recapture of slaves and servants are best seen as a missing link between capitalism and servitude in Benjamin Franklin's America. Masters, of course, did not need print to keep slaves, collectively, in place. The law, despite uneven enforcement, accomplished that. As Franklin intimated in his memoir, strangers of the wrong look, dialect, or color were regularly committed to jail and, if their masters did not appear, were sold to recoup the expense of their incarceration. But even country jailers began to rely on the newspapers to help the long arm of the law across counties and colonies.

Benjamin Franklin's newspaper succeeded because it spread crucial information between participants in translocal markets. The news and advertisements served similar functions, letting people know what goods were available, where and when. His *Pennsylvania Gazette* very quickly emerged as an important institution for the sale and recapture of unfree laborers. When Samuel Keimer started the paper in 1728, he offered each subscriber a free advertisement every six months: the first three ads to appear in the paper were for land, a runaway servant, and the sale of a Negro man. The latter ad epitomized the epistemology of market life that the paper advanced: "enquire of the printer, and know further."[39]

During the nineteen years Franklin owned and managed the paper, growing wealthy enough to retire at the remarkably young age of forty-two, the *Gazette* carried such ads in every issue. Between one-fifth and one-quarter of the paper's advertisements directly concerned unfree labor. The profit generated was considerable, not to mention essential to the life of Franklin's entire printing business, for ad revenue was far more dependable than subscriptions, which so often remained uncollected. Indeed, Franklin kept extremely careful records of moneys collected for ads. By the early 1730s ads cost five or, for longer ones, seven shillings, as compared to ten shillings for a full year's subscription. If only because of the ads for the sale and capture of slaves and indentured servants, Franklin, from a young age, was deeply invested in the system of unfree labor: its profits helped make him free, property owning, and wealthy.

Masters seeking fugitives encouraged those who caught a runaway and claimed a reward to bring the slave or servant to the print shop, where, presumably, he or she would be held by Franklin himself, much as a merchant might store or transport retail goods for a customer. He participated directly as well as indirectly in the local slave and servant trade, selling goods and persons alike and acting as a true middleman—not just a provider of information—in their exchange. In his own advertisements for his printing shop he offered soap, goose feathers, sugar, coffee, servants, and slaves, sometimes in the same ad: "TO BE SOLD, A Dutch Servant Man and his Wife, for Two Years and Eight Months, a genteel riding Chair, almost new, a Ten Cord Flat with new Sails and Rigging, a Fishing Boat, and sundry sorts of Household Goods." The language of the ads was the same whether the commodity was sundry or genteel, indentured like the German couple or enslaved like the "Two likely Young Negroes, one a Lad about 19. The other a Girl of 15, to be sold. Inquire of the Printer."[40]

Sometimes Franklin acquired these goods as payment, and sometimes on speculation; sometimes he held them as a favor. Especially in the case of slaves for sale, masters often used Franklin as a screen, asking prospective buyers to contact them through Franklin—a strategy that kept information from the human commodity who might try to affect the conditions of his or her sale. Printers like Franklin, and the market-oriented people who read their newspapers, increasingly celebrated the free market in information that the spread of print seemed to represent. Anyone who read the paper could gauge opportunities in public life: the republic of letters and its polite rules came to seem a counterpoint to promising, but often corrupt, political and economic systems.[41] Those rules and opportunities simply did not apply to the unfree.

And what of Franklin's own household? Franklin's ownership of slaves has traditionally been seen as a function of his middle-aged rise to wealthy status. The first mention of household slaves in his letters appears in the late 1740s, when he was beginning to remove himself from the daily workings of the print shop. Seen in this way, Franklin's investment in and ownership of slaves becomes an unthinking and late decision. Franklin took a long time to let go of his slaves, but they were never especially important to him. Slavery was a larger moral issue, and his conversion to antislavery a larger process, a "sea change" by which a provincial Pennsylvanian became a cosmopolitan *philosophe*. As in other realms, the comforting conclusion goes, he did not always apply his principles to his private life.[42]

One problem with this admirably humane view of Franklin's limitations and his eventual progress is that it underestimates the economic importance of slavery and unfree labor in Franklin's Boston and Philadelphia. Franklin's involvement with slavery was actually quite typical of Pennsylvanians. For all his expressed distaste for the work habits of Peter and Jemima, the slaves who worked for him and his wife Deborah in the 1750s, the Franklins never sold or freed them, probably because the scarcity of labor simply made it against their interest to do so. The Franklins divested themselves of slaves gradually, over several decades, through their slaves' own mortality and escapes. It was emancipation, not slaveowning, that was an unthinking decision.[43]

The humane view of Franklin also dates his initial ownership of slaves at the very moment when he began to speak of divesting himself (and America) of slaves.[44] Two bills in his surviving papers suggest, in fact, that he did hold slaves or mixed-race indentured servants earlier. A shoemaker named Warner itemized Franklin's purchase of a pair of shoes for his "negro boy" in December 1735. Charles Moore, a hat-maker, sent him an outstanding bill for a beaver hat for "your man Joseph" in 1742 and another made of raccoon "for your Negro" in 1745.[45]

Who was "Joseph"? Who were Franklin's "negro boy" of 1735 and his "Negro" of 1745? Were they one person, two, or three? Joseph may have been Joseph Rose, the son of a printer who died in 1723 and an apprentice of Franklin's from 1730 until at least November 1741. The other person or persons could also have been servants, through clearly they were of African descent. This ambiguity itself suggests the gradations of unfreedom and race in Franklin's Philadelphia. These documents are no smoking gun, no DNA test, proving some kind of transhistorical guilt. They tell us, however, that we do not know as much as we think we do about Franklin's early life. Very soon after he became a self-sufficient property owner, before his thirtieth birthday, and at a time when he might still be described as a rising artisan, Franklin probably invested in at least one slave. Perhaps his name was Joseph.

Or perhaps Joseph was an indentured servant, white or mixed race or black. It did not greatly matter. It mattered so little that it went almost unrecorded: only another tradesman to whom Franklin owed a few pounds thought to record it. The absence of Franklin's first servants and slaves from the otherwise vast documentation of his life, including his autobiography, is striking. It suggests that there are unplumbed dimensions to Franklin's experience in a world of runaways and self-made men. Like other freemen, and like other fugitives, he had reasons to tell only part of the story.

TWO

Fathers, Brothers, and Masters

Franklin's famous autobiography impresses so much with its description of self-made manhood that it is easy to forget that he begins with family. He does so thematically and chronologically, by first telling the story of his male forebears, in a kind of upheaval of traditional genealogical pride. He was not the eldest son—that is, the privileged one—but the youngest son of the youngest son for five generations back. He also begins with fathers and sons literally, by addressing his memoir to his own eldest son, William Franklin, the royal governor of New Jersey. Imperial controversy put the Franklins on different sides of a widening political divide when Ben Franklin began the work in 1771. It was an awkward time to reflect on patrimonial duties. He declared his dependence on family traits and traditions in an effort to allow William Franklin to retain a similar balance, preferably one that could include loyalty to Franklin, to the colonies, to the mother country, and to himself.

Much of what Franklin revealed about his childhood and his eventual flight from his family he wrote to prevent a similar break by his only surviving son. The gesture begged the question: Is it ever possible to follow a self-made man? Can the revolution commenced by the first generation be continued by the second? William's dilemma had been faced by the young Ben Franklin himself. His family had been religious dissenters in England, but in Boston Puritan dissenters were the establishment. His position in 1723, when he ran away, was more complicated still, because his brother and master was engaged in some of the most strikingly rebellious activities seen in Boston to that time, when he began to print in opposition to the government and the pulpit.

Franklin dealt with this dilemma in his memoir by trying to turn re-
belliousness and independent-mindedness themselves into virtuous family traits, ones that had led his grandfathers, uncles, and father to be
somewhat contrary but always public-spirited. Uncle Thomas was behind all the public works of his generation in Ecton, Northamptonshire.
Peter Folger, his mother's father, criticized the authorities for oppressing
Quakers and dissenters yet, lest he be labeled a despised "libeller,"
courageously signed his name. His father hid his dissenting practices
while in England by strapping his illegal version of the Bible to the un-
derside of a stool, emigrated to Boston for reasons of conscience, and became a model, if humble, churchman and citizen. Uncle Benjamin took
down sermons and collected pamphlets with an eye toward the spread of
knowledge, piety, and understanding in controversial times.[1] Each lega-
tee presages the mature Benjamin Franklin whom the reader of the
memoir, like his son William, already knows for his independence of
mind and action. I rose from obscurity, I left my origins, says an old Benjamin Franklin, but I remained faithful, I followed in the footsteps of my
father and his brothers.

Yet the forefathers' England, and their Boston, were not his. Franklin's experience led to a break both like and unlike theirs. Much of that
story would turn on his being the youngest and on being, like his father
before him, bound to an elder brother caught in the midst of his own crisis of vocation. His abandonment of his brother and Boston turned him
into a runaway—a rebel, for a time, against family and against mastery.
If he could not be a servant and a family member, he would have to create new bonds and new meanings for them.

The Franklins had lived in the village of Ecton, Northamptonshire, for
three hundred years—that is to say, the eldest sons had managed to remain there, as blacksmiths, until Franklin's father's generation came of
age during the tumultuous third quarter of the seventeenth century. The
Franklins held three hundred acres for those three hundred years and
were not inclined to split the freehold. But by the seventeenth century, if
not before, they could hardly expect the younger sons to stay in the borough. They pursued a different family strategy. While the eldest son,
Thomas, took over the smithy and also became a scrivener and an important man in the town, the second eldest, John, became a woolens dyer

and settled in Oxfordshire. Benjamin Franklin, for whom his famous nephew would be named, apprenticed to a silk dyer in London. By the time Josiah, Franklin's father, came of age to be apprenticed, John was ready to take him into his own shop.[2]

Dyeing worked out well enough for John that he was able to support his aging father, Thomas. But it was a trade literally dependent on fashions. Textiles, and the finishing trades generally, suffered a downturn in late-seventeenth-century England, and neither Josiah nor Benjamin prospered. A combination of religious and economic motives probably accounts for Josiah Franklin's decision in 1683 to remove, with his wife and two children, to Boston; his widowed brother Benjamin would finally follow him thirty-two years later.[3]

Puritan New England forced Josiah Franklin to take a step down, possibly because Puritan sumptuary laws made dyeing even less profitable than it had been in England. He took up the trade of a tallow chandler, or soap and candle boiling. He managed to wring a profit from this less prestigious but safer hot-water work, profit enough to be able to start another family when his first wife died giving birth to their seventh child in 1689. Abiah Folger, Josiah's second wife, brought seven more Franklins into the world before Benjamin was born in 1706, the fifteenth of seventeen, the youngest son, eleventh of the thirteen who survived infancy.[4]

In doing so Josiah fared far better than his brother Benjamin, who chronicled his ups and downs in verse. Early on these brothers had been very close, but when in 1715 they reunited in Boston, they quarreled. After moving into Josiah's new, enlarged house, Uncle Benjamin failed to make much of a contribution, leading Benjamin the younger to recollect that his father disapproved of lengthy family visits on principle, believing that it was very common for those with great affection for each other at a distance to argue, vehemently, in close quarters.[5]

It was very like Josiah Franklin to turn a personal argument into a wise maxim—a skill his son would perfect. Perhaps this experienced family man was the first to utter in young Ben's presence the immortal line "Fish and visitors stink in three days." Josiah may have objected to a more particular kind of interference, for there was a striking similarity between Benjamin the elder and his young namesake. Both were opinionated and fond of words. Two of the few surviving anecdotes about Franklin as a young boy stress his verbal abilities. He managed to talk a group of playmates into building a wharf from stones that had obviously been left for construction of a house; when he was caught, he expounded to his father on the "usefulness of the project." The same little boy was capable of turning his father's combination of piety and economy on its head: the other anecdote has the young boy telling Josiah, who was busy salting down a cask of meat or fish for winter, "I think, Father, if you were to say *Grace* over the whole cask—once for all—it would be a vast *saving of time.*"[6]

Families often ease tensions over their everyday differences precisely through such jokes and, later, by retelling them as stories. Certainly by the age of six or seven Benjamin's precocity was his most distinguishing characteristic and put his father in mind of his elder brother, for whom he had, providentially enough, named the boy, for the uncle was already sending verses back across the Atlantic about little Ben's rhymes. Later, Josiah may not have thanked Providence for putting, however briefly, two jesting Benjamins under the same roof, where the uncle proceeded to further encourage his namesake nephew in versifying. Josiah's response to this was to observe that verse writers were usually beggars—a point that Uncle Benjamin probably heard as intended, for he would soon write in his notebook: "Four years they [my kin] did me kindly treat, / But noe Imployment did present, / Which was to me a burden great, / And could not be to their content." Benjamin perhaps hoped to compensate through the young boy and suggested that he might make a fine preacher. He could even set him up with stock in trade—the sermon abstracts he had recorded in shorthand, then carried across the Atlantic and continued in his ample spare time.

That advice apparently echoed recommendations by Josiah's friends, probably fellow members of Old South Church, for very soon after Uncle Benjamin's arrival the wordy youngster was enrolled at Boston Latin School, the town's best. The way Josiah described it, nine-year-old Benjamin would be the "tithe" of his sons and enter the ministry.[7]

This was an ambitious choice, if one that seemed natural to the boy's talents. It did not last long, however, even though Benjamin vaulted to the top of his class in less than a school year. Franklin remained, or later became, too loyal to his father to express any open resentment, but in his memoir he is oddly taciturn about the reasons for his removal, an event that he must have known would change the course of his life. He put it in the kindest way: "my Father in the mean time, from a View of the Expence of a College Education which, having so large a Family, he could not well afford, and the mean Living many so educated were afterwards able to obtain, Reasons that he gave to his Friends in my hearing, altered his first Intention." Instead, Josiah enrolled him in another school—with a "famous" teacher but no college preparatory curriculum.

It is likely that the failed strivings of the gifted student's elder brothers disillusioned Josiah.[8] In 1715 his thirty-year-old prodigal son, Josiah Jr., returned from the East Indies for the first time in nine years. Josiah had never approved of his eldest son a-voyaging overseas, a great temptation to many Boston boys in the eighteenth century and one that his youngest also toyed with, much to his father's concern. Merchant seamen faced harsh discipline, horrifying working conditions, and as often as not, an early, watery grave. The seaman's return must have been a moment of great joy and expectation. A record thirteen Franklin children gathered around the family table, with newly arrived Uncle Benjamin rounding out the reunion. Benjamin the elder composed a poem for the event, praising God for returning his nephew alive. But Josiah Jr. chose that moment to make it very clear, probably in the brash style that already marked English sailors, that he had been "unaffected by God's great goodness."[9] Certainly his resistance to the older generation's style of piety was less subtle than young Benjamin's over the saltmeats, though doubtless no less colorful. Before long he shipped out and was never heard from again.

Josiah had better luck with his other sons and daughters. The eldest son, Samuel, had been trained as a blacksmith, and Elizabeth, Hannah, and Anne were all married by 1712. Peter, later a merchant, wed in 1714; we can assume he was self-sufficient by then. At the same time, John, who had apprenticed to his father at the tallow vats, had reached his early twenties, started a family, and announced his plan to move to Newport, Rhode Island, to set up on his own. Viewed from the sometimes-precarious balance sheet of household economy, before Josiah removed Benjamin from the Latin School he was up one grandson but down one skilled apprentice and prospective partner, as well as the cash he may have given John to help him get his start. At even greater expense, he had sent James Franklin, the brother closest to Benjamin in age (nine years older), to London to apprentice as a printer.[10] In short, the needs and desires of his elder brothers and father had much to do with why Benjamin Franklin lost the chance to graduate Boston Latin School and go to Harvard, or even to remain in school more than another year.

Sometime in 1716 he began working for his father in the tallow shop. He hated the work and began to think about the sea, thoughts a talkative eleven-year-old in a port town does not easily keep to himself. Role models abounded: his elder sister Elizabeth had married a shipmaster, as did sister Mary in 1716. And then there was the rebel, the rough-talking Josiah Jr. To his father, the threat was an urgent one. As Benjamin recalled with gratitude, Josiah Sr. took his youngest all around town to see other artisans at their work. The smart boy would get to choose his master, or so it seemed. In the end, the logic of the family strategy, by which younger sons waited their turn, prevailed; Josiah resolved on his own to apprentice him to Uncle Benjamin's son Samuel, a cutler in Boston. Perhaps Josiah viewed this as payback for boarding Samuel's father. If so, Samuel didn't get it. Only recently removed from London and perhaps struggling himself, he asked for a fee—a common demand in the higher trades there—not realizing that the scarcity of even apprentice labor in the colonies had rendered that hoary guild practice unworkable in Boston.[11] An Americanized Josiah found the demand not only ungrateful but unnecessary—another example of how pervasively he sought to make economic conditions conform to his family strategy, and vice versa.

James Franklin's return from England, complete with type and press, solved the problem, for a time. Benjamin, eleven years old, began to work for James, twenty. Starting out, James was clearly in debt, probably to Josiah as well as to others; even though it might not make sense to put two boys in the same trade, it would help James get on his feet and solve the problem of the precocious little one. "I liked it better than [the shop] of my Father, but still had a Hankering for the Sea," Franklin would remember. A frustrated Josiah, spying a seemingly neat solution, badgered his youngest son to sign indentures to be bound to his brother: James would gain a hand, and Josiah would have one less mouth to feed, and perhaps to hear. But Benjamin rarely made things so easy. More than a half-century later he proudly recalled that he "held out for some time" before signing away the rest of his youth. Eventually, he capitulated and bound himself for nine years, or until the age of twenty-one.[12]

The economy of maritime Massachusetts depended on the young men whom New Englanders produced in such abundance. Many, perhaps most, future freemen passed through a period of unfreedom; certainly all aspiring seamen and merchants, as well as artisans, earned their standing as they learned their trades, by doing the unskilled dirty work of the shop, the wharf, the shipboard. It is tempting to see apprenticeship and the indentured servitude of immigrants as a temporary stage in the lives of men like the older and younger Franklins.[13] Yet their difficulty in getting settled as freemen suggests otherwise. There were no guarantees. Establishing self-sufficiency often proved difficult. Some took advantage of the labor shortage and did well; others found they had to move on to move (or grow) up, if they ever felt they did in their own or their fathers' eyes. Both the expansion of opportunity and the common failure of younger sons reflected the ups and downs of trade in a growing imperial outpost.

So did the rise of slavery in Franklin's Boston. The years when Josiah Franklin entered the tallow trade and continued to have children constituted Boston's economic and demographic golden age. The town emerged as a major supplier of timber and ships for the entire North Atlantic and an entrepot for fish captured off the coast and for goods imported from England. Imperial warfare only increased the demand for goods made there by artisans like Josiah Franklin. Surviving merchants' inventories place his candles on ships bound for Jamaica, where they lit the taverns where wayfarers and gentlemen quaffed rum and other fruits of the sugar islands. On the mainland they prolonged the working day so that ambitious artisans could pursue greater profit—requiring indentured servants and slaves to work longer, candle-lit hours.[14]

During the 1710s warfare on the high seas slowed the supply of white indentured servants and further increased the demand for slaves. While population figures that exist are imprecise, it appears that as of 1708 there were only several hundred people of African descent in Boston; by 1720 there were five times that many in the province as a whole, and blacks constituted as many as one-sixth to one-fifth of the city's population.[15] As Boston's streets and wharves came to look like those of "any English seaport," the city also began to look especially like a colonial seaboard town, where the presence of slaves signified to all who cared to notice the inseparable trends of capital accumulation, successful production for the Atlantic market, and an increasing diversity of persons arriving and departing with the ships that carried the goods. Provincial government found itself responding to the dictates of London; Boston religion, more than ever, found itself making way for new syntheses of Anglicanism and the New England way.[16]

For Josiah, not only did religion and the pursuit of profit jump together, so did tradition and modernity. By impressing his neighbors and fellow members of Old South with his sobriety and honesty, he managed to borrow money to buy a much bigger plot on Union and Hanover Streets and thus expand his business. One fellow parishioner sold him the house; another provided the mortgage. The burdens of getting so many sons and daughters on their feet meant that Josiah did not pay off the property for another quarter-century, when he was eighty-two years old. He died five years later, in 1744, still owing—but admired as an honest tradesman.[17]

Such pressures account for why an advertisement in one of the two Boston newspapers in 1713 told of six slaves "to be Sold by Messieurs *Henry Dewick* and *William Astin*, and to be seen at the House of Mr. Josiah Franklin at the Blue-Ball in Union Street near the Star Tavern, Boston." Josiah Franklin was not a successful enough tradesman to actually own or deal in slaves; while he did later own at least one indentured servant, most of his capital went into the house or to his sons and daughters. Rather, the ad reflected his attempt to raise the margin of his savings above his average of about three pounds a year by taking boarders into his new house, in this case the merchants Dewick and Astin and their imported human property. Perhaps a friendly neighbor, passing through the Star Tavern across the street, recommended the room in the Franklin house, recently vacated by departing younger Franklins. Regardless, family, debt, and economic creativity drew Josiah and his family into a newly intimate knowledge of slavery.[18]

For Boston's clerical and judicial leaders, the presence of more slaves in their midst seemed a price of economic progress, but one they did not always want to pay in the manner the issue presented itself. By the early 1720s the white community associated a rise in theft and several arson scares with unsupervised slaves. The General Court passed resolutions about the preferability of indentured servants, but in the short term New Englanders' desire for cultural homogeneity was outweighed by their demand for cheap labor.[19]

Nevertheless, Benjamin Franklin's Boston was also notable as the venue for some of the first attempts by British North Americans to ameliorate, to attack, and then to defend the institution of slavery. The presence of slaves reflected larger changes that needed justification or divination.

The most forthright critic of slavery was himself a merchant who dealt in West Indian goods: Samuel Sewall. Josiah Franklin knew him well as a fellow member of Old South Church and an attendee of special weekday religious meetings at private houses. Other Bostonians knew Sewall as a judge of the superior court, in which capacity he had condemned the witches at Salem, only to repent and ask forgiveness at Old South five years later, in 1697. In 1700 Sewall took to task his fellow judge John Saffin, who had promised his slave Adam freedom after several years' service, only to renege later because of Adam's allegedly bad behavior. He wrote a pamphlet, *The Selling of Joseph*, that placed slavery in the context of men's sins against their fellow men and God's design for universal regeneration: all men, potentially, were Adam, just as they were in fact sons of Adam. He buttressed his surprisingly extreme antislavery argument by reassuring his audience that he thought white servants preferable: so many Africans were clearly unassimilable.[20]

Saffin replied by stressing racial differences: Africans were so untrustworthy that they had to remain slaves until the (probably far-off) day when they would be eliminated from colonial society. It is revealing that Sewall and his fellow merchant and jurist Saffin disagreed in their conclusions about slavery's ultimate justification but agreed on the necessity of drawing distinctions between these foreigners and true members of the Puritan community. Such debates were part of the eighteenth-century process whereby slavery was brought into question even while racism provided a reason to deny the equality of all men, before either God or law.

Cotton Mather, scion of powerful clergymen, the foremost clerical intellectual of his day, and another of Salem's hanging judges, had a strikingly different solution. In response to the signs of social change all around him, he put forward a model of traditional, holy extended families that would be so strong that they would triumph over less meaningful differences like race. In *Bonifacius: or Essays to Do Good* (1706), a book that Benjamin Franklin would describe as a major influence on his intellectual development, Mather denounced the slave trade as "a spectacle that shocks *humanity*" absent a commitment to Christianizing slaves and bringing them into full membership in godly communities. Religious activism, such as the labors of the Society for the Propagation of the Gospel in Foreign Parts to convert slaves, had to be vigorously encouraged despite its control by the suspect Church of England. Otherwise the city on a hill threatened to become the frontier of sin: another West Indies, driven solely by profit, not by pious purposes.

Mather forthrightly addressed the new social reality of slaves in New England—and their resistance to their enslavement. He found a place for slavery and mastery in his social vision, a place that reinforced the importance of piety and patriarchy. He declined to put slaves into a special racial or caste category. They were servants, even family members not much different from ideally obedient children. "You are the *Animate, Separate, Active Instruments* of other Men," he said, directly addressing the servants and slaves in his pews. "Servants, your Tongues, your Hands, your Feet, are your Masters, and this should move according to the will of your masters."[21] The year he published his *Essays to Do Good* and another pamphlet called *The Negro Christianized*, his grateful congregation bought him a slave, whom he named Onesimus. In the ensuing years Onesimus delighted him with his ingenuity and frustrated him with his unwillingness to be an appendage of his master's will. In response Mather, to his credit, practiced what he preached. He remonstrated with himself again and again in his diary, seeing in his slave's recalcitrance his own limitations as a master and religious instructor, as a spiritual and real father.[22]

The great drama in Mather's life had been his effort to live up to the the example set by his grandfathers, Richard Mather and John Cotton, and by his father, the legendary Increase Mather, who lived during these years under his son's roof. He resolved this tension by identifying profoundly with the Puritan search for spiritual—and worldly—authority that generations of Cottons and Mathers had furthered. Like wayward youths, slaves, with their strange ungodly customs, were his generation's cross to bear, an opportunity to be saved or damned.[23] And so he wrote on, by the light of some of Josiah Franklin's candles, taking in and taking on new books and new people that came on the ships that brought the other goods, including slaves, to his beloved families.

Meanwhile James Franklin returned from London and set up his print shop, joined by his twelve-year-old apprenticed brother. London connections meant something rather different for the young printer than they did for Mather, a fact that both would learn before long. James probably apprenticed in London with Benjamin Harris, the "noisy dissenter" who had published Boston's (and the colonies') first newspaper in 1695, only to be censured by the authorities. Harris returned to London but printed work for Samuel Willard, the pastor of Old South Church—a connection that father Josiah certainly appreciated and probably had relied upon. From Harris or other printers, James learned to think of the possibilities of the printer's vocation in a more expansive way. Working with men of education and some standing, a printer could make a distinct contribution to religious and political affairs, even the public good in the broadest sense. He could introduce the new products of the press and, with a little ingenuity and attentiveness to trends, could even turn a profit from his fellow citizens' hankering for worldly and otherworldly news.[24]

The Franklins printed pamphlets. "In a little time I made great Proficiency in the Business, and became a useful Hand to my Brother," remembered Franklin. And his brother's library proved very useful to him, much more so, he would later insist, than the works of "polemic Divinity" that filled Josiah's shelf. The print shop soon attracted tradesmen like Matthew Adams, whose poetry books Benjamin consumed. Despite his warnings about the fate of versifiers, Josiah encouraged Benjamin to write some occasional poems on local events, such as "The Lighthouse Tragedy" (a drowning) and "The Taking of Teach the Pirate" (the capture of Edward Teach, also known as the pirate Blackbeard). The poems were printed as broadsides, and the single sheets were hawked on the street by the author himself.

Master and apprentice put Ben's literary instincts to strikingly productive use: the sentimental exercise concerning the drowned seaman, at least, "sold wonderfully."[25] Yet there was more promise and more portent in the brothers' trade than simply being an outlet for a scribbling apprentice. The proliferation of print genres in London had led the printing trades to become highly specialized, if competitive. There a printer made books or pamphlets or newspapers or jobs like broadsides—but rarely all of them. When the Franklins noticed the popularity of the newspapers in which reports of local events appeared, they crossed genres, mingling entertainment with news to realize a heretofore untapped source of profit.

Up to that time news had been strictly tethered to the official pronouncements of the government and to the theologically based worldview of Puritanism, in which everything—and especially tragic and fortuitous events—had divine origin and meaning. Cotton Mather labored long and brilliantly to cast contemporary events and New England's own history in light of Puritan values and Puritan politics. Franklin would later look back on this literary tradition, upheld by his father, and deride it as "polemical Divinity" and "Books of Dispute about Religion." For Mather's and Ben's parents' generations, issues of divinity and church politics *were* public life—and entertainment enough for Josiah and Uncle Benjamin, who both took notes on sermons and collected public pamphlets. It is tempting to deride this tradition as the bastion of autocratic clerical intellectuals, as indeed the son and nephew would. But to do so would be to miss the fact that religious debates connected ordinary people to their ministers as well as to their provincial and imperial English governments and certainly provided them a wealth of reading material.[26]

The magistrates of Massachusetts expected the press to serve God and His servants, not particular men and certainly not multiple audiences in a marketplace. For leading Puritans like the Mathers, who still hoped to preserve their city on a hill against the incursions of an increasingly jealous imperial and Anglican establishment, the printed word should be an echo of the authoritative word of local ministers and magistrates. Broadsides and similar popular literature had been around long enough for Mather to complain about them in his diary five years before the ink dried on Ben's "Taking of Teach the Pirate." Mather himself tried to meet and redirect the demand by publishing graphic crime narratives that culminated in overwrought hanging confessions (and occasionally saving grace). The "synergy" of the brothers Franklin in melding doggerel and late-breaking news suggests that Matherian diligence and creativity in the service of authority and ambition had, for the first time, met worthy opponents, ones who understood that the printed word could bring the wider world that Bostonians already cared about to their doorsteps.[27]

The Franklins' new literature was neither religious nor even civic in the traditional sense. It took commentary out of the confines of the church (and later out of the state as well). When Uncle Benjamin wrote a poem about a seaboard journey—Josiah Jr.'s—it ended with God's providence. When the younger Ben tried his hand with the "Lighthouse" and "Teach the Pirate" verses, they did not. Little wonder that father

Josiah "Ridicul[ed] my Performances."[28] The emergence of a secular popular literature, however, like the creation of a freer press, was as gradual as it was occasionally stark and abrupt, and in 1721 it lay mostly in the future. James and Benjamin Franklin did not know they were initiating, or catalyzing, or participating in a secularizing cultural revolution. They were busy trying to become free men. For more than a brief moment, master and apprentice, elder and younger brother, worked together.

James's London experience got him a major break when a new postmaster asked him to collaborate on a new newspaper to rival John Campbell's *Boston News-Letter*. The *Boston Gazette*, from its use of more fonts to its attractive woodcuts to its increase in advertisements, reflected James Franklin's cosmopolitanism and formed a real contrast to Campbell's sedate style, even as it mimicked Campbell's strategy of identification with local authorities and their pronouncements. After six months, however, the postmaster was replaced by a Londoner who decided immediately to go with a more established printer.[29]

James did not wait to be chosen again. He went to his father, who cosigned two loans totaling £346—more than Josiah had invested in the new house. James printed pamphlets and calico cloth, a skill quite possibly derived from the dyers in the family.[30] But he had greater ambitions. Apparently he had won enough friends to consider going it alone with an unprecedented third Boston paper, one that would offer a real alternative and would read more like a genuine English newspaper. He chose a propitious moment to launch the *New England Courant*, initiating a polarizing controversy that would shape his younger brother's life far more than either brother would ever care to admit.

On April 22, 1721, HMS *Seahorse*, a West Indies ship, docked in Boston harbor with the most unwelcome of passengers: the smallpox virus. By May 8, town authorities had discovered that a person of African descent who had been on the vessel had brought the disease into town. This was hardly the first time the pox had arrived on a trading vessel; Bostonians knew about the nature of contagious disease and its effects on people of different genetic backgrounds, thanks to outbreaks throughout the seventeenth century and most recently in 1702 and 1713. The ship was quarantined. But by May 27 eight cases had been reported; in June the town recognized the reality of another epidemic. Over the next six months more than half the town would catch the disease; 844 townspeople would perish.

What made this epidemic different from its predecessors was the emergence of the distinctly modern controversy over inoculation as a preventive measure. Historians of medicine disagree over how knowledge of inoculation first arrived in England and New England: reports of its success in Ottoman lands appeared in the publications of the Royal Society in 1714, early enough for Bostonians to consider it even as the 1723 epidemic advanced. Cotton Mather left no doubt as to where he had first heard of the practice: his long-term interest in medicine had resulted in his cutting-edge learning at the hands of his slave Onesimus, "a pretty intelligent fellow" who described the procedure, showed him his own scar, and with other slaves Mather subsequently interviewed, led him to conclude that inoculation was "often used" in Africa by the Coromantee, or Akan nation. Having lost his wife, several servants, and children in the outbreaks of 1702 and 1713, Mather was willing to take some risks. He circulated a letter to Boston physicians advocating the cutting of arms and application of infection to bring on mild, survivable cases of smallpox.[31]

African scientific knowledge did not impress ordinary Bostonians; nor did it persuade most of their physicians. The remedy, after all, seemed to attribute divine powers to medical hands. Perhaps understandably, doctors and populace alike thought that a health crisis was no time to experiment with the counterintuitive logic of producing the disease in order to combat it. When Dr. Zabadiel Boylston, the sole supporter of inoculation among the doctors, experimented on his six-year-old son and two of his slaves, some also realized that this freelance spreading of the disease could itself become a secondary cause of epidemic, because Boylston did not quarantine his patients as others stepped forward to be inoculated. Besides, it was common knowledge in town that the smallpox had been brought into the city by people of African descent. The town selectmen responded in part by ordering a special street cleaning by the free black and mulatto men, who usually did such work in lieu of militia service.[32] Both the smallpox and its remedies, in other words, were seen as black.

Dr. William Douglass, a Scotsman and the best-educated doctor in town, certainly did so. There was something very wrong, in Douglass's more cosmopolitan view, with a medical community that took its cues from ministers and their slaves. Douglass, who was skilled in polemic as well as in medical practice, implied that Boylston and Mather, with their advocacy of a "negroish" cure, had flouted not only medical knowledge but also "the all-wise Providence of God Almighty." "There is not a Race of Men on Earth more False Liars" than Africans, he insisted. For Douglass, indeed, Mather's reliance on slave testimony evoked the worst "infatuations" of the past, such as the witch inquisition of 1692, which Mather had indeed led.[33]

A pamphlet war ensued, one that held out a special opportunity for James Franklin the enterprising printer. Mather and five other leading ministers, including his father, Increase Mather, replied in a public letter defending Boylston. It was a matter of life and death, of science and faith, but also of authority, for as James Franklin, William Douglass, and the others who helped fill the *New England Courant*'s first issues realized, Mather and the other clergymen had staked their reputation on the value of inoculation. The scientific verdict, indeed, would not quickly be conclusive. The reasons and the rhetoric—the claims to authority and the nature of the criticism—became the real issue, as the town moved to ban inoculation and quarantine those exposed, and as the Mathers asserted their right to lead without rude rebuttals from recent immigrants and young artisans.[34]

Even if it got a good launch by opposing inoculation, the *New England Courant* was far more than a one-issue paper. The group of "friends," as the paper's apprentice remembered them, shared varying kinds of disaffection with provincial culture and an appreciation for the more cosmopolitan literature then on the rise in London. Some of the Couranteers were Anglican, or more sympathetic to the Church of England, than the majority of Bostonians. Others simply wanted a chance to write the kinds of social commentary best exemplified by their contemporary Joseph Addison's serial essays in the aptly named *Spectator*.

What is most revealing about the *Courant*, from the outset, was that while its essayists were concerned with many of the same questions that had long occupied the courts and churches of New England—sexual behavior, uses of the streets, the achievements and failings of the people at large—it divorced them from those traditional settings and authoritative voices that had hitherto controlled them. The anonymous, unsigned essays of the *Courant* made possible a certain kind of voice, one that was

largely conservative in its actual prescriptions but radically different in
its creation of authority. The authoritative voice was disembodied by the
Couranteers, vested in fictional and collective personae who appealed to
an equally invisible reading public even while alluding to the urban
public's most visible bodies with suggestive detail.[35]

Mather's insistence on his authority enabled Franklin and his colleagues to justify their independent paper as an alternative to official
government and church-sponsored discussions, at a time when religious
denominations and nascent political factions depicted each other as sub-
versions of order, reason, and godliness. The inoculators' only argument,
asserted Douglass in the first issue, was "the merits of their characters."
The antiauthoritarian tendencies of the Couranteers were immediately
apparent, even and perhaps especially because Douglass and Franklin
also insisted that they were speaking both for the doctors—the real ex-
perts—and for the people. They used humor to suggest the confluence of
bad ministers and bad government in Boston. The *Courant* also reflected
another relatively new English fashion, but one the Bay Colony elite did
not care to see applied to themselves, when it asserted that political
"jealousy" was necessary for the people—but not for the magistrates.
This new oppositional language united the Couranteers. James Franklin
himself specialized in wedding to it a populist piety that asserted the importance of God's presence in the epidemic—a strategy even more subversive insofar as it mimicked the sermonic style while criticizing the
usual sermonizers. And when the Mathers and their allies accused
Franklin of libelous speech and an intention to defame ministers, he
found still more justification in quoting contemporary "Whig" or opposition writers who defined libel narrowly and the rights of Englishmen
broadly.[36]

The Mathers and their extended network of kin and friends tried to
play the game of anonymous rebuttal—and found themselves bested.
They responded in a manner that in a post-Franklinian world seems excessively personal, if not irrational. To them, though, keeping it personal
was not just a preference; it was the point. Authority, correction, and the
evaluation of godliness must not be separated from their moorings in the
local community, the church, and the actual persons who led them. So
Cotton Mather delivered a personal chastisement to James Franklin in
the street. James waited two weeks and responded carefully, in print, re-
inforcing points that the various Couranteers had made before. They
stood for the town, not themselves. The press ought to be open to oppos-

ing views. A certain clergyman ought to be judged on the merits of what he said, which was "as groundless in his *Invectives* as in his *Panegyricks* [to inoculation]."

The exchange, however, contained another new dimension, one that would ultimately trap James Franklin and open up an opportunity for his brother. Mather's direct personal confrontation forced Franklin to claim authorship and ownership of the *Courant*. He signed his name to the piece, as he did to a follow-up retort that responded to someone else's written version of Mather's precise words and an elaboration of them. The Mathers forced James's hand by beginning to refer directly to him and perhaps especially by calling attention to James's youth. "Young man," began Cotton Mather's harangue directed at the twenty-four-year-old, a theme continued a month later by father Increase Mather, who singled out James as an example of New England's declension: "I that have known what *New England* was from the Beginning, cannot but be troubled to see the degeneracy of this place. I can well remember when the Civil Government could have taken an effectual Course to suppress such a *Cursed Libel*! which if it not be done I am afraid that some *Awful Judgment* will come upon this Land . . . I cannot but pity poor Franklin, who tho' but a *Young Man*, it may be *Speedily* he must appear before the Judgment seat of GOD, and what answer will he give for printing things so vile and abominable?"

James knew the risks of going toe to toe with such hellfire damnations, and it is a mark of both his own religiosity and his straining desire to escape domination that he continued to maintain that he acted in a godly fashion while appealing to a rather different standard of judgment. He criticized the very basis of ministerial authority beyond that of the congregation by seeking to separate the debate about inoculation, and the emerging debate about the debate, from the participants themselves.

> I confess, I have not treated this Gentleman [Cotton Mather] as his Character deserves; but (whatever is the Matter with me) I can't help being so metaphysical as to separate his Person from his Character. He has no Business to curse any Body out of his own Congregation. My own Pastors are as faithful to their Flock as he can be to his, and they have not yet thought proper so much as to reprove me for inserting any thing in the *Courant*, since No. 3.
>
> Dec. 4, 1721   J.F.

What James Franklin meant by being "metaphysical"—the divorce of speech from speaker—was precisely what the *Courant* had begun to do—and precisely what its printer was no longer doing in his eloquent, yet personal, responses to the Mathers.[37]

In the meantime, his brother had been listening carefully, reading, often secretly, sometimes on Sunday when everyone else was in church, in the *Courant*'s library, and trying his hand at the Addisonian essay. The result was the first of his Silence Dogood essays, which he slipped under the door of his brother's printing house.[38]

Ben's "Silence Dogood" essays wedded the mission and style of the *Courant* to his own particular dilemma as an apprentice, as Josiah's son, and as James's brother. The very nom de plume suggests a prior silencing amid a challenge to authority (literally, as "Dogood" nods to and mocks Mather's *Essays to Do Good*). Silence is an orphan who was born at sea, on the way from England to America. In what is surely a parody of early New England's absorption of everyone into a patriarchal household, she was taken in by a minister. As his servant, she educates herself in his library, until eventually the minister proposes marriage. Silence actually laughs—but accepts: a telling commentary on the continuing power of ministers and masters even as their cultural influence on their charges waned. Silence serves seven years as a wife—a female apprenticeship or term of servitude—and then becomes a widow. This frees her, it seems, to become an author. She no longer belongs to another.[39]

By inventing a widow named Silence who dares to do good by, among other things, turning the gossip and unruly speech of older women, youths, and servants into rational social criticism, Ben Franklin, the sixteen-year-old apprentice, generalized, tamed, and liberated the outspoken female figures, young and old, who were at the center of recent cultural crises—such as the witchcraft episode in Salem, which was very much within living memory.[40] Intriguingly, fathers and husbands, ministers and masters are conflated in Silence's thumbnail autobiography—and are dispensed with very quickly, except as objects of mild humor. Once Silence is alone (and writing, with the encouragement of a new "ingenious minister" who is her tenant, reversing significantly the power dynamics of the household), she can not only speak but announce her character as virtuous, "A Hearty Lover of Clergy and all good Men, and a mortal Enemy to arbitrary Government and unlimited Power"—precisely the pose of the Couranteers. She is also "naturally very jealous for the Rights and Liberties of my Country," a set of terms that directly puts her in the rhetorical position of the English "Whig" champions of liberty against the corrupt administration. The persona of the secular critic is spiced by the admission of a womanly tendency to discourse long on the faults of others. This is not an anonymous male persona, a middling-to-gentlemanly everyman, as had been the case with Addison's *Spectator.* Silence Dogood is a person with an author standing far behind—shielded by her wit, her eccentricity, her sex, her story, and even her apparent rhetorical excesses. She persuades by giving the reader the option to agree or disagree or to partly agree, to relish Silence's untied tongue or to laugh at her, or to do all these things at once.[41]

After her first-person narrative introducing herself, the first piece of social commentary Silence contributed was a blistering satire on Harvard College and its students. Composed at a time when Franklin might himself have been attending the college had his father kept him in school, it reflects the personal dimension of Silence Dogood's iconoclasm. Her ridicule of the students' and faculty's quite worldly motives, and their neglect of real learning and wisdom, linked Ben's personal frustrations with those of the Couranteers—learned men who were Anglicans, dissenters, or doctors, and whose authority, they thought, was underrated if not dismissed by the clerical elite who made Harvard their home. Needless to say, the Dogood essays delighted the *Courant* circle—so much so that the apprentice could not resist confessing his authorship.

This revelation apparently worsened an already difficult relationship between Benjamin and James. "I began to be considered a little more by my Brother's Acquaintance, and in a manner that did not quite please him, as he thought, probably with reason, that it tended to make me too vain." Why would James have cared about his young brother's vanity, especially if it provided him with good copy? "Tho' a brother, he considered himself as my Master, and me as his Apprentice; and accordingly expected the same Services from me as he would from another; while I thought he demean'd me too much in some he requir'd of me, who from a Brother expected more Indulgence."[42] It is easy to condemn James on Ben's evidence, for he was undeniably at the center of the arrangement that Ben found so oppressive. On the other hand, James *was* master and Ben *was* his indentured apprentice, brother or not. His growth as a writer or a printer did not change that; it only made him more valuable as an underling, at least insofar as "vanity" did not spoil him. Ben's increasingly valuable labor was one of the *Courant*'s few unencumbered assets.

Ben, though, was hardly without resources. Both brothers still lived under Josiah's roof. The situation created a contradiction in authority, one that the father seems to have handled with some tact. Josiah did not, for example, consider Benjamin to be "under his Care" enough to require of him "Attendance on public Worship," as he had earlier. Yet the brothers were too young not to need, or still desire, his help. Ben remembered the results of his father's mediation with relish, in a passage that, given his famously forgiving attitude with respect to "fancy" and vanity, needs to be carefully read:

> Our Disputes were often brought before our Father, and I fancy I was either generally in the right, or else a better Pleader, because the Judgment was generally in my favour: But my Brother was passionate and had often beaten me, which I took extremely amiss; and thinking my Apprenticeship very tedious, I was continually wishing for some Opportunity of shortening it, which at length offered itself in a manner unexpected.*

> **Note*. I fancy his harsh and tyrannical Treatment of me, might be a means of impressing me with that Aversion to arbitrary Power that has stuck to me thro' my whole Life.[43]

This passage is generally understood as if its narrative elements had progressed in a straightforward fashion: Ben and James's arguments are brought before Josiah, who favors Ben; James beats Ben; Ben looks to escape apprenticeship and learns to hate tyranny. Franklin's syntax is more carefully vague than that. It implies less a clear succession of events than a vicious circle that can be clarified only if we consider James's feelings and experiences as well as the full severity of what Ben had experienced at his brother's hands. James "*had*" beaten Ben, which is probably why the sixteen-year-old went to his father, and why his father was sympathetic. Ben clearly had been acting like someone who thought his apprenticeship tedious, which had something to do with why James felt threatened by his secret writing as Silence Dogood and why their fights escalated. Ben's resistance, in effect, was not merely an end result but a cause as well. And the description of "harsh and Tyrannical

Treatment"—the beatings—leading to a constitutional "Aversion to arbitrary Power" is a justification that does not tell the whole story.[44]

Franklin's reminiscences of this episode are shot through with an ambivalence that clearly had something to do with a sense of his ultimately not having done his duty to his brother or, perhaps more especially, to his father. To his credit, at least some of this ambivalence may have had to do with his sympathy for the difficult fix James was in. Here the timing of events is critical. Silence Dogood first ran in early April 1722 and continued through October. On June 11, 1722—before Ben revealed his authorship—James printed a blurb satirizing the government's minimal action against a pirate ship, which moved the General Court to order his arrest. James spent a month in jail.

Benjamin, as his master's apprentice and apparently his most expert assistant, took over the paper and found that with his brother in trouble he could serve both his family and his own ambition. Probably it was at this time that he revealed himself as author of Silence Dogood, to justify taking an editorial as well as a manual role in putting out the paper during his brother's confinement. On June 18 he published an essay by "Janus," a new persona, who promised to be all things to all people. He was a dangerous democrat, insinuating because—like an ideal servant?—"I can screw myself into as many shapes as there are different Opinions amongst Men."[45] Ben also enlisted Silence Dogood on behalf of his brother, supplementing the series with excerpts from *Cato's Letters* on liberty of the press and religious hypocrisy.

He also screwed himself into an obedient, silent servant when he himself was brought to testify against his brother. "I did not give them any Satisfaction," Franklin remembered, "they contented themselves with admonishing me, and dismiss'd me; considering me perhaps as an Apprentice who was bound to keep his Master's Secrets." James "took very kindly" Ben's silence and his artfully presented words in the paper. When the assembly refused to continue the prosecution of James's paper (apparently not feeling especially implicated in the attacks on the provincial government or the ministry), James returned to work, Silence Dogood continued her social commentary, and the *Courant* continued its lively wit and its successful search for customers.[46]

James Franklin evidently still felt he had something to prove, and his brother Ben had gained a similar reputation "as a young Genius that had a Turn for Libelling and Satyr." For a few months they worked together,

seemingly in the open. The *Courant* proved itself quite likely to comment acerbically on whatever controversies came up, from treatises in
praise of Christmas (which Anglicans celebrated but Puritans hated), to
vindications of the Yale College faculty who scandalously converted
to Anglicanism, to warnings about court flatterers and "hypocritical
zealots." In January 1723 the General Court got a committee of the legislature to agree that the paper "disturbed" the province's ministers, "his
majesty's government, and peace and good order." Future issues would
have to be cleared with the secretary of the province of Massachusetts.
James ignored the edict, was ordered arrested, went into hiding, and
when caught, served another week's time before being released. It was at
this point the House ordered *"that James Franklin should no longer
print the Paper called the New England Courant."*[47]

Nothing if not consistent, the Couranteers sought a literary solution
to their legal and political problem. Rather than change the name of the
paper, which would have been, as Franklin recalled, economically "in-
convenient," they changed the name of the printer. From February 10,
1723, throughout the rest of its existence, the *New England Courant*
came out as printed by "Benjamin Franklin." James Franklin and his
circle in effect reinvented the apprentice and fellow author in order to
save the paper and protect James. In the ultimate legal and literary fiction, they signed over his indenture to him while having a new, secret indenture drawn up to be produced later when necessary. In effect they
split the teenage Ben in two. He was a free man for their purposes—and
a servant for their purposes. His name and fictitious freedom preserved
the rest of the group's right to debate and contribute to the public good,
and James's ability to make a living.

Yet wasn't what they had done to Benjamin something like what the
Mathers, and now the government, had done to James? Had they not
given him a bad name in town and saved the privileges of authority for
themselves?[48] Perhaps that did not seem the case in the short term, as
Benjamin himself picked up his pen to explain to readers that the
Couranteers' new leader was "Old Janus," their friend with a split face
and sixteen characters. The irony and injustice of the situation may have
at first seemed unimportant in light of the danger James faced. Surely
Benjamin felt a renewed sense of privilege in being a real member of the
group of anonymous scribblers after spending a couple of weeks actually
editing the paper. But one wonders how long any sixteen-year-old, even

one as brilliant and precocious as Benjamin Franklin, could have dealt with the complex set of inversions involved in his seeming to have been freed when he wasn't; in seeming to be the editor when he was really still under his brother's command; and perhaps most of all, in being the most gifted writer of the group while getting all of the responsibility and risk of authorship. He was living in a hall of mirrors. He had become Janus, a double-face, a mask: a tool for every use but his own.

In the meantime, subscriptions rose. And James Franklin felt secure enough to do something he had warned his fellow young men never to do, in the first poem he wrote for his paper: he got married. His brother, still working without pay, was his get-out-of-jail-free card. He had written himself the ultimate pass—his brother's name.

Ben would prove an effective tool even when absent. The *Courant* appeared under Benjamin Franklin's name for almost three and a half years, most of that time after Benjamin Franklin had fled James's service. And so James Franklin became a self-made man. Even after the *Courant* folded in 1726, James prospered as a printer in Newport, Rhode Island. He died young but never saw the inside of a jail again. He had become the first printer-editor in America, in fact, to stand somewhat independent of authority.[49]

Like his famous personae, Franklin had "his reasons for not divulging all."[50] In the *Autobiography* he dismissed the name on the paper's masthead as a "flimsy Scheme" that lasted for only "several Months"—that is, until it actually provided him with a weapon against his brother. The hidden indenture signified the fakery of his freedom. If James brought them out, he would expose the illegality of the paper and risk going another round with a grand jury.

In the meantime, though, it was more than seven months, from February to September 1723, before Ben dared claim his freedom. The "flimsy Scheme" worked all too well. Franklin remembered that when he revealed his plan to expose or threaten to expose the false indenture, claim his freedom, and set out on his own, James secured promises from all the other Boston printers not to employ him. He implied that this took place just before he ran away, yet Franklin telescoped all these events in his short narrative. What did James actually say to the other printers, and when did he say it? Did he give Ben a still worse name, or somehow blame illegal acts on his younger brother, threatening the other printers with being implicated or victimized at some future date? Or did they, despite their competitions, prize the solidarities of masters, or privileges of older brothers, over any market advantage they might have gained by hiring Ben? It is impossible to know for certain, but James was a man who had looked tyranny in the face and found that his most effective recourse was deceit. He could have been tempted to say anything, especially if his anger at his less-than-obedient younger brother-apprentice remained as strong as it had been earlier. What we do know is that over the course of seven months the scheme became less, not more, tolerable to Benjamin Franklin. It put the younger man whose name it named, whose unfreedom it mocked, at risk of something worse: prison. Instead of making him more of a man, as apprenticeship might ideally have done, it made him more of a thing, a cipher, a mystery known only to members of a family.

In the meantime, he stewed—and wrote. A previously unnoticed and unattributed piece in the July 15 *Courant* suggests his mindset, as well as the context for his continued oppression. The brief essay purports to have been written for "an aged Negro Man (and a slave to a Gentleman in this town)" named Dingo. The subject, as well as the sympathetic friend who contributes "the Advantage of using a Pen," claim inspiration from an earlier *Courant* essay, also attributable to Ben Franklin, which had railed against the traditional definitions of libel, "especially the part which tells of a famous Country Justice who sent a Warrant after poor *Jeremiah Levett*, because he *being of no good name and Fame, did upon the 19th of* March *give out and utter reviling and blaspheming Words against a Justice of the Peace.*"[51] What is unfair about this kind of justice—precisely the kind that had been applied to James Franklin—is that it is meted out in favor of the powerful, against those with "no good name." The process creates a situation in which the lower orders—here, natives and slaves—visit their troubles on those beneath them, thus mimicking the wrongs done on behalf of gentlemen. As Dingo put it:

[I] took the opportunity of a great Indian Dance which happened here lately, to sell a few Jills of Rum of my own, in order to gain a little Money, since Age had render'd me almost incapable to do it by hard Labour; and an Indian Fellow, named *Ben*. Living with Mr. *Ephraim Delator*, applying to me for a Dram upon Trust, and

I doubting his Credit, and refusing to let him have it, he was so highly exasperated, that truly he gave me an *ill Name* to his aforesaid master *Delator*, and inform'd that I sold rum by the Jill. Mr. *Delator* being a Man of a very tender Conscience, and not being able to bear that the Laws should be so notoriously abused, thought it his Duty to report this *evil Fame* of me to the Justice of the Peace for our Town; and he being under Oath to prosecute law-breakers, issues out a Warrant to the Constable to take me up, and bring me before his Worship; who after hearing the Matter but cursorily, I having no Advantage of Council, my Master being also absent, order'd that I should pay the Cost of Court, and give £20 Bond with two Sureties, not to sell any more Rum by the Jill as long as I continu'd in this Town: Which Judgment I am not able to abide, as not having sufficient Estate to defray the Court Charges, and my Master (upon his Return) and other Friends upon whom I had a great Dependence, refused to be bound with or for me; so that I am out of Gaol only upon my *Parole*, which is a very *tickleish Condition*, and I can't expect that the Justices good Humour will last always: Therefore I publish this my Manifesto, in hopes some tender hearted Gentleman will undertake to be bound with me, and relieve from rigorous Justice

Your aged Humble Servant,
The Mark   X   of
Dingo

As in the earlier Silence Dogood and Janus essays, the writer scores points for James Franklin and the Couranteers by morphing into a persona to discover injustice and censorship. The unorthodox voice of Dingo proves the absurdity of orthodox practices, like arresting and fining people for defaming their "betters." Enforcement of the law against free speech here worsens the rising social problems of Native American alcoholism and the quickly growing, unruly slave population.

The story within the story, however, is a parable about the Couranteers', and particularly James Franklin's, hypocrisy. Ben the Indian causes Dingo—an enterprising bound servant loyal to his master's economic interests—to lose his good name so that Ben can keep his own, much as James caused "Benjamin Franklin" to be known as the editor and author of the libelous *Courant*. It is one thing to be complicit in the

Courant, especially as its servant; it is another to be "bound" to pay the price for all its possibly illegal activities. The Indian's freedom to participate in Indian dancing and drinking, like the Couranteers' ability to carry on their paper, demands the unfreedom, or at the least a "tickleish condition," for Ben Franklin, as for the slave. Ben Franklin, and the slave, have friends and patrons; but they hang back, unable or unwilling to solve the problem—much like Josiah Franklin. All Dingo can do is to write for the paper, which seems to be all Ben Franklin could do. Dingo, like Benjamin Franklin, is taken advantage of by his Janus-like double, his partner in crime—who in the story actually goes by the name of "Ben." The irony is cruel, for who else (besides a slave) could understand what it meant to have "no good name" in New England society better than an Indian—or James Franklin?

If Ben Franklin identified with a slave at this moment, it does not mean that he triumphed over endemic racism at age sixteen. Rather, he was helping to inaugurate a tradition by which oppressed North Americans would don blackface in order to protest being treated as less than human. That said, the black "other" whom Franklin invoked and identified with was far from imaginary, either in the *Courant* or in Franklin's Boston. In the wake of the smallpox epidemic in which they were implicated as bringers of disease, a decided trend toward scapegoating, possibly in response to increased black acculturation and collective strength, emerged in Boston and became quite visible in the pages of the *Courant*. A series of suspicious fires led to periodic arrests and convictions of Afro–New Englanders during the spring of 1723; at least one slave was hanged, initiating a pattern that would recur in the aftermath of economic, political, and health crises in the eighteenth-century North. That same year blacks, mulattoes, and Indian slaves were banished from Boston Common after sunset.[52] If Ben Franklin at sixteen found himself becoming simultaneously more and less free, better able to navigate his town's social rituals yet ever more suspect by the authorities and by his own master, he had something real in common with the slaves of the town, especially perhaps the older and more privileged ones like Dingo, the fictional good slave whose special talents—and entrepreneurship—had been made the very rationale for his oppression.

Ben remembered, without specifying, a "fresh Difference arising between my Brother and me," quite probably resulting from Ben being treated as a servant. Or perhaps it was something he wrote. Regardless, he played his trump card: "I took it upon me to assert my Freedom, presuming that he would not venture to produce the new Indentures," a course Ben felt justified in because of "the Blows" his brother's "passion too often urg'd him to bestow upon me." He proposed to leave town, as his brother John had, but this time Josiah took James's side.[53]

A friend helped Ben out by inventing for him another New England persona of the era: that of the man who got his sweetheart pregnant but had no intention of paying the legal cost. In that guise, and with money earned by selling part of his library, Benjamin Franklin finally boarded one of the ships of his dreams, though not as a seaman. The servant had become the runaway.[54]

It was left to Cotton Mather to wonder what the events of 1721–23 had done to New England, to the institution of slavery—and perhaps also to Benjamin Franklin. Like other fathers of the town, in the wake of the smallpox epidemic he "feared a slave revolt" in the form of a great fire. Unlike others, he asked in his notebook whether such a revolt would be justified: "whether our conduct with relation to our African slaves be not one thing for which God may have a controversy with us."

Mather was no modern antiracist—he was outraged when Dr. Douglass called his evidence "negroish" and even more so when another anti-inoculator satirically renamed his own slave "Cotton Mather." He had once accused Samuel Sewall of treating his father Increase "worse than a Negro": it was apparently the worst insult he could imagine. Yet he included slaves among the reasons why God's authority, and his own, could not be mocked. He could condescend to his "pretty intelligent" African and damn a talented young man like James Franklin. What he could not do was forget about them, turn them into mere objects, or stop trying to save them. "I would always remember," he wrote, "that my *servants* are in some sort my *children*." For Franklin, such an equation had been all too true. If slaves were members of the family, then members of the family could be enslaved.[55]

Sometime during his last months in Boston Benjamin Franklin visited Cotton Mather in his study. We do not know what prompted the visit, but we do know that young Ben had been there before, probably to deliver his father's candles. Half a century later Franklin recalled his pleasure in being "condescended" to by the spiritual father whom his brother, and he, had already done so much to challenge. Why was Mather so kind to the young rebel, who had earned a bad name even at seventeen for his "indiscrete Disputations about Religion"?

Franklin learned part of the answer on his way out of Mather's house. "As I was taking my Leave he accompany'd me thro' a narrow Passage at which I did not enter, and which had a Beam across it lower than my Head. He continued Talking which occasion'd me to keep my Face partly towards him as I retired, when he suddenly cry'd out, Stoop, Stoop! Not immediately understanding what he meant, I hit my Head hard against the Beam. He then added, *Let this be a Caution to you not always to hold your Head so high; Stoop, young Man, stoop—as you go through the World—and you'll miss many hard Thumps.*"[56]

This was Mather's favorite kind of advice: literal and allegorical at once, for the moment and for all time. Ben soon took it quite literally, stooping below the deck of a departing ship, avoiding, from that moment forward, the thumps that marked his brother as his master.

THREE

Friends, Saviors, and Slaves

By the age of seventeen Benjamin Franklin had traveled widely in Boston. He had been groomed for Harvard and relegated to menial duties. He had been encouraged by an uncle, guided by a father, and embraced and abused by a brother. He had taken a place at the storm center of the era's culture wars. He had experienced at first hand the ways in which one person's freedom was another's bondage. And then, spinning stories, he had set off a chain of events that left him suddenly without family, without Boston, and without a job. He was free.

Authorship had made possible these opportunities and these crises. So had a situation of scarce labor and political conflict. What, after all, was a printer—and who, after all, was Silence Dogood—but someone finding a place amid division, dissent, and controversy? During the early eighteenth century, printers and authors remained men in between. Printers were, without a doubt, artisans, but they could create special links to patronage networks, and they played increasingly creative roles in religious and political battles. Authors, too, were hardly the professional class that they became in another century; most often their writing activity derived from another role, another project, such as the ministry or the law. Yet the writer—often, the anonymous writer—increasingly played a special role in Anglo-American society, voicing new and radical ideas, explaining half-visible changes to everyone.[1]

One way of thinking about Benjamin Franklin is to see him as a runaway as well as a self-made man. Seen this way, he becomes emblematic of how in colonial America freedom and bondage were two sides of the same coin: joined and yet opposite. But the peripatetic young men of the early eighteenth century existed on a wider spectrum than this peculiarly American antinomy of slave and individualist suggests. As displaced laborers, peddlers, persons bought, and seekers of fortune crowded into the byways of the Atlantic world, new genres of literature emerged to comment on these mobile heroes and villains. Crime narratives, autobiographies, novels, and "news" items took as their subject these people of shifting identities. Printers and authors, then, actually made people like themselves into a part of the goods they sold. The situation led to a degree of self-reflexiveness and humor in the literature of the day (which sometimes reminds contemporary scholars of our own mobile, media-saturated age).[2]

Over the course of his long life, none of the printers and authors Franklin knew most intimately ever matched his own success. In his *Autobiography*, he offered justifying explanations: the others lacked industry, or were too plebeian, too intellectual, too fanatical, or too well bred. Fairly characterized or not, most of those so described have been consigned to the dustbin of history. But their experiences help us understand Franklin better. Knowing about their lives and how they saw contemporary events opens up another aspect of Franklin's life and thought. Why did he describe his rivals, protégés, and co-workers with such a mixture of love and loathing? Probably he had a sense that there but for the grace of God went Ben.

Or was it truly the grace of his talent and industrious habits? His friends and sometime enemies among his fellow printers and writers had a different explanation for their failures: they complained, again and again, that printers and writers like themselves were treated like slaves. They were worked too hard, then abandoned. They had to carry out the wills of others. Their acts of self-fashioning only made them more vulnerable. They were fortune's fools.

If Franklin was not representative of printers and writers generally, then what does his incredible success mean? It has always been tempting to see in the young Franklin a post-Puritan exemplar of modern freedom and secular culture. Nevertheless revolutions, especially cultural ones, are not so easily made. The dozen years following Ben's flight from Boston would see his rise to self-sufficiency and mastery, and they would require of him even more shape-shifting, inventiveness, and struggles with authority. He sought at first to abandon religion along with his father's and brother's control, but later found that Christianity, however various in the Anglo-American world, remained the common coin in which a public man had to trade.[3] Eventually he found a way to reconcile his libertarian and freethinking tendencies with his own transformation from apprentice to wage laborer to owner of others. The key to his moral reconciliation lay in his embrace of progress and the exemplary role of the printer, the writer, and the citizen in public life. Franklin, a runaway, became the proponent of a role-playing approach to public life, an approach that turned aside the absolutes of contemporary religion.

One of those absolutes, held by a small minority whom Franklin knew intimately, concerned the immorality of slavery. Unlike Cotton Mather, these early antislavery radicals questioned the complacencies of paternalism among slaveholders at a time when family life did not by any means protect slaves from abuse or dehumanization. Franklin knew all of the most prominent and outspoken critics of slavery in Boston and Philadelphia during the first half of the eighteenth century. His ever-more-cosmopolitan worldview allowed him not so much to escape the problem of slavery as to redefine the issue as he redefined himself. The result was a Benjamin Franklin equally—or at least sufficiently—at home with theoretical antislavery and slave-ownership. He would not justify slavery; nor would he attack it, as some of his own favorite radical reformers began to do in these years. His careful rejection of and accommodation to religious worldviews, especially those of the Quakers, saved him from the more difficult paths trod by God-inspired enemies of slavery, a group of men whose often tragic lives he knew at first hand. This phase of his life, then, cannot be properly understood without a careful consideration of the zealots, wastrels, and antislavery activists whose paths ran across his own. There but for his own grace went Franklin.

In truth Franklin was and was not a typical runaway servant when he fled Boston and his family. After all, he carried his signed-over indenture in his pocket.[4] On the other hand, the events spurring him to flee were so complex and multifarious that he could hardly speak of them. Indeed, his salvation or survival depended on *not* representing them accurately. Mainly he needed to be perceived as a young man of at least some promise who could labor—which was true enough, but hardly the whole truth.

According to the *Autobiography*, this was by no means the first time he chose to disguise his "real" identity. By the time he was a teenager, he had after all become sophisticated enough about the use of personae not only to invent literary characters but also to play with the relationship between their fictional trials and and his own. For at least a few years, however, his in-person performances became more important. Without them, he would not get to use his literary gifts.

On the way to Philadelphia his boat experienced a near shipwreck. He had to walk fifty miles to Burlington, New Jersey, to get another boat, and the next night he straggled into a lowly tavern, where he "cut so miserable a Figure too, that I found by the Questions ask'd me I was suspected to be some runaway Servant, and in danger of being taken up on that Suspicion." In the next tavern he discovered the proprietor to be a fellow literary man; in Burlington, while he waited for his third boat, a local woman was sufficiently impressed with him not only to lodge him but to suggest that he set up shop there as a printer. Before he ever got to Philadelphia, then, the road had taught him the variability, and the cost, of first impressions. He later commented ironically on how, to end the voyage, he overpaid for his passage despite having shared the rowing, "a Man being sometimes more generous when he has but a little Money than when he has plenty, perhaps thro' Fear of being thought to have but little."[5]

He had first set out for New York, "the nearest Place where there was a Printer." William Bradford, the printer in question, may or may not have known about the young Franklin's troubles with authority in Boston or his troubles with his own brother. He certainly knew at first hand that a colonial printer's fortunes depended on the outcome of religious controversies. Earlier Bradford had become the first printer in Pennsylvania because he had apprenticed to the Quaker printer Andrew Sowle of London, married his daughter, and converted. In the schism over taxation for defense that afflicted Pennsylvania Quakers during the early 1690s, Bradford took the side of pacifist George Keith, got arrested, and eventually left for New York, where he was appointed government printer.[6]

By the time Franklin appeared in the sixty-year-old Bradford's doorway, the elder printer had buried his wife, remarried a wealthy New York widow, and set up his younger son, Andrew, as a printer back in Philadelphia. The New York Bradford did not have work for Franklin but suggested that his son might, having recently lost his main assistant, Aquila Rose, to an early grave. In his paper, the *American Weekly Mer-*

cury, Andrew Bradford had championed the rights of the Couranteers against the repressive measures of Boston's authorities. The father had actually been about to leave for Philadelphia when he had met the youngster in New York and, thanks to Franklin's misfortunes on the water, actually got there before him. Franklin remembered being greeted by the younger Bradford (later his rival) "civilly," but the more precise and accurate terms would probably be *graciously* and *carefully*. He could not offer Franklin a permanent job—he had just taken on another journeyman to replace Rose—and could not think of expanding in the midst of a depression. But he saw that it was in his interest for Franklin to remain in Philadelphia. He offered him lodging, held out the prospect of future work, and let Franklin know what he would have found out anyway: that another printer had just set up in town.[7]

The Bradfords set into motion a series of events that eventually made Franklin into a free man and a master printer himself, but not without a good deal of artful dissimulation. They sent the young Franklin to their new rival's shop as a mole, teaching him (if he needed the lesson) how to give and withhold information about himself and others to his advantage.

Strictly speaking, the Bradfords were following the informal rules of fellowship within the trade. As master printers they knew that if they did not share with rivals the restricted pool of workers, they would end up without workers, or having to pay more for them. But the Bradfords were not going to give away such a skilled young worker for nothing. The elder Bradford accompanied the young prospect to the rival Samuel Keimer's shop. William did not reveal his identity as Andrew's father and partner but instead greeted Keimer as a "Neighbour" and claimed to wish to do him a favor. An excited Keimer, new in town and looking for backers, spilled all his plans to the older man, who doubtless looked like a rich Quaker merchant. Bradford "drew him on" by asking questions. It was an impressive performance. "I who stood by and heard all, saw immediately that one of them was a crafty old Sophister, and the other a mere Novice." That was not all. After Bradford left, Franklin made it clear to Keimer that he could be of considerable use; he began by telling him exactly who the old visitor was.[8]

At the very beginning of their relationship, Samuel Keimer and Benjamin Franklin found their interests to be both in common and at odds. Their primal scene, according to Franklin himself, placed the vulnerable teenager between two possible patrons and employers, a situation in which both silence and truth-telling constituted complicity in their rivalry over their livelihoods and his labor. We can hardly expect Franklin to be able to tell us the whole truth about Samuel Keimer. Indeed, in the *Autobiography* Keimer comes off as a colossal fool as well as a novice, the antinomy of everything Franklin would become. He describes Keimer as saddled with "an old shattered Press" and "worn-out" type, simultaneously writing and typesetting an elegy in memory of Aquila Rose. This rather efficient literary bravado is depicted by Franklin as almost premodern, a ridiculous neglect of the division of labor that reduces the master printer to a "mere Compositor." In two paragraphs Franklin dismisses Keimer as a former "French Prophet" who, mixing faiths, concocted his own personal religion. Despite being a religious virtuoso and "something of a Scholar," Keimer was nonetheless "very ignorant of the World" (compared to the seventeen-year-old Franklin!) and "had . . . a good deal of the Knave in his Composition." Later Keimer appears as a glutton, as ridiculously ambitious, as jealous of the attention the young genius receives, and as an exploiter of Franklin's well-rounded skills as a printer.[9]

Who was Samuel Keimer? He was all the things Franklin said—and much more. The printing trade and religious controversy combined to make and break Keimer—as it had the Bradfords—several times before Franklin ever met him. As an eighteen-year-old apprentice in London, Keimer had seen his older sister Mary become one of the first English converts and lay preachers of the Camisards, or French Prophets, a group of Huguenot refugees who began to draw crowds in London in 1705–6. His mother joined the sect soon after, as did Samuel, to his later regret. At the time enthusiasm must have made economic sense, because the market for printed matter was expanding with the proliferation of Protestant sects. When Keimer was asked to print Prophet-inspired works, his mother and others were quick to realize the possibilities and bought him out of the last months of his apprenticeship. In 1713 he married a fellow Prophet and in doing so secured a dowry to open up his own shop, where he printed for Daniel Defoe, among others. But success went to his head, and he failed to keep his books accurately. Some of the Prophets bailed him out but insisted on taking an operating interest in the shop. Perhaps as a result, Keimer found himself embroiled in factionalism within the sect. Disillusioned, he sought to extricate himself from the Prophets (and possibly their control over his press), only to be "slandered" by his former mentors and thrown into Ludgate prison for debt.[10]

In his autobiography and exposé of the Prophets published in 1718 as *A Brand Pluck'd From the Burning*, Keimer describes a youth not so different from Franklin's, except that he embraced a minority faith rather than simply dissenting from the state church, and he failed to avoid prosecution as Franklin, still an apprentice, had done. The prospect of quick advancement—from apprentice to master, thanks to patrons who recognized his talents—inflated his ego and led him to think he could get away with not only religious but also political dissent, including some outright fakery, in order to keep his independence. In 1715 he printed a spurious account of the victory (actually a defeat) of the rebel pretender to the English throne and other items "offensive to the government." Made a state prisoner, his sometime partner continued to print under his name. The Prophets cut their losses and again denounced him. Keimer wrote his exposé from the Old Bailey prison, seeking to capitalize on his knowledge of the cult and to clear his name. He promised to pay his debts and suggested that he was about to pledge himself to the Quakers, whom he warned to watch out for his evangelical sister, who was apparently on her way to Pennsylvania to propagate the Camisard "Spirit of Confusion."[11]

Whether to spite his sister or to join her, Keimer followed her to Pennsylvania in late 1722 or early 1723. He proceeded to try to pass for a Quaker, or at least enough of one to occupy a central place in Philadelphia culture—an effort that, for Keimer, seems to have been at least partly sincere. Even after the Quakers notified the public in print that he was not one of them, he paid little attention to clothes, wore a long beard, and employed the Quaker *thee* and *thou* in written correspondence. He seemed desperate to fit in and to revolutionize at the same time. Very soon after arriving in the province he advertised in Bradford's paper that he intended to start a school for teaching male slaves how to read the scriptures. The school, which would be free, would be held every morning until eight o'clock except on the sabbath: "all those concerned about their souls" (their own as well as their slaves') should bring the Africans to him. Keimer's rivals later saw his school for slaves as the epitome of his pretensions to learning, his general eccentricity, and his "Matchless Talent at Scandal." It could just as easily be seen as a sign of his ambition and his genuine sympathy for the oppressed, perhaps even of his shock at seeing Quakers, in whom he had placed his hopes of a purifying community, holding slaves. Eventually he would wind up in Barbados, where he turned a fledgling newspaper into a grand cultural, if not financial, success that energized a Caribbean literary culture and a nascent West Indian colonial identity.

Keimer's problem, it seems, was less his strangeness or his lack of economy than his distinctly religious approach to print—his inability to separate himself from doctrine or to relegate doctrine to anything less than a primary purpose of running a press. He did better in Barbados, where his taste for poetry stood him well, but still had run-ins with authorities who found him too independent and libelous. Nor could he resist preaching slavery reform—or comparing himself to a slave when his readers failed to pay him for his efforts.[12]

There was nothing inevitable, then, in Keimer's eventual failure as a printer in Philadelphia; both before and after his close encounters with Franklin, the vicissitudes of the printing trade dictated his peripatetic, enthusiastic career, at least as much as his character and his commitments did. Deliberately or not, Franklin misremembered when he depicted a just-arrived Keimer pathetically struggling to put out his first printing, his elegy for Bradford's journeyman and the clerk of the Assembly, Aquila Rose. Actually, he had already drawn mixed reviews but real attention for some controversial printings. Joining the Aquila Rose tear-fest was a safe way to showcase his own talents beyond the specificities of sect and to make some quick change. In Keimer's hands, the dead printer-poet Rose became a unifying force. All the civil authorities were joined at the funeral by "Church-Folks, Dissenters . . . each differing Sect agree, / To grace his Fun'ral with their Company."[13] A different Samuel Keimer came to life in the elegy Franklin put to press: a sentimental and perspicacious man of the town, a lover of virtue with an eye for the main chance.

Even as Keimer exposed himself to the Bradfords by taking Franklin in, he got his elegy printed quicker by the strong-armed newcomer—and made some money off of Andrew Bradford's loss of Rose, his best hand. Keimer continued to show an inventiveness and knowledgeability that led him to introduce not only religious disquisitions but also important examples of enlightened knowledge to a middle colonies readership. In 1724 he became the first colonial printer to reprint *The Independent Whig*, a serial by the Englishmen John Trenchard and Thomas Gordon, authors of *Cato's Letters*, which would become of great importance in the development of a colonial political voice. Four years later, when he tried to beat Franklin, who had quit, to the punch by starting a newspaper, he created one much more interesting than Bradford's. Keimer's distaste for the Church of England and any state religion made him especially sympathetic to speculative thought and science.[14] Keimer may have been too enthusiastic, and a poor businessman as well, but he was no fool. Like his new hand, at the moment they met, he was rising.

In eighteenth-century America one grew in stature as well as in mind only with the help of friends and patrons (and workers). Part of the drama of life—and politics—in that America lay in the construction of "interest" among men and their families. Keimer succeeded in making Franklin a part of his interest, though not, reminisced Franklin, a part of his household. In a typical put-down of Keimer, he noted that the thirty-six-year-old man, separated from his wife, had rented a house "without Furniture." Keimer would not hear of Franklin staying with the Bradfords, so he procured him a bed at the house of his landlord, John Read. Franklin remembered his first months with Keimer as a happy time. He began to make friends among "Lovers of Reading" his own age. He saved money and missed Boston less and less.[15]

If he did not immediately seek patronage and family, his talents led patronage and family to seek him. His elder sister Mary's husband, a shipmaster named Robert Homes, wrote him a letter, asking him why he had left Boston and suggesting that he might safely return. In the *Autobiography* Franklin does not convey, or did not recall, exactly what he told Homes in reply, except to suggest that "I . . . stated my Reasons for quitting Boston fully, and in such a Light as to convince him I was not so wrong as he had apprehended." Whether it was the story of the smallpox controversy and his role in editing the paper, or his brother's cruelties, or some combination, it made an impressive story. Homes related it to William Keith, the royal governor of Pennsylvania. Not long afterward the governor and another gentleman came to Keimer's shop—but not, as Keimer excitedly hoped, to offer him a government contract. They were there to see Franklin. Keimer "star'd like a Pig poison'd" while the governor exerted the full measure of his charm on the teenage journeyman and invited him to a tavern for a glass of madeira. One can only imagine how Keimer felt, over the next weeks, as the governor ignored him while regularly inviting his journeyman to dinner, and what suspicions he entertained when Franklin suddenly announced he was going back to Boston to visit "friends." Were he suspicious, he had grounds: Keith had proposed that the young artisan go into business for himself; he should get his father to advance him the money; Keith would get him the Pennsylvania government's printing contract.[16]

Brother-in-law Homes had not sent word back to Boston, so when Benjamin strolled back onto Union Street, it came as a complete surprise to all the Franklins, including Josiah and James. Given his luck with other fugitive sons, the return of the prospering Benjamin after seven months probably pleased Josiah immensely, though not enough to pry open his shallow pocketbook. A few days later, when Robert Homes got back to town, Josiah took the opportunity to ask his son-in-law, in Benjamin's presence, what he thought of Governor Keith and his flattering letter promising patronage. Homes "said what he could in favour of the Project." Josiah answered "that [Keith] must be of small Discretion, to think of setting a Boy up in Business who wanted yet 3 Years of being at a Man's Estate." Besides, "he had advanc'd too much already to my Brother James."[17] He suggested that Benjamin return to Philadelphia, save his earnings, and continue to impress the locals and "avoid lampooning and libelling." In three years, if he came near having enough to set up shop, Josiah would "help me out with the rest."

Benjamin Franklin had his father's approval but remained the younger son. His resentment is apparent in his decision to visit his brother during work hours, "before his People," where he behaved in such a way that James said "he could never forget or forgive it." He showed up in a "genteel new Suit"—"better dress'd than ever while in his Service"—and proclaimed the virtues of Pennsylvania to James's very impressed workers, whom he also made sure to let see his silver money and his pocket watch.[18]

A little revenge, and a lesson learned from William Keith, who, as Josiah had divined, traded more on impressions than on sober planning or deep pockets. As Franklin looked back on this period, he depicted a world full of real and false friends, of possible patrons and substitute fathers, of good-hearted men and "hypocrites, deluders, and pretenders." It could not have been clear to him at the time, however, who was which, especially since Keith was the governor and offered several kinds of concrete assistance. His true brothers—Homes and John, who "always loved" Benjamin and whom he visited in Newport on the way back to

Philadelphia—seemed very enthusiastic. The eighteen-year-old kept making a good impression, good enough for one of John's friends, a man named Vernon, to give him a note for £35 against a favor: to receive and remit £35 owed him by a fellow Philadelphian. This was a common enough request at a time when each colony had its own currency in addition to English and continental specie. But Franklin soon found himself drawing on that money, thanks, he recalled, to one of his own friends. Collins, a boyhood chum and an impressive scholar who "seem'd to promise making a good Figure in Life," had decided to follow Franklin back to Philadelphia. By the time they got settled, it was obvious that Collins had become an untrustworthy, leeching drunk. In one memorable incident of the sort the later Franklin loved to make into a life lesson, Collins refused to take his turn at rowing a boat; the friends argued about it, and Franklin pitched him overboard. Soon after, Collins took off for Barbados, never to repay his debts.[19]

Franklin had left for Boston in a new suit and with money in his pocket; he returned to Philadelphia in debt to Vernon, a man who never intended to loan him a shilling. He arrived as a prodigal and a prodigy and left, once again, as a younger son, reminded of his nonage. He could afford neither to accept paternal authority nor ignore his need for paternal figures as well as brothers and friends. When Governor Keith dismissed Josiah's demurrals and pronounced that he himself would outfit a new printing shop if Franklin would go to London to pick out the materials, Benjamin Franklin made plans to sail on the next annual ship.[20]

In the meantime he had to pretend to Keimer that nothing unusual was going on—a situation that put him in an ethical bind. He and Keimer "liv'd on a pretty good familiar Footing and agreed tolerably well" at this time. They took mutual pleasure in arguing about anything and everything; Keimer developed so high an opinion of Franklin's skills that, in his quintessential style, he proposed they extend their unequal partnership from printing to prophesying—to start a new sect in which Keimer would "preach the Doctrines" and Franklin "confound all Opponents."

Franklin drew amusement and profit from humoring Keimer. He agreed to Keimer's unattractive doctrines, including not shaving and keeping the sabbath, only on the condition that Keimer follow his own vegetarian practice. In the *Autobiography* Franklin stresses how he saved some money by creating a two-man vegetarian cooperative with his boss, but there was more to this episode. Franklin introduces it by reminding us that he had been a devotee of "my Master" Thomas Tryon's *The Way to Health* (1683), an influential ethical tract proposing dietary moderation and avoidance of all animal flesh. In his brother's house he had followed a similar diet and in doing so gained time apart and money for books. In re-creating this moment, however, he avers that *before* setting up his vegetarian scheme with Keimer, he had actually given up the regimen.

> I believe I have omitted mentioning that in my first Voyage from Boston, being becalm'd off Block Island, our People set about catching Cod and hawl'd up a great many. Hitherto I had stuck to my Resolution of not eating animal Food; and on this Occasion, I consider'd with my Master Tryon, the taking every Fish as a kind of unprovok'd Murder, since none of them had or ever could do us any Injury that might justify the Slaughter. All this seem'd very reasonable. But I had formerly been a great Lover of Fish, and when this came hot out of the Frying Pan, it smelt admirably well. I balanc'd some time between Principle and Inclination: till I recollected, that when the Fish were opened, I saw smaller Fish taken out of their Stomachs: Then thought I, if you eat one another, I don't see why we mayn't eat you . . . So convenient a thing it is to be a *reasonable Creature*, since it enables one to find or make a Reason for every thing one has a mind to do.

What were the implications of such a change of heart? With regard to Keimer, it meant that he could treat his employer less as a brother or a father than as another fish in a hostile sea.[21]

The transformation takes on still more meaning if we take seriously Franklin's early devotion to Tryon and his doctrines, as Franklin did himself by mentioning it twice in the *Autobiography*. Tryon's vegetarianism was grounded in a conviction that flesh eating was inherently violent. "The Tyranny of Man over his fellow-Creatures" violated the golden rule. In *The Way to Health* Tryon included not only recipes but impromptu speeches by cows, sheep, birds, and horses, against their oppression. In other works he applied this religiously based logic to become one of the earliest and most widely read critics of colonial slavery. The very year after the publication of *The Way to Health* he brought these themes together in a persuasive demonstration of the British colonies' military-sugar-skins complex.

As an enthusiast of Tryon in the 1710s and 1720s, Franklin could hardly have been unaware of Tryon's bracing critique of slavery. For the Franklins' youngest son and apprentice, Tryon's egalitarianism was probably what made his vegetarianism appealing in the first place. Ben could also relish Tryon's accusation that West Indian planters' invocations of Christianity, like those of Boston's authorities, served as a mask for their power. But the follower of Tryon did not have to face up to any incendiary call for revolt. Despite his devastating critique of the system, Tryon carefully called upon owners to treat their slaves in a Christian manner and predicted obedience by the slaves in return.[22] Tryon's advice, in short, was for masters, not for servants. In giving it up, Franklin distanced himself from more than vegetarianism. He also gave up whatever trust he still had in the benevolence of masters, and any hope of a world without slavery. Especially for little fish, it was a fish-eat-fish world. Doctrinal consistency would not well serve a fish in his own position.

That position turned out to be more vulnerable than he imagined. Even as the ship for London lay in wait, Governor Keith postponed providing Franklin with the letters that would introduce him to his friends in London and speed his way. They never came. Franklin must have been rather nervous when, on arriving in London, he took what turned out to be the ship's random group of letters addressed to stationers and printers to their addressees, hoping that one of them would be from the governor and mention him. The very first letter he delivered turned out to be not from the governor but from one William Riddlesden (aka William Cornwallis), an attorney and former convict known for his illegal land deals. The stationer, who recognized the ex-convict's name, turned on his heel and ignored the bearer of the swindler's letter. In his very first attempt to make a connection in London, Franklin found himself caught up in the trail of someone else's confidence game.[23]

As Thomas Denham, the Quaker merchant who befriended him aboard ship, put it, Governor Keith had neither money nor a good name; he traded on promises and appearances. Why not take a position in a London printing house, Denham asked: "When you return to America you will set up with greater Advantage." In a sense, that is exactly what Franklin did by working in the establishments of John Watts and Samuel

Palmer—but in a quite indirect manner. Readers of the *Autobiography* see his London persona through his later maxims on work habits and the evils of "Saint Monday," the hung-over workman's day off. He describes his own healthy water-drinking habits, compared to the tippling of his besotted fellow workers, who dubbed him the "water-American." Actually, Franklin also makes it clear that in London he lost his faith and probably his virginity. His friend and companion on the voyage, James Ralph, helped him spend his money in theaters and his time in vain literary endeavors of precisely the kind his father had always warned against. Ralph had left his wife and child, intending never to return. Franklin "forgot" his engagement to Deborah Read, the daughter of his Philadelphia landlord.[24]

Ralph had faked being a merchant to get out of his marriage; in London he tried to be an actor, a scrivener, and a writer. He would eventually succeed at the latter, surviving long enough to collaborate with Henry Fielding, earn the ridicule of Alexander Pope, and gain a sinecure to stop satirizing the government. He eventually wrote one of the first protests against the immiseration of professional authors, in which he declared that "there is no Difference between the Writer in his Garret, and the Slave in the Mines." But in the 1720s he was less sure of his professional or personal identity and more impressed by the necessity and possibility of changing and disguising it. In the preface to his first book of essays, published in 1728, he would declare himself a Janus-like figure, "rarely known by two Persons by the same Name, and to no body, by my true one." He proceeded to take Franklin's name when he went to the country to earn some money as a schoolmaster. Benjamin repaid the theft by trying to steal Ralph's girlfriend. To complete the typically Augustan comedy of errors, Ben's advances were repulsed, Ralph's intimate told on him, and Ralph declared his monetary debts to his friend completely void.[25]

Franklin had been there before. The events he experienced in London—the excitement of literary fellowship, the disappointment in patronage—can be seen in some ways as magnified aspects of his Boston experience. Boston's crime wave, its cultural ferment, its new levels of anonymity and anomie were after all muted or refracted versions of what was going on in the much larger capital of the empire. In that context, as much as in Boston, Franklin began to use whatever means he could to try to distinguish himself—and keep himself solvent, not just as a water-quaffing artisan but as a man-about-town. For example, he managed to sell an asbestos purse and a few other "curiosities" that he had brought over with him to the great naturalist Hans Sloane in what may also have been an attempt to find another patron and an identity as an interesting provincial.[26]

Not coincidentally, his most ambitious effort drew him back to the question of religion and faith. He wrote and printed a hundred copies of an impressive pamphlet animated by deductive reasoning and fueled by the desire to trump a work he himself had set to type. *A Dissertation on Liberty and Necessity, Pleasure and Pain* mocked the attempts of the liberal divine William Wollaston, the highly regarded author of *The Religion of Nature Delineated*, to square order, truth, human nature, and free will in a systematic theology. Franklin did not dispute the existence of God, though he remembered being a "thorough deist" at this time of his life. Instead he argued that God's existence and all-powerful nature offer no assurance that there exists another world where reason and justice reign, much less that religious devotion is necessary. Rather, God's sovereignty over man in every respect means simply that nothing that is can be condemned as outside of God's plan. Distinctions between the good and the bad, or vice and virtue, are in this respect meaningless; good and evil, pleasure and pain cannot exist without each other.

To illustrate what was at stake, Franklin turned to the revealing examples of theft and servitude. Averring that he did not mean to promote stealing, he insisted that if theft is wrong because property is "truly" inalienable from its owner by nature, it was just as easy to say that it is in the nature of the thief, who is evil, to steal. By a similar logic, the slave is as happy as the "monarch," for pain is the absence of pleasure, and vice versa: the slave experiences as much pleasure on ceasing from labor as the monarch experiences pain whenever his pleasures are ended.[27]

Commentators have understandably disagreed on what to make of this seemingly nihilistic doctrine. It is easiest to dismiss it, as Franklin did, as an "errata" he would later correct and perhaps as another indication of Franklin's disaffection from the orthodoxy of his parents. Nevertheless, a "dramatic leveling" takes place in the essay, one that rejects the hierarchies of conventional belief (and morality). Franklin was so concerned to puncture the pious certainties of churchmen, their judgments about who was and was not virtuous, and their warnings that sought to keep everyone in their place, that he allowed more relativism to slip in than he may have intended. The logic, in any case, was fairly impressive. Samuel Palmer, his employer, began to think of him "more . . . as a young man of Ingenuity." A reader went out of his way to introduce him to Sir Bernard Mandeville, the scandalously cynical, nonbelieving, materialist author of *The Fable of the Bees*.[28]

Nothing more appropriate could have occurred. By taking religion seriously enough to point out ways in which it could not be squared with Enlightenment naturalism and rationalism, and by taking the tenets of the Enlightenment seriously enough to show that it created problems for anyone of deep faith, Franklin showed himself to be on the cutting edge of culture in mid-1720s London. Experiencing heady introductions while barely keeping his head above water financially must have seemed to match his theory about the inescapability of pleasure and pain. The only thing he could be sure of was that if someone was watching and guiding him from above, he had no access to the knowledge or benefit.

What he did learn was that those who rejected religion did not, in the end, treat him any better than did the worshipful patriarchs he mocked. If his stay in London was in fact a "pivotal experience" for Franklin, it was not only because he learned more about his trade there. He also faced a vocational and intellectual, if not spiritual, crossroads, where he had to choose from among different kinds of careers and different ways of thinking. He actively considered whether he would do better in printing or in teaching young gentlemen to swim—precisely the type of adventure and opportunity that his more roguish London friends embraced.

The freethinking Franklin found himself drawn back to a model of stability in the person of Thomas Denham, the Quaker merchant he had met on the voyage over a year before. Denham offered to teach him how to become a merchant if he would serve, for wages that constituted a pay cut, as his assistant. Eventually, when they returned to Philadelphia, Denham predicted, Franklin would become his agent, traveling to the West Indies with consignments of flour and other provisions, a prospect that both men apparently assumed "would be profitable, and if I manag'd well, would establish me handsomely."[29]

Franklin leaped at the chance and found in Denham a new kind of patriarch: the father as kind partner. It was the kind of fatherhood he had sometimes had in Josiah, at least until his brother's interest and authority had intervened.[30] In the *Autobiography* Franklin carefully used the language of mutual care and respect: Denham "counsell'd me as a Father, having a sincere Regard for me: I respected and lov'd him." Both men, however, took ill only a few months after they returned to Philadelphia in October 1726, and Denham's death a year later ended the partnership.

Denham did more than help Franklin find his way out of debt and back to America. (Though he insisted on his own budding frugality, Franklin somehow owed more money after Denham died than he had eighteen months before.) As a Quaker, Denham may also have encouraged Franklin to find more positive uses for religion, and to realize that religion could be an aid to virtue and to self-realization. Religion, in short, might be less the authoritative voice of paternal masters than the voice of assurance from within: the path to self-mastery. He confidently fashioned a plan of conduct that included a self-criticism that he "had never fixed a regular design in life" and resolved to be frugal, honest, and industrious. Strikingly, on the voyage back from England he distanced himself from the "loud stinking rabble" of indentured servants. Rogues, he wrote in his journal, are always found out: some slip gives them away.[31]

Two years later he would systematize his new beliefs in a private devotional he called "Articles of Belief and Acts of Religion." He had shifted, it seems, from a Calvinistic insistence on theological rigor that required him either to accept God's heavy hand or to utterly reject it, to a figurative if not literal belief in a plurality of gods—demigods really, children of the "Author and Father of the Gods themselves." These minor deities represent the varieties of human goodness, which imitate the divinity that smiles on that goodness. While there is only one "Powerful Goodness" whom we must revere, the fact of lesser gods permits the convenient illogic of worship as a practice and in the process allows one to meld self-improvement with dutiful thankfulness. For this new Franklin, as for Quakers like Denham, prayer and godliness were less a doctrine or theology than an attitude and a practice. Franklin fixed a "countenance of filial respect" and asked for help from the heavenly "father" but in doing so named the many acts and powers that, however humbly described, were ultimately his to exercise.[32]

In coming to manhood, Franklin had found a way to turn God—and fathers—into friends. Once again in the printing shop, he found himself confident enough to identify with the great Father and Author in composing his own epitaph:

The Body of
B. Franklin,
Printer,
Like the Cover of an old Book,
Its Contents torn out,
And stript of its Lettering and Gilding,
Lies here, Food for Worms.
But the Work shall not be wholly lost:
For it will, as he believ'd, appear once more,
In a new & more perfect Edition,
Corrected and amended
By the Author.

Who is the author of Benjamin Franklin? Clearly, it is God. Yet his cheerful, joking obeisance to the theistic perspective on death and rebirth only provides a gilded cover, as it were, to Franklin's inflated claim for his own trade as an almost divine form of power and inspiration. One could not be much further from Samuel Keimer's, or James Ralph's, pleas for the printer or writer as slave.[33]

Denham's lengthy illness and his death, in 1727, cost Franklin his prospects as a merchant. Homes, his brother-in-law, suggested he return to printing; Keimer came along "with an Offer of large Wages by the Year to come and take the Management of his Printing-House, that he might better attend his Stationer's Shop." Franklin had met Keimer's wife and "her Friends" in London and, not surprisingly, had heard much that led him to doubt Keimer more than ever. If he had been able to find a position with another merchant, he later noted, he would never have gone back into printing. In the *Autobiography* he emphasized the inevitability of Keimer's failure and his own conflict with his less proficient boss— not the more evident fact that, at the time, Keimer was prospering in Philadelphia without Franklin, prospering enough to expand his business and staff.[34]

Keimer, in fact, was doing well in part because he had learned to use

the labor market to his better advantage.[35] Franklin himself became part
of that design. Keimer had five workers, each of them "raw" in terms of
the printing trade. Hugh Meredith and Stephen Potts, former farmers
with intelligence but little experience, worked at low wages in the hopes
of learning the trade. Along with these wage earners Keimer had procured three bound laborers. George Webb, a former Oxfordian, had run
to London to become an actor, descended into debt, and sold himself
into servitude. David Harry was a "country boy" turned apprentice. And
finally Keimer had bought a "wild Irishman" off a ship. Franklin's high
wages were to make up for the fact that Keimer hadn't the time or,
Franklin contended, the skill to teach these men the trade; they would
learn it from Franklin, while the owner of the shop handled the over-the-
counter business.

After about six months, after Franklin had taught them much and
earned their loyalty, Keimer asked for a rebate on his wages and "put on
more of the Master." The last straw came soon, at some point in the autumn of 1727, when Franklin stuck his head out a window to observe a
commotion on election day. Keimer rushed down from the shop to upbraid his foreman in front of not only the other workers but within
earshot of the crowded street. To be not only embarrassed in this manner
but also denied equal participation in public life—the pleasure and the
necessity of watching—especially galled Franklin. The two men argued;
Keimer gave him his three months' notice. He responded by quitting on
the spot.[36]

Underappreciated and upbraided, Franklin almost ran off again, contemplating a return to New England. But a very loyal Hugh Meredith
prevailed upon him with a different plan. Meredith not only admired his
friend and fellow worker but had conveyed, intentionally or not, to his
father, Simon Meredith, that Benjamin had influenced him to drink less
and to improve himself. Hugh was certain that the elder Meredith would
support them in their own printing venture. They could order a press and
type from London; in the meantime Hugh could serve out his last six
months with Keimer. Keimer himself facilitated the plan by asking for
Franklin's help with a big job he had already contracted printing money
for the colony of New Jersey (out of fear that Franklin would do it himself under Bradford's auspices if he did not make the offer). Meredith
and Franklin kept their plan secret from Keimer—a very consequential
deception that Franklin never numbered among his "errata."[37]

At this very moment Franklin turned his desire for fellowship, and his delight in literary companionship, into the Junto, a club for mutual and public improvement. Among its members were some men who would remain his friends for life, including his fellow employees in Keimer's shop: Meredith, Potts, and Webb. Part of the Junto's logic was the necessity of secrecy. The group in effect sought to reinvent social relations from the ground up, to use their deliberations and their knowledge collectively to benefit themselves individually, one another, and ultimately the public. Franklin always defined the group as a public-spirited enterprise, but strikingly it emerged at a moment when he first began to understand the importance of keeping a strict confidence, not only within the trade or the family (as with the Couranteers) but also outside the trade and outside the family.

When Franklin brought his revised theological speculations before the group, he must have realized that his mutual improvement society had not only taken its model from the small congregations and prayer groups of Puritan Massachusetts but had begun, in a small way, to substitute for them as well. The Junto proved to be of quite material use in turning the peripatetic printer into a master and his own man. Members bailed him out of his partnership with Meredith when it became clear that Hugh could not hold up his end. Like his father's friends at Old South Church, they provided key loans and helped give Franklin the confidence to envision a new project, a newspaper. But when he told Webb, who still worked for Keimer, about his plans, he embroiled himself in further dealings that did not match the "*Truth, Sincerity*, and *Integrity* in Dealings between Man and Man" to which the Junto, and his new religious devotions, had been dedicated.

Webb had asked if Franklin might have work for him when his time of service was up. In a scene that echoes the competition for labor that Franklin had experienced as a worker, he offered Webb the prospect of work when he started a newspaper—in effect, planning to steal Keimer's remaining trained hand as soon as it was possible to do so. Webb immediately told Keimer, and in doing so strengthened his own position, as Keimer planned to spite Franklin by beating him to the punch with a new paper.

In the heroic telling of American journalism, Franklin's paper is considered a great literary and practical triumph, a vast improvement over Bradford's and Keimer's efforts. The truth is rather more complicated.

Keimer's proposals for the paper abused Bradford's *American Weekly Mercury* and promised a more lively and informative sheet—the very challenge Franklin had planned, probably thinking of how the *New England Courant* had trumped the establishment paper in Boston through a mix of urbane wit and strategic antiestablishmentarianism. Keimer knew better than Bradford how to bring metropolitan literature to the middle colonies and creatively sought to combine the function of a newspaper with that of a general literary magazine (a strategy that would work fairly well for him in Barbados). When the *Universal Instructor in All Arts and Sciences, and Pennsylvania Gazette* first appeared in October 1728, its pretentious-sounding title indicated its ambition. The paper began by admitting a lack of news but promising to reprint the very innovative Chambers *Cyclopedia*, a project that would later inspire Diderot and the French Encyclopedists. With characteristic literalism, Keimer started with the letter A, and not even his most committed critics—including Franklin—ever said that the encyclopedia entries were as dull as they must appear to us now. The paper's limited success more likely had to do with Keimer's other debts, his labor problem in the wake of Franklin's and Meredith's departures, and the fact that he started his paper on the cusp of a harsh winter.[38]

Keimer may also have struggled against local orthodoxy: his articles and printings against superstition and speculative theology rendered him suspicious in the eyes of local Anglicans and Quakers alike. Franklin seized the opportunity presented by Keimer's reprinting of the *Cyclopedia* article on "ABORTION" to try to undermine his rival by contributing some satire to the *Weekly Mercury*. In a series called *The Busy-Body*, presented in a female voice, he contrasted the man of true virtue with Keimer, whom he depicted as a credulous and pretentious philosopher: "wilt thou never understand that the cringing, mean, submissive Deportment of thy Dependants [Webb?], is (like the Worship paid by Indians to the Devil) rather tho' Fear of the Harm thou mays't do to them, than out of Gratitude for the Favours they have receiv'd of thee?"

Keimer responded by depicting the Busy-Body as a two-headed monster, part "Free-Thinker of the Peripatetic Sect" and part "obscure" manual laborer, an "Understrapper to a Press" who was "Not one but every Ape's epitome."[39] The two were quickly engaged in the old New England (and Grub Street) game of who-owns-religion, a dangerous game indeed for young men on the edge of solvency. Meanwhile, Bradford reaped the rewards, expanding the *Weekly Mercury* to a full sheet for the first time.[40]

Franklin and Keimer might have gone on like that and ruined each other had not Keimer's creditors caught up with him first, securing him in debtor's prison in June 1729. Keimer survived this episode long enough to publish a brief account of his trials, in which he called himself a white Negro. But by September he had sold his press to his former apprentice David Harry, and the *Gazette* to Franklin, and left for Barbados. Harry did not turn out to be the "powerful rival" that Franklin at first feared, thanks, according to Franklin, to his desire to live too well. Soon he too left for Barbados, where, in a turn that clearly delighted Franklin, Harry hired Keimer as a journeyman and fought with him incessantly. Franklin enjoyed the story of their mutual decline in the sweltering heat so much, in fact, that he failed to report in the *Autobiography* that Keimer eventually triumphed over Harry and reestablished himself as a master and entrepreneur of letters. Keimer remained a man of the margins, a schemer and reformer, probably not happy when too successful. For Sam Keimer, perhaps moving to the Caribbean was for the best, as well as what Franklin saw as the worst. As other friends of Franklin would learn, it took a strange mix of ambition and resignation to succeed as a printer in a land of would-be grandees, absentee landlords, and many, many slaves.[41]

Supported by friends and noticed by leading members of the Quaker-dominated Assembly as an upright and sober young man, Franklin had found independence. With it came debt and risk. At several junctures during his partnership with Meredith, the printing enterprise could have easily gone belly up. In perhaps the best-known section of the *Autobiography*, he described the period from 1729 into the early 1730s as a time when he set in place the personal habits that would make him a successful printer. Franklin's adherence to these habits, along with his abilities as a writer and printer, won him "Interests" among the leading men.

But the process was not as linear as he later depicted it. Even as he outlasted Keimer and began to get some of Bradford's business, he had "Intrigues with Low Women that fell in my way," one of whom probably bore him his first son, William, in 1728 or 1729. He courted the niece of the Godfreys, with whom he shared a house, but broke off the engagement when they refused to provide a dowry. Less than three months later he did marry Deborah Read, his girlfriend from six years before, who had recently experienced her own embarrassment when her ne'er-do-well husband skipped town for the West Indies and was not heard from since.[42]

He opened a stationery and bookshop, hired one of his London co-workers, Thomas Whitemarsh, and took on Joseph Rose, the son of Aquila Rose, as an apprentice. Deborah contributed in many ways to the business as well as to the family economy. By the early 1730s the runaway had become a patriarch, a master, and in 1732 a father again, when Deborah gave birth to Francis Folger ("Franky") Franklin, a child named not after his own father or any of his brothers or uncles but after his mother's father and, to all appearances because of the nickname, the father himself.

Franklin expanded his market activities in order to pay off his debt. He also acquired his first African American slaves and servants. He would soon add the topics of marriage and labor to his repertoire of social commentary and satire, ever balancing the opportunities and costs that close relations with other persons always afford. In the meantime, he expanded the *Pennsylvania Gazette*, taking real chances by offering more commentary on local and international affairs. He had made his peace with religion as a positive good and a social fact, and with a God who, like his father and his patrons, "sometimes" intervened to relieve human suffering. And yet he continued to find that as a printer and public voice, he had to tune his perspective on things sacred very, very finely. In pluralist, Quaker-dominated Pennsylvania, religion was not an easy commodity in which to speculate.[43]

In April 1730, for example, his "Letter of a Drum" ridiculed ministers who believed in witchcraft and spirit possession; he followed it up in the next issue of the *Gazette* with an equally anonymous defense of true religion and the printer, whose willingness to print this reply showed his receptiveness to religiosity. In July, when Franklin printed several essays on the origins of Christianity from a London newspaper, he heard that several divines were outraged and invited them to please reply at the same length as the original essays. The next spring, after he printed an ad from a sea captain who forbade his ship to "black gowns" (clerics) and other pests, he had to defend his press as not anticlergy but rather open to all. This first, landmark defense of freedom of the press and the market rationale for its workings, was, in other words, a plea that he was not, despite persistent rumors to the contrary, irreligious.[44]

His rival Bradford, following Keimer, did not miss a chance to stoke those rumors. Everyone knew his newspaper's attacks on blasphemers and revilers of religious establishments were aimed at Franklin and his friend and patron Andrew Hamilton, speaker of the Assembly. At a time when Franklin was beginning to embrace the opposition ideals of the nonproprietary, Quaker-dominated faction in Pennsylvania politics, these debates were quite politicized. When he could not resist putting forth his views on religion—as in an August 1734 parody that depicted true religion as a source of joy and confidence as opposed to morbid thoughts on mortality and the state of the soul—he was taking a significant risk. No matter how serious and respectably liberal his views may have been in the Anglo-American theological spectrum, they no doubt struck some as deistical deviation. No strong adherent of a sect, and no atheist, could have made the *Pennsylvania Gazette* please all its various constituencies; he had to remain open and liberal, providing a space for religious controversy without taking it, or its awe-inspiring implications, too seriously. He understandably remained extremely sensitive to accusations of imbalance or partisanship on the topic of religion—so much so that when a new Presbyterian preacher, Samuel Hemphill (the first minister to keep him in a pew for successive Sundays) came under attack in 1735 for insufficient orthodoxy and lost his position, Franklin uncharacteristically identified with the charismatic young preacher, mistook a parish fight among Presbyterians for a full-scale assault on liberty, and started his first extended pamphlet war.

The Hemphill affair, as it came to be known, was as much a product of Franklin's ambition as anything else; Hemphill might actually have kept his position had Franklin not been so inflamed by the revocation of his friend's pastorate as to rush into print three anonymous pamphlets in his defense. Why would the otherwise temperate Franklin, who had learned the hard way that printers who challenged religious authorities tended to lose out, go on the attack? If Franklin was at such pains to prove himself sympathetic to true religion and not hostile to clergy, why would he risk taking sides in a Presbyterian church court affair?

Two aspects of Hemphill's struggle against the church elders suggest its importance to a Franklin who was making the transition from fugitive iconoclast to liberal-thinking, post-Puritan patriarch. First, Hemphill's new style of preaching, and possibly his embrace of modern rationalist doctrine, led him to be silenced by church elders, including Jedediah Andrews, the minister whom he was supposed to help ease into semiretirement. Secondly, Hemphill insisted that the doctrinarian approach of the church elders, especially Andrews's opposition to emphasis on grace rather than good works, "make[s] us Presbyterians rather than good Citizens." As a result, in his second pamphlet Franklin pulled out all the stops and accused the clergy of being enemies of "truth and Liberty." He contrasted true "Christian liberty," a "Privilege common to Mankind," to a clergy "too fond of Power" who seemed most interested in "enslaving people's minds." "Nothing, in all Probability, can prevent our being a flourishing and happy People, but our suffering the Clergy to get upon our Backs, and ride us, as they do their Horses, where they please."[45]

In Franklin's emerging vision of a pluralist colony guided by the tolerance of its Quaker business and political leaders, there was no place for moral absolutes of the kind he understandably associated with Presbyterian orthodoxies. They were bad for business and bad for him. They subverted the expanded notion of citizenship he had already begun to build with the Junto. Ironically, but perhaps in the end appropriately, Franklin found himself descending to the all-too-familiar level of "polemical divinity" and prophet-centered feuding that he had hoped to supersede.

Franklin deserves much credit for his consistency. He did not merely become the Quakers' pet printer, for he actually opened the *Gazette*'s pages to the first major Quaker antislavery dissenters. To understand the choice Franklin made, we need to consider the substance and the logic of their attack on slavery.

In March 1729, at a time when Franklin was mocking Keimer in the pages of the *Weekly Mercury*, a Quaker merchant named Ralph Sandiford came to him with an antislavery manuscript. A cautious Franklin agreed to publish it, though without his name as printer on the title page: Sandiford would have to purchase and give away most of the copies. Like Thomas Tryon and most early opponents of slavery, Sandiford had seen slavery at first hand in the Caribbean and in South Carolina. He had moved to Philadelphia in the late 1720s only to find slavery on his doorstep, in the form of sales occurring literally right down the street from his shop, especially after the legislature lowered the duty on slaves imported by 90 percent, from £10 to 20 shillings.[46]

Like Samuel Sewall, whom he cited at length, Sandiford defined slavery as an immoral and wicked kind of trade. He countered the argument that it had biblical sanction. He went further, though, and suggested that the church everywhere—and perhaps especially its ministers—was threatened by this iniquity. Taking a page from Tryon as well, he described the immorality of oppressing any beasts of burden. He even identified and updated a particularly North American version of Tryon's slavery-military-colonialism complex: when South Carolinians sold captured Indians into slavery, they encouraged Indians, and Spanish, to do the same, provoking wars. The entire skin trade, and the exploitation of the Indians, appeared to Sandiford as part and parcel of the same colonial reliance on exploitation: "we go to the very Indies for fans and Umbrella's, which are for the same Service to us; for which the very Indians upbraid us, for Robbing the Creatures of their natural Covering, and yet cover ourselves with borrowed Hair, which is unnatural, which shews the great Degeneracy & Fall of Man from his first Creation." Sandiford defined Africans as a captured nation who had not "forfeited their Country and Liberty" and whose captivity was not being redeemed in any way, as all biblical precedents required.[47]

Although Sandiford begged his readers to disregard the fact that his sentiments had not been approved by the Quaker yearly meeting, he was banished from the sect for publishing without the meeting's approval. He died a broken man at the age of forty, in 1733. By that time he had been befriended by another refugee Quaker merchant, Benjamin Lay, who bought copies of Sandiford's book from Franklin and continued to distribute them gratis.

Lay, a regular customer of Franklin, defined himself as a direct disciple of Sewall, Tryon, and Sandiford. A sailor who had settled in Bermuda as a merchant, he had earned the hostility of his fellow white islanders for his attempts to ameliorate slavery. Immigrating to Pennsylvania in 1731, he hoped to find a more sympathetic audience but discovered instead that slaveholding was on the rise among Quakers, as in the colony as a whole. Lay would prove to be a twenty-five-year thorn in the side of the Quaker majority. He took Tryon's injunctions so seriously as to embrace vegetarianism, refuse to eat with slaveholders, and refrain from wearing any garments that were the product of slave labor. During the 1730s he sought a mutually supportive relationship with the animal world, raising vegetables and flax, keeping bees, occasionally living in a cave, and engaging in at least one very public fast. He received admiring visitors, including Franklin and the governor of Pennsylvania, and for more than a decade sought new ways to demonstrate the ways in which slavery was the "Mother of all Sins."[48]

Lay might be called the first modern abolitionist, not only because of his religiously based conviction that slavery was a sin, but because of the way he insisted that slavery corrupted the entire community. Believing so, he testified regularly in Quaker meetings and churches and was often forcibly removed from them. During the 1730s and 1740s he developed more and more dramatic ways of making his point. On one occasion he publicly destroyed his late wife's china as a symbol of the violence wrought by the tea trade and refined appetites. In the most famous episode he stood up in the Burlington, New Jersey, regional yearly meeting of 1738 to denounce slaveholding among Quakers as not only a violation of the golden rule but the ultimate warlike act. Friends might as well renounce their pacifism and put on armor, he exclaimed, opening his overcoat to reveal his military garb below. He then took out a sword and stated that slaveowners committed a sin as grievous as murder—then thrust his weapon into a Bible that hid a bladder of red pokeberry juice, spattering himself and those who shared his bench with the ersatz blood.[49]

Above all Lay sought to make slavery a *personal* matter. His other recorded protests include a pseudo-kidnapping, in which he detained the child of a neighboring slaveowner, asking the worried parent if he did not suppose that his slaves' parents or grandparents had once felt that way. On one cold winter day he stood outside a meeting house with one bare foot in the snow, comparing his self-imposed plight to the daily shiverings of the parishoners' underclothed slaves. Slaves, as Cotton Mather had insisted, were members of the family. Even if servants were part of the natural order of things (Lay and Sandiford, like Tryon before them, explicitly distanced themselves from any attempt to delegitimate all relations of mastery and servitude), ungodly dealings with servants could be the most mortal of sins.

It is clear that Franklin and Lay had an interesting relationship. Franklin assembled and printed Lay's 1737 collection of testimonies and reflections, *All Slave-keepers That Keep the Innocent in Bondage* (though again without the printer's name on the title page), and reported his more spectacular doings with some respect in the pages of the *Pennsylvania*

Gazette. Lay seems to have visited Franklin's shop regularly when he ventured from his country home in Abingdon to purchase paper, ink, legal forms, and books to give away. He also subscribed to the newspaper. Twenty years later, Deborah Franklin still admired Lay enough to keep a portrait of him displayed in their home.[50]

And yet during these same years Franklin began to profit from slavery in multiple ways and owned slaves himself for the first time. Franklin's ambivalence might have been best captured in his only recorded reminiscence of Lay. When the man he respected enough to call the "Pythagorean-cynical-christian Philosopher" walked all the way to Philadelphia to visit him during his famous fast, Franklin found his breath "so acrid as to make his eyes tear and pain."[51] There is no better picture of Franklin's engagement and distance from the dangers of antislavery than Lay's presumption and the printer's sense of an actual physical discomfort in the presence of his words.

Sandiford and Lay attacked vanity, inhumane waste, and the pretensions of ministers. Franklin's early appreciation of Tryon, and his appreciation for Quaker sobriety and egalitarianism, made him receptive to their religiously based criticisms of the entire social order. They knew what they were doing when they approached the young printer for help. Eventually—fifty years later—he would take credit for printing the first antislavery pamphlets in the province. As the Hemphill affair showed, Franklin could get genuinely excited about the contemporary indictment of religious authority as "enslaving." He might even sympathize with an attack on religious hypocrites who sought moral authority in the community but were guilty of holding slaves.[52]

For these reasons, however, he needed a rationale for keeping a sympathetic distance from antislavery. He found it in religious pluralism, his commitment to freedom of the press, which suited his desire to expand his market beyond any one denomination. This pluralism, which took God seriously but denied the power of divine judgment and church discipline, ignored one crucial aspect of the emerging antislavery argument from faith. Slaves, in this vision of Mather, Sewall, Tryon, Sandiford, and Lay, were not only members of the human family, but also members of a society of families who were subject to the government of church as well as state.

In the long run, Sandiford and Lay proved prophetic. More patient activists like John Woolman and Anthony Benezet guided the Friends toward the antislavery vanguard, and Franklin, somewhat grudgingly, with them. But in the shorter run of the mid-eighteenth century—for most of his adult life—Franklin's agenda made him a rather strange friend of antislavery. He brought it into the marketplace of ideas only to leave it there.

In the *Pennsylvania Gazette*, people of African descent were understood rather differently. In a 1730 annual census of corpses added to the Philadelphia burying ground, Franklin reported 81 "Church" [Anglicans], 39 Quakers, 18 Presbyterians, 8 beggars, and 71 "Strangers"—41 whites, 30 blacks. People of African descent were classed with vagrants and other people not of the community, whatever their nativity and despite their economic and personal importance to the households in which they lived, worked, and died. Six months later, after another wave of smallpox had hit and left the town, Franklin announced another body count: 288 people had died of the disease. He added that "64 of the Number were Negroes; If these may be valued one with another at £30 per Head, the Loss to the City in that Article is near £2000."[53]

Citizens had religious identities; strangers had only racial ones. Race, in turn, made it easier to define certain strangers as property rather than as children. Our understanding of Benjamin Franklin and the role of slavery in eighteenth-century America depends on our ability to see such definitions as a creative choice made by men who defined themselves, and quite often their economic and political enterprises, against "slavery" but wanted—or needed—to have their slavery, too. In Benjamin Franklin's America, the community would be redefined as secular, public, and free to practice any religion as long as that practice did not interfere, as Mather and Lay sought to interfere, with the consciences, privileges, or property of others. That body of citizens, in the pages of the *Pennsylvania Gazette*, came in many creeds but only one shade: white.

PART TWO

Enterprises: Slavery, Capitalism, and Empire

To be SOLD,

At Christiana-Bridge, within the County of New Castle,

A Good Dwelling House, with two Brick Chimneys, a large Stone-wall'd Cellar, and a small Loft, lying convenient in the Town for a Store or a Tradesman to Live in. Together with Thirty Acres of good rough Land (just by the Town) two or three Acres of it is newly clear'd for Meadow; there may be made 10 or 12 more of Meadowing. Whoever inclines to Purchase the same may repair to Lewis Howell at the Place, or to Messirs. White and Taylor, Merchants, in Philadelphia, and know further.

THere was lately taken up and are now in Burlington Goal, Two Negro Men, who belong to Baltimore County, in Maryland.
The right Owner is desired to pay the Charges and take them away.

For JAMAICA directly,

THe Sloop Elizabeth and Mary, William Burrows Master: For Freight or Passage agree with said Master at Mr. Beun's Wharfe, on very reasonable Terms. She will Sail for the above Port with all convenient Speed.

RAN-away from William Rumsey on the 26th of September past, an indented Irish Servant Lad named Benjamin Mozley, about 19 Years of Age, middle Stature, fair Complexion, large Nose, light brown Hair pretty much Sun-burnt, he talks good English; had on an old yellowish colour'd Coat of CottonRibb (somewhat like Fustian) too long Wasted for him, and trimm'd with white Metal Buttons with wooden Moulds in them, and an old red Duffil Great Coat, Oznabrigs Breeches and Jacket, an old fine Hat, and old Jockey-boots, his Linen uncertain, had Oznabrigs Shirts, but 'tis supposed he took one or more Garlick Holland Shirts with him ruffled at Bosom and Sleves. Rode away on a fine large natural Pacing Bay Mare branded R S, shod Before, and one of her Hoofs being broke Shoing is cut shorter than the other, had also an old Breasted Saddle and a snaffle Bridle.
Whoever apprehends the said Servant and secures him, and the aforesaid Mare, so that their Master shall have them again, shall have Fifty Shillings Reward. And if either of them be brought Home to their Master living near the Head of Bohemia in Cecil County, Maryland, shall have a sufficient Reward and reasonable Charges, Paid by
William Rumsey.

RAN-away on the 22d of August last, from Joseph Gumly of the Mannor of Mooreland in the County of Philadelphia, an Irish Servant Man named Martin Farril, a pretty lusty Man, of a sandy Complexion; he has large grey Eyes, no Hair but wears a Cap; he had on a light colour'd Kersey Coat without Cuffs, and has Pewter Buttons with a flap over the Button holes, a pair of Trowsers and Drawers, homespun Shirt, good Stockings and Shoes, and a Castor Hat.
Whoever takes up the said Servant and brings him to Philadelphia Goal, shall have Six Pounds Reward, and all reasonable Charges, paid by
Joseph Gumly.

RAN-away, the 26th of August last, from William Beasin of Cecil County in Maryland, an Irish Servant Man named Will Flanoom, aged about 20 Years, of middle Stature and well set, very much Pock fretten, short dark Hair and very little Beard, he has a very large Scar on his right Foot above the Toes, lately cut with an Adz; had on when he went away a Felt Hat half worn, two Shirts one of Ozenbrigs, an old Flannel Jacket, a linsey-woolsey Vest with large flat Metal Coat Buttons down the Breast, a pair of half worn Buckskin Breeches with some white Metal and some Brass Buttons and three streight Seams down each Knee, two pair of old Trowlers one of Ozenbrigs the other striped Linen, mix Yarn Stockings and old Leather-heel'd Shoes He is by Trade a Miller, but may pretend to be a Sailor or Plowmaker. He speaks pretty good English, but can neither read nor write
Whoever takes up and secures the said Servant, and gives Notice thereof to Bohemia Ferry in Cecil County aforesaid, so that his Master may have him again, shall have Fifty Shillings Reward and reasonable Charges,
paid by William Beasin.

To be Sold by George M'Call,

A Very likely Young Negro Woman; also Broad Cloaths, Kerseys, Druggets, Shalloons, plain and strip'd Calamincoes, Tammies, plain and strip'd Camblets, Ruggs, and Stockings, Worsted Caps, Muslins, Garlick and Irish Linens, Writing Paper, and London double Refin'd Sugar, Iron Pots, Nails, Short and Long Pipes, Hats, & sundry other sorts o Goods, on reasonable Terms.

TO be Sold by Humphrey Garland, at the House late of Mr. Spragell, in Second-Street near Arch-Street, Worsted Damasks, Silk and Worsted Crapes, Plain Calimincoes, Camlettees, Mantua Silks, Persians, Tickens; sundry Haberdashery, Cutlery and Iron Wares, at very reasonable Rates.

For BRISTOL directly,

THe Snow Pompey, James Wyllie Master, will Sail with all convenient Expediton: For Freight or Passage agree with William Hellier, or the said Master.
☞ N. B. She will have very good Accommodations for Passengers.

ALL Persons Indebted to Reese Meredith, are desired to come and Settle with him, and Pay their respective Balances, he designing to leave the Province by the first convenient Opportunity.
To be Sold by said Meredith, at his Store on William Fishbourn's Wharfe, Three quarter Garlicks, Plain and Corded Dimitys, Broad and Narrow Shalloons, Tammys, Worsted and Cotton Caps; Mens, Womens and Childrens Stockings, Stuffs, Calimincoes, Crapes, Sagathees, Mohair and Buttons, Metal Ditto, Fine Hats, Bohea and Green Tea, Coffee, Single and Double refin'd Sugar, Sail Duck, Cutlery and Iron Ware, Guns, Anchors, a set of Blocks and Pumps for a Ship and Sloop, Logwood, Short Pipes, Earthen Ware, and Manchester Goods: All very reasonably for Ready Money.

CHoice good LAMP-BLACK made and sold by the Printer hereof.

Philadelphia: Printed and Sold by Andrew Bradford, Post-Master, at the Sign of the Bible in Second-Street, where Advertisements are taken in, and all Persons in Town or Country may be supplyed with this Paper.

American Weekly Mercury, October 2, 1735. (Courtesy of the American Antiquarian Society)

FOUR

People and Capital

For more than a century, scholars looking for the root of things American and middle-class have scrutinized Franklin's writings in the *Pennsylvania Gazette*, the annual *Poor Richard's Almanack* (1733–58), and the parts of the *Autobiography* in which he candidly yet enigmatically reflected on his remarkable rise to wealth and public prominence. Yet Franklin remains famously elusive, and his reputation famously divided. Was he the avatar of the common man's rise to wealth and patriotic service, as historians long insisted, or the prophet of a repressive bourgeois capitalism, as modernists like D. H. Lawrence concluded?[1] The confusion arises in part because of his penchant for mixing business and politics, self-making and philosophy. To understand Franklin's ethos, it is necessary to look at what he was doing as well as what he was saying. And with a man who sought so diligently to make silence a virtue, it is important to notice what he avoided saying, or said less often.[2]

Consider one well-known remark from the *Gazette* written in the summer of 1736: "The Printer hopes the irregular Publication of this Paper will be excused a few times by his Town Readers in consideration of his being at Burlington [New Jersey] with the Press, labouring for the publick Good, to make Money more plentiful."[3] In a typical double entendre, Franklin gently conflated the printing of money with the creation of actual wealth. His own labors became synonymous with the public good. His audience—his customers—were turned from annoyed readers into chuckling co-workers. The strenuous and rapid expansion of his role from a local Philadelphia printer to an intercolonial businessman and proponent of paper money was reduced to everyday terms, to labor, to humor, and most of all to the creation of a form of capital that was supposed to benefit all of his readers. In one sentence Franklin emerged as a populist, a capitalist, a local citizen, and a man on the move.[4]

As a former unfree laborer seeking to expand the market for secular print, Franklin saw unfettered trade as a new source of wealth and freedom. As no one quite had before, he learned to make his printed manufactures—the newspaper and the annual almanacs—essential goods in the booming economy. Even as his printed and self-authored products explored the religious, ethnic, and economic differences among his audiences, Franklin also addressed their commonalities, helping to advance a new civic world and marketplace in which virtue and dollars were the only differences that mattered, at least for white men. As part of his relatively egalitarian campaign to expand the marketplace and the civic realm in an orderly, improving fashion, he himself became a regulator of unruly persons—especially the women, servants, and slaves who at times threatened to turn his "new American order" on its head.[5]

His printed paper commentaries became commodities that regulated the circulation of other commodities, including people who were bought and sold. Simultaneously, he experimented with paper money and a related set of abstractions. If money contained no self-evident essence, such as the value of metal, if it was the product of the marketplace, of opinion and perception, of the value placed upon the labor it represented, then money was not a foreign object; it was a metaphor, a representation not merely of human labor but of people themselves. The corollary was that people could be seen as capital.

Franklin's writings of the 1730s and 1740s pivot repeatedly around these notions of money as akin to people, and people as capital. Playing with such tropes helped him to trace the liberating features of the capitalist marketplace. Indeed, they helped him to emphasize those features from the perspective of those with a greater measure of control over their own persons and capital. Individuals could, in fact, seize that liberating control. And he managed all this while minimizing the fact that even though everyone might become like a commodity in a world where an individual and his labor were evaluated in public, some people were literally commodities. The roots of Franklin's capitalism and his glossing of slavery lay alike in his practice as printer and producer of knowledge about a credit economy in which speculations in people's lives and labors could accrue paper wealth to the speculators with remarkable speed and efficiency. The artfully mixed metaphors of people and capital added up to Franklin's first great master story, a set of experimental morality tales that suited his ambitions as a one-time commodity turned tradesman and trader. Their ironies have always been delicious to those who could imagine themselves in Franklin's place. With respect to persons abstracted into capital—especially women and slaves—the story got increasingly difficult for Franklin to manage. It is at these junctures in his story that we see the hinges and rough edges of his philosophy, his politics, and his practice. There traditional morality and traditional prejudices, which Franklin himself was quite capable of questioning, would come to have new, compensatory uses.

What kind of businessman did Franklin become? In the *Autobiography* he stressed the measures he took to become independent of debt. Patronage and public opinion were essential to success in the marketplace, but they could be managed through the careful projection of being a credibly hardworking, sober citizen. Efficiency was essential, but it was of limited use if it was not perceived by customers. Franklin seems to have let the reader backstage, as it were, when he wrote of his self-conscious decision to wheel his own loads of paper through the streets. It is easy to forget that the telling of such anecdotes itself continues the performance of a virtuous, penny-pinching author who was once again allying his interests with those of his reader. Pushing the wheelbarrow, Franklin was no capitalist middleman: he eliminated the middleman— and the porter or servant who might otherwise do the pushing.[6]

Actually, from early in the 1730s Benjamin Franklin's print shop was a much more diversified enterprise than he made it seem in the *Autobiography*, and it was all the more successful for being so. Diversification served many ends in a cash-poor economy, and many of the measures Franklin took to save money actually removed various aspects of his printing from cash exchange. At the same time, taking and selling goods involved him in the complexities of contemporary merchant capitalism, where exchanges of goods for services, and in kind, could become quite intricate and quite speculative. Barter required double-entry bookkeeping and an increasingly savvy approach to costs and receipts. Penny-saving through not spending had implications for every transaction. Money could potentially be saved, or made, anywhere.[7]

Franklin was this kind of businessman. If we begin with the advertisements in the *Pennsylvania Gazette* and supplement them with his surviving account books, we get a vivid picture of his business practices. Many of the merchants who advertised in the *Gazette* included a whole shop's or ship-bottom's worth of goods—including, sometimes, indentured servants or slaves. The newspaper functioned as a clearinghouse of information about the arrival of goods and workers, indicating where they could be seen and from whom one could learn more about them. By 1730 Franklin himself had become one of these merchants—by virtue of holding and selling both workers and goods for sale. These goods were hardly limited to the crown soap and candles made by his Yankee siblings, or to the lampblack he began to make in a side venture to supply himself with the raw materials for ink. His book and stationery shop, opened in 1730 on the floor beneath his press room and tended after 1733 by Deborah Franklin, gradually became something of a general store, filled with a wide assortment of merchandise supplied by his own merchant customers: sugar, coffee, rice, and other new necessities of life, all of them unthinkable without plantation slavery.[8]

The men with whom Franklin did business existed along a continuum of barter and transatlantic trade. Consider William Crosthwaite, a local wigmaker, hairdresser, and owner of several slaves and servants who worked in his own shop during the 1730s. Crosthwaite regularly took out ads in Franklin's paper, advertising his wigs and occasionally one of his workers (a slave or servant) for sale. He also came to Franklin to offer rewards for stolen wigs—and for runaway laborers. For the ads he probably paid Franklin much-needed cash. He also bought "bonds" (printed contracts), blank paper, indenture forms, almanacs, books, sealing wax for his own correspondence, an account book, and at least once, some of the New England Franklins' crown soap. These purchases may have been made on credit: Franklin kept accounts of such transactions—receipts and expenditures—both by date and by the customer's name. Crosthwaite may have been one of the artisans from whom Franklin took services in lieu of cash payment. Later a hairdresser earned a subscription to the *Gazette* in return for a regular shave.[9]

Taken alone, William Crosthwaite might appear to have been a mere artisan, getting more efficient perhaps but hardly possessed of an adventurous, much less capitalist, spirit. But he had a brother who sailed the coastal route. Thomas Crosthwaite advertised berths aboard his sloop, the *Charming Betty*, in the *Pennsylvania Gazette* when he was ready to depart on his regular runs to South Carolina. When he returned, he advertised his goods for sale: rice and slaves who could be inspected at his brother William's wig shop. Both were available "for Ready Money, flour or Bread." Franklin's paper goods, Thomas Crosthwaite's ship, William's wigs, the grains grown by farmers north and south, and slaves formed inseparable commodity chains. Any link in the chain could be a source of profit or sustenance.[10] The process turned savvy, well-connected artisans like Franklin and William Crosthwaite into merchants—and slave-dealers. Indeed, the increased availability of slaves in the 1730s made these roles practically the same.

When the hairdressing Crosthwaite died in 1748, the executors of his estate held a public auction of his effects, including "a young Negroe Man, who can shave and dress wigs very well, and a Negroe woman, who can wash, iron, and is a very good cook; also a servant man's time, who has but two years and three months to serve." Trading with the slave colonies and dealing in slaves themselves made Franklin, like William Crosthwaite, more likely to own or rent them.[11] As early as December 16, 1735, Franklin purchased shoes for his "negro boy," and he purchased a beaver hat for his "man Joseph" in 1742 and a raccoon one for his "Negro" in 1745.[12] Given what Franklin himself said about his household economy during these years, it is certain that most if not all of the slaves and servants he owned worked in the shop. They would have freed his wife, Deborah Franklin, to tend the increasingly busy counter where goods were bought and accepted as payment.[13]

The Crosthwaite-Carolina connection may have helped Franklin imagine and enact the extension of his business toward the plantation societies of the new world. In 1731 he sent his trusted assistant Thomas Whitemarsh, whom he had first met in London, to Charleston, to collect a bounty offered by the South Carolina Assembly for the establishment of a print shop. Two years later, after Whitemarsh died, he sent Louis Timothée as a replacement. This was the first of a string of limited-liability partnerships that brought Franklin healthy profits and, even more important, extended his mercantile enterprise. Partners in other colonies became conduits of news for his paper, provided a bigger market for his stationery supplies, books, and almanacs, and even became an outlet for excess dry goods accumulating in his own shop, including tobacco and wheat. He sent five hundred copies of the third run of *Poor Richard's Almanack* to Timothée, via Crosthwaite.[14]

As a merchant who communicated essential mercantile information like the arrival of ships and the availability of goods, Franklin was in the best position of all to understand and profit from Atlantic trade. In an everyday sense, this meant controlling information about servants and slaves, but it also meant something as traditional as bartering food-stuffs—trading in marked-up goods while avoiding markups when it came to his own household's needs. His arrangements with his workers partook of this historic mix of forestalling, bartering, and wage-paying. Stephen Potts, a friend of Franklin's and fellow employee of Sam Keimer, regularly worked for Franklin as a bookbinder and pressman and kept a little bindery shop of his own in his room. He rented this room from Franklin's mother-in-law, Mrs. Read, sometimes boarded with the Franklins, and at other times partly fed himself out of Franklin's stores of rice and codfish. Franklin's ledgers recount regular deductions for sundries as well as cash payments to Potts.[15]

Evidently Potts preferred to keep his life as simple as possible, even if it meant usually being in debt to his landlord and friend. It certainly served Franklin well to have his friend available as a worker and a con-sumer of goods in precisely the casual manner that seems to have satis-fied Potts. When Potts died in 1758, Franklin recalled him as happy despite his lack of funds or goods: "a Wit that seldom acted wisely . . . in the midst of Poverty, ever laughing!" He had been a relatively wise fool, in other words, whom Franklin contrasted favorably to another deceased compatriot, a rich friend who "fretted" away his wealth. Not everybody took advantage of the market in goods and people; some, like Potts, pre-ferred to let others, like Franklin, do the worrying—and take the profits. In the *Autobiography*, it is fairly clear what happens to these kinds of men: they wind up working for others, often in places like Barbados.[16]

Potts was a fellow founding member of the Junto, Franklin's mutual improvement society. Early members included established tradesmen, others just starting out, and others working as journeymen, for wages. The activities and concerns of the Junto included debates that would sharpen the minds of its members for public service and their own pur-suits. Yet very early on Franklin identified the Junto's goals as those of *master* artisans and tradesmen, rather than all "leather apron men." These men not only sent one another business but collectively sought ways to avoid paying more for their workers than necessary. In his own set of queries for the Junto copied into his notebook in 1731, Franklin asked, immediately after an initial question about why water forms on the outside of a cold metal tankard, "Does the importation of Servants increase or advance the Wealth of our Country—Would not an Office of Insurance for Servants be ~~advantageous~~ of Service; and ~~how~~ what methods are proper for the erecting such an office."[17] Franklin was thinking of the wealth masters had invested *in* servants as well as the wealth servants produced. The importation of unfree people would certainly increase the polity's overall wealth (and their own) if they all were destined to become wealth-producing freemen, but in 1731 Franklin knew that that was an uncertain proposition and that his own quickly improving prospects were as much an exception as the rule. Nor, it seems, could servants be counted on to always be a good investment for their masters—least of all if they tended to become free as Franklin had done, by running away. Hence the follow-up question: might there be a way of leveraging the capital that Franklin and his fellow master tradesmen invested in servants? An insurance scheme could save employers from the risks of their competition with one another in the labor market, as well as from the risks of losing bondsmen who stole away.

No runaway in 1731, Franklin identified the wealth of masters with that of "our Country." These were the men of virtue who he imagined would bind together and effect a kind of revolution. His *Pennsylvania Gazette* essays of 1730–32 reveal that he was giving a great deal of thought and energy to the question of how such tradesmen should behave. They needed to obey certain rules for their own interests to meld with the public's good. He carefully distinguished "lying shopkeepers" from honest ones, insisting that credit in the marketplace should be a reflection of true character, and that double-dealing only increased the distrust and guile of the consumers, who then would be encouraged to lie themselves. In the ideal world Franklin described in the pages of the *Gazette*, free sellers and buyers recognized common interests and acted by the same standards. They left "cunning" and double-dealing to runaways and bondsmen—the "sordid and Ignorant Servants, and dishonest idle vagabonds, [who] often attain to the highest Perfection of it."[18]

The equity and transparency Franklin sought, which would bring credit to merchants like him, had to be dissociated from the aspects of the market historically associated with fairs and the much-less-differentiated group known as "the people," who claimed the street and its transactions (licit and illicit) as their own. Nowhere does Franklin appear more quintessentially bourgeois than in his writings penned before the publication of *Poor Richard's Almanack*. In them he criticized the bipolar class distinctions thrown about in the popular politics of the day for underestimating the virtues of both the wealthy and "the people." Instead, he sought to regulate not only elite disdain for merchants and marketplaces but also, and less subtly, the actions of ordinary people, especially the unfree, who gave the streets and markets a bad name.

During the fall of 1731 he began a campaign against the traditional fair. In doing so he invoked all the classic terms of dirt and disorder that scholars of Europe have identified as crucial to the nascent bourgeoisie's attempt to distance themselves from traditional popular culture.[19] Like his contemporaries in England, Franklin appreciated the ways in which the commercialization of culture and society could lead to degradation as well as to progress. He sought to expand and improve the market in general and the readership of the *Gazette* in particular, creating a larger respectable audience of producer-consumers. His protest against the fair typifies his writing, business, and political strategies of the 1730s. But Franklin's American version of the reform of traditional popular culture contains a peculiarly American twist: it is unfree people—servants and slaves—whose freedom is the greatest threat to mercantile mastery.

The trade in "trifling commodities" available at fairs was not to be confused with real commerce, which Franklin defined as open, visible, and honest. Rather, it took place in "Booths" and continued into the night. Worse, it was the occasion for "the insolent and dangerous and scandalous Collection of Negroes, mixing with low white servants and Boys in their petty and noisy Games" in the streets. Servants who attended fairs got drunk and "contrive[d] to run away." Franklin elaborated on this sordid picture, which he initially published in the *Gazette*, in a draft petition to the Pennsylvania Assembly that survives in the same notebook where he recorded his devotional exercises and his queries for the Junto concerning insurance. There he also noted "That Servants who by Custom think they have a Right to Liberty of going out at those Times, commonly disorder themselves so as to be unfit for Business some time after; and what is worse, having perhaps done some Mischief in their Liquor, and afraid of Correction, or getting among ill Companions, they combine to run away more than at any other Time." Fairs, in short, encouraged theft—of money, of goods, and of the people without whose labor neither money nor goods could be efficiently produced.[20]

In presenting a public voice that was favorable toward commerce but critical of its excesses, Franklin's articles adapted not just the form but also the substance of his models, the *Spectator* essays of Joseph Addison.[21] Because he was both creating a literary persona with a critical voice and guarding his investments as a proprietor, Franklin continually expanded the purview of his market-regulating activities. The illicit, money-devaluing activities of theft and counterfeiting especially concerned him. In the *Gazette*'s pages he successfully spread information regarding the commission of theft and counterfeiting, the pursuit of these criminals, and their often harsh punishment. Like runaways, thieves and counterfeiters turned rational production and consumption on its head and introduced distrust into the process of buying and selling. Unfortunately, the spread of the market, and the circulation of people in and through Philadelphia and its hinterland that signaled growing trade, made theft and false coinage harder to prevent.[22]

Franklin's war on criminals continued throughout his editorship of the *Gazette*, but it took especially intense forms during the 1730s. In the New England of Franklin's youth, ministers like the Mathers had guided the public interpretation of the meaning of crime. They allied theft, murder, and moral failings, like adultery and buggery, with sin and guided a system of punishment that sought to expunge evil from the community. Sinners' public renunciations of sin, on the way to or even at the gallows, served as rites of purification, where God's rule and community standards could be reinforced and mutually strengthened.[23]

Franklin's far more secular reports on crime inaugurated a different tradition: one in which criminals themselves were singled out and defined as outsiders by nature—their crimes being windows onto their bad character rather than symptoms of omnipresent deviltry. In a series of reports on the arraignment, trial, and reprieve of two indentured servants in 1730, we can see him transforming the form and the ritual of crime reportage, emphasizing less the roots of crime in sin than the secular causes and consequences of thefts and punishments. James Prouse and James Mitchel had allegedly broken into a barber's house on Front Street and, with the help of their drinking companion, the barber's own servant, stolen seven pounds and ten shillings. Prouse, only nineteen years old, confessed to being in on the plot but tried, unsuccessfully at first, to argue for Mitchel's innocence. Franklin's report of their trip to the gallows, Prouse's confession, and Mitchel's protest of innocence showed the servants appealing to the magistrates and the crowd by narrating their lives as a series of misfortunes that had led them into servitude in the first place. They confessed their responsibility and, in almost identical form, separated the question of their actual punishment for theft from their guilt of sin before God, affirming their religious identity in their last words: "I die a Protestant."

Franklin, however, turned the crime and the governor's last-minute reprieve into a commentary on the problem of servants and the compensations offered by the increasingly polite and virtuous people and their magistrates. Several "compassionate people" appealed for clemency despite their knowledge that "the great Increase of Vagrants and idle Persons, by the late large Importation of such from several Parts of *Europe*," had rendered it necessary "for the common Good to make some Examples." Mitchel, the innocent man, displayed "fortitude" and "manly Constancy"—until he was actually pardoned, when he appropriately thanked God and the governor and shed visible tears of joy that were reflected in faces of the well-meaning "Multitude" looking on. The streets became a theater of education, not only in the traditional virtues of religiosity but in the newer ones of manners, of secular grace under duress. For Franklin, the spectacle became a lesson not in the ubiquity of sin or in the inevitability of God's will but in "the general laudable Humanity even of our common People, who were unanimous in their loud Acclamations of *God bless the Governor for his Mercy*." Franklin the editor scrutinized the events of the day for signs not of divine intervention but a very human, secular goodness. God was still present, unquestionably, but more in the invocations of the people and the convicts than in the editor's own framing of events. Franklin had turned a godly ritual into one defining public virtue. Servants were still suspect but were worthy of redemption if they acted according to the relatively new norms of politeness that his paper celebrated.[24]

This secular, reforming perspective on business and crime extended to an even more ample stream of writings on the theme of consumption, culminating in the persona of "Richard Saunders," the fictional author of Franklin's *Poor Richard's Almanack*. In the first edition, published in late 1732, Richard explains that he has taken his almanac to market only because his "excessive proud" wife Bridget threatens to keep him "excessive poor." The next year public patronage of the almanac has created an embarrassment of riches. While Richard has bought only a secondhand coat with the almanac's profits, Bridget has purchased shoes, two new shifts, and a petticoat (a potent contemporary symbol of fashion). Franklin was always tempted to make women the symbol of overconsumption, even as he also made them symbolic of the broadening of respectability that print, and good market manners, could bring.[25]

He was toeing a fine line, in other words, between advancing the liberating possibilities of the marketplace, and maintaining the kind of traditional order on which stable market relations depended—an understandable position for a young, up-and-coming tradesman. Also in 1733 he published a short essay in the *Gazette* signed "BLACKAMORE." Its author, a self-described "mechanick," satirizes a would-be "molatto gentleman" for the purpose of decrying not racial intermixture (he seems to take that phenomenon for granted) but the overweening "ambition" of the would-be gentleman. The mulatto is like the would-be gentleman insofar as both are trying to be what they are not, the one a gentleman and the other white. The racial phenomenon is not an exception but rather the rule about proper modesty, the limitations of self-fashioning in a world still made up of two classes, the ordinary and the genteel: "our *half Gentry* are exactly in the Case of the *Mulattoes* abovementioned. They are the Ridicule and Contempt of both sides."[26]

The essay cites several examples of the social "Mungrel," one of whom is compared to "a Monkey that Climbs a Tree, the higher he goes, the more he shows his Arse." Franklin was so intent on ridiculing people who would too quickly turn money into gentility that he relativized notions of race, even as the motif of his essay depended on the idea that blackness, even half-blackness, could determine status in the last instance. His casting of race as no more (though also no less) real than other forms of social distinction is a side effect of his goal: to regulate all those on the bottom, whose excessive striving could make deserving aspirants (like himself) look bad. By concluding with the thought that while "there are perhaps *Mulattoes* in religion, in Politicks, in Love, and in several other Things, none appear to me so monstrously ridiculous as the *Molatto Gentleman*," he would seem to have it both ways. He has not challenged racism or extended it; he has used it to keep bondsmen, a category that after all included virtually all mulattos, in their places. The signature "BLACKAMORE" itself compares the self-identified author, a mechanic, with a happy slave, content to remain in a subordinate position.

And yet, at its most revealing—before it turned race into a metaphor for social order—the essay did something else. Like the Dingo piece he had written before his flight from Boston, Franklin actually tried to see things from the perspective of a person of color and even implied that many people were sharing the experience of in-between status mediated by everyday public perceptions in a growing city.

> [Mulattoes'] Approach towards Whiteness, makes them look back with some kind of Scorn upon the Colour they seem to have left, while the Negroes, who do not think them better than themselves, return their Contempt with Interest: And the Whites, who respect them no Whit more for the nearer Affinity in Colour, are apt to regard their Behaviour as too bold and assuming, and bordering upon Impudence. As they are next to Negroes, and but just above 'em, they are terribly afraid of being thought Negroes, and therefore avoid as much as possible their Company or Commerce: and Whitefolks are as little fond of the company of *Molattoes*.

Contempt returned "with Interest," "Company or Commerce": racial discrimination appears as another entry in the marketplace. Even when he was decrying the effects that quick moneymaking could have on social relations, Franklin was relying on a distinctly economic language to describe the process. His publications—market products that helped people prepare themselves for market activities—tended with greater and greater regularity, and creativity, to think of people as products of a marketplace, and about the marketplace as a distinctly human place.[27] It was an exciting time in the study of man and institutions, and Franklin's contribution was to improve upon the idea that people, in society, acted like capital—and that capital, if carefully monitored, multiplied like people in a new country.

In the Anglo-American world of the early eighteenth century, few topics commanded as much attention as the problem of credit and its representation in money. The British fiscal-military state and the "financial revolution" that made it possible faced a reckoning after its seeming (but strikingly, not actual) collapse in a colonial stock speculation scheme.

The so-called South Sea Bubble of 1720 raised the question of what exactly was happening in a world where great fortunes could be made and unmade through the trade in paper wealth. In the colonies, provincial governments tussled with the question of whether to turn to paper money to alleviate chronic shortages of coin and manage the confusions arising from the many sorts of coin circulating along Atlantic routes. If paper wealth, with its basis in overseas trade, threatened to displace the material wealth of land and precious metals, perhaps paper currencies could be based on land values in the land-rich colonies. Thus the first, controversial banking schemes in New England were based on the notion of paper currency as coined land, to be issued by chartered land banks.[28]

It was obvious to all that issues of paper money favored debtors over creditors, striving men and small property holders over wealthy landed proprietors. As a result, paper became the issue around which some of the first organized political factions coalesced in Massachusetts, New York, and Pennsylvania. Franklin had seen it as a young man in Massachusetts in the 1710s: the Couranteers had picked up on some of the antiestablishment themes voiced there by the "popular" pro-bank party.[29] As a tradesman in debt, he had special reason to give the matter of money very serious thought. The result was his first major political intervention, a pamphlet entitled *A Modest Enquiry into the Nature and Necessity of a Paper-Currency* (1729). Franklin did not try to hide which side he was on: he hardly could in these politicized debates. He explicitly argued that the emission of paper money was justified precisely because it would benefit artisans. The justice of the measure could be seen in who stood against it: moneylenders, large landowners, speculators in land, lawyers, and the "Dependants" of these rich and powerful people. In the strain of contemporary political thinking fashionable in the colonies, landowners were supposedly the basis of the body politic, the virtuous remnant set against the corrupting powers of urban speculation. Franklin turned the virtuous remnant into the "lovers of trade"—not merchants (who were invisible in his sociology) but rather the "Labouring and Handcrafts Men which are the chief Strength and Support of a People." When such people were discouraged by the scarcity of capital, they did not migrate to Pennsylvania. Lack of immigration in turn depressed the price of land and led to the loss of more specie, which went to pay for imports that could be supplied by local artisans if they were better encouraged to come and stay.[30]

Two crucial arguments follow from these observations. First, real wealth in the community derived from its working people. Government policy should aim to increase their numbers without lessening overseas trade. Second, and more important, paper money was merely a means to that end. The real issue was people and their labor, because labor—not land or capital—was the real source of wealth: "The riches of a country are to be valued by the quantity of labor its inhabitants are able to purchase, and not by the quantity of silver and gold they possess." Money, being merely "whatever it will procure," ought to be mobilized to save real wealth—that is, labor. Money, then, was not only "coined land," as the land-bank advocates maintained, but also, even primarily, coined labor. Since labor was nothing if not human time, the very circulation of a currency that saved time and money would actually create real—not just paper—wealth.[31]

It is tempting to cite Franklin as an early champion of artisans', and thus working people's, economic interests. Karl Marx himself credited Franklin's essay with an important conceptual advance: he called it "the first conscious, clear and almost trite analysis of exchange value into labor value." But Marx also realized that Franklin did so in a fundamentally bourgeois vein that "abstracted" and "alienated" labor. In this case, Marx came closer to the truth than some of his modern adherents, who would make a working-class hero of Franklin. Far from championing the interests of all laboring people, Franklin practically apologized for identifying labor as the source of wealth. The definition of wealth's ultimate source was not really the point; the real point was to increase "the quantity of labor its inhabitants are able to purchase." As in his queries to the Junto, Franklin was greatly concerned about the cost of laborers to artisans and tradesmen who worked, to be sure, but who also purchased workers' time and oftentimes workers themselves. He was an apostle here not of the labor metaphysic (the Marxist ideal) but of labor's commodification (Marx's nightmare).[32]

The most important influence on Franklin's political economy, the English statistician and physician William Petty, had sought to quantify the value of Irish land and labor in order to rationalize England's colonization of Ireland, secure title for absentee landowners, and turn that country into a source of stable revenue for the crown. The problem for Franklin was to adapt Petty's analysis to the colonies without allowing the white colonists themselves to be reduced to so many monetary units (since they, after all, were the colonizers, not the colonized; like the English in Ireland, not the Irish themselves). When Franklin indulged his developing "habit of quantifying" by multiplying the cash value of slaves lost in the smallpox epidemic of 1731, he made a distinction between people who had a monetary value and people who did not. He also revealed, however, that his particular application of Petty's theories was a distinctly colonial one that conceptualized money not just as coined labor but, in its ideal form, as coined unfree labor.[33]

The originality of Franklin's theory of money is less important than the reason he came to have this particular theory and the purposes it served in his developing worldview. For at the same time as he was arguing the case for paper money as a labor-saving device, he was developing the carefully calibrated public persona described in the *Autobiography*: a person whose appearance of mercantile virtue was worth at least as much to him as his parsimonious habits and careful bookkeeping. He was writing pieces, like the one signed "BLACKAMORE," in which women, blacks, and ordinary artisans experienced reputation as a problem of credit in a marketplace of gossip, of circulating words.

There were compelling similarities between print journalism, the printing trade, the trade in reputation in an increasingly impersonal yet still face-to-face community, and the actions of people one owned—or invented in print. In the marketplace, the people and personae acted like commodities. Paper commodities, as the early paper money advocates had predicted, generated wealth—like busy workers. The process soon came full circle when Franklin began to make money by printing the colony's paper money, a development he attributed to the success of his own anonymous pamphlet on the subject.[34]

Printing and writing, embracing the marketplace and helping to regulate its excesses, made Franklin solvent and soon a secure property-holder. It is in this light that we should approach *Poor Richard's Almanack* and its famous maxims. What were the almanacs really about? Life-deadening assertions like "Time is Money"? Sermons against miserliness and in favor of virtue? The delightful bawdiness, earthiness, and (today) sheer offensiveness of its reflections on women and marriage? Commentators often celebrate or denigrate one strain in the maxims and ignore the others. What did the maxims have to do with one another, and with Franklin as a rising printer and observer of his times?[35]

Taken as a whole, the almanacs illustrated the promise and perils of the marketplace. The openings or prefaces set their tone and reach. Poor Richard invites us into his household and informs us that he enters the marketplace only under duress. His wife, Bridget, is not content to sit spinning in her tow-linen shift while the would-be astrologer Richard spends his time with books and instruments. She insists he make them "profitable." So he dares to go to market with his calculations, speculations, and advice. His first prediction is wholly absurd: he insists that his friend and now rival almanac-maker, Titan Leeds, will die at a precise hour during the coming year. The following year, thanks to the success of the almanac, Bridget is pacified, though to Richard's mind she overspends on her textiles.

Titan Leeds, however—the real Titan Leeds—was not at all content to be considered deceased. In his almanac for 1734 he called Saunders (Franklin) "a Fool and a Lyar," for reporting his demise. Franklin then took his play with paper personae and their real market effects a step further and in his 1734 *Poor Richard* had Saunders call this Leeds a fraud. *His* friend Leeds, he wrote, would never use him so! The insults to him must be a scheme perpetrated by the printers—Franklin's real market rivals, the Bradfords—to make money despite Leeds's death as predicted. In 1735 he pronounced that Leeds must be dead: why else would his almanacs be getting worse and worse each year? Franklin kept up the conceit of Leeds's death for years, bringing it back even after the real Leeds actually kicked the bucket: Leeds's spirit returns to Poor Richard in the night to guide his hand in an attack on the Bradfords. Similarly, with each progressive year Poor Richard's predictions about the weather and its economic effects appear in an ever more tongue-in-cheek fashion. He insists, for example, on the accuracy of predicting rain—give or take a few days or a thousand miles. All the while he thanks his audience for their generous patronage of a well-meaning poor man not unlike themselves.[36]

Why the odd, labored justifications of prediction, the rivalry among printers, and the emphasis on the bottom line? Today we tend to think that we are the first to wink at astrology, weather prediction, and the like, but Franklin and his knowing readers were doing precisely that. Franklin had taken the very name Richard Saunders from a series of English antiastrological almanacs.[37] He did the rationalism and realism of seventeenth-century antiastrology one better by not only insisting on but repeatedly discussing the economics of almanac publication and marketing. Franklin's almanacs were not satire: they were well-developed examples of a popular culture innovation that kept the genre going by acknowledging the reader's suspicion (after more than a century of popular annual almanacs) and even encouraging and rewarding it. Their very humor made them in the end more effective as a vehicle for both morality and for teaching market savviness. The readers were in on the joke; it was up to them to decide when to laugh and when to listen carefully.

And Franklin invited them in at every turn. Has it been said that "there is no such a Man as" Richard Saunders, that there is only Benjamin Franklin? Then "how is it possible I should appear publickly to hundreds of People, as I have done for several Years past, in print?" Are there too many warnings in the almanac about women who spend money? Bridget tears up the 1738 preface and writes her own, insisting that the tea she's been drinking was a gift from the printer; she theatrically throws some sunny days into the predictions so that women can put their clothes out to dry. Is Poor Richard no longer poor? The printer gets the profits, Richard reminds us—but he is such a good man that he deserves ten times more. Richard and Bridget Saunders were as real as their audience cared to make them, their sayings as true as believed. Their entire personalities were artifacts of the marketplace, nothing more—but nothing less either. Their homespun virtues, and failings, were a salve offered by Franklin, a relief from the market's, and the almanac's, often disappointing results.

The maxims and the prefaces, then, are best understood as they were read in their time, in tandem. In light of Franklin's other writings of the early 1730s, they appear to be a reflection on something that would have been known to Franklin's Philadelphia patrons: his own rise to solvency and even wealth, which the best-selling almanacs did so much to promote. Franklin knew very well that to print an almanac was to enter into an often fierce competition with the other printers. Sam Keimer had fought this battle royal and found himself accused of stealing by the Bradfords. The almanacs warn of the virtues of silence and the care that one must take around once and future enemies. Turn your competition into an asset, Poor Richard argues—much as the maxims advise people not to hold grudges and to be kind to those who wrong you, putting them instead in your debt. Franklin's almanac did not steal Titan Leeds's name or his predictions, as Keimer had in fact done. Instead it treated Leeds's paper identity as a public commodity—and made something new with it.

Franklin had an even more direct inspiration for Poor Richard and his shrewish, or at least calculating, wife. That inspiration grew from a very real romantic disappointment, one that supports the notion that *Poor Richard's Almanack* is a studied reflection on the commodification of human relations experienced—and promoted—by Franklin. After he left Keimer and started the partnership with Hugh Meredith, Franklin had rented a house and taken in Thomas Godfrey and his wife and children as tenants. Franklin boarded with the Godfreys, who were approximately his age, and knew them intimately. Thomas was a glazier who, according to Franklin, "worked little, being always absorb'd in his mathematics." An original member of the Junto, he authored a single-sheet almanac that Franklin printed from 1729 to 1731. Sometime in 1730 Mrs. Godfrey "projected a Match for me" with her "very Deserving" niece or cousin.

> The old Folks encourag'd me by continual Invitations to Supper, and by leaving us together, till at length it was time to explain. Mrs. Godfrey manag'd our little Treaty. I let her know that I expected as much Money with their Daughter as would pay off my remaining Debt for the Printinghouse, which I believe was not then above a Hundred Pounds. She brought me Word they had no such Sum to spare.

The negotiations proceeded. What is striking is how much they still rankled Franklin forty years later. A hard bargainer, he suggested they "mortgage their house." The parents responded by going to William Bradford and getting the old "sophister" 's prediction that Franklin would "soon follow" Keimer into bankruptcy—a downgrading of Franklin's chances that must have driven the young printer up the proverbial wall, because nothing would injure his prospects more than failure to receive a £100 dowry like the one that had guaranteed Bradford's own solvency decades before.[38]

Thanks to Bradford, the would-be in-laws "did not approve the match." Or did they? Franklin years later still suspected "Artifice"— that they had banked on the youngsters' passion, which they hoped would lead to an elopement and so no need to give a dowry. In other words, a bargain for the parents. They forbade their daughter to see the young printer, withholding her from the market for a better price. He stopped attempting to see her. Franklin used the (for him) strong term "resented" to describe his own feelings about the incident, a term appearing only one other time in the *Autobiography*—to describe how he felt after his brother's beatings.

> I was forbidden the House, & the Daughter shut up.—Whether this was a real Change of Sentiment [or not] . . . I know not: But I suspected the latter, resented it, and went no more. Mrs. Godfrey brought me afterwards some more favourable Accounts of their Disposition, and would have drawn me on again: but I declared absolutely my Resolution to have nothing more to do with that Family. This was resented by the Godfreys, we differ'd, and they removed, leaving me the whole House, and I resolved to take no more Inmates.

What Franklin resented was interference, which here was both of a traditional kind and of a particular marketplace kind, namely that of his competition. Both the Godfreys' relations and the Bradfords had used their position to try to rob him of money. If, as biographers often complain, Franklin became hard to know, if he avoided not only household "Inmates" but also certain kinds of intimacy, it was because he had learned, the hard way, to count the cost.

The Godfreys left the house, and Franklin soon married Deborah Read, his former sweetheart, whose husband of two years, the potter John Rogers, had disappeared to the West Indies with one of his in-laws' slaves. In her ambiguous, deserted state, Deborah was a very special kind of bargain. Having once opposed it, her mother now approved the match with Franklin. As owners of the property on Market Street, the Read family had something as good as a dowry to offer. A few months later Deborah also agreed to take in Franklin's infant son William, born in 1728 or 1729 to another woman whom Franklin apparently would not or could not marry.[39]

Suddenly Benjamin Franklin was a patriarch. In all it was a dizzying series of events. The Godfreys chose to cut their losses and went to Bradford to print their next almanac. Franklin responded with a series of essays in the *Gazette* in which women consume, gossip, and calculate the costs of both activities so carefully as to require a ledgerbook. In one piece quite possibly aimed at the Godfreys, printed in the *Gazette* on July 10, 1732, a tradesman, Anthony Afterwit, gets himself into hot water by counting on £200 he expects to get as a dowry. The "old Gentleman," his intended's father, tricks him into eloping. His wife, who desires to be a "Gentlewoman," then gets Anthony to buy her a mirror, a tea table, and a fashionable horse. Faced with bankruptcy, he sells the horse and the table when his wife is away, replacing them with a spinning wheel and piles of flax. They also turn away their servants, keeping only an ambiguously mentioned "boy" of Anthony's, presumably an apprentice but quite possibly a slave.[40]

The maxims in the first almanacs reflect Franklin's concerns of the early 1730s: solvency, debt, and the opportunities and risks represented, literally and figuratively, by women. In the 1733 almanac risk is represented baldly: "Ne'er take a wife till thou hast a house (& a fire) to put her in." Or even more disturbing: "Love well, whip well." By March the reader has been through domestic love and domestic violence to arrive at short verse where kisses are referred to as "stakes" in a game of lovers, where the woman gets the better of the man. In June "the proof of gold is fire, the proof of woman, gold; the proof of man, woman." The next month, we learn that "many estates are spent in the getting, / Since women for tea forsook spinning and knitting." The almanac's traditional catalogue of the births of kings and queens culminates with *"Poor Richard*, an American Prince, without Subjects, his Wife, being Viceroy over him. [Born] 23. Oct. 1684."

Unwise marriage, and women in general, continue in later almanacs to be the greatest risk to a man's money and happiness. Yet they are also an essential foundation for the careful garnering of capital that the almanacs recommend more and more clearly by the mid-1730s. Women remain the epitome of dangerous consumption, yet they become the perfect exemplars of saving money by staying out of the cash economy as much as possible. The link between Franklin's encomiums about women and about money lie in his appreciation for the way women helped him save money. Women, as well as slaves and servants, helped him understand the relationship between labor and money—building on his understanding of people as capital, while creating a realm of escape from its dehumanizing implications.

Women came with a cost, but they were the essence of the household and of men's property. In a sense, they were the best example of the people-as-capital principle. In the case of women, Franklin began to reverse the equation of the laboring or spending person with money, to describe cash money (as the land-bank advocates had) in warmly personal terms: "There are three faithful friends, an old wife, an old dog, and ready money." This was especially true of the wife when she produced more people, as Deborah did in 1732, giving birth to Francis Folger Franklin, their son soon known as Franky. In the 1748 compendium *Advice to a Young Tradesman* appear not only "Time is Money" and "Credit is Money" but "Money is of a prolifick generating Nature. Money can beget Money, and its offspring can beget more, and so on." If the creation of capital was a blessing on the order of human reproduction, its destruction could be a metaphor for true evil: "He that murders a Crown, destroys all it might have produc'd, even Scores of Pounds." This fertile analogy between people and money had its logical culmination in Franklin's famous "Speech of Miss Polly Baker" (1747), in which an unwed mother escapes judicial punishment by persuading one of the judges (who subsequently marries her) that because she has produced wealth in persons, she has added to the commonwealth.[41]

That seemingly radical optimism emerged in its full form only after the Franklins' economic successes of the 1730s, which Debbie Franklin made possible. The Franklins *lived* the conflicts, the alternatives, the hesitations, the maneuvers, and even the denials between men and women, around money, that were alluded to in the almanacs. Franklin thanked Deborah in his autobiography for her economy during these early years; but he also blamed her for introducing "Luxury," in the form of a china bowl and silver spoon, to their breakfast table, on the rather manipulative grounds of her pride in him. We know that in addition to childrearing, cooking, cleaning, sewing, and mending, Deborah Franklin stitched books. After 1733 she also kept the stationery shop—in precisely the years when it expanded to become something of a general store. Franklin signed a power of attorney for Deborah, and by 1738 she was recording the over-the-counter sales in their "shop book." The more money the couple made, the more their sexual division of labor blurred, and the more Deborah's economic activities mattered.[42]

Around this time—before 1735—the Franklins had apprentices, servants, and at least one "Negro boy."[43] It is impossible to know whether there were other slaves and servants of African descent, and which ones worked for Deborah in the household or the store, and which for Benjamin in the printing house. They all lived in the Franklins' house or in the house of Deborah's mother a few doors down Market Street, and together—the slave or slaves, the servants, his wife, and himself—they became part of one enterprise known as Franklin's shop. The servants and slaves surely underwrote the couple's own hard labors, as well as their own search for something greater than self-sufficiency.

Franklin's strikingly quick rise in the early 1730s may well have depended as much on his own careful use of the full range of available kinds of labor, especially the unpaid kinds, as it did on his and his wife's famous industry and frugality. In the *Almanack*, he did not so much forget or deny the importance of servants, slaves, and wives as conflate them all together in the fungible mix of money-producing people. Labor and its fruits were generally claimed for ordinary men, even to the point of raising labor to a great virtue: "No man e'er was glorious, who was not laborious" (1734). Servants were potentially wasteful: "If you'd have a servant you'd like, serve your self" (1737).

Yet gradually an admission creeps in that even the ideal penny-pinching money-saving farmer or artisan probably had servants. Watching the servants emerges as an important kind of labor for the middling sorts. Especially because they were bought with significant capital outlay rather than paid wages, servants of all kinds presented a capital risk, which first appeared in the almanacs as an extension of the woman question: "Let thy Maid-Servant be faithful, strong and homely" (1736). In 1742 Poor Richard defends himself from "the perpetual teasing of both Neighbours and Strangers, to calculate Nativities, give Judgment on Schemes, erect Figures, discover Thieves, detect Horse-Stealers, describe the Route of Run-aways and stray'd Cattle." Next year, "the Eye of a Master, will do more than his Hand." In 1748 he presents a poem about how husbandmen should not stop working even if their lands seem to produce wealth without oversight: "Tho' his collected Rent his Bags supply, / Or honest, careful Slaves scarce need his eye." Three years later: "Not to oversee Workmen, is to leave them your Purse open."

This combination of self-reliance with warnings to watch over servants was addressed to free men with and without bound laborers, helping them to come to grips with the rise of a cash economy that depended on both free and unfree labor. The maxims' presentation of servants, wives, and one's own failings as a series of risks to good economy allowed the people-as-capital theme to present its great usefulness to the greatest number of men and women. In a social context where bound servitude was often a means for the repayment of what immigrants, bankrupts, and young people owed for their debt service, maintenance, and training, Poor Richard glorified the independent householder and urged him not to fall into debt. Where freedom could literally mean the absence of debt, and servitude its presence, it made all the more sense to equate capital with freedom and with command over others' labor. A casual, market-friendly slavery, in which the relative numbers of slaves and servants rose and fell with supply and cost, reinforced an awareness of the commodification of everyone's labor time. Poor Richard, then, was a master—but one who knew what it meant to feel reduced to an equation of time and money and hoped to control the process.

For all his protestations of poverty, all his complaints and acceptance of subjection, Poor Richard gave advice intended for masters and those who aspired to be masters. The almanac's comments about servants, few but rising in number over the years, reflected the growing wealth of the middling sorts and the diversifying market for servants and slaves. Yet their relatively rare appearance, when compared to the ever-present maxims that emphasize self-control and a monetized vision of human affairs, suggests a desire to deflect the problem of dependence on servants—much as the runaway ads alluded to but argued against the importance of fugitives' skills, knowledge, and actual worth in the marketplace. Perhaps because he knew more than a little bit about working for others, or perhaps because his transformation into mastery made it necessary for him to forget the ubiquity and importance of unfree people, Franklin sought ways of talking about labor that emphasized freedom, self-sufficiency, and owners' work—not the immiseration of workers.

The commentary concerning women and relations between the sexes in the almanacs served as a kind of a compensation—one that made a great deal of sense given women's crucial role in household production. Women's labor was essential to most colonial households, perhaps especially those that engaged in production for extralocal markets. Later on, in the nineteenth century, women's household work would be defined, by the middle class at least, as existing essentially outside the marketplace. Franklin's middling sorts did not have that luxury.[44] To them, especially to the men among them, women's work was the first, most easily joined battle in the rationalization of production. In the mercantilist household disinclined to pay for work in a cash-poor, labor-dear economy, women could stand in ideologically for the entire domestic labor force, familial and bought, free and unfree.

During the 1730s, as he gained solvency, a family, servants, and slaves, Franklin began to celebrate the virtues of labor and the importance of a good wife. At the same time, slaves became less visible in his writings. He wrote no more pieces disguising himself as a person of color. When slaves and servants did appear in his writings, they were cast as evil outsiders with no organic relation to the body politic.

The trope equating people with capital allowed for—if it was not actually inspired by—the buying and selling of people, even as Franklin turned it toward the very interesting wealth-creating, autonomy-enhancing possibilities of paper money in a market society. Thanks to the logic of people as capital, Franklin did not have to resolve the problem of whether the slaves and servants that he and his readers bought and sold were members of the family or mere commodities. They remained in a kind of suspension, both goods and people, subject to the negative and constraining, rather than positive and liberating, possibilities of human commodification. Indeed, one purpose of Franklin's market products—his newspaper and the almanac—was to keep them in that profitable suspension, to make sure that the market freed their masters to use them, rather than freeing them to act in the marketplace. Such an interpretation does not explain everything about Poor Richard, but it does help explain Franklin's increasing silence about slaves and mixed-race people, not to mention the virulent racism that would soon meet them when they forced their way into the conversations of their masters.

Art, even Benjamin Franklin's art, is not life. Problems not addressed by Franklin's brilliant performances had a way of coming to the surface, as they did in two incidents that might serve as portents of things to come: signs of the inherent, even inevitable, limitations of the solutions Franklin had devised as the one-time runaway moved into a position of mastery, profit, authorship, and leadership. Both cases concern aspiring employees: one an apprentice, one a free man. One ended in tragedy, the other in something of a farce. In each case Franklin found himself accused of dishonesty, of covering up the truth, of using his position as printer to keep himself aloof from real events and real people. In the second, more public affair, he stood accused, as he would often come to be accused, of manipulation, greed, and craftiness: the obverse of the virtues of Poor Richard—or, if you prefer, the very vices of runaways.

In 1731 Franklin joined the new lodge of Freemasons in Philadelphia. Apparently he enjoyed the order's combination of fraternity, secrecy, mutual aid, and public service. For at least some of his brothers, however, the lodge proved as meaningful for its exclusions as for its inclusions. When the chemist Evan Jones's apprentice, Daniel Rees, displayed an annoying inquisitiveness about Freemasonry, Jones and several friends devised a fake initiation ceremony for the young man, complete with an oath to the devil and a ritual rump-kissing. The real Masons enjoyed the mockery so much that they agreed to repeat the fun a few days later by initiating Rees into a higher degree of their faux order. During that ceremony Rees either became frightened or began to have suspicions. In an effort to get a rise out of the apprentice, Jones raised a flaming bowl and either accidentally or purposefully threw it, setting the boy's clothes on fire. Daniel Rees died of the resulting injuries a few days later.[45]

Franklin reported this event in the usual cursory fashion in the *Gazette*. He had heard about the first evening and laughed along with the joke enough, at least at first, to ask for and circulate a copy of the devil's oath written for Rees. But after Rees died, Jones was indicted and Andrew Bradford used the incipient scandal to attack the Masons. Franklin went to the authorities and at the January 1738 trial testified for the prosecution. Though two of the Masons were convicted of manslaughter, one gained a pardon, and Jones himself received only a brand. Some thought he deserved a murderer's punishment of death. One of Jones's defenders called attention to Franklin's striking reversal, even change of sides, charging that he had not only been in on the joke but had helped continue it, saluting Rees with a "secret" sign in the street.

Franklin printed a defense in the *Gazette*, denying that he had encouraged Jones or Rees in any way. His circulation of the oath had been an accident; he had asked for it out of curiosity, only to have others come by to read it. He implied that the accusations were a ploy of Bradford to injure his reputation. Despite presenting two witnesses willing to swear that he had not heartily approved of the practical joke, he never answered the question of his accuser: if Franklin had really been appalled by the treatment of Rees from the moment he heard of the devil-play, not to mention the display of posteriors—if he had, as he claimed, sympathized with the boy—why had he not acted to warn him?[46]

No lasting damage marred Franklin's business or his reputation. But the ambitions of a young apprentice, and the arrogance of his own fellow masters, had put Franklin in a delicate position, one not so easily papered over by the rituals of reportage or law. Local events could have extralocal implications: the Rees controversy saw print in Boston and New York. His theories and maxims did not always match the realities of life in the streets and the workshops.

Nor did they always imitate life among the printers with whom Franklin competed for government patronage, small jobs, subscribers, and—repeatedly—employees. In 1737 Franklin won the postmastership of Philadelphia and with it the very helpful guarantee of having his newspapers carried by the post riders, a right that the previous postmaster, Bradford, had denied him. Bradford had grown delinquent in remitting fees, and the deputy postmaster general for the colonies, Alexander Spotswood, went so far as to order Franklin to stop carrying Bradford's *American Weekly Mercury* unless Bradford himself paid postage, or paid the extant balances.

Franklin later insisted that unlike Bradford he played fair, continuing to allow the riders to deliver the *Mercury* upon Bradford's promises of payment. Bradford may not have thought so. Certainly they had been mocking each other surreptitiously for some time. Franklin, in the voice of Poor Richard, had ridiculed Bradford's reliance on an almanac author whose formulas were so tired he might as well be dead. Bradford, in turn, was not content to have spoiled Franklin's courtship with the Godfreys. For the rest of the 1730s he lambasted the *Gazette* and its editor as irreligious and dangerously populist whenever he had the chance.[47]

One of the writers who had enlisted on Franklin's side in political debates was an Irish-born lawyer named John Webbe. When the postmaster general asked Franklin to act on his behalf and sue Bradford for the unremitted postal fees, Franklin retained Webbe to handle the case. Their business relationship soon extended to a new venture: a monthly "general magazine" for the British colonies of America, imitating a successful London version that specialized in reporting parliamentary debates and digesting the news. Franklin asked Webbe to edit the magazine, a task that he insisted would require only several days' work each month; he would print it and take a full three-quarters of the profits. Webbe, perhaps rightly, wondered about the terms. Why would he be an unequal partner? Would it really take only a fraction of his time? One way or another, he voiced his frustration to Bradford—and received a better deal. On November 6, 1740, Bradford's *Mercury* published an announcement of his soon-to-appear *American Magazine, or a Monthly View of the Political State of the British Colonies.*

Franklin had been through this sort of thing before, with Keimer; he had also seen the Bradfords' divide-and-conquer strategy more than once. He replied immediately with an ad for his own magazine in the *Gazette*, which included aspersions on Webbe, "to whom the Scheme was communicated *in Confidence*."[48]

Webbe replied with scorn and outrage in the pages of the *Mercury*. Franklin did not own the idea; they had developed it together, with Franklin committing mainly to a proposal about his responsibilities as printer. Only after beginning the work and finding that it took up all his time had the lawyer considered himself "relieved from such a Contract." He would not "suffer himself to be made his [Franklin's] Bubble," insisted Webbe. The lawyer pressed his case against Franklin eloquently, comparing the printer's actions to the "*sneaking* Villainy" of a "Pickpocket." When Franklin continued to print his own ad, including the accusation of Webbe's dishonesty, and brought forward Spotswood's letter to justify his aspersions on Webbe and Bradford, the lawyer accused Franklin of trying to keep Bradford "under his thumb" with the postmaster general's order. Franklin lacked "candour" and "sincerity." He was a trickster who engaged in defamation by indirection.[49]

The magazine affair reveals another Benjamin Franklin, one with enemies who cannot be accused of not knowing him. He was earning those enemies by practicing the very sort of sharp dealing, distrust, silence, and elusiveness recommended by Poor Richard. Biographers have usually dismissed these characteristics as irrelevant, charming, all-too-human flaws.

We do Franklin a disservice by not investigating the close relationship between his advice and his experiences; these flaws, or skills, had a deeper structure in his psyche and in his world. Caught by the able prosecutor Webbe, he responded with humor—but of a disturbing kind. The February 12, 1741, edition of the *Gazette* contained a mock version of Webbe and Bradford's latest announcement in the *Mercury* about the terms for subscription to their magazine. It was written in Irish dialect and appeared under the heading "TEAGUE'S ADVERTISEMENT."[50] Though signed by Bradford, the boasts in brogue referred to Webbe's own descriptions of how he would make the compendium original, and to Webbe's elevation of his own clear and open writing style over Franklin's in his recent defenses in the *Mercury*:

> *No Shweepings, but dose of my own Shcull shall have plaish;*
> *And dose, you must tink, will be vhery fine:*
> *For do dis Advertisement my Printer does Shign,*
> *To tell you de Trute, de Shense is all mine.*

Webbe had become a servant of Bradford, Franklin implied—but such an illiterate "Teague" should hardly write, much less advertise as masters did. At a time when more and more Irish indentured servants were filling the ranks of the unfree, and were described in runaway ads as members of a swarthy foreign nation, these were fighting words. When the logic of mutual interest in the marketplace, and the language of people and capital, failed to get the job done, Benjamin Franklin was ready to stake his claim as a master and as an Englishman.

FIVE

Children and Colonies

Though it did not turn a profit, Franklin's *General Magazine* reveals the breadth of his ambitions and the value he placed on being part of the British Empire. It took as its purview "all the British Plantations in America." From the first he saw no conflict at all between improving intercolonial communication and being British: indeed, for the printer, the two seemed to complement each other. The first issue included extracts from Robert Beverly's twenty-year-old *History of the Present State of Virginia*; an account of the new colony in Georgia; and letters about the itinerant ministry of George Whitefield, who had by then turned southward from the middle colonies. These historical and contemporary portraits of the South were accompanied by accounts of northern industry: the manufactories and land banks of New England and export statistics from the port of Philadelphia. During King George's War (1739–48) such numbers demonstrated not only the economic value of the colonies but the interdependence of the empire's constituent parts. The "fertility" of the "Provision Colonies" fed not only the slaves but also Britain's navy and soldiers in the Caribbean, "which shows that these Colonies give Great Britain a considerable Advantage over its Enemies in an American War, and will no doubt be an additional Inducement to our Mother Country to continue us in its Protection."[1]

"America" meant more territory to Franklin in 1741 than it would later, or than it does to us today. The same was true for Britain. The growth of the empire made the growth of the colonies possible, and vice versa. As a rapidly growing entrepot, Philadelphia stood at the center of a trade network that spread from the fisheries of Nova Scotia to the sugar plantations of Antigua, encompassing of course many other points, legal and illegal, to which an Atlantic or coastal vessel could sail, unload, and load. During the mid-eighteenth century the Americas got caught up in the dynastic and trade conflicts of the European powers, only to quickly become the catalysts and the stakes in wars that Europeans fought by land and sea. The extension of trade and empire, and the desire for news created by imperial warfare, made it possible for Franklin to imagine himself, and to serve, as a citizen of the empire. He did not so much abandon Philadelphia as seek to envision the larger landscape beyond the local squabbles and competitions. In an era when he devoted himself more and more creatively to solving local, even urban, problems, his political solutions, as much as his business, helped bring the empire to Philadelphia.

The exchange of goods and ideas that Franklin championed made Britons out of provincial Americans as never before. The process has been represented as commercial, as intellectual, as political; yet with Franklin it was always practical and personal. Looking beyond the local helped him avoid traps set by local controversies, especially religious ones, even as Pennsylvania entered a period of deep political division over its Quakers' pacifist values and the demands of its own proprietors, the Penn family. In the case of the Penns, it was all too clear that traditional values and traditional patriarchal relations had not been handed down intact. Indeed, heredity had become the excuse for the worst abuses of privilege.[2]

By contrast, during the 1740s and 1750s Franklin emerged as a citizen of the world who championed voluntary relations between peoples and rational experimentation in politics as well as science. His electrical experiments, artfully publicized by friends, made him the first North American scientist to win European acclaim, confirming his emerging vision of equality within the empire, of expanding networks of knowledge, profit, and power. For Franklin and the colonies, the 1740s and 1750s were a period of convergence, when his various real and invented personae flowed together. As he became the patriarch of a larger extended family, he extended his printing concern across land and water. As postmaster he became a literal servant of the crown and helped improve the communications infrastructure that carried his printed goods. His activities exemplified both the energetic, independent, labor-intensive mentality of Poor Richard's sayings and Richard's encomiums to watch over one's own holdings, including servants and dependents.

He began to participate in an emerging debate about the nature of such oversight, a conversation about the nature of colonies and the mother country, that held broad implications for the world he inherited and the world he was helping to make.

What was a colony? When was it a child, and when a trading partner? What happened when children *grew*? At a time when successful British Americans like Franklin imported more and more young Englishmen, Irishmen, Africans, and Germans, it was easier to think of the colonies as children, and to continue to balance their growth with their obedience, than to notice that the very integration of empire, and the very wars to extend and secure empire, had given the colonial children a growth spurt, and the empire itself severe growing pains. By 1757, when he finished the *Poor Richard* series with a flourish and took his son and two slaves to England, Benjamin Franklin had emerged as the great poet and propagandist of a new American identity, one that wavered uneasily between its filial relation to England and its less ambivalent but no less fraught relation to its own subordinated peoples. The question would be not only what kind of children were Benjamin Franklin and his fellow Americans but what kind of masters they had become.

In the voice of Poor Richard, Franklin registered jokingly the portents of change that war brought. Inserting politics into astrology, he wrote: "This year [1741] there will be but two eclipses . . . Neither of which will be seen in these Parts of the World: But to the present Inhabitants of Cuba, and other Spanish Settlements in the West-Indies, these are like to appear very great Eclipses."[3] Wars had often been considered as regular, even natural events, if disastrous; yet the terms of Franklin's playful prediction reveal still more. They suggest that even though European events like the wars of the Spanish succession might seem far off to colonials, they derived in large measure from Europe's competition for the seas and new world colonies. The British-Spanish conflict of 1740–41 had been catalyzed by the alleged mutilation of British Colonel Robert Jenkins, a shipmaster and accused smuggler, the most famous one-eared man in Western history before Van Gogh. From the North American perspective, the future of the West Indies was a matter not just of guns but of bread and butter, fish and sugar, and rum.

Britons and Americans interested in the growth of the northern colonies had objected to the provisions of the Molasses Act in 1733. Intended to disrupt a competitive advantage enjoyed by France's sugar colonies, the act undid trading advantages of North American colonial suppliers over their British West Indian customers. The West Indian planters won the resulting battle in Parliament thanks to their far greater direct economic importance and more powerful lobby. Yet mid-Atlantic "provision colonies" began to argue themselves into something like parity with the West Indies, which after all could not produce such prodigious quantities of sugar without mid-Atlantic supplies. At a time when promoters of the empire argued that "there are no Hands in the *British* Empire more usefully employed for the Profit and Glory of the Commonwealth" than those of the West Indian slave, North Americans stood to gain distinct advantages from imperial warfare: it offered not just a short-term risk to safe trade but the prospect of long-term health for a wealthy Atlantic British Empire.[4]

The imperialization of the mainland colonies in wartime, however, quickly came up against real colonial autonomy—particularly in Franklin's Pennsylvania. The Quakers, dominant in the Assembly, took their pacifism very seriously, refusing to participate officially in the raising of troops, though they did appropriate £3,000 for the king's wartime use. Lacking a draft act, volunteers lagged behind a reasonable quota. Officers responded by accepting runaway servants into the royal service.[5]

Masters petitioned the legislature, charging British officials with encouraging servants to run off by concealing their names once enlisted. However sneaky the practice, imperial officers had acted within their commander's edict, which called upon "all subjects" of the crown to serve. Local law conflicted with imperial community—a fact that the Pennsylvania Assembly confirmed when it passed a resolution declaring servant enlistments illegal without the consent of individual masters. The controversy ended, for the time being, in a telling stalemate: the empire continued to maintain the king's right to call on "the service of all his subjects," free or unfree. The Pennsylvanians, meanwhile, appropriated £2,354—more than three-quarters of the amount they had paid toward the war chest—to compensate the 250 to 300 masters who filed complaints of lost human property. The governor expressed shock and outrage at the provincials' daring insistence on serving their own needs and customs. It was a portent of things to come.[6]

Franklin took a great interest in the problem of the fugitive as a British soldier. In the *Gazette*'s pages during the spring of 1742, he reported an incident in which recruiting officers had taken on several servants, only to be countermanded by their ship captain, who feared being taken to court by their owners: "As the enlisting of Servants is on all hands allow'd to be a great Hardship to the Province," wrote Franklin, " 'tis a Pleasure to observe, that the Proceedings of the Officers in that Respect are now not countenanc'd by the Government." The optimism was not warranted: the issue would recur with a vengeance during the continental phase of the Seven Years' War. In 1754 Franklin, now a member of the Pennsylvania Assembly, would be appointed to get an overly enthusiastic recruiting colonel to release enlisted servants. In 1755, after eight years of struggles to create a military force in Pennsylvania, he drafted a Militia Act that explicitly forbade servants or apprentices to enroll themselves without "consent of guardians." Just months later he would remonstrate with the governor and royal commander in chief, William Shirley, about the taking of servants.[7]

Evidently his fellow members perceived him as a specialist in the matter of labor recruitment and runaways—which, as proprietor of the *Pennsylvania Gazette*, he in fact was. He had admitted as much in a letter to New York council member and surveyor general Cadwallader Colden in 1747, advising Colden to get their mutual friend John Hughes to locate a runaway, just as Franklin had helped Hughes recover one who had absconded a full year previously. It was a matter of reciprocity and common interest, not unlike the Junto or his scheme to build a subscription library for the mutual benefit of readers. In wartime the fugitive problem increasingly worked both ways, especially during the drawn-out Seven Years' War, when desertion became a real problem. British and provincial officers, including Franklin's own son William, went so far as to advertise, chase after, and prosecute deserters. New York and Philadelphia newspapers featured ads for both deserters and runaways who, their masters feared, might be hiding in imperial uniforms, on land or sea. There is no more vivid example than deserters and runaways of the importance of labor to imperial growth—and the ways it caused English and Anglo-American property-owners' interests to converge and, dangerously, to diverge as well.[8]

Franklin's rise to a new level of fame and fortune depended on the laborers and the increasing need for intercolonial coordination in economics and politics. The success of *Poor Richard's Almanack* and his paper money ventures themselves tended to set his sights beyond Philadelphia, while the *Pennsylvania Gazette* gained subscribers and advertisers in the Pennsylvania hinterlands and beyond. In "becoming intercolonial" Franklin, like any good businessman, both responded to customers' needs and created them.[9] The magazine controversy of 1741 revealed the peculiar mix of entrepreneurship and patronage networks by which Franklin sought to extend his sphere of influence. As Philadelphia postmaster, he could seek to transcend a local rivalry and create a new product, the magazine, with continental, even imperial, reach. At the same time, he would be making contacts with elites in other colonies and pushing public policy in directions that might reap long-term rewards.

It is striking how consistently Franklin tried to re-create the conditions of his local success, but on a larger scale. In 1743 he helped form the American Philosophical Society, an "intercolonial junto" of scientifically minded men desirous of overcoming the distinct disadvantage that men of learning experienced at such a distance from European centers of knowledge. The proposal Franklin wrote celebrated the "long tract of Continent, from Nova Scotia to Georgia," that was in English hands, turning the problems of intercolonial communication and geographical distance into virtues, even a subject of philosophical inquiry. Later in the decade he sought to overcome Pennsylvania's religious and ethnic provincialism by founding an academy that, he wrote enthusiastically to a prospective president of the institution, might lure young men from as far away as the West Indies. Meanwhile he supported the remarkable itinerant ministry of George Whitefield by publishing favorable accounts of it in his newspaper and printing the evangelist's sermons and notebooks. Even religious revivals, if they brought people together across time and space, could be profitable, cosmopolitan, and productive of the public good.[10]

Franklinian ventures tended to knit colonists together where they lived while simultaneously facilitating their range of motion in the republic of letters and the world of goods. Best of all were those ventures that did both simultaneously, such as his emerging network of printing concerns. Beginning with his limited-liability partnership with Thomas Whitemarsh in South Carolina (who was succeeded by Louis Timothée and later by Timothée's wife and son), Franklin established a string of such partnerships stretching from Newport, Rhode Island, to Antigua. Most of these printers, like Whitemarsh and James Parker (whom he sent to New York in 1741) began as apprentices or journeymen in Franklin's own shop. Parker himself had run away from Franklin's rival Bradford and would remain loyal to Franklin for the remaining three decades of his life. Franklin took considerable pride in setting these men up in business and extending the reach of the printed word farther across the British Atlantic. He also took considerable profit: these enterprises usually gave him 50 percent for a significant period of time.[11]

The printing concerns were more than investments. Like modern holding corporations (or early modern imperial ventures), these satellite shops were simultaneously customers for supplies and suppliers of locally grown goods. Whitemarsh, in South Carolina, returned sugar and rice, which were easily retailed through Franklin's shop. He and the others also sent their newspapers and informal reports, which guaranteed that Franklin, as postmaster, would receive them before his rival printers did. Because Franklin had men who owed him favors in several places up and down the seaboard, he was in an especially good position to retail the information that traveled along with the goods. He could also stockpile supplies like the paper he imported or the lampblack he made, selling it to these customers as needed; the guaranteed business made it easier for him to expand his stock to supply even more printers and to receive their disposables on good terms. Indeed, by the mid-1740s Franklin was the largest dealer in paper in North America.[12]

He had learned his mercantile lessons well and was applying them to a loosely joined enterprise that was itself increasingly analogous to the British Empire in the age of "salutary neglect," or permissive central management. In the *Autobiography*, Franklin stressed his equitable arrangements "by which several families were raised": his partnerships, he implied, lasted only six years and led to his partners' complete independence. As in other arenas, including imperial relations, Franklin simplified in retrospect. Even his most grateful protégés in printing would eventually find their business arrangements with Franklin frustratingly ambiguous; they had little doubt that they remained dependent on his desires and quite often on his patronage as a retailer and as postmaster. Peter Timothy, the son of Louis Timothée who anglicized his name, provided a glimpse into the network when he wrote to Franklin to apologize for not being able to send a prompt payment for paper in 1754.

Part of the problem lay in erratic voyages headed to Philadelphia that season, and part in his own servant problem. He had found it necessary to discharge his main apprentice—a drunk—two years early and was alone in the shop "excepting a Negro Boy whom I am teaching to serve me at the Press." Timothy later sent the money in, and a new shipment of paper appeared. But by 1755 Timothy felt emboldened to wonder if Franklin, who was no longer writing him, wasn't stretched rather too thin and not paying him the attention due a loyal customer. Patronage required care, and Timothy was right to ask if Franklin's new involvement in "Electrical Arcana, and public affairs" had caused the breakdown in their previously regular contact. His wounded tone suggests that he had felt what can only be called a traditional paternal bond with Franklin as well as a contractual one. While in the 1754 letter he provided lengthy excuses for his own lack of remittance, a year later, when he had held up his part of the bargain, he vented frustration at not receiving a single "line" from Franklin. Yet temporary irritation did not prevent Timothy from identifying with Franklin enough to later name his second son Benjamin Franklin Timothy—a third generation of Timothys shaped by Franklin's intercolonial ambitions.[13] If Franklin freed his apprentices and protégés, he freed them to become part of a larger network, with himself at the head.

The profits from his various enterprises enabled Franklin to move into more province-wide and even intercolonial forms of civic participation, especially after he retired from the active management of his Philadelphia printing house in 1748. Doing so, however, meant bringing the logic of partnership home. Rather than shutting down the enterprise, he found someone else to keep it going for him and continued on in the role of a not-so-silent partner. The story of how David Hall became Franklin's partner reveals as nothing else does the great chain of working, buying, and selling that allowed him to make the transition from urban artisan to man of empire.

The Franklin-Hall relationship may have become a Philadelphia story, but it began as an imperial one. Their relationship could neither have existed nor gotten far off the ground had it not been for William Strahan, a London printer and later Franklin's closest friend and associate in England. David Hall had been Strahan's fellow apprentice in Edinburgh and in 1729 followed him to London, where he worked as a journeyman in Strahan's shop. Hall was apparently an ambitious and capable printer, and when Franklin saw a letter Strahan wrote recommending Hall to his wife's cousin, the lawyer James Read, Franklin wrote directly to Strahan—their first correspondence, apparently—inquiring whether Hall might be interested in becoming Franklin's third managing partner, somewhere in the West Indies. He promised a year of work in Philadelphia and the cost of passage.[14]

Hall arrived in Philadelphia a year later, in 1744, somewhat the worse for wear and with ideas of his own. He found Franklin off-putting, or at least not especially friendly or confiding. The young Scot cast about, considered opening a coffeehouse in Philadelphia, and even wrote to Strahan about sending the materials for him to open his own Philadelphia print shop. Meanwhile, Strahan and Franklin had begun to correspond regularly. Strahan was impressed by the Philadelphian, who in turn praised Hall as "obliging and discreet, industrious, but honest." When conveyed by Strahan, Franklin's approval seems to have been news to Hall himself, who toyed with returning to England; but Strahan urged him to trust Franklin and stay put. By late 1745 Franklin was ready to send Hall to the Caribbean but hesitated because of the "hazardous Times" and because of his own need for Hall's services in the home shop.[15]

In 1746 Franklin named Hall foreman of the Philadelphia printing office. By then the Hall connection had reaped greater dividends. Franklin began to rely on Strahan for London periodicals and books. For the next quarter-century Franklin maintained a close friendship with "Straney," even as Hall kept his own. From Strahan, Franklin ordered the books he consumed and sold in ever greater numbers, as well as the new presses and fonts that he retailed to the new members of his expanding coastal network. As imperial politics drew more and more of his attention, the first-hand news and gossip that Strahan could offer became irreplaceable, and among Franklin's first thoughts on contemplating his semiretirement in 1747 was a trip to London, where his first stop, he promised, would be Strahan's shop. That event did not occur for another decade, when Franklin was a more eminent man and in London on an official political mission, but their encounter gained in intensity through anticipation. Hall, in turn, as the new editor of the *Gazette*, besieged his old friend with orders for supplies, the latest periodicals, and, increasingly, political news. Their exchange of information was inherently unequal, even as the English grew more and more interested in the other side of the Atlantic. Still, the American trade developed into an important part of Strahan's notably large and diversified operation, helping to make Strahan, in a sense, the Franklin of England—the printer of an important newspaper; the publisher and distributor of many books, including some by the nation's best authors (David Hume, Samuel Johnson); and a wealthy man who could contemplate passing his large business on to his son, William Strahan Jr.[16]

Hall and Franklin were both relatively punctual remitters of bills—far more so than some of Franklin's other partners, whose operations remained relatively marginal, and far more than James Read, the London-trained lawyer who linked the three men and turned out to be a ne'er-do-well and schemer. Like many a London tradesman during the eighteenth century, Strahan never collected on all the debts that Americans owed him. Yet he got much more than money out of his relationship with Hall and Franklin, his two fellow English-trained printers who, despite their partnership and close physical proximity, never between themselves breached the formality so obvious in their letters, in which they addressed each other as "Mr. Hall" and "Sir." Hall (who called Strahan "Will") gratefully named his first son after Strahan (who called Hall "Davey"). Only afterward did Hall follow the trend among Franklin partners and name his younger children after Benjamin and Deborah Franklin. He showed special gratitude to Strahan by apologizing for not always paying immediately and by asking his friend to join him in buying lottery tickets on both sides of the ocean, as if they were still apprentices scheming how to get out from under presswork.[17]

To Strahan, Hall remained forever like family. He named a son after him and longed for his old friend "Davey" to return, at least once, to England, so that they could relive their romps in the Scottish hills. Franklin, in turn, became part of Strahan's adopted, extended family, one they both sought to make real through their women and children. Long before Franklin ever arrived in London, both men encouraged their respective wives to correspond, and they played with a not-so-mocking courtship of their youngest children—Deborah and Ben's Sarah (Sally), born in 1743, as the intended of the Strahans' young son Billy. The conceit went on for years, so long that it became real: a loving attempt to recreate a family of affiliation by ambitious men who had left their home provinces and in the process lost their real brothers and first friends.[18] The empires that Strahan and Franklin made, in the business of culture and politics, were empires of flesh and blood. Through their letters and travels, as much as their ledger books and printings, these men's empires became substantial at mid-century. Predicated on oceanic distances, their very financial and emotional successes made them yearn to turn Britannia, already a far-flung nation of shopkeepers, into something more real and more human.

Franklin had his share of human drama in these years. As of late 1735, his house contained three young Franklin boys (as well as a number of teenage apprentices, servants, and at least one slave). The youngest, Franky, Deborah and Benjamin's first child and clearly a favorite, died of smallpox in 1736, at the age of four. The oldest in residence was Ben's nephew James (Jemmy) Franklin Jr. Benjamin had promised to his now-reconciled brother on his deathbed to bring his son up in the printing trade. While Jemmy's mother ran the print shop in Newport, Jemmy came to Philadelphia, where he studied with a private tutor alongside his cousin William, who was less than a year his junior. Then the two boys' paths separated: William would attend the Pennsylvania Academy that Franklin had founded; in 1740, at about the age of ten, Jemmy signed an indenture to his uncle.[19]

Franklin remembered his nephew as "always dissatisfied and grumbling," particularly about clothes. He promised him a "new suit of Cloaths" in the indenture, "besides his common Apparel." Clothes were often an apprentice's sole remuneration, and sole personal possession of any value, but for Jemmy they seem to have taken on special meaning as a source of aspiration—and as a site of adolescent rebellion. On some Sunday mornings he fussed over his appearance so long that he almost avoided having to go, with the family, to church. At a time when his cousin William was being treated indulgently, and was apparently being groomed for greater things than the print shop, Jemmy probably expressed his teenage jealousy through such subterfuges. In 1746, while his uncle was out of town, his aunt Deborah encouraged him to buy himself a new suit. He chose one that Franklin claimed cost half again as much as any he had ever bought himself. When Franklin wrote his maxims about avoiding frippery and saving money, he was thinking not only of himself, his wife, and his very young daughter but also of his nephew, who was also his apprentice. When his sister Jane's son, Benny Mecom, complained about the clothing supplied by his master, Franklin's partner James Parker, he remarked that such was the way of all boys. Doubtless the very boyishness of Jemmy's maneuvers helped Uncle Benjamin to distance his immature nephew's actions from his own twenty years earlier, when he had been apprenticed to Jemmy's father.

When his apprenticeship ended, Jemmy returned to the shop in Newport. In 1753 Franklin offered him a new place in his coastal network of printers, a shop in New Haven. Franklin assumed his nephew would jump at the chance. Jemmy turned it down. In one sense, James Franklin Jr. was the first in a long series of young sonlike figures whom Franklin sought to mold. In another sense, he was the first to realize that being patronized by Franklin did not necessarily lead to independence of the kind his uncle so prized.[20]

William too began to test the boundaries of his own freedom, and the meaning of being Benjamin Franklin's (illegitimate) son. In light of the limited evidence, biographers disagree about how close Franklin was to William during his formative years. Clearly Franky had been something of a favorite. Deborah did not give birth for another seven years after her natural son's death. The Franklins focused on building the business and running an expanding household that included a number of dependents, none of them the natural child of them both. They may have played favorites; for the sake of household order, they may have kept a careful emotional distance, in what would have been traditional early modern fashion. It is clear that by the time William was twenty-four, if not before, relations with his stepmother, Deborah, were quite tense. She did not hesitate to call him a "villain" to a casual acquaintance. This may have been partly a result, not of William's illegitimacy, but of his success in embodying his father's aspirations to move in circles beyond Market Street.[21]

At first, it had not been clear what to do with William, if he was not groomed to run the print shop. William had his own ideas. In 1745, at the age of fifteen or sixteen, he boarded a privateer and attempted to ship out, only to be hauled back home by his father. Franklin consented to his enlistment as an ensign in an expedition to Canada about a year later, a post more suitable to the family's genteel pretensions. His father gave him that freedom—but meanwhile solicited letters from "his Captain and Brother officers" about his son's conduct (which they reported on favorably). At this very moment, in 1746–47, Franklin decided on his course of retirement and set the terms of his partnership with Hall.

Franklin seems to have consciously rejected for his son the kind of harsh discipline he himself had received at the hands of his brother. Instead he used all the skills that had helped him succeed in business, and were beginning to make him a force to be reckoned with in politics as well, to see his son well placed. As a mode of parenting and mentorship, it was a choice that suited the enlightening, expansive times.[22]

William loved the army: perhaps most of all, he loved its acceptance of men who followed rules. At the age of seventeen he was sent back to Philadelphia on a special mission to collar deserters, a task he performed with gusto and efficiency. The next year he volunteered to join Conrad Weiser, the Indian agent, on a treaty mission to the Ohio River valley. He may have returned thinking that, as an officer and a budding gentleman in an empire regularly at war, he need not find a regular peacetime profession. His father let him know otherwise, proudly reporting to his own mother in Boston that William, who had "acquir'd a Habit of Idleness on the Expedition," was now, under his oversight, "applying himself" to legal studies. Father and son planned a trip to London, asking Strahan to register William's name at the Middle Temple of the Inns of Court and to send the important English law books.

Blood ties, invented families, and empire had already come together when Franklin asked Strahan for his help in collecting William's officer's pay. Within just a few years William would become "of Great Use" to Franklin as a militia colonel, treaty negotiator, and active participant in the Pennsylvania Assembly's battles with the Penns and their party. When Benjamin Franklin left the clerkship of the Assembly to run for the office of assemblyman in 1751, William became clerk. When Franklin gained the deputy postmastership for all North America and set out to rationalize the mails, he immediately appointed William to his old job of postmaster at Philadelphia. (Later on brothers, cousins, and his printer protégés would be drawn into this parallel extended postal family, which constituted a political and financial empire with Franklin at the head.) As Franklin's phenomenal rise to intercolonial importance began, his illegitimate son gained the polish to move in genteel circles. This was the ideal son for the intercolonial and British Benjamin Franklin. Together they began to dream and scheme about the western lands William had tramped, presumably in his British uniform—the kind of imperial dreams that would catalyze the next war for North America and send both on a mission to England.[23]

If William represents the sunny side of Franklin's refashioning of family and empire during the 1740s and 1750s, his other printing nephew, Benjamin Mecom, epitomizes its risks. Benny was just a little younger than his cousins William and James Jr. His father, Edward Mecom, a financially strapped and periodically disabled Boston saddle-maker, apprenticed Benny's elder brother himself but could do little for his other children. A younger Mecom apprenticed with the soap-making Franklins in Boston. For Benny, their second son, Jane and Edward Mecom looked to the uncle after whom they had named him. In 1744, at the age of twelve, Benny sailed not for Philadelphia but for New York, to apprentice in James Parker's shop. Uncle Benjamin had promised to raise Benny up in the trade himself, but his experience with Jemmy may have made him conclude that that was not the best course to follow. Or perhaps he did not want another teenage boy of ambiguous status, and potentially rebellious impulses, in his household. And he very much trusted Parker, who was raising boys of his own and may have especially needed an apprentice after the New York shop had survived its first few years. In any case, if Franklin saved his own household further compli-cations, he set himself up to be a middleman between his close family and his own former apprentice and most trusted partner. He could have been thinking of Jemmy, of his own past as an apprentice, or of his friend Parker's needs when he wrote his sister and brother-in-law to "advise [Benny] to be very cheerful, and ready to do everything he is bid" in New York, "and endeavour to oblige every body, for that is the true way to get friends."[24]

But by the spring of 1748, Benny had reached a crisis with Parker. He tried to run away and enlist on a privateer. He sent letters to his mother, which Jane anxiously forwarded to her brother, along with one of her own to Benny asking for clarification of his complaints and suggest-ing that Benny might confront his master and with his uncle's help be "discharged" from the terms of his apprenticeship. She added some ac-cusations that Benny had made not to her but to someone named New-port (probably a slave or servant of African descent).[25]

Franklin responded by quashing this plan and seeking to calm Benny's mother. Newport was probably lying; and Benny's own com-plaints, "as you [Jane] observe, do not amount to much." They seem to have concerned requests that Benny go on small errands; neglect by the Parkers' house slave while he (and Mrs. Parker and their daughter) lay ill during a smallpox epidemic; and the by-then classic complaint about clothes. All this sounded quite familiar to Franklin, who patiently rehearsed for Jane his own experience with Jemmy and William to prove that Benny was just acting the part of a normal sixteen-year-old. Later on, he assured her, Benny would become a more valued hand and be spared annoying tasks. Besides, he added, "there is a negro woman who does a great many of those errands."

Rarely do we see such direct evidence of the way relations between masters and servants could turn on the presence of slaves in households that were also workplaces. For Benny, apparently, being ignored by the Parkers' female slave epitomized his base treatment and immiseration. For Franklin, the slave's presence would smooth the conflicts between master and servant, helping to guarantee Benny progress from teenage apprentice to skilled young artisan.

It is tempting, on reading the letter, to follow Franklin's lead and normalize these conflicts. Ever the gifted writer, Franklin started with his best case—the unreliability of third-person, and possibly slave, testimony. He saved for the end the more disturbing facts and perhaps the root cause of the tumult. Parker himself had written to his patron to explain that Benny had been "staying out nights" and refusing to say where he had been, with whom, or what he had done. This was a probable violation of the indenture contract, and Parker responded by "correcting"—beating—Benny. Franklin justified the rod to his sister: "If he was my own son, I should think his master did not do his duty by him, if he omitted it, for to be sure it is the high road to destruction. And I think the correction very light, and not likely to be very effectual, if the strokes left no marks." He promised to inquire further of Parker, who had himself asked Franklin to intervene and judge Benny's complaints and his responses.[26]

Corporal punishment remained the norm at midcentury, as Franklin's rhetorical contrast of such "correction" versus "destruction" implies. And yet Franklin still had to justify Parker's actions to the boy's mother. There is an inherent tension between his justification of the physical punishment of a sixteen-year-old and his normalization of Benny's extreme responses to life as an apprentice in the Parker household. "I have a very good opinion of Benny in the main, and have great hopes of his becoming a worthy man, his faults being only such as are commonly incident to boys of his years, and he has many good qualities, for which I love him," he concluded, assuring Jane that the crisis would pass, much as it had for Jemmy and William. Two years later he was still mediating between the parents and the master: when Benny sailed for New England to visit his kin, his uncle tried to head off trouble by writing Jane that since the New York Assembly was meeting, the print shop would be busy and doubtless Parker would be wanting his eighteen-year-old best hand back in the shop as soon as possible. How Benny may have felt about having such an omniscient uncle, one who thought of his partner's needs before his nephew's, is not hard to imagine—unless, that is, he managed to feel grateful for being spared further "correction."[27]

All parties had tired of the situation by the summer of 1752, when Franklin came up with a solution. His partner in Antigua had died. Why not send the twenty-year-old Benny to run the shop? It might make his fortune. After eight years of apprenticeship, he clearly had the skill. Parker did not hesitate to agree, especially after Franklin made sure that Benny indebted himself to Parker for the equivalent of journeyman's wages for his remaining time. It was a typical Franklin masterstroke: it had something for everybody and made his own interests—in Parker's shop, in the Caribbean—consonant with Benny's own, or so it seemed to him. Jane expressed motherly concern about sending the young man so far away, to which her brother responded by insisting that "that Island is reckoned one of the healthiest of the West Indies"—hardly a balm to a worried Yankee matron. True, his old Antigua partner, Thomas Smith, had died there, but he had been healthy for four years until he started frequenting taverns (that is, behaving as most white men did).[28]

Although Franklin himself had already begun to write critically about the West Indies, disparaging its economy and culture compared to the mainland (and especially northern) colonies, he did not reveal any second thoughts to the Mecoms—or to Benny, who stayed at his house before sailing out of Philadelphia. But then something about the trip— and what he saw on his arrival in the Caribbean—shocked Benny Mecom to the core, and the letters he sent to Franklin disturbed the older man. He forwarded them to his sister and brother-in-law without much comment, aside from casting doubt on Benny's fortitude: "I fear I have been too forward in cracking the shell, and producing the chick to the air before its time . . . In my opinion, if Benny can but be prevailed on to behave steadily, he may make his fortune there. And without some share of steadiness and perseverance, he can succeed no where."[29]

Proud of his own seeming success with protégés and children,

Franklin seems to have been less inclined to weigh the rather different challenges Benny Mecom faced in New York and Antigua. In fact, Benny lasted longer in New York and in Antigua than the young Ben Franklin had lasted in Boston, in his first stint in Philadelphia, or in London. If Franklin showed "steadiness and perseverance," it was not until his twenty-third year, and in a much less crowded trade at that time, in which he could maneuver quite successfully without being called to task by an uncle who took the side of his master. It had been precisely such a situation that he had rejected in Boston. Yet Franklin biographers have seized upon these early moments to accuse Ben Mecom of a congenital "instability of character" that led inexorably to insanity and his mysterious demise a quarter-century later. Such a one-sided account is possible only if one does not listen to the voice of Benjamin Mecom, who did his best in a very difficult situation and who loved his uncle and aunt dearly. Had he not been so loyal, perhaps he would have fled the Caribbean immediately, as he had once tried to flee in New York. Ben Mecom's only surviving letters from this period avoid the topic of his uncle's harsh judgment and his mother's anxieties. They are addressed to Deborah Franklin, to whom he sent sweetmeats, oranges, and the frightening information that twelve of his acquaintances died in the "sick time" of 1754. So many deaths occurred that the Antiguans had developed a bell-ringing ritual: nine tolls for a dead man, six for a woman, three for a boy, and two for a little girl.[30]

Mecom succeeded nonetheless in resuscitating the *Antigua Gazette*. Optimistically, he ordered a large shipment of books from Strahan. Franklin had approved a "little cargo" of stationery and books in 1753, but Thomas Smith, the previous printer, had gone into debt the same way: West Indian planters did not promptly pay their bills, as Sam Keimer had lamented in verse a decade before. In the spring of 1754 Franklin thanked Strahan for *not* sending the books Mecom had requested. "Pray keep him within Bounds," Franklin wrote, as if discussing a servant rather than a partner. Much as Parker had used his connection with Franklin to keep Mecom in line, for what both considered the young man's own good, so Franklin relied on his deepening ties to Strahan to save Mecom, he thought, from the occupational hazards of being a printer in the West Indies.

Such bottom-line strategies, however, served the not-so-silent partner better than the young proprietor. Like most men who dealt with planters in the new world's slave-labor zones, Ben Mecom found that to construct an "interest" meant to take gentlemen and would-be gentlemen on their honor about paying up. Benny was a young man working, as Franklin had pointed out to Jane, in the seat of the government of the British West Indies—still the wealthiest sector of the empire, dealing with a turnover of grandees, managers, and ship captains. What was a printer—an artisan more lettered than most of the rich men but also dependent on them—in such a place? It had driven the pretentious Keimer to satire. Little wonder that Smith had started quaffing rum in the taverns. Mecom took a more genteel route, one his cousin Jemmy would have understood very well. A few years later in Boston an apprentice witnessed Ben Mecom recently returned from the Caribbean, "handsomely dressed" in "a powdered bob wig, ruffles and gloves," while sweating, expertly, over a press. A rather different kind of display than the one young Franklin had affected in Boston and Philadelphia seemed to be the way to wealth in Antigua.[31]

The debt issue came up again a year later; this time Mecom persuaded Strahan to send the goods without Franklin's prior permission. "I do not at all approve," wrote Franklin, in what was for him very strong language, "and shall write to [Mecom] about it." Within ten weeks Benny had written back, saying he wanted to leave the island. "I have no objection to it," Franklin wrote his sister. They quarreled about arrangements. The debt question had led Benny to rethink the entire agreement with his uncle, which he realized had more than a whiff of the antique about it. If Uncle Benjamin was going to insist on cash accounting in all cases, what exactly did he—Benny—owe his patron-partner? Franklin replied that his arrangement with Smith had been for one-third of the profit, but that "after he did well I relinquished that" in favor of an annual payment to his mother, Abiah—now a widow with dependents— "and some rum and sugar to me." Franklin, in short, asked for a quitrent and a tribute: feudal legacies that would soon come under attack in the revolutionary Atlantic world.

Mecom replied by asking precisely how long that debt would continue. And what about the earlier debts—would they be canceled? As Franklin recorded it, his nephew "finally insisted that I would name a certain Sum that I would take for the Printing House, and allow him to pay it off in Parts as he could, and then the Yearly Payment to cease; for tho' he had a high Esteem for me, yet he lov'd Freedom, and his

Spirit could not bear Dependence on any Man, tho' he were the best man living."[32]

Mecom's frankness, not to mention independence, left Franklin speechless. He admitted to his sister that the letter lay "long unanswer'd." Benny took further "offence" at this neglect and finally demanded the terms on which he could leave the island. Franklin told him to send the press home and pay his debts to Strahan. Mecom remained at Antigua for a few months, collecting debts full time. He eventually settled with his uncle, choosing to return to Boston with the printing press in hopes of making a go of it there. Franklin was satisfied with his payment to Strahan, accepted a bond from Benny for £100 (part of it a new loan), and stressed his evident "industry and frugality" in a later letter to Jane. But these events may have been on Franklin's mind when he wrote enigmatically in the 1757 *Almanack*, "The *Borrower* is a Slave to the Lender; the *Security* to *both*."[33]

Like his cousin Jemmy, Ben Mecom turned down Franklin's offer of the New Haven printing office. Back in Boston, he began to print small jobs, pamphlets, and books. Declaring independence in much the same way as Franklin and other master printers had, he got married. He showed his continuing loyalty by printing the first pamphlet editions of Franklin's most important writings of the period: *Father Abraham's Speech, The Interest of Great Britain Considered*, and "Observations on the Increase of Mankind." In the short-lived *New England Magazine* that he edited and dedicated to "a good old gentleman," Mecom reprinted *Plain Truth*, Franklin's 1748 call for the mobilization of the Philadelphia citizenry, and his uncle's filial tombstone epitaph for Abiah and Josiah Franklin. But when Franklin, now deputy postmaster for North America and in charge of all the regional postmasterships, gave the Boston job to Tuthill Hubbart, the stepson of the late incumbent John Franklin but not a printer, Benny raged, and his mother lamented bitterly enough that word reached her brother in Philadelphia.

What could be done? Ben Mecom was the nephew and namesake of the self-made man, the apprentice of the self-made man's apprentice. Culturally, he was caught between Boston and Antigua, while being manipulated from Philadelphia. He may not have managed those routes any better than he improved upon his roots, but then again, he came of age in a different time and place than did Benjamin Franklin, all the while being saddled with Franklinian expectations of the kind Franklin him-

self could never have conceived at such a young age. Isaiah Thomas remembered Benny in his Boston years as "queer," sweating away in his
ruffles, but also as an excellent printer, recognized as such by his peers.
The wonder may be not that he eventually went crazy but that he did not
go crazy sooner. All Benjamin Mecom wanted, it seems, was what he
could never have: a truly fair chance to prove himself worthy of his
name.[34]

Extending the sphere of his interests and operations complicated Franklin's relations with his protégés and his family. The problem of slavery, in
turn, came to symbolize, for Franklin, much that was dangerous, or at
least unresolved, in the household and wider world. When the Quaker
pacifists and the proprietors could not agree on a mode of defense in
1747, Franklin, writing as a tradesman, called on the citizens to form a
militia. If "we, the middling people" did not take up arms against the
privateers who had raided as close as New Castle, Delaware, "your Persons, Fortunes, Wives and Daughters, shall be subject to the wanton and
unbridled Rage, Rapine, and Lust of *Negroes, Molattoes*, and others, the
vilest and most abandoned of mankind." For the patriarchal property-
holders whom *Plain Truth* addressed—not the rich, but the ordinary
"Tradesmen, Shopkeepers, and farmers of this Province and City"—
mulatto seamen were made by Franklin to symbolize all the disorders of
a world turned upside down. Their possible invasion justified not only
the call to arms but a populist revolt grounded in a patriotic middling-
class rhetoric, one that was valid even without the leadership of "the
Great" of Pennsylvania. "Great Numbers of our People are of the BRITISH
RACE, and tho' the fierce fighting Animals of those happy Islands, are
said to abate their native Fire and Intrepidity, when removed to a Foreign Clime, yet with the People 'tis not so; Our neighbours of New England afford the World a convincing Proof, that BRITONS, tho' a Hundred
Years transplanted, and to the remotest Part of the Earth, may yet retain,
even to the third and fourth Descent, that *Zeal* for the *Publick Good*,
which has in every age distinguished their Nation." The problems of the
colony and of patriarchal descent were solved by the invocation of blood,
as the language of race entered Franklin's politics for the first time.
Adding praise for the "Brave Irish protestants" and "brave and steady
Germans" who would fill out the ranks did not so much pluralize the

British community as reinforce the notion that nationhood was race, and race was destiny.[35]

Racial nationhood was a notion that Franklin did not so much literally believe as find useful in the emerging political context, and in his personal life.[36] Around 1750 a racial and imperial British nationhood held out an expanded sense of possibility for his own second career. It suggested ideological and practical solutions to the most intractable dilemmas of Pennsylvania politics: enthnoreligious diversity and the Penns' proprietorship. Moreover, racial nationhood might help resolve the problem of slavery: that is, the problem of the institution's inherent injustice (which Franklin, as much as any of his contemporaries, was prepared to see), and the practical problem of slave resistance, in the form of a fifth column in the household and on the home front.

At this pregnant moment in his career and his political thought, a domestic incident involving two of his slaves led Franklin to contemplate divesting his household of slaves. On April 12, 1750, he wrote confidentially to his mother of the affair and its aftermath:

> My Leg, which you enquire after, is now quite well. I still keep those Servants, but the Man not in my own House: I have hired him out to the Man that takes care of my Dutch Printing Office, who agrees to keep him in Victuals and Clothes, and to pay me a Dollar a Week for his Work. His Wife since that Affair behaves exceeding well: But we conclude to sell them both the first good Opportunity; for we do not like Negro Servants. We got again about half what we lost.[37]

There is no other evidence that sheds light on these enigmatic remarks except Franklin's own report months earlier that he had been "lame" for two weeks. It seems reasonable to say that some sort of domestic accident or altercation occurred that caused a significant injury to Franklin's leg and damaged some goods or cost some money.[38] Most important, he not only blamed the slave couple but invoked their race as an explanation. It was better not to have such people around. Typically, he used his printing network—in this case, the German printing establishment of Johann Boehm—as a cash-producing holding pen. Whatever the enslaved couple had done, and whenever they were sold (their fates, too, are unknown), they suffered from the easy convertibility of their membership in the Franklin household into the extended family of Franklin's business interests.

Sometime the next year Franklin penned his "Observations on the Increase of Mankind," a calculated effort to imagine the British Empire without slaves or a permanent class of servants—particularly non-British servants. The essay has often been pointed to as an early version of the frontier, or safety-valve, theory of American history, whereby the lower classes shake the dust off and move to unclaimed land rather than remaining where they are and becoming a depressed and exploited peasantry or proletariat. But the essay's roots actually lay in the conjunction of slavery, to which it refers repeatedly, and imperial regulation. The Iron Act of 1750 had imposed restrictions on the colonial iron industry, out of fear that if the colonies worked their own raw or pig iron into their own manufactured goods, thousands of Englishmen would be put out of work. Arguments in its favor were arguments about population and its relation to wealth in England and in the colonies, a subject Franklin had been considering for some time and was prepared to reduce to the new science of "political arithmetic." He posed his intervention in terms of a problem in natural history as well as political economy: what do we know about the growth of nations and empires in numbers, and thus in wealth, and what does it imply for the peopling of the colonies and how its economy should be organized?[39]

The central facts of the new world—the availability of land and the expense of labor—created possibilities for upward mobility. These opportunities would allow people in the new world, specifically North America, to marry sooner, which would lead to a rapid rise in the population: "our People must at least be doubled every 20 Years." The population boom would create a market for consumer goods made in England. Both colony and metropolis would thrive in these circumstances, so that even if industrious colonists began to manufacture, Britain should not interfere. Labor was and always would be expensive in America because of the availability of land, and the high cost of labor would make it impossible for colonial manufactures to compete with British imports in any serious or lasting way.

The main threat to this prosperous empire—besides conquerable Indians, ill-advised imperial taxation, and overconsumption of luxury goods—was not the slave-fueled economic expansion of the colonies (the iron industry was itself typical in its innovative and flexible use of both slaves and servants) but rather the mistaken metropolitan idea that "by the Labour of Slaves, *America* may possibly vie in Cheapness of Manufactures with Britain." It was mistaken because slavery was an inherently bad investment with interest rates high in the colonies, wages low in England, and "every slave being *by Nature* a thief."[40] Only the tendency of white servants to graduate or run away from servitude lured strapped masters to buy slaves, a strategy that in the long run only stunted the economy and, Franklin implied, could easily be regulated out of existence. The number of whites in a nation, whose labor was equivalent to true wealth, actually diminished in proportion to the number of slaves. Counterintuitively (as far as the view from London was concerned), Franklin argued that the increasingly wealthy, cash-crop-growing slave societies of the Caribbean and the southern parts of the continent did not represent the future of empire in America, because their white populations—the true measure of wealth—remained stagnant. Slaves and their owners did not exhibit "frugality and Industry."

Dismissing how much wealth continued to be expropriated directly and indirectly from enslaved bodies enabled Franklin to boldly address the slavery question, which, the wars of the 1740s had taught him, was also a question of imperial policy. When in 1750 a treaty with Spain awarded the *asiento*, or right to supply slaves, to the British, this was even more the case.[41] He turned slavery into a question of the larger trade in people, in which it looked like a bad bargain. Slaves were taking up spaces that could be occupied by white immigrants who would in the long run add more wealth to an expanding empire. If the English thought correctly about their common interest with their fellow Britons across the water, they would use race, instead, as a benchmark for economic policy. Colonists and Englishmen were white Britons; they deserved preferment over all darker races.

Should the doubling propensities of the English not be hemmed in by Indians or "Palatine [German] Boors" who managed to live more cheaply (though failing to assimilate), Franklin exulted, "the greatest Number of Englishmen [would] be on this Side the Water." Hedging his bets about how Englishmen might respond to this prediction, he defined it as a collective benefit: "What an accession of Power to the British Empire by Sea as well as Land! What increase of Trade and Navigation! What numbers of Ships and Seamen!" The prospect underlined how important it was to make sure that the postwar treaties supplied more than a little el-

bow room for the North American colonists: rather than giving back good
mainland like Quebec for a southerly island port like Minorca, as England had done in 1748, the empire ought to be conceived as growing, not by the accession of islands and slaves, but by the whitening of
America:

> Which leads me to add one Remark, that the Number of purely
> white People in the World is proportionably very small. All Africa
> is black or tawny; Asia chiefly tawny; America (exclusive of the
> new Comers) wholly so. And in Europe, the Spaniards, Italians,
> French, Russians, and Swedes, are generally of what we call a
> swarthy Complexion; as are the Germans also, the Saxons only
> excepted, who, with the English, make the principal Body of
> White People on the Face of the Earth. I could wish their Num-
> bers were increased. And while we are, as I may call it, Scouring
> our Planet, by clearing America of woods, and so making this
> Side of the Globe reflect a brighter light to the eyes of Inhabitants
> in Mars or Venus, why should we, in the Sight of Superior Beings,
> darken its People? Why increase the Sons of Africa, by planting
> them in America, when we have so fair an Opportunity, by ex-
> cluding all Blacks and Tawneys, of increasing the lovely White
> and Red?

From this extraterrestrial height, substituting scientific perspective for
God's watch, Franklin ratified white Anglo-American solidarity at the
expense of a swarm of racial others: blacks, Indians, and Europeans not
(yet) white. Whiteness, metaphorically but importantly, was nothing less
than enlightenment: a brighter light.

The problem was that anyone reading this essay in England or in
America would have noticed that most people in America were, by the
measure Franklin proposed, black, tawny, or swarthy. So Franklin concluded with a brilliant, ironic, and self-reflexive turn that, to some
scholars eager to retain a usable, liberal Franklin, mitigates the frank, if
strategic, racism of the preceding paragraph: "But perhaps I am partial
to the Complexion of my Country, for such Kind of Partiality is natural to
Mankind." There is indeed an attractive, even modern relativism here—
but it is racism itself that is relativized, and thus excused, in support of
complexion as nature. The comment sealed the whiteness of Franklin's

country, which, in the essay's most important and central argument, was simultaneously the colonies, the British nation, and the empire.

The effect was as astounding as it was confounding, which may explain why Franklin did not publish the piece for another four years. He had taken his innovative political economy, and his argument against the Iron Act, into relatively uncharted territory. He had argued against slavery at a time when the loudest voices in London were actually celebrating the African trade as a pillar of the empire.[42] He had done so by using cosmopolitan relativism to naturalize racism even while hinting that maybe racial distinctions were mostly in the eye of the beholder. He had resolved the contradiction in this argument—Were darker peoples inferior or not? If they were inferior, why not keep them as slaves? If not, why not keep them as citizens?—by imagining that a division of labor in the empire, supported by the infinite availability of land, would actually enable Americans, *sans* slaves, to be the empire's enlightened future, without the corruptions of earlier, more primitive imperial ventures. America would float the British nation of manufacturers and shopkeepers who would supply it with its surplus white children. The bonds across the Atlantic would be at once imperial and familial. The future looked free and bright, fecund, profitable, and white.

In *Poor Richard's Almanack* for 1752, Franklin included excerpts from Richard Savage's "On Public Spirit" (1737), with altered lines suggesting Philadelphia's recent public improvements and the lush lands available on Pennsylvania's frontier. The poem praises science, improvement, and liberty and allies them with the appropriation of the neglected lands of the "blameless Indian" and a criticism of African slavery, on which a carelessly "revolving Empire" might otherwise meet its "doom." Franklin's version, however, omitted two lines that called Africans by "nature equal meant."[43]

Franklin was more than up to date in pairing enlightenment and progress with racism and opposition to slavery: he was at the cutting edge. During the late 1740s David Hume began to argue that slavery had spoiled the republics of the ancient world; he simultaneously insisted that Africans were innately inferior. It would not be long before Hume and Franklin became good friends, with Hume singling out Franklin himself as the first new world genius, precisely the kind of natural flow-

ering that he contrasted to Africans. Like Hume and other thinkers of
the Scottish Enlightenment, Franklin had obvious incentives to write the
provinces into the history of a greater Britain and its imperial progress.[44]
Ironically, perhaps portentously, in beginning to propose union and
equality within the empire, he called attention to the very things that
made America different.

In these writings of the early 1750s, circulated among influential
colonial administrators and later anonymously in print, we see an
"American" consciousness legitimated, or at least emboldened, by the
very British nationalism it sought to broaden and join.[45] Immigration,
and the labor supply, were the keys, both practically and symbolically,
as "Observations" suggested. The supply of people in America, after all,
could hardly be separated from their image, or identity, as children of
the mother country.[46] Around the time he drafted the "Observations,"
Franklin collected a series of reports of crimes committed by convict laborers in the mid-Atlantic and published them in the *Gazette*. The forced
transportation of convicts "for the better peopling of the Colonies" put
into practice the idea of the colonies as a satellite for inferiors, a pun-
ishing ground for misbehaved children: a land of Britons who were yet
half-citizens, laboring for the benefit of others. The results, in Franklin's
sensationalistic editorial, epitomized the reverse of freedom and advancement in a transoceanic empire: a Maryland servant who, poised to
stab his mistress to death, cut off his hand instead, only to add, *"Now
make me work, if you can."* In such a deranged world, virtuous natural
increase was replaced by sin, disease, and filth:

> What good *Mother* ever sent *Thieves* and *Villains* to accompany
> her *Children*; to corrupt some with their infectious Vices, and
> murder the rest? What *Father* ever endeavour'd to spread the
> *Plague* in his Family!—We do not ask Fish, but thou givest us
> Serpents, and worse than Serpents!—In what can Britain show a
> more Sovereign Contempt for us, than by emptying their Jails into
> our Settlements; unless they would likewise empty their Jakes
> [privies] on our Tables?

The follow-up essay (which Franklin signed "Americanus," the first time
he invoked an American identity in print) developed the symbol of the
snake as a figure for this unnatural sin of empire. Franklin insisted that

America's native rattlesnakes, "Felons-convict from the Beginning of the World," should be sentenced, not to death, but to transportation to England. Perhaps some change in climate would change their nature, he remarked in a satirical reversal of both continental speculation on the effects of new world weather on racial characteristics, and English justifications for exporting felons in the first place. He further questioned, ominously, where the empire's original sins lay—in the garden of the new world, or with the master planters?[47]

Who were the real snakes? Some Parliament courtiers, he added, were already all too reptilian in their venal, seducing habits. Yet just a few years later the threat of attacking Indians, and the uneven integration of the Americans into British priorities during the next imperial war, inspired Franklin to create a symbol of a possible American unity in his famous "Join or Die" cartoon of the colonies as a chopped-up snake. Joined, the colonies would become forceful, effective, and dangerous to their French and Indian enemies. Together, the sinuous line of provinces along the Atlantic coast would suggest a body politic.[48]

The metaphorical richness of the snake image at midcentury, however, was merely the tip of an iceberg that was just then coming into view. The growth of the colonies, their rising importance to the imperial economy, and the relative autonomy that the colonies had enjoyed during the second quarter of the eighteenth century—an autonomy that fueled their exciting and problematic growth—led to innovative attempts on the part of the colonial administration to rationalize and even centralize the administration of the colonies. Royal vetoes of colonial laws, the reorganization of the Board of Trade, and the use of explicit instructions, to be followed to the letter by colony governors, may not have succeeded in the short run from the perspective of Whitehall, but it led to a transatlantic discussion of what exactly the colonies were and what their relation to England and empire might be. The metaphor of parents and children formed the crucial idiom of this debate. Like contemporary childrearing theories, it could accommodate everything from an emphasis on the children-colonies' dependence and deference to the mother country, to an emphasis on the common good, mutual interest, and even the relative equality of the members of the family-empire.[49]

Once the Seven Years' War did begin, with skirmishes and sieges in and around the forts of the Ohio River valley, military events highlighted the colonies' need to belong as well as the evidence of inequality in the empire. The Plan of Union that Franklin presented at the Albany Congress of 1754 failed not merely because it tried to find a workable union of politically distinct and jealous colonies, but also because it sought to unify the empire into a tighter overall political framework—a trend the various colonies were selectively, and successfully, resisting even as they reveled in the glory of their Britishness and the prospect of a frontier cleared of Frenchmen and their native allies. "Britain and her Colonies should be considered one Whole, and not as different States with separate Interests," wrote Franklin. Colonies were like "so many Counties gained to Great Britain." Imperial instructions should reflect "Fatherly Tenderness and Affection," not "Masterly harshness and Severity." He continued to set German immigrants, a political wild card in Pennsylvania politics, against a true transatlantic English interest. Despite the Germans' "habitual Industry and Frugality," they did not measure up because they were a drag on the developments Franklin most prized: the prospect of becoming British in the most expansive sense of the word, of moving from the extremity to the center of the empire, which he increasingly depicted as a process of growing into maturity, even a parallel paternity: "O let not Britain seek to oppress us, but like an affectionate parent endeavour to secure freedom to her children; they may be able one day to assist her in defending her own." This organic, healthy set of developments would prevent disease in the body politic, "whereas a Mortification begun in the Foot may spread upwards to the destruction of the nobler parts of the Body."[50]

This was the bird's-eye view, an attempt to see the empire from outside the perspectives of metropolis or colony. Its diagnostic language suited Franklin's anonymous pamphlets and letters to his friend Peter Collinson, the man who was simultaneously advancing Franklin's scientific reputation in the Royal Society of London. On the ground, in specific interventions, the stakes were clearer. To Governor William Shirley of Massachusetts, a kindred spirit who was about to be appointed second in command of all the British forces in North America, he complained pointedly that the plans afoot to regulate and tax the colonies through parliamentary law would amount to "treating them as a conquer'd People, and not as true British Subjects." He went on to name the stakes more explicitly. A tax on land would be a "Discouragement" to the "Growth and Increase" of the colonies, a zero-sum game that neglected the ways in which trade regulations already taxed British colonists in effect by forcing them to pay more for goods. Besides, such taxation contravened the "native rights of Britons, which they think ought rather to have been given them, as due to such Merit, if they had been before in a State of Slavery."[51]

Americans, "who have most contributed to enlarge Britain's empire and commerce," deserved to be treated as the opposite of slaves—even if they had once been considered slaves or akin to slaves. It was a bold statement but one that was only necessary in a world in which colonists might be mistaken for the unfree people who actually produced so much of the wealth they owned, wealth for which Franklin claimed credit in the imperial scheme of things. The more closely Franklin dealt with actual policy issues, the more often the labor question reared its head, taking its central place in his expansionist, cosmopolitan, and pro-master politics. In a wartime plan for settling the lands beyond the Appalachian Mountains, Franklin anticipated arguments against slow expansion by stating that western North America would become "a populous and powerful dominion," whether it was in the hands of England or France. If French North America grew thanks to restricted British settlement, "many of our debtors, and loose English people, and servants, and slaves, will probably desert to them; and increase their numbers and strength, to the lessening and weakening of ours."[52]

The threat of the runaway returned again, as the war expanded and the empire pressed for American recruits: Franklin's own Militia Act for Pennsylvania specifically forbade the enlistment of servants or apprentices without their masters' consent. In September 1755 Governor (now Major General) Shirley ordered his officers in Pennsylvania to avoid recruiting servants. But servants themselves had other ideas, and their ability to get into uniform inspired Franklin, as an Assembly member, to draft a protest petition to the governor of Pennsylvania. Any encouragement to servants was a double threat to the colony. If servants could be taken away or tacitly permitted to run away at any time, "the Purchase, and of course the Importation, of Servants will be discouraged, and the People driven to the Necessity of providing themselves with Negro Slaves, as the Property in them and their Service seems at present more secure. Thus the Growth of the Country by Increase of White Inhabitants will be prevented, the province weakened rather than strengthened (in as much as every Slave may be reckon'd a domestick Enemy) one great and constant Source of Recruits be in great Measure cut off," and Pennsylvania, the breadbasket and recruiting ground, would start to look like "the Slave colonies now do," requiring expensive protection rather than protecting themselves. The enlistment of servants would amount to nothing less than "a most severe, unequal, and oppressive Tax on Purchasers, often falling on People in low Circumstances . . . A manifest and grievous Injustice and Oppression."[53]

Even if masters were compensated after the fact—as provided for in a law passed by Parliament in 1756—for making servants and slaves into uniformed Englishmen without racial distinctions, it would decisively upset the economics and the politics of the empire Franklin held dear. In a private letter to his supervisor, the postmaster general of the colonies, Franklin allowed himself a personal example: "Taking the compositors from a Printing-House (my own Case) the servants who are Press Men, tho' left behind, not knowing how to compose, must remain idle." Besides, the name-changing, shape-shifting runaway confounded the stable identity of the temporarily "British" arms-bearing enlisted freeman: "he may repeat the Frolick as often as he pleases."[54]

There could be only one result: more slavery. It was precisely such a set of ineluctable political problems that prompted the Pennsylvania Assembly to appoint Franklin as their agent to London, empowered to argue the colony's case against the Penns and, secondarily, to seek the end of proprietary government itself.[55]

On June 5, 1757, he boarded a ship along with his son and Peter and King, their personal slaves. Before leaving, he wrote a will in which he freed Peter and the wife he had forced Peter to leave behind. This may have been the same couple he had resolved to sell seven years before.[56] Franklin did not "like Negro Servants," perhaps on personal, maybe on moral, but definitely on geopolitical grounds. Nevertheless, he was finding it as difficult to extricate them from his family as from the empire. As a result, the path from British to American nationhood, a path that took him across the ocean and back, would be traced not only around, but also directly through, the problem of slavery.

SIX

Printers, Agents, and Blackened Men

In the part of the *Autobiography* written after the Revolution, Franklin delicately reviewed his role in Pennsylvania's rancorous politics of the 1750s. "Disputes" abounded, despite goodwill and genteel standards of conduct. Even when the provincial governor who had been sent over from London, Robert Hunter Morris, was someone he knew and liked, Franklin was drawn into a cycle of harsh public invective between the Assembly and the executive.

At least Morris had a sense of humor about the situation, and grace enough to remain cordial. Their jesting friendship made possible an informal exchange that Franklin thought significant enough to write down three decades later. One evening "in gay Conversation over our Wine after Supper he told us Jokingly that he much admir'd the Idea of Sancho Panza [in Cervantes's *Don Quixote*], who when it was propos'd to give him a Government, requested it might be a Government of *Blacks*, as then, if he could not Agree with his People he might sell them."[1]

Such were the wearied fantasies of a colonial governor. Would that the provincial elites were as tractable as slaves! It was an especially potent idea for Morris, whose dependence on the Penns for his position and salary forced him to fight their battles with the Assembly. One of Morris's friends at the dinner recognized the aptness of the fantasy and pushed it further. "Franklin," he exclaimed, "why do you continue to side with these damn'd Quakers? had not you better sell them? the Proprietor would give you a good Price." Suddenly Franklin was the governor, the master of men, whose best move would be to sell out to the owner of them all. But Franklin resisted the joke, much as he and the antiproprietary "Quaker" party had resisted the political terms set forth by the Penns and the governors they appointed. Instead, he turned the joke around: he suggested that the real issue was not the unwillingness of Penn's colonists to act like slaves but the proprietors' habit of thinking and talking about them as if they could be bought or sold. He would not sell out the Quakers, he retorted: "The Governor, says I, has not yet *black'd* them enough."

The joke worked when Franklin first told it because mid-eighteenth-century Anglo-Americans understood viscerally the connection between slander, racial prejudice, and the institution of slavery.[2] It still worked thirty years later, when he extended the joke, in the past tense, in light of subsequent events: "He [Governor Morris] had indeed labour'd hard to blacken the Assembly in all his Messages, but they wip'd off his Colouring as fast as he laid it on, and plac'd it in return thick upon his own Face; so that finding he was likely to be negrify'd himself, he as well as Mr. Hamilton [the previous governor], grew tir'd of the Contest, and quitted the Government." As funny as Franklin was here, he presented a bleak view of Anglo-Pennsylvanian politics in the era of the Seven Years' War. It was a contest to see who could be controlled—or sold: to see who was the owner among owners and who could be "blackened" into submission.

For the rest of his life, as he moved in the corridors of power and continued to write for the press, Franklin's political action partook of this heady mix of bon mot and slander, of personal battles and simultaneous struggles to represent large groups of people. Skills he had honed as a printer, civic leader, and ideologue he applied in the provincial and British imperial arenas. Because of all that had passed during the past thirty years, the stakes—personal and political—were only greater. He leaned all the more on his canny, careful conflation of British and American interests, the language of wise parents and industrious, faithful children.

Another imperial war accelerated colonial maturity and confidence during the late 1750s and early 1760s. The Seven Years' War, a result of both the colonies' economic importance and their own aspirations to more territory, put strains on their finances and those of the imperial government, which made taxes, and the right to demand them, an issue in the first place. In this sense, the battle over raising revenue for defense in Pennsylvania during the Seven Years' War prefigured the imperial controversy of the 1760s, even though it was at first Thomas Penn and family who refused to be taxed. The point can be extended to apply to the larger conditions of life in the empire. The levying of taxes to cover costs like those incurred fighting Atlantic wars grew the British state and created new areas of common interest and identity. Victories created more national glory to rejoice over and more spoils to fight over; they also generated more bills to pay, and more land and ships to speculate on. When the Americans seemed to act rebelliously just as they began to exult, more than ever, in their Britishness, it seemed as if the empire might be falling apart at the moment of its greatest triumph.[3]

With rising stakes, the identities and character of the players themselves became an issue. Representative figures like "the Great Commoner" William Pitt, the populist journalist John Wilkes, and the "patriot King" George III played roles beyond their elected, appointed, or hereditary offices because they, and figures like them, crystallized the aspirations and actions of the greater numbers of people who were taking an interest in the affairs of the nation.[4] First in Pennsylvania and then in London, Franklin became one of those figures. It not only became more difficult to separate Franklin and his image from the causes he espoused, it was also beside the point, since he so literally represented them: sometimes quietly or anonymously, in print; sometimes diplomatically, as a designated agent at the seat of government; and often publicly, in song and satire. Personality and reputation became profoundly political, and the gibes and snubs of both the press and the court reverberated indoors and out of doors, even across the ocean.

The empire itself created new kinds of mercantile and speculative wealth that freed some Englishmen to become newly minted gentlemen. Whether they bought land and access to the House of Lords or settled for a place in the House of Commons, this "open elite," along with their supporters in the streets, changed English politics into a much more contested, popular affair even as the North American colonies achieved political and economic significance. The rising men of the eighteenth century, like Franklin, were also insecure men, because of the newness of their stature and wealth. The entry of Scotsmen and Irishmen into metropolitan life, even as the mass of their countrymen remained provincial, made mid-eighteenth-century British culture a swirling festival of opportunities—and stereotypes. Add to that mix absentee West Indian planter "nabobs," Protestant dissenters both homegrown and foreign, increasing numbers of Africans even in London, and the occasional visiting North American Indian, and we have a recipe for profound acts of identity-mixing and self-creation. Out of this cauldron came a patriotic British identity, a widened palette of negative stereotypes, and a great deal of confusion. The presence of far-flung colonies lent ballast to the patriotic claims of John Bull, but it also raised the question of who counted, and how, in an expanded national identity.[5]

The colonists, in short, were not the only ones to experience an identity crisis. What, after all, was a freeborn Briton? Who belonged in the category that Franklin had invoked in his 1747 *Plain Truth* and his 1751 "Observations," only to exclude various newcomers from consideration? The answers were not much clearer in London or Edinburgh than they were in Philadelphia. Much as in our own time, a ubiquitous national popular culture with near global ambitions grew in tension with calls for diversity and tolerance. Name-calling escalated because it was the coin of both claims for inclusion and struggles for identity.[6]

In this context blackness remained a living metaphor. So did slavery. In the mid-nineteenth century, Melville's great narrator Ishmael, feeling himself oppressed by the shipboard labor system and the conditions that forced him to labor within it, asked rhetorically, "Who ain't a slave?" It was an apt question, both straight and ironic, asked at a time when many oppressed people were comparing their oppression to human bondage despite the fact that most people then, in most parts of America, were not slaves. A century before, when there were slaves in many more parts of British America, Franklin and other Britons asked simply, who is a slave? and subsequently, who is being treated like one? The questions, oddly enough, both did and did not have implications for the Africans whom many of the questioners held in bondage.

Real political problems entailed rhetorical debates filled with allusions to slavery and race, debates that in turn had real consequences. During the third quarter of the eighteenth century, most Anglo-Americans still recognized a world of dependencies, of slave-likeness, or varieties of liberty and unfreedom. Precisely because freedom was a relative matter and racial slavery a legal status, slavery and blackness provided potent ways of talking about power: about dependence on others and the ownership of others, and its abuses. To have one's property taken or used at the will of another, to be an appendage of another's will, was slavery. The man who was the subject of abuse, who lost reputation or honor, was "blackened." And the one who held others in a position of dependence enjoyed the truest mark of independence.[7]

The stark symbolics of the matter, the neat dualities—free and slave, black and white, colonist and Englishman—help explain what happened to Franklin and his contemporaries in the late 1750s and 1760s and why it mattered so much. But not entirely; things were not that black and white—not yet. The expanded opportunities, the expanded freedoms of the era, made the language of slavery and freedom all the more meaningful for being relative. Franklin, in this sense, was representative even as he began to serve distinctly representative functions in the polities of Pennsylvania and Great Britain. His status as a colonial agent exposed him to remarkable and revealing forms of freedom and constraint. It also opened him up to surprising varieties of abuse and forced him—hardly against his will—to blacken others.

In the meantime, his printer protégés suffered the growing pains of American and Franklinian empire. Sadly, some of the printers who remained most faithful, or most obedient, to Franklin fared the worst. They were left wondering how they had managed to become so unfree. Others, including one who declared his own independence, joined the growing ranks of Englishmen and Americans willing to sacrifice Franklin to their own ambitions.

Franklin did not turn decisively against the proprietors of Pennsylvania until the Seven Years' War, but when he did so, he became the leader of the struggle against the Penns' "feudal" governance. Earlier, Franklin had participated in controversies against the Quakers in the Assembly, especially when they did not appropriate funds for defense. Once the Assembly did, the onus of raising the funds fell on the Penns, who refused to be taxed to pay for military or any other costs. The Penns' lordly exemptions inspired Franklin and his fellow assemblymen to angrily denounce the Penns' tendency to define themselves as owners but not members of the community. Pennsylvanians under this scheme, they argued, were technically "Vassals fighting at their Lords Expence, but our Lord would have us defend his Estate at our own Expence! This is not merely Vassalage, it is worse than any Vassalage we have heard of; it is something we have no adequate Name for; it is even more slavish than Slavery itself." When the governor accused the assemblymen of trying to make him look like a would-be enslaver and thus defaming his majesty's government, they insisted on their ultimate loyalty: "we make wide Distinction between the King and Government and the Governor's conduct." For it was the governor who exhibited a disturbing tendency to describe Pennsylvanian rights as "crimes."[8]

The rights to protest, to refuse the enlistment of servants and slaves, to appropriate funds, and to tax all the land in the province: these belonged to the Assembly as rights of "freeborn Englishmen." The Pennsylvania assemblymen argued that they themselves were model citizens of the empire—as opposed to "Plantation Governors" of the southern and Caribbean colonies, who were "frequently transient Persons, of broken Fortunes, Greedy of Money, without any regard for the People." Did the Penns want to substitute a "French" constitution, characterized by absolutism, for the English one at the very outset of a war against France? The disallowed bills for defense, vetoed by order of Thomas and John Penn, meant that the Assembly had to defend the country without being able to raise the means to do so: "this is *demanding Brick without Straw*, and is so far *similar* to the Egyptian Constitution . . . we will . . . become servants to our Pharoah, and make him [the governor] an *absolute Lord*, as he [Penn] is pleased to stile himself *absolute Proprietary*." In 1756 Franklin and his fellow committee members equated the rights of political representation under threat from the Penns with their rights as masters of other men: "if this new-claimed Negative in the Proprietaries takes Place, the People will not have it in their Power to reward the Man that serves them, or even to pay the Hire of the Labourer that works for them, without the Governor's Leave first purchased."[9]

The impasse sent Franklin to London, as agent of the Assembly. Once there he quickly learned, to his surprise, that neither the proprietors nor most high British officials believed that a royal charter or customary rights granted a colonial assembly the ability to legislate without the supervision of the proprietor or the king's designated authority, the Privy Council. Franklin tried to shame Thomas Penn into recognition of his father William Penn's intentions as laid out in the 1701 Charter of Privileges. Had not William intended to grant "all the Power and Privileges of an Assembly according to the Rights of the Freeborn Subjects of England"? If such rights did not exist, hadn't all the settlers been "deceived, cheated and betrayed"? When Penn trivialized this charge, Franklin wrote directly to Isaac Norris, the speaker of the Assembly, venting his anger at the proprietor's "triumphing laughing Insolence," and compared Penn to a "low Jockey"—a horse salesman chuckling at a customer who felt cheated. What was worse, Penn had the audacity to "meanly give up his Father's Character," a transgression of shared values that so upset Franklin that he had "conceived that Moment a more cordial and thorough Contempt for him than I ever before felt for any man living . . . I believe my Countenance expressed it strongly." The letter leaked back to the Penns, which only increased the animosity between the proprietors, Franklin, and the Assembly.[10]

The recriminations multiplied. The Penns asked for "some person of candour" to replace Franklin. Franklin refused to meet with their imperious lawyer, Ferdinand John Paris. The proprietary party planted articles critical of Pennsylvania and its Assembly in the London press, as the Penns brought a brace of recent Pennsylvania laws to the Privy Council for review. Franklin did not hesitate to call the Penns "damned rascals" to Prime Minster William Pitt. The Assembly brought the unctuous William Smith, provost of Philadelphia's new college and a proproprietary writer, up on slander charges, which the Privy Council disallowed. Franklin and his allies went after the Penns for their famously fraudulent Indian treaty of twenty years before, known as the "walking purchase" for inflating a distance that was to be measured as a day and a half's walk by "running," and for then leaving Pennsylvanians vulnerable to frontier violence by angry natives in the aftermath. The Penns, in other words, had caused the war on the frontier. A compromise brokered by Lord Mansfield and other Council members in early 1760 allowed both sides to save face—Franklin reported being literally invited behind closed doors to devise the language by which the Penns would grant funds for defense while saving the appearance of their exemption from taxation. It helped a great deal that Parliament, under Pitt's sympathetic guidance, had committed itself to reimbursing the expenditures of the colonies, and that Lord Loudon, the commander general in the colonies, had pressured the new governor to pass the appropriations bill despite contrary instructions from the Penns.[11]

Franklin, however, was not content to fight such battles forever. He began to work for an end to the proprietorship, whether by decree or by purchase. The antiproprietary struggle partook of classic court maneuverings and outsider politics, by which early modern subjects appealed to higher powers over a local or provincial lord. Not surprisingly, Franklin and his allies even managed to scare up a pretender to the throne: young Springett Penn. As the heir of William Penn from an earlier marriage, Springett had a plausible claim to being the real proprietor. His uncle Thomas was trying to wrest from him a large chunk of Pennsylvania land and send him off to Russia or India. Such dynastic (though in this case, not very dangerous) maneuvers worked well or innocuously precisely because they were pursued, as Franklin pursued his campaign against the Penns, within traditional channels and in the name of the king.[12]

For Franklin sought not to overthrow constituted authority but to reconstitute it rationally, under the king: Pennsylvania as a royal colony. The idea seems ludicrous, a throwback or anachronism, only in retrospect. Colonials and Englishmen had long celebrated the king as the guardian of English liberties. While controversies over royal versus parliamentary authority still surfaced, the growth of a ministerial authority, which linked policymakers near the king to Lords and Commons, gave the concept of King-in-Parliament persuasive weight. Given that the Pennsylvania Assembly's claims for self-government originated in the king's right to grant them, and Franklin already had a sense of the policymakers' belief in Parliament as the ultimate lawmaking body for the entire empire, then the notion of royal proprietorship and stewardship seemed the most likely path between the Penns and the other lords of the realm.

Royal intervention also made practical sense because Franklin was himself a royal officer. In 1753 he had been appointed joint deputy assistant postmaster general for North America, a £300-a-year plum that came on the heels of his fame as an electrical experimenter. The post increased Franklin's ability to offer patronage to his extended family and his network of printers. He immediately appointed his son William Franklin comptroller, much as he had secured for William the clerkship of the Assembly and the Philadelphia postmastership. Various friends of Franklin became local postmasters, securing, or at least furthering, their footholds on the local printing trade. Enemies of Franklin began to notice that while he was in London, he was spending the colony's money generously: to gain willing ears for the Assembly's cause, surely, but perhaps also to gain a still higher office for himself. His friends and enemies mentioned various possibilities over the next decade: Would

Franklin gain a seat in Parliament? A colonial governorship? The post-master generalship itself? William Smith marveled at Franklin's ability to be the courtier in London and the "demagogue" at home, even as his mission proved to be much less than a complete success. The Penns and the Pennsylvanians who found themselves on the other sides of the issues worried that Franklin's international fame worked like electricity itself, shocking into stunned wonder all who came near him.[13]

Franklin was no universal conductor, but what else could they have thought when William Franklin suddenly emerged, at the tender age of thirty-one, as the designated new royal governor of New Jersey? The shocked aristocrat Thomas Penn exclaimed that the position should have gone to a real "gentleman," and Franklin's enemies quickly spread word of the younger man's bastard beginnings, but to no avail. The link to the crown was too strong: it ran through the Earl of Bute, a particular friend of Franklin and young King George III's favorite adviser since childhood. The rationality of the Franklins' royalism arose from the closeness to real power they achieved when they gained the favor of Bute. Out of gratitude Franklin, in fact, never quite gave up on Bute, even when he became a distinctly unpopular figure in London and colonial politics. Along with the images of the king and queen they brought back to America in 1762, father and son hung portraits of Bute in their homes.[14]

It was actually William Franklin who, in many ways, emerged as the more typical courtier. The aspiration was evident in the larger sums he spent on clothing, the deftness with which he impressed his father's friends, and the ease with which he evaded both his fiancée at home, the impressive and wealthy Elizabeth Graeme, and the match Franklin began to envision for him with their landlady's daughter, Polly Stevenson. After fathering an illegitimate child, named William Temple Franklin after himself and an elite friend, William parlayed his new governorship into a match with a slightly older and somewhat frail though apparently charming woman, Elizabeth Downes, whose father was a rich Barbados sugar planter. William Franklin could not have more quickly integrated himself into the structures of empire. He continued to be extremely loyal and "very serviceable" to his father, and quite useful politically, as he kept a watchful eye on Pennsylvania politics when Ben returned to England. Yet Franklin was surprised by his son's initiative as well as his choice of a bride, and possibly hurt enough to take a ship back to Philadelphia before the wedding in London.[15]

Perhaps he sensed how much a West Indian connection might do for William on his own someday. In Franklin's family as in the empire, war and imperial growth laid bare contradictions even as they opened opportunities. The Anglo-American triumphs at Quebec and Guadeloupe presented the pundits and policymakers of the increasingly expansive empire with a dilemma: if one of these territories was to be returned to the French in a peace treaty, which should it be? Did the future of empire lie on the North American continent or in the sugar colonies? If it lay in North America, rather than the more obviously "dependent" and profit-making Caribbean, how would a wholly British North America be prevented from becoming a great empire of its own?[16]

Franklin's response, *The Interest of Great Britain Considered* (1760), struggled to find new ways to explain that colonial growth did not mean competition. Colonies and empires were not like parents and their offspring after all: "The human body . . . is limited by nature to a certain stature . . . in the case of a mother country and her colonies, it is quite different. The growth of the children tends to encrease the growth of the mother, and so the difference and superiority is longer preserv'd." To arguments that the French and Indians provided a natural "check" on the colonies, Franklin retorted that " 'Tis a modest word, this, *check*, for massacring men, women and children." According to that kind of logic, it would be more efficient to "let an act of parliament be made, enjoining the colony midwives to stifle in the birth every third or fourth child. By this means you may keep the colonies to their present size."[17]

Economic growth in the colonies and the costs of the war at home created an entirely new political situation in 1763, in which colonial agents like Franklin found they had to deal not only with obstreperous provincial governors but also with new imperial policies, including taxes. These new policies, developed in the wake of an expensive war that was perceived as having protected and benefited the colonists, assumed a divergence of interests within the empire that needed to be redressed to keep the colonists in line. But the strains of expansion, and of colonial agency in every sense of the latter word, were felt among Franklin's associates at home before 1763, as Franklin began to revel in his international stature and his cosmopolitan Britishness. He did not allow, or admit, that the interests of his personal colonies—the printing and family network that increasingly mimicked, as well as participated in, the structures of the British Empire—might grow apart from his own, especially in the wake of his (perhaps salutary) neglect. As a result, the printers who owed their vocation to Franklin found themselves blackening each other in their own struggles for liberty and livelihood.

So begins a tale of four printers, Franklin protégés in three cities, their families, and their efforts to avoid being what they called enslaved. It is a tale of confidences betrayed, of neglect and recrimination, of competition, of patriotism and profit and patriarchy. It is an intercolonial story, of men on the move trying to profit from other men on the move. It is about their failures to become Benjamin Franklin, and Franklin's buoyancy on their shoulders: a buoyancy that helped him begin a revolution. It may or may not say something about the American Revolution that the only true scoundrel among these four was also the only one to be remembered as a Son of Liberty.

When Franklin departed for England in 1757, he left much in the hands of James Parker, his New York partner and designated comptroller of the post office. Thanks in part to Parker's management, the postal system simultaneously expanded and began to yield a handsome profit. The possibilities of the postal system excited both men and probably inspired in Parker as much ambition as they did in Franklin, including perhaps the hope of a Franklinian early retirement. In any event, Parker had hardly been in a position to say no to his senior partner when Franklin first asked him, in 1754, to find some solution to the problem of the still-empty New Haven postmastership and printing office. As Parker simply expressed it, "He was my Patron." Even though he himself had begun to expand, taking on a partner of his own in New York and opening the first printing office in New Jersey that same year, he agreed to manage New Haven himself.[18]

At about the same time, Franklin also asked Parker to take in John Holt, the brother-in-law of his co-deputy postmaster, William Hunter. Parker was to teach the thirty-three-year-old the trade. Holt, a bankrupt merchant, had literary pretensions and was enough of a gentleman to have served a one-year term as mayor of Williamsburg, Virginia. With his good inheritance prospects and genteel ways, he must have looked like a promising partner, though Franklin and Parker would have been better served had they looked more closely into the shady circumstances that caused Holt to flee his home colony. Parker took Holt first to his new establishment at Woodbridge, New Jersey, and then installed him in New Haven.

Supplying the printing needs of New Haven was secondary to Franklin's interest in the postal network: he wanted to continue to improve service along the New York–Boston corridor. Yet he also believed that a printing establishment and a newspaper, Connecticut's first, could survive on the postal fees and perquisites. More than ever, printing houses depended on elite and government patronage. Franklin, who had been invited to New Haven to receive an honorary degree from Yale, had been evidently promised both. Increasingly, however, printers also relied on good postal routes—to ensure that newspapers were distributed, of course, but also to receive extralocal news in a timely, competitive fashion. An out-of-town paper that too often scooped the local paper could siphon off essential subscribers. Though Parker had been granted the postmastership of New Haven by Franklin, this proved an insufficient edge. He personally had to invest in a special post rider in order to cover New Haven's northern hinterland extending to Hartford, the colony's capital.

New Haven's postal and printing ventures, in other words, were neither integrated nor especially well conceived at first. Parker's *Connecticut Gazette*, with Holt at its head, did not do well. In late 1755 Holt decamped for Boston to pursue some other main chance. He returned a few months later, though, after Yale and its new president came through with some printing, at which point he offered to buy the establishment from Parker outright. Parker hesitated. He had New Haven in mind for his nephew, Samuel Parker, who had three years left as an apprentice. Holt and Parker agreed on a fifty-fifty partnership, with Sammy Parker and Holt running the shop. Holt paid half of his £500 share in the business with a loan from a member of his wife's family. The rest he owed Parker.[19]

And here the troubles began. Sammy Parker, perhaps disappointed at losing his prospects for a shop of his own, decided he couldn't stand Holt or New Haven and went home. Not long after, Holt's servant, Charles Roberts, asked to buy his freedom. Then the batch of lottery tickets Parker had sent up from New York disappeared, and Holt fingered Roberts and took him to court, getting his term extended to forty years. Afterward the business appeared to prosper, but Holt sent little or no money to Parker, whether in the form of profits or payment toward his debt. Holt did buy a large house, however, apparently out of the postal funds.[20]

Parker might have noticed such irregularities more if he had not been trying to establish himself in Woodbridge, New Jersey, where he had inherited some land and slaves and had become an active member of the community. (He later served as a justice of the peace and a deacon in the Episcopal church.) He was working hard at his new position as comptroller of the entire North American postal system. He also had to navigate an increasingly difficult relationship with his former employee and now partner William Weyman, who was managing their previously very successful New York newspaper and printing shop. Weyman, too, stopped remitting any money or rent by 1758—the conclusion of a typically difficult triangle of maneuverings between Parker, Weyman, and another former worker and now rival, Hugh Gaine. After trying to buy Weyman out so he could install Samuel Parker in his place, Parker was apparently double-crossed: Weyman instead started up a rival paper and managed to win the New York government printing contract away from the Parkers. Meanwhile, nephew Samuel descended into alcoholism: in early 1760 he absconded with more than £300. In such a situation Parker had little choice but to gratefully accept Holt's offer to come to New York and take over the shop.[21]

What caused these printers to act so poorly toward each other, and yet to take chances on each other again and again? Doubtless it was the same pressures of competition that had turned young Benjamin Franklin into a resentful worker and a hard-fighting competitor with Keimer and Bradford in Philadelphia. Parker's biographer suggests another reason: a stamp tax initiated by New York authorities to try to offset some of the costs of the Seven Years' War. Two years after the tax was passed Parker felt moved to write a small pamphlet in defense of printers and himself. Parker's *Appeal to the Publick of New-York* (1759) is, in many ways, Parker trying—and largely failing—to be Franklin. But in doing so he reflected an astounding loyalty to Franklin's ideas, plans, and politics.[22]

Friends of "Religion, Liberty, and Vertue" value a free press, insisted Parker. Any tax discouraged that freedom, but this tax would "crush me more than others." The reason, he implied, was that he, unlike his competitors, was honest and did public work at little or no profit. The founders of printing in New York, William Bradford and John Peter Zenger, both "died poor"; Bradford and his sons did better in Philadelphia, perhaps in part because it was easier to get apprentices there, where grateful families would give the master printer money as well as keep their teenage sons in clothes. In New York, Bradford had been "obliged to take of the lowest People." Unlike in England, where printers could survive without printing newspapers and papers were paid for daily, colonial printers lost a full quarter of their sales through nonpayment for newspapers delivered through the mails. Yet under the new law these were to be pretaxed regardless. Printers, in short, had all the risks of merchants who advanced goods on credit, and all the drudgery of artisans who made things with their hands. Unlike silversmiths, whose luxury products might have been taxed, printers, he argued, did not even have cheap skilled labor: "we cannot well teach Negroes our Trade; but are obliged to work like Negroes, and in general are esteemed but little better." The tragic irony, to Parker, was that because they disseminated essential political news, no one had a better claim than colonial printers to the identity of "British Subjects and Lovers of Liberty."

Given Charles Roberts's skilled work at John Holt's New Haven press, Parker's insistence that black illiteracy hampered printers should be seen as more rhetoric than reality.[23] It is a revealing bit of rhetoric nevertheless. In the hampered trade, at the center of the growing "English Atlantic," one of the most ambitious and favored printers said publicly that being squeezed between gentleman patrons and his former workers-turned-derelicts-turned-competitors made him like a Negro, a slave. While saying so, he did not mention that he had once run away from William Bradford. He had put his runaway status behind him and come to depend not on the Bradfords but on Benjamin Franklin, with whom he had lived "many years." Franklin had set him up in New York and supplied him with nephews for apprentices before Parker's own nephew and son grew old enough. Now Franklin had moved on and up, taking Parker a step with him, into the imperial service as comptroller. But the tax on paper had prevented Parker from starting a paper mill and thus consolidating his interests as Franklin had.[24]

Holt continued to make things worse for Parker. He came to New York to take over Parker's office and newspaper there and then sought to simplify the terms of their arrangement. Perhaps seizing the chance offered by Parker's troubles, Holt offered to lease the New York establishment outright for £100 a year. The arrangement would free Parker, who was forty-eight and beginning to feel his age, to concentrate on his New

Jersey establishment. Parker, himself in debt to Franklin for post funds and several orders of books (some of which Franklin had ordered for him without his approval, and which Holt had not managed to sell), asked for the money up front, hoping that Holt would commit some of the £1,000 that his wife, Elizabeth Hunter Holt, had recently inherited. Holt paid only £80, though. Parker accepted this, afraid of offending Holt and turning yet another protégé into an independent rival. He began to change his mind when he found out that Holt's successor in New Haven, Thomas Green, had been sending Holt, not Parker, the post office returns as they trickled in, and Holt had pocketed the money without saying a word. The best Parker could do in response was to replace Green with Benjamin Mecom.[25]

Meanwhile, in November 1762 Franklin returned to Philadelphia and threw himself into reforming the postal system. The desire to do so derived in part from the need to settle matters after the death of William Hunter, his co–postmaster general and Elizabeth Holt's brother, and in part from an initiative of his superiors in London. Much like the colonies in general, the postal system, when it expanded and began to turn a profit, began to look less rational and efficient, and as a result it began to receive far greater official scrutiny. Franklin and John Foxcroft, his new co-postmaster, were pressured to centralize operations in New York, which led Franklin to try to get James Parker to move there, despite Parker's protests about the effects of Manhattan on his health. Franklin and Foxcroft also began to try to force local postmasters to turn in their books and forward missing payments.[26]

The result was a new cycle of failure and blame that highlighted the problems of colonial printers and agents. John Holt, now in New York, refused to account for his postal funds, leaving unclear how he had paid for the sizable house he had bought in New Haven, which he had no intention of selling or giving back to the post officers. In late 1763, when relations between Parker and Holt had already soured, Franklin asked New Haven attorney Jared Ingersoll to file suit against Holt in the king's name to recover £320.

Parker and Franklin held their own reunion and settlement, which resulted in Franklin taking one of Parker's slaves, a man named George, back to Philadelphia in lieu of a £100 payment. It was an indication of what was to follow. Parker began to have trouble making up his own debt to Franklin, a fact that made him both increasingly uneasy and less able to even consider refusing any of Franklin's demands on his time. Even before the Currency Act of 1764 disallowed much-needed issues of paper money by the colony legislatures, an economic downturn made it even harder for printers to part with available cash reserves. Worse for the postmasters, the London office took away the "franking" privilege of free postage for all post officers but the postmasters general, Franklin and Foxcroft. Parker complained that the ability to mail one's own newspaper for free was the only thing that made the smaller post offices worthwhile. As the Woodbridge postmaster, he had to take a ferry at ungodly hours to deliver a few pieces of mail for fees that amounted to little more than the cost of the transport.[27]

A despairing if apologetic tone began to enter Parker's letters to Franklin during these years. Not all of Franklin's protégés were as polite. William Dunlap, a printer, Philadelphia postmaster since 1757, and the husband of Deborah Franklin's niece, resigned under Franklin's aggressive scrutiny of his accounts. Something that passed between Franklin, Foxcroft, and Dunlap deeply disturbed the man: or possibly it was the experience of being treated in an officious, rather than familial, manner. In October 1764 he offered the deputy postmasters, as a settlement, a tract in Chester County, Pennsylvania, and a bond from the late William Hunter. These, he maintained, constituted his entire estate. "[N?]othing but a Disire to get from under the Weight of your merciless Oppression" should have induced him to go so far; the arrears, he steadfastly claimed, were due to the neglect of the previous postmaster, William Franklin.

Dunlap felt he had been slandered as a "Rogue, Rascal, &c.," by Franklin's accounting. In reply, Franklin and Foxcroft maintained that it was not in their power to forgive a debt to the crown. When Franklin departed for England shortly thereafter, Parker, as usual, took care of the land deal for him. Dunlap left for Bridgton, Jamaica, where he had an interest in a printing shop. A year and a half later he wrote Franklin in England, seeking financial assistance in the form of aid securing the post of customs officer. Franklin refused. Dunlap completed his unFranklinian descent by taking ordination in the Church of England and a parish in Virginia, a fate in which Franklin saw not a little humor, considering what he perceived as Dunlap's angry, uncharitable personality.[28]

It was far easier to read moral, rather than practical or personal, lessons into the fates of other printers, especially when their failures became increasingly costly to Franklin and Parker themselves. Such was the case with Ben Mecom. Franklin's nephew returned to his hometown of Boston from Antigua in 1757, sold books out of the first floor of his print shop, and took on prestigious projects like a new psalter and the *New England Magazine*, neither of which earned him any money to speak of. He soon married Elizabeth Ross, whom he most likely met in New York or Philadelphia, before his Caribbean sojourn. He hoped to get the Boston postmastership when his uncle John Franklin died, but it went instead to his step-cousin Tuthill Hubbart, a decision of Franklin's that probably rankled all the more because Benny desperately needed the secure income if he was to make it as a printer. Yet he did not nurture a grudge; he was, after all, still in debt to his uncle and still eager to prove himself worthy of his relation. The most striking pattern in his enterprises during these years is his close attention to his uncle's own words. He was the first to realize the commercial potential of Franklin's compendium of Poor Richard's sayings, *Father Abraham's Speech*, and printed it as a pamphlet, as he did *The Interest of Great Britain Considered*. He also put some of Franklin's unpublished writings, like his tombstone epitaph for his parents and his humorous paean to "Plain country Joan" (Deborah Franklin), in his short-lived monthly magazine. His mother Jane sent good reports of Benny's industriousness to Franklin in England; his uncle sent him books and stationery to sell at the standard commission rate. Mecom reported that he was prospering in Boston and had no regrets about leaving Antigua. The next year he printed twenty titles. The young Mecoms named one of their daughters—they would have five—after Aunt Deborah Franklin.[29]

Yet two years later Mecom came to Philadelphia to meet with his uncle, who had returned from England, and discuss the possibility of his moving to New York. Quite possibly there were family reasons, or prospects: Benny's brother John, a goldsmith, had relocated there. His wife was from nearby Elizabeth, New Jersey; her father had been mayor of the town. The Mecoms made the move in 1762. Unfortunately, their timing could not have been worse. Parker and his former workers were maneuvering around one another, and an ambitious, polished, and unscrupulous Londoner named James Rivington was trying to corner the book market. Hard times failed to impress his uncle. By June 1763, Franklin disapprovingly passed on word that William Strahan considered Mecom "shamefully behind" on his payment for books and materials. Franklin promised Strahan he would check in on Mecom personally when he passed through New York on his post office tour. Strapped, Mecom hopefully launched a new newspaper, the *New York Pacquet*. The first issue featured the beginning of a short novel called "The History of Tom Varien, By a Gentleman of St. Kitts," a West Indies tale that revolved around being spoiled by slavery and the wealth that slavery brings. The paper folded after seven issues.[30]

Mecom liked to take risks of the kind his uncle no longer did. What other choice did he have, if he was to raise himself out of the usual cycle of failure and reach a position of economic and cultural significance worthy of the namesake of the great Franklin? This time Parker rescued him, offering the New Haven shop and postmastership. Given its recent history, that New Haven was viewed as promising for Benny spoke volumes. Parker and Franklin agreed to repossess Mecom's press and book inventory and auction it to satisfy Strahan. In June 1764 Mecom announced his plan to renew the *Connecticut Gazette*. The broadside included a Franklinian paean to newspapers and their ability to bring all the colonists together as "British Brothers."

By January 1765, though, Parker was nervous about Mecom. He hadn't heard much from New Haven, had received no post office accounts, and had noticed that Mecom, while printing, had not yet revived the newspaper as planned. Two months later he wrote Franklin that Mecom was getting small job work, just enough to get by, "but I believe he will never do any great Matter."[31]

Benny still thought otherwise, and the controversy over the Stamp Act gave him the chance to prove it. He asked that "Gentlemen of serious Reflection" not judge him too quickly for any failure to be careful or circumspect: he wanted above all to avoid the "dishonorable" taint of merely imitating his uncle, printing's only "GRAND CONDUCTOR" in the colonies. At a time when New Englanders were beginning to compare their oppression under colonial laws to slavery but were also hoping to keep the implications for chattel slavery at bay, he asked, in his first issue: "The reigning Question now is, *whether* Americans *shall be Freemen* or *Slaves*? Every free Man, nay every Slave is concern'd in the Question; for, Who would not rather be a Slave to Liberty, than a Servant to Slavery?" Perhaps he was thinking of the West Indies novel he had serialized; whatever the reason, Mecom could not let the issue or the language of slavery alone.

He pushed the logic further. Reporting on a seasonal festival, possibly Negro Election Day, an annual event celebrated in New England in which Africans elected their own governor for the year, he wrote:

> According to an old Custom, the Negroes of both Sexes meet in this Town every Spring and Fall at a Tavern, here they are allowed to indulge themselves in many innocent Recreations of a free People. Last night they got together to enjoy their established Privileges; and it was observed that their Frolicking was conducted with regularity and Sobriety.—How Contented are the slaves of Freemen? how truly miserable the Slaves of Slaves![32]

What was Benjamin Mecom doing, simultaneously criticizing slavery and affirming a special, happy slavery for African Americans? In one sense, he was being absolutely consistent: American slaveholders were beginning to insist that their properties, including slaveholdings, were the liberties they contended for—a logic Mecom soon affirmed by printing (perhaps also writing) another piece that named "a Property of his own,—his Estate" the true "Birthright of every *British* Subject." Enslavement of any kind was impossible for the true Englishman, if not for Englishmen's slaves. To say so was to be a true patriot. And yet he apparently could not say so without at least gesturing toward the African slaves. By 1765 he had more than once gone out of his way to say that slavery was wrong, or at least had very bad effects on slaveowners. He groped toward a position he and his readers could live with. To avoid "Imitation," to truly signalize himself as a writer and a printer, he needed to at least begin to push the slavery envelope.[33]

In 1764, when Mecom went to New Haven, Franklin, in Philadelphia, became newly vulnerable to attack. As settlers surged westward after the Seven Years' War, Pennsylvania's natives objected to the postwar status quo. The proprietary party sought to make frontier outrage against postwar Indian attacks into a rallying cry against the Pennsylvania Assembly. Franklin led the counterattack against the "white savages" of Pennsylvania. The "barbarous" Paxton Boys and their allies, he argued in an influential pamphlet narrating the massacre of Christian Indians at Conestoga, had acted "to the eternal Disgrace of their Country and Colour." They made much of their whiteness, and the Indians' inherent, racial savagery, but even "the Negroes of Africa" knew that it was wrong to condemn people to death because of their race. Franklin's challenge to racism was real but subtle and even double-edged, given that it affirmed the white identities of his readers, only to say that the Paxtonites hardly deserved to be considered similarly white. Meanwhile, Penn stepped up his campaign to get Franklin removed from his postmastership.[34]

The ensuing Assembly campaign reached a level of invective hardly matched before or since. Franklin helped begin it by reminding readers that the Penns continually sought to reduce their settlers to "the most abject Slavery." Another writer reminded the public that the pro-Penn men had "encouraged the wantonly inlisting and robbing you of your Servants, in the last two Wars," and had then proceeded to "blacken and abuse the former Assemblies" for objecting to the proprietors' tax exemption. Isaac Hunt labeled the Penns and their party descendants of "London fishwives, huckstering street sellers, and daughters of convict servants." William Smith, clergyman and Penn supporter, came in for special scorn as a sexual deviant, "consumate Sycophant," and trans-oceanic author of "*blackening* Lies."[35]

One of the responses hit the Franklins hard. In the mock-epitaph style Franklin himself had perfected, *What is Sauce for the Goose is Also Sauce for the Gander* described Franklin as an "ingrate" who stole "other Men's *discoveries*" and translated them into fame and money. He had risen, politically, by insults and attacks on good government but only faked a populist sensibility. Having taken large sums for his diplomatic expenses, he also faked poverty.

> *His principal Estate*, seeming *to consist*,
> *Till very lately*,
> *In his Hand maid* BARBARA
> *A most valuable* Slave,
> *The* Foster-Mother
> *Of his last Offspring*,
> *Who did his dirty Work,—*
> *And in two* Angelic *Females*,
> *Whom Barbara also served*,
> *As Kitchen Wench and Gold Finder [privy cleaner].*
> *But alas the Loss!*

Providence for wise, tho' secret Ends,
Lately depriv'd him of the Mother
Of EXCELLENCY.
His fortune was not however impair'd,
For he piously witheld from her
MANES [spirit],
The pitiful Stipend of Ten Pounds per Annum,
On which he had cruelly suffered her
to STARVE;
Then Stole her to the Grave, in Silence.

This personal accusation probably did not cost Franklin nearly as many votes as did William Smith's reminder to Pennsylvania Germans that Franklin had once called them "BOORS." In this final damning accusation in the pamphlet, however, what exactly were Franklin's enemies accusing him of? Sleeping with a household slave? Of illegitimately fathering "his Excellency," Governor William Franklin? The ambiguity was, of course, the point: the character of Barbara seems to conflate William Franklin's mother, a woman of known lower status who relied occasionally on Franklin for money, with alleged ill treatment of slaves and/or servants by Franklin.[36]

Such sexualized slander occurred often enough in eighteenth-century Anglo-American politics. The interestedness of the accusers, however, does not prove the falsity of the statements.[37] If the verse hardly proves the existence of "Barbara," much less her race or servitude, it does tell us where Franklin's enemies perceived him vulnerable. His own personal relations might not withstand close scrutiny; he too exploited others. For this reason alone, his use of blackening rhetoric was beginning to haunt him.

Franklin lost his Assembly seat in the election but was nominated to return to England as agent, charged with pressing the Assembly's formal request for royal government. Once there he sought to turn the new taxes on sugar and stamps toward a more equitable system of colonial integration in the empire, such as a crown-supplied paper money system complete with loan offices, clerks, and trustees. He failed but saw it as a collective failure of the American agents, and one to be reversed through economic action, persuasion, and perhaps a happier turn in English domestic politics. He trusted boycotts of enumerated goods like molasses to bring the administration to its senses and generally saw the legislation as a temporary aberration. Things could not be all that bad: after all, head of the Treasury George Grenville had consulted with him and the other American agents to make the act as unobtrusive as possible. Franklin even believed he could circumvent the special threat to printers represented by the Stamp Act by rushing a special load of extra-large paper to his partner, Hall. The law, in fact, showed a special misunderstanding of the situation of American printers, taxing them at a penny per sheet but two shillings per advertisement—each time the ad appeared. Franklin and Strahan themselves showed just as little understanding of how strapped colonists, and especially printers, were for cash, when they advised Hall to use the occasion to rationalize the business by printing only for ready money.[38]

Twenty-twenty hindsight suggests that in cooperating with the ministry Franklin miscalculated badly, leaving himself and his friends open to attack. Because the opposition of the American agents had occurred largely behind the scenes and anonymously in print, when American outrage began to swell over the stamp duty, the pro-Penn party in Pennsylvania accused Franklin of having engineered the Stamp Act as part of his plan to bring in royal government. After all, had not the man who had most energetically defended Franklin against personal attacks in the Assembly, John Hughes, been appointed Philadelphia's stamp collector? Hughes was in fact an old chum, and Franklin made matters worse by urging him to stand "loyal" against "the madness of the Populace or their blind Leaders." Warned that his house (and Franklin's) would be pulled down, he "determined to stand a siege." His resolve, understandably, broke under extreme duress and what seemed like a conspiracy. Forced to resign, Hughes lost his Assembly seat—Franklin's allies cut their losses—and found himself despised even by his own brother. He was among the first, but not the last, of Franklin's friends to gamble on the empire and lose.[39]

Meanwhile, in New Haven much of Benjamin Mecom's energy went to safeguarding his uncle's reputation, as it was not at all clear whether Benjamin Franklin opposed the stamp tax. In the pages of his *Gazette* Mecom tried to dispatch that problem as a fiction invented by the proprietary party in Pennsylvania, with apparently mixed results, because Franklin had recommended Connecticut's agent, the ubiquitous Jared Ingersoll, to the post of stamp collector. Ingersoll had resigned only in the face of violence; he had justified his actions, and received more abuse for it, than almost any other collector. Other newspapers, reported Mecom, were calling Ingersoll "a Dictator, a Negro Soul, a voracious mad Creature." Mecom argued, however, that the man deserved sympathy. He followed his uncle's cues for the rest of the controversy. Loyal to Franklin in a moment of crisis, he was not making friends: in April 1766 the New Haven grand jury indicted him for "willingly and obstinately" refusing to attend worship "at any congregation," a surprising development considering that a few years earlier his aunt Deborah had written of her nephew's pious doubts about a freethinking minister.[40]

David Hall, still Franklin's partner even though Parker was engaged in the laborious process of settling their accounts, also found himself in a difficult position. Despite his publication of a black-bordered issue mourning the Stamp Act, out of loyalty to Franklin he refused to say he would not publish with the stamps. He also failed to print the harsher invectives against the Act, including any of the proliferating attacks on Franklin that blamed him for the law. He knew these to be untrue, but the decision nevertheless caused him to lose at least five hundred subscribers. In the end he followed the majority and joined the boycott actively: a sensible decision, given that his partnership with Franklin was due to expire. He probably also suspected what James Parker reported the next year: rather than Hall needing to pay off Franklin for his share of the materials to end the partnership, Franklin owed Hall a good deal of money, not least because Hall, along with paying Franklin upward of £600 every year, had supplied Deborah Franklin, for whom he took a special responsibility as a cousin by marriage, with cash upon request at a time when the female Franklins built a new house and entertained many friends and relatives. Despite his successes, Hall remained financially vulnerable.[41] And despite joining the boycott and severing his business relations with Franklin, he also remained loyal. Along with Strahan, he continued to form a crucial link in Franklin's transatlantic publicity chain, printing praise of Franklin's accomplishments and seeing to the wide distribution of his influential testimony before Parliament on the repeal of the Stamp Act.

Unfortunately for Hall, though, his declaration of partial independence from Franklin angered two of his important patrons, New Jersey governor William Franklin and Pennsylvania Assembly speaker Joseph Galloway. During the 1766 election season, Hall decided to print accusations that Galloway had justified the Stamp Act, along with Galloway's rebuttal. William Franklin, smarting from attacks on his careful smothering of resistance to the tax in New Jersey and on his continued involvement in Pennsylvania politics, chose to blame Hall as the source for the assault. "He has no friendship for you," wrote William to his father, describing Hall as "a snake in the grass." Without consulting Benjamin, William Franklin and Galloway engaged William Goddard to start a new antiproprietary paper, the *Pennsylvania Chronicle*, in direct competition with Hall's *Pennsylvania Gazette*. They appropriated Franklin's old house and Mecom's old press, putting the elder statesman in a tricky situation, as Franklin was contractually forbidden to be engaged in any other printing establishment in Philadelphia while still concerned with Hall, as he was officially until January 21, 1766 (and longer as he did not settle his debts to Hall, preferring to contest Parker's computation of them).[42]

Hall was deeply hurt by the Franklins' actions. Ironically, at the very moment Hall chose to make a stand for a truly free press of the sort Franklin had always supported, Franklin's family and friends seemed out to destroy him, even as they owed him almost £1,000. He chose to vent to his old friend William Strahan: "to be Served so, by a Branch of that House, to which, I have been so faithful a Slave, for so many Years past, vexes me not a little." He was further dismayed when Franklin, in reply to his protests, averred that he could not stop a paper from being published for the common good—which Hall understandably took to imply that his own was not—and argued strongly against Hall's view that the spirit of their agreement implied that Franklin should never set up as a rival to him in Philadelphia. Meanwhile, Debbie Franklin continued to receive more money from Hall than even Franklin's share of the printing house's income would have represented. Hall never, in fact, got any settlement out of Franklin. Fortunately, the business he helped build remained solid enough to support his sons after his death in 1772.[43]

John Holt had better luck—in part because of his unhesitating support for the resistance in New York, but also because of his utter lack of conscience when it came to his debts and his workers. Together these two facts set in motion a series of events that led both to his triumph and to James Parker's greatest trials.

The Sons of Liberty in New York, dedicated to resisting the Stamp Act, faced stiff and daunting official disapproval and eventually realized that they needed a printer they could depend on. Holt had little to lose.

His press, after all, belonged to Parker, and any property he had was under threat of legal judgment anyway. And for a change, taking a strong political stand, it seemed, could actually boost sales. (When there was actually danger from the authorities, as in printing a "Constitutional Courant" filled with essays no one else would touch, Holt encouraged Parker's apprentice William Goddard to sneak off to Woodbridge and borrow Parker's press without his knowledge, a move that almost got Parker arrested.) When jail loomed for Holt because of a £440 debt to a merchant (for books), the Sons of Liberty put up the money. Soon they helped him buy the printing press of the late Joseph Royle, a Virginia relative of his wife. Thus subsidized, Holt engaged in a remarkable series of maneuvers to keep from paying James Parker or the postmasters any significant sum.[44]

Parker was used to Holt's skill at "parrying a Dun" and his disinclination to manual labor, which he occasionally attributed to Holt's drinking problem, but he did not expect Holt to use Parker's own cautious libertarianism, much less his loyalty to Franklin, against him. When Parker asked Holt to publish a piece urging only careful, legal resistance to the Stamp Act, Holt attributed it to Joseph Galloway and mocked the piece as too timid in a preface. Holt then began a regular practice of suggesting that the reason Parker, and Franklin, pursued him for debts was that they actually favored the stamps.

Parker was stuck. If he exposed Holt as a liar or successfully turned him out, he would not recover any of the £1,500 Holt now owed him. After the end of their four-year rental agreement and another round of threats and promises, Parker took back the *Gazette*, but Holt promptly started his own newspaper, the *New-York Journal*, put the cash he might have paid to Parker into a new press of his own, and kept most of the subscribers. Parker took out warrants for Holt's arrest on the debt charges, but Holt claimed illness and literally stayed indoors for months at a time to evade the sheriff, apparently leaving the actual work of the press, as usual, to his servants and apprentices.

If one overlooked a few inconveniences, John Holt had arrived as the writer-politician, gentleman printer, and solvent patriot. He was living Benjamin Mecom's fantasy: or was it Franklin's life? In recognition of his success and his identification with the patriot cause, he began new projects like an essay series and an almanac under the name of "Frank Freeman."[45]

By contrast, Parker's semiretirement had turned into something else entirely. The Stamp Act, that "fatal Black Act" as he called it, dashed his hopes of being able to get by on New Jersey jobs and the postmastership at Woodbridge. He had rather unwillingly returned to New York for the sake of the postmasters Foxcroft and Franklin. To make it more worth his while, they got him another sinecure, a position as an inspector in the customs service. This turned out to be a mixed blessing: for a small salary that it took years (and Franklin's help) to actually collect, he had to walk the docks two to four miles a day on his gouty legs and face not only the brazen fraud of smugglers but also its newly fashionable patriotic veneer, in the form of outright mockery of imperial officials. Worse, being a royal customs officer gave verisimilitude to the rumors about his politics.[46]

What Parker did not know made things worse. He trusted Jared Ingersoll, who was also handling the postmasters' suit against Holt, with his own, not realizing that Ingersoll and Holt were quite friendly and that the New Haven lawyer was actually representing Holt in other matters. Holt apparently managed to overcome his outrage against stamp men where it came to Ingersoll. He paid his lawyer's bills on time.[47]

Parker vented, regularly, almost ritually, in his reports to Franklin, then in England. When Parker scored a scoop with a new essay series against the Townshend Acts in 1768, Holt not only reprinted them—a standard practice—but made it appear as if they had originated in his paper. Holt was "always a Creeper into other Man's Labours particularly mine." How had this "Master in Chicanry," whom Parker compared to Tom Bell, the most famous colonial confidence man, succeeded in making him out as the villain, "fighting me with my own weapons"?[48] Could anyone stomach such "base undeserved Ingratitude and Injustice"? How could Holt turn patriot, while making the man who had taught him the trade be liable for debts to the king and their mutual patron, Franklin? A man of estate, Parker nevertheless found that "both my self and People go in Rags," in part because he had to keep sending available cash receipts to Franklin on behalf of the postal system.

James Parker's resentments, his faith in God, and his debts kept him fighting on. He got little help from a rather preoccupied Franklin, who advised him to "possess a placid Temper" and promised only that all would be resolved when they met again. He took some pleasure in small victories, like getting Benny Mecom out of New Haven. Benny failed to pay his rent to Parker and only contributed his part of the post rider's salary, remitting nothing else out of whatever he collected as postmaster. Parker had hoped for better and kept pressing for the postal accounts. Blaming Mecom's "lethargic Indolence" for the lack of communication between them, Parker threatened lawsuits or repossession of Mecom's press, but without much success. Their letters assumed a nasty tone as they took out a decade's worth of frustrations on each other. Clearly the New Haven postmastership did not bring in much to Mecom, for in early 1767, tired of Parker's nagging letters, he simply resigned. In perhaps the worst insult he could think of, Parker complained to Franklin that "Mecom's soul and Holt's seem to have a good deal of resemblance."[49]

Benny kept up the *Connecticut Gazette* for another year. In November he paused to ask those who had not agreed to pay in kind to please pay their debts in cash: he wanted to keep his family in New Haven. It was not to be. Soon Parker demanded the use of the press, which he gave back to Thomas Green—the printer who had once sent all the post office money to Holt. He advised Mecom to go back to the West Indies, "but [Benny] was highly affronted even at the proposal." Parker wrote Franklin what he then told Mecom: "I now think he has not a Capacity for a Master"—words Mecom surely did not want to hear from his former master, from whom he had once tried to run away. At the age of thirty-five, Benny had no desire to become anyone else's hand. In the last issue of the *Gazette* Mecom begged in as genteel a fashion as possible for some of the citizens of Connecticut who owed him money to give him enough so that he could move out of town with dignity.[50]

He went to Philadelphia, where he hoped—delusionally, according to some—that his uncle would become his patron. The men in the family—Benjamin and William Franklin—said his troubles were his own fault for having too many children, and declined to set him up. Briefly, Mecom worked as a pressman for William Goddard's *Chronicle*, the pro-Franklin paper William Franklin and Joseph Galloway had bankrolled. But he soon argued with Goddard, who offered him 35 shillings a week but reported that Benny "insisted on coming and going just as he pleas'd." Perhaps Mecom wondered why Goddard, not he, had been given a subsidized shop identified with the Franklins. Besides, according to Benny, Goddard did not pay wages on time.

Sadly, even this turn of events became a war of words and reputation: the male Franklins, father and son, took Goddard and Parker's side, while Deborah stood up for the struggling Mecom family. Benny tried to publish a paper on his own but did not get many subscribers amid the highly politicized competition already existing among Philadelphia printers. As his fantasies of gaining real help from his uncle the royal postmaster and colony agent dwindled, he submitted a beautifully printed application for a liquor license to the city authorities in 1770. It was denied.[51]

That same year James Parker suffered a fatal stroke. David Hall died two years later. John Holt survived them all. By 1778 he and Goddard were so confident of their place that they connived to expose Franklin as a double agent. Eventually, though, Holt decided there was room enough in America for him and the man who had given him his second chance after he ran away from Virginia. When he died in 1784, he was eulogized as "a gentleman of unblemished character" and buried at St. Paul's Church, under a large slab cut with letters designed to look like newspaper type. He was remembered as the great patriot printer of the Revolution in New York.[52]

By the summer of 1776, Benjamin Mecom was a confirmed lunatic incarcerated in Middlesex County, New Jersey. Franklin paid for his support. In the confusion of the Battle of Trenton, he disappeared.[53] It is easy, far too easy, to say that he had always been crazy. It is better, more honest, and a good deal more revealing to call him a casualty of several battles for independence, including his own.

PART THREE

Politics: Slavery, Identity, and Revolution

† abolishing our most valuable Laws

for taking away our charters & altering fundamentally the forms of our governments

for suspending our own legislatures & declaring themselves invested with power to legislate for us in all cases whatsoever:

he has abdicated government here, [by declaring us out of his protection & waging war against us. withdrawing his governors, & declaring us out of his allegiance & protection:]

he has plundered our seas, ravaged our coasts, burnt our towns & destroyed the lives of our people:

he is at this time transporting large armies of foreign mercenaries to compleat the works of death, desolation & tyranny, already begun with circumstances of cruelty & perfidy unworthy the head of a civilized nation:

he has endeavored to bring on the inhabitants of our frontiers the merciless Indian savages, whose known rule of warfare is an undistinguished destruction of all ages, sexes, & conditions [of existence:]

[he has incited treasonable insurrections of our fellow-citizens, with the allurements of forfeiture & confiscation of our property:

he has waged cruel war against human nature itself, violating it's most sacred rights of life & liberty in the persons of a distant people who never offended him, captivating & carrying them into slavery in another hemisphere, or to incur miserable death in their transportation thither. this piratical warfare, the opprobrium of infidel powers, is the warfare of the Christian king of Great Britain. determined to keep open a market where MEN should be bought & sold, he has prostituted his negative for suppressing every legislative attempt to prohibit or to restrain this execrable commerce: and that this assemblage of horrors might want no fact of distinguished die, he is now exciting those very people to rise in arms among us, and to purchase that liberty of which he has deprived them, by murdering the people upon whom he also obtruded them: thus paying off former crimes committed against the liberties of one people, with crimes which he urges them to commit against the lives of another.]

in every stage of these oppressions we have petitioned for redress in the most humble terms; our repeated petitions have been answered only by repeated injuries. a prince whose character is thus marked by every act which may define a tyrant, is unfit to be the ruler of a free people who mean to be free. future ages will scarce believe that the hardiness of one man, adventured within the short compass of twelve years only to lay a foundation so broad & undisguised for tyranny over a people fostered & fixed in principles

Draft of the Declaration of Independence, with Franklin's edits marked by Thomas Jefferson. (Library of Congress)

SEVEN

America the Enslaved

Word had reached America of the Revenue (or Sugar) Act and future taxes by the time Franklin returned to Philadelphia in 1764. That autumn he revived and updated Poor Richard Saunders. Richard's annual paeans to "industry and frugality" became recipes for making, among other domestic staples, beet sugar to replace the enumerated French and Dutch West Indian molasses. After the recipes came a homily contrasting God's gifts to the Caribbean and those to the "Northern Colonies." West Indians had "the Sugar Cane, from which, by the *forced Labour* of Slaves, Sugar and Melasses are extracted, for their Masters Profit. This is denied to us of the Northern Colonies: But then we have an Infinity of Flowers, from which, by the *voluntary Labour* of Bees, Honey is extracted, for our Advantage." Well-kept hives might even render "Great Profits" as well as economic independence.[1]

As a young man in London, Franklin had been introduced to Bernard Mandeville, the famous author of *The Fable of the Bees*, who had described disturbing but undeniable links between private vices like luxury consumption and public benefits like full employment. Franklin's updated fable of the bees depicted North America's relative poverty as a virtue and those colonies as places where hard labor and the unforced servitude of the animal world combined with the supervisory intelligence of men to produce the good things of the earth. Explicitly he suggested that the slaves' "forced labour" in the West Indies tainted the British planters' pro-tax position. Implicitly, he maintained that there were not significant numbers of slaves in the northern mainland.

Yet even this denial was not sufficient for Franklin's purposes. He concluded by making it clear that consideration of labor and morality in this political controversy should not extend too far. Whether because of their natures or because of "the nature of slavery," Africans were still the opposite of free Americans, who could if need be support themselves without slaves or the molasses their forced labor produced. If the Americans themselves could only "see and know, the extreme Slovenliness of the West-Indian Slaves in making Melasses, and the Filth and Nastiness suffered to enter it, or wantonly thrown into it, their Stomachs would turn." Neither the labors, the injuries, nor the identities of African slaves should be confused with those of "the People of the Northern Colonies."

The other most widely read protests did not allow themselves the luxury of assuming that Americans could boycott their way out of their economic and political ties to the West Indies, much less out of slavery. Boston merchants politely pointed out that the tax-induced hike in the price of molasses would affect the entire Atlantic trade, including the African voyages that supplied slaves to the Caribbean and mainland alike.[2] Stephen Hopkins, the governor of Rhode Island and a resident of Newport, a hub of the slave trade, described a "circuitry of commerce" that depended on northerners distilling French and Dutch Caribbean molasses. The Sugar Act, he argued, would ultimately destroy the triangular trade.

Still, Hopkins, like Franklin, could not resist using the slavery issue against the Caribbeans. What could possibly have led the British West Indian planters to expect support for duties that benefited only themselves? It could only be "that as these people are used to an arbitrary and cruel government over slaves, and have so long tasted the *sweets* of oppressing their fellow creatures, they can hardly forebear esteeming two millions of free and loyal British subjects, inhabitants of the northern colonies, in the same light."[3]

James Otis, the American resistance movement's first ideologue, went further. Unlike the Caribbean colonies, the northern colonies were not a "compound mongrel mixture of *English, Indian,* and *Negro,*" but rather were populated by "freeborn *British white* subjects, whose loyalty has never yet been suspected." For Otis, who would drive himself and others crazy with his tendency to push arguments to their logical extremes, it was not enough to make Boston sound racially more British than Barbados. Instead he grounded his objection to taxation without representation in "natural rights." Doing so led him almost immediately—within pages—into a classic attack on racial slavery. Black slavery explained the planters' advocacy of the Sugar Act and their neglect of natural, and historically British, liberty: "Is it to be wondered at if when people of the stamp of a creolean planter get into power they will not stick for a little present gain at making their own posterity, white as well as black, worse slaves if possible than those already mentioned?" Otis echoed Hopkins and Franklin in his treatment of hypocritical slavedrivers. He differed in that he brought out the latent antislavery, and antiracist, implications of his assault.[4]

According to conventional understandings of cause and effect in American history, this approach should not have been possible in 1764. It is usually said that the issue of slavery entered the political realm only after the contest between the colonies and the mother country was under way. Once colonists began complaining of their prospective political enslavement by parliamentary legislation, the argument goes, it did not take much imagination to see the relevance of such arguments to African slavery. A "contagion of liberty" ensued; rising antislavery thus derived most substantially from the political arguments for American rights.[5]

The idea that the American Revolution deserves credit for antislavery is reassuring. It keeps the Revolution wholly—or at least in the end—on the side of the angels. Unfortunately, facts intervene, for slavery came to the fore as an issue in 1764, at the very origins of the controversy: in short, slavery was present at the creation. The first of Parliament's newly enforced taxes singled out sugar, the great slave-driven engine of colonial profits. This occurred in part because British West Indian planters had more power in the halls of Parliament than did the North American mainlanders—again, because of slavery. The Revenue Act not only highlighted the economic links between the colonies with the fewest slaves and those with the most; it took the side, as it were, of the most profitable Anglo-American economies: the ones with the most slaves.

The responses of Franklin, Hopkins, and Otis opened up the possibility of fusing colonial protest and antislavery: not so much because of an affinity among arguments against tyrannical power as because of the line-ups on each side of the debate. And while the sides changed somewhat—the British West Indians and North Americans found more common ground after 1765—the issues of slavery and colonial rights could not be easily uncoupled. The debate over imperial arrangements, of which slavery was a central part, led to a controversy over authority, property, and power, in which the issue of African slavery could never be wholly subordinated because slavery was central to colonial authority, colonial property, and colonial power.[6]

Why else would Hopkins and Otis, much less the ever-cautious Franklin, leap so quickly down this rhetorical road? New England had hardly divested itself of slavery or slave-produced profits. Hopkins, who feared a complete collapse of Rhode Island's economy, was willing to risk criticism of slavery only because slavery could be more directly identified with the Caribbeans. Indeed, that identification, rather than antislavery, was the point. Like Franklin and other northern writers, he leaned heavily on the worsening image of West Indian "nabobs," who in an era when sugar became Britain's most valuable import played an increasingly conspicuous role in the life of London and its far-flung empire. They were an easier target than Parliament itself.[7]

For these writers, it was more than a flight of eloquence to compare the loss of economic and political control to real—that is, racial—slavery. Such a loss *was slavery*. Property, as well as power, made the comparison obvious, not far-fetched. As Hopkins would put it, "those who are governed at the will of another, and whose property may be taken from them by taxes, or otherwise, without their own consent, and against their will, are in the miserable condition of slaves." In a world of slavery, debt, patronage, and contingent liberties, it was not only that discussing liberty raised the issue of slavery; discussing slavery played a role in the struggle over liberties.[8]

Americans and Britons would debate the political implications of this linkage for the next twelve years. Their varying responses, and the very length of the controversy, reflected the varieties of freedom and unfreedom in their world and the complexities of politics in an age of empires that were themselves made up of composite states. What was the relationship of the colonies and colonists to the English? What was the relationship of the colonial slaves to the English? Did the eighteenth-century union of England, Ireland, and Scotland into a "British" nation set a precedent—or did it create a contrast between commonwealthmen and mere colonials? Did it matter that increasing numbers of convicts had been sentenced to transportation to the colonies, implying that North America was an inferior place, one appropriate for Britons who had fewer rights?

If the answer to any of these questions was affirmative, it raised the stakes tremendously. If colonists were by their nature lesser subjects, were African slaves, then, colonists? If colonists had some "British" rights, did slaves? If slaves' rights were limited or nonexistent because of their slave status, were not colonists' rights similarly limited?

In the wake of the Atlantic wars that had "propelled the colonies to the center of the empire," three ways of thinking about American colonists remained available. One, the most traditional, viewed Americans as fellow nationals, as Britons enjoying a common identity with other Britons in a larger empire. Franklin had relied on this view for more than two decades. The second cast the Americans as foreigners who were, nevertheless, part of the empire: subjects of the king and possibly of Parliament, but with the limited rights of a defeated or subject people. The third option—where much of the debate would occur—placed the Americans beyond the English nation but still part of the expanded British political community, a people whose rights and duties had to be as carefully calibrated as those of any British outlanders (like the Irish and the Scots). That the latter two options were possible, even increasingly popular, as the English gained a sense of the diversity of their empire suggests why Franklin, and later Otis and Hopkins, so early and insistently put forth a view of Americans as Britons and Britons as the opposite of slaves.[9]

The temporary clarity that some northern Americans thought they saw in 1764, when the West Indian grandees wielded their political muscle as outrageously as they displayed their fine carriages on the streets of London, dissipated within months. When Britons in the Caribbean and in Parliament joined them in opposition to the Stamp Act, a different clarity began to emerge. Viewed from London, it appeared as if colonial slave-drivers with special slave-driving perquisites were asking for special dispensations. Because the colonial protests concerned property as well as power, because the rights under discussion were first and foremost (if not solely) rights to property, the questions of imperial union and colonial slavery could not easily be kept distinct. Increasingly, however, the colonial wish was to do precisely that. After 1764 the linkage of the colonial issue and the slavery issue caused more trouble than triumph for those, like Franklin, who championed Americans' British rights. To keep these issues distinct, Whig leaders had to keep the potential rights of Africans off the table.

Just as there were three ways of thinking of colonists—as British, as foreign, and as provincial—there were three notions of African American identity useful for separating oppressed colonists from their oppressed colonial slaves. They all fit most logically with the Franklinian understanding that the Americans were free and equal Britons. They had different uses, though, in different arguments, and all remained present in the debate that culminated in American independence. Indeed, all three were necessary to the American Revolution and the continuation of slavery.

One view of the Africans embraced race and racial justifications for African slavery. Franklin had experimented with these before. But during the 1760s and 1770s the enlightened company he kept made racialism, at least taken alone, less than effective as a defense of mainland interests. Moreover, race was not the absolute or biological category it became later in the nineteenth century. Race, in other words, was necessary but not sufficient to keep the question of slaves' rights from interfering with colonial protest.

Another was a sense of British national identity and citizenship strong and restrictive enough to exclude Africans from membership. British citizenship—if Americans held it and Africans did not—had tremendous implications for the laws that kept slaves in their places. Slavery might be unjustifiable in light of national and natural rights, but to free slaves would infringe on the property rights of Britons—and thus effectually enslave the slaveholders. Placing Africans outside the pale of British nationality would make slavery a problem, but one best dealt with by the Americans themselves; to interfere would be to oppress fellow nationals. Inconsistencies and evident self-interestedness, however, marred such arguments, leading Americans, Franklin among them, to resort more and more often to racial differences and sometimes to racial inferiority.

The third, and perhaps most lasting, idea seemed easier to swallow some years after the Sugar Act debate, when intricate and extensive discussion had invigorated ideas of British and natural rights. It held that slaves, or their labor, were unimportant in mainland America or were not even present at all. This argument was weakest as it flew in the face of the well-known facts. On the other hand, it avoided the limitations of racial and nationalist arguments. It avoided, also, the problem with natural rights: the threat that once they were embraced by Americans, they could be applied to enslaved Africans. For this reason, the underrating of North American slavery proved to be a crucial idea in the making of the American Revolution. It reassured Americans like Franklin who wished to imagine, or create, America as free.

As a polemicist, politician, diplomat, and international symbol of America, Benjamin Franklin occupied the storm center of debate. He handled the confluence of American identity, colonial resistance, and slavery with all the considerable subtlety and care he could muster. He had heard all the important arguments against slavery decades before, so his revealing silences and careful interventions reflected much more than the personal enlightenment he began to confess, at times quite strategically, to antislavery friends and activists. Anything he said meant much more than the private or theoretical musings of a well-informed American. (Even his surviving "private" thoughts on the subject were written to people conducting public antislavery campaigns often critical of the colonists.)[10] Antislavery had less and less to do with conscience and more and more to do with politics.

After 1764 the relationship between slavery and the politics of the American Revolution crystallized in the remarkable public dialogues that Franklin conducted with British politicians and pundits like David Hume, former Prime Minister William Pitt, Chief Justice Lord Mansfield, Colonial Secretary Lord Hillsborough, Undersecretary William Knox, and Samuel Johnson. Many of these key interlocutors were Irish and Scottish born and were themselves fascinated with the problem of provincial identity. These men, Franklin's mirror images as ambitious culture brokers and political actors in the empire, provide the context for understanding Franklin's increasing, but carefully directed, antislavery statements. Again and again they felt compelled to raise the question of slavery as a way of cutting to the heart of the matter of British rights and American identity. They forced Franklin to be creative—and often downright crafty—in making the case for North American innocence.

Ultimately Franklin projected the blame for slavery onto England and the West Indies. He traded rhetorical maneuvers with the rising antislavery movement and with the antislavery opponents of colonial protest, incorporating their ideas and language just enough to blunt their criticisms of the North American mainland. These carefully calibrated maneuvers should not be confused with what came later. His own dream of independence untainted by coercion, displayed so memorably in the memoir he wrote in 1771, began in large measure as a defense of American identity at a time when it was under attack. By 1776 that defense, including its elements of fantasy, had jelled into an enduring, mythic portrait of America without its slaves.

That mythic portrait merged with Franklin's sense of himself and his public identity. As colonial agent and the first internationally acclaimed American scientist, he knew that his own value in England could hardly rise above that of the colonies he represented. He also knew that on the larger European stage, he himself was evidence in the controversy over the new world.

David Hume, the Scottish philosopher who suffered his own sense of being underrated as a provincial, wrote in 1762 to lament Franklin's impending return to Philadelphia: "America has sent us many good things, Gold, Silver, Tobacco, Indigo, &c. But you are the first Philosopher, and indeed the first Great Man of Letters for whom we are beholden to her: it is our own Fault, that we have not kept him: Whence it appears, that we do not agree with Solomon, that Wisdom is above Gold." According to mercantilist theory, colonies were all about providing "good things." In this letter, Hume went out of his way to devalue those usual colonial things by stressing particularly those goods that—controversially—had required the extinction of natives or the importation of slaves to work the land.

Franklin, representing wisdom, was a different story. His ascent to the seat of empire portended a different America, even a different colonial relationship, one that could include such philosophical repartee precisely because it included philosophically astute people. It would not have been lost upon Franklin that Hume himself, in his few earlier writings on these matters, had argued that slavery spoiled the republics of the ancient world. At the same time Hume, like Franklin, had argued that Africans could be considered inferior because Africa had not produced poets or scientists. Franklin had earned a great compliment indeed. His very existence made America more than a colony, more than an inferior. As a new world man of letters, he was the opposite of an American slave.[11]

In response, Franklin depicted himself not only as a person worthy of the attention but also as a Briton of a different, nonmercantilist kind. Hume's "Compliment of *Gold* and Wisdom" was unnecessarily "injurious to your Country." "DEMAND," not a zero-sum game of supply, determined value. With more geniuses (like Hume) in England, Franklin should naturally return to the better market in America![12] In this dialogue Franklin accepted American intellectual inferiority, yet the way he did it proved his ability to participate equally in the conversation.

He also made the case for the market as a fair arbiter of metropolitan-colonial relations—for free trade over traditional colonial service to the metropolitan economy. Since the late 1740s Franklin had publicized a view of colonial economy in which land-rich, labor-poor North Americans would never compete with British manufacturers in any sustained or injuring way. At the time of the Iron Act of 1750, he presented a deregulated America as a place of opportunity, of farmers whose productivity would help themselves and the British empire at once. Britons east and west could have their unrestricted trade and their mercantilism, too.[13]

During the 1760s Franklin subtly altered his understanding of political economy: no longer did he stress labor as a source of wealth. A decade after his argument in "Observations on the Increase of Mankind," after the accession of even more Caribbean territory to Britain, it was even harder to credit profit to labor while depicting the cheapest form of labor—slaves—as unprofitable. Instead he began to describe land itself, and secondarily trade in agricultural products, as the true mainsprings of wealth and civilization. This change in perspective had distinct political uses amid rising controversies over the taxation of colonial produce. To tax the colonies was to siphon off, and thus discourage, the most productive and virtuous of economic activities. The colonies were not rival traders, budding manufacturers, or slave-driving planters. They were simple farmers and local tradesmen whose fields fed the empire.[14]

This crucial shift in economic reasoning helped the colonial agent compensate for the difficulties he faced with his American constituents when he did not directly throw down the gauntlet at the introduction of the Sugar and Stamp Acts. His desire to be an equal Briton as well as his inability to predict the extent of American protests, which certainly surprised everyone else in London, helps to account for his relative patience with postwar changes in policy. So do his more direct, personal interests. He and William Franklin had pressing land grant proposals before the administration, and in light of William's success at getting a governorship, some had begun to speak of Benjamin Franklin as a candidate for a far greater, more lucrative office.[15]

In the process the inventor of the lightning rod became a lightning rod of sorts for imperial relations. At a time when some colonists were effectively, and illegally, taking matters into their own hands—through riots and boycotts—Franklin insisted that the cause of the difficulties and the hope for their resolution rested with Parliament. If the stick was economic self-reliance, the carrot remained an appeal to British community, enlightened political traditions, and imperial wealth. Why not more fully integrate the colonies into the empire through, for example, a uniform currency and banking system? A cartoon he drew and distributed at this time, entitled "Magna Britannia her Colonies Reduced," embodied the argument about mutual interests. As depicted on these "political cards," which he handed out to friends and acquaintances (he also employed a man to give one to each member of Parliament while they debated repeal of the Stamp Act), the colonies, the limbs of the empire, have been severed from the body, leaving Britannia defenseless and unable to work. Brooms on the masts in the background signify that the ships, the circulatory system of the body politic, are also out of commission. The right, laboring hand of the British Empire—Pennsylvania—holds a laurel branch.[16]

The image is a study in the paradoxes of colonial power and Franklin's own embodiment of these paradoxes. The colony-limbs did the work: but then who had lopped them off? Could Pennsylvania, or Franklin as its representative, really offer an olive branch if it was a subordinate part of the empire rather than a separate country? As in so many cases, colonial remonstrances raised as many questions as they resolved. As the stakes rose, the war of words and images accelerated in 1765–66, and the rhetoric reflected the sense that the entire colonial relationship was at stake. Weeks before his famous Examination before the House of Commons on the Stamp Act and the printing of the cards, Franklin responded to a newspaper piece that lambasted wealthy colonists as "selfish," "mean," and "void of public spirit." If taken seriously, wrote Franklin, such words would "incite the mother country to sheath the sword in the bosom of her children."[17]

Franklin went to war with his pen, relying on the press as vigorously and imaginatively as ever. Again and again he objected to the charge that Americans lacked "gratitude" (even as he wrote allies at home that it would not hurt matters to show some). Were Americans supposed to be grateful for the dumping of convicts, for being identified with these in-voluntary immigrants as "housebreakers and felons"? It was only a small step from there to the extreme of alienation—the colonists as Britons' slaves: "But every master of slaves ought to know, that though all the slave possesses is the property of the master, his *good-will* is his own, he bestows it where he pleases; and it is of some *importance* to the master's *profit*, if he can obtain that *good-will* at the cheap rate of a few kind words, with fair and gentle usage." Yet Franklin stepped back from the undeniable fact that the colonies were, in more than one very real sense, children and servants of the metropolis, and that many English saw Americans primarily in that way. Writing in the guise of an Englishman, Franklin insisted that the Americans "are not, never were, nor ever will be our slaves." The colonists who settled New England were "English gentlemen of fortune" who remained loyal to the king.[18]

The Americans' allies in Parliament during the Stamp Act repeal de-bate eloquently objected to the pro-tax lobby's tendency to talk of colo-nial subjection. As the "great Commoner" William Pitt put it, "When were they made slaves?" They were brothers, wives, sons—anything but slaves. They might be made slaves—if they accepted the taxes. Indeed, Pitt went so far as to spy a danger to all Britons: "Three millions of peo-ple, so dead to all the feelings of liberty, as to voluntarily submit to be slaves, would have been fit instruments to make slaves of the rest." This type of rhetoric ranged far afield from Africans or from chattel slavery. But there were always more cards to be played once the word *slavery* had been uttered.

In 1765 and 1766 defenders of the pro-tax Grenville ministry chal-lenged the rhetoric of political enslavement with the reality of colonial slavery: a rhetorical move for which Franklin did not always, or even of-ten, have a convincing reply. In one exchange, a newspaper essayist pre-dicted that the colonists would bend and accept the taxes because they could not possibly do without the products of the empire, sugar in-cluded. Franklin, in the voice of "Homespun," replied that Indian corn, along with other American grain staples, made suitable and varied breakfast foods. The same writer seized upon this remark to charge that Indian corn was especially objectionable: everyone knew it was primar-ily food for slaves. Franklin's reply defended American hoecake but begged the question about colonial difference. Slaves ate Indian corn, he wrote, precisely because of its wholesomeness: "Our slaves, Sir, cost us money, and we buy them to make money by their labour. If they are sick, they are not only unprofitable, but expensive."[19]

To twenty-first-century eyes, this is a bizarre colonial, slaveholding perspective: self-sufficient colonists who boasted about the independence that came from being able to feed their slaves all by themselves; independence that was born of dependence, freedom arising from the unfreedom of others. These disturbing themes in Franklin's outraged anonymous letters to the press—particularly these less-well-known ones—force us, as sure as we are that Franklin and the colonial protesters were as *right* in 1766 as they would be ten years later, to take more seriously the arguments coming from the other side. For despite Franklin's protests, the logic of slavery and the logic of colonialism did have something important in common: they both presumed inequality, that one group operated for the benefit, and to a very real extent constituted the property, of the other. If the Americans were going to compare colonial subjection to the state of slavery in order to make clear the constitutional and future policy implications of taxes, how were they to escape the antislavery implications of their arguments?

Perhaps the easiest way out was to justify both slavery *and* American colonial subjection, to keep the status quo. More people on both sides of the Atlantic accepted that option than later generations have wanted to believe. But there were other solutions. Why not simultaneously reform both colonial relations and that subset of colonial relations known as African slavery?[20] Franklin's was not the only way out of the tangle of chattel slavery, colonial identity, and policy. He developed his strategies in dialogue with British alternatives.

In the middle of these dialogues stood a man who might be called Benjamin (and William) Franklin's imperial alter ego: an ambitious, steadfast, somewhat self-made, and very smart servant of empire named William Knox. He was born in Ireland in 1732 of Scottish parentage. His father converted from Presbyterianism to the Church of England and in doing so helped pave the way for William to secure a patronage appointment as provost marshal in the relatively new colony of Georgia. Much of that job consisted of holding runaway slaves in jail until their masters claimed them and auctioning off the ones who went unclaimed, deducting expenses to support his office.

Knox learned the ways of the province quickly. Realizing the accumulative possibilities of its bounty system, whereby those who owned or sponsored laborers (free or slave) could claim grants of new land, he bought fourteen slaves with money borrowed from home. By the age of thirty he was a substantial plantation-owner, with more than three thousand acres to his name, and was chosen a member of the Governor's Council—his first royal appointment.[21]

Like many a province-born planter in these years, Knox found through plantation profits a way to the center of the empire. He angled for and received an appointment as Georgia's agent in London, leaving his substantial estate (in which he would continue to invest until it included 122 slaves) to the care of efficient overseers. He soon proved as adept at gaining the confidence of authorities in London as he had in Dublin and Savannah. Arriving from a young colony where (unlike the situation in Pennsylvania, Massachusetts, and even South Carolina) the governor and council still effectively ruled over the legislature, he perceived the integrating drift of imperial policy after the Seven Years' War. In a remarkable series of acts that even his sympathetic biographer calls a "double agency," Knox began to advise the administration to restrain colonial growth by strengthening royal appointees and stationing troops. Both should be paid for by export and import duties. Appointees to governor's councils should be supported by generous salaries not derived from the votes of colonial assemblies.[22]

Knox had become a man of empire—not of Ireland, nor of Georgia, nor even of London, but of Britain. Yet his version of thinking and living imperially differed dramatically from that of Benjamin Franklin. He saw the empire not as a body politic with working colonial limbs but rather as a hierarchy, a series of concentric circles with London at its center. Having ascended to that center, he joined sympathetically in any and all plans to reform the empire's workings. In a 1763 memo to the Earl of Shelburne, he proposed a general tax to support imperial government. Such measures were necessary because the British Empire in America was no longer a series of settlements in the wilderness needing help only in "subjugating the old Inhabitants" and "extending Dominion" over land. Rather, it had become a commercial enterprise requiring careful regulation. The economy had changed; more government was needed, not less: "The British Colonies are to be regarded in no other Light, but as subservient to the Commerce of their Mother Country; the Colonists are merely Factors for the Purposes of Trade, and in all Considerations concerning the Colonies, *this* must always be the leading Idea."

Consequently, during the Stamp Act crisis Knox did not hesitate to publish an attack on *The Claim of the Colonies to an Exemption from Internal Taxes Imposed by Authority of Parliament*. He gave no quarter to any seemingly authentic voice of the people against taxation. Speaking as an American landowner, Knox insisted that Parliament had "a full and complete jurisdiction over the property and person of every inhabitant of a British colony." He replied directly, and in terms no one could have missed, to his fellow American agent Benjamin Franklin, "the only man whose account of North America, it is said, should be regarded." Franklin had been heard making the ridiculous claim that Parliament's supposed right to tax "is equivalent to an authority to declare all the white persons in that province Negroes." This was absurd; the charter of Pennsylvania itself allowed taxation by Parliament. Knox topped off his pamphlet with an assertion that the jurisdiction in question belonged to Parliament and remained "supreme and uncontrolled . . . internally and externally" because "the property of the colonies has arisen from, and is connected with, the right of Parliament to exercise jurisdiction over the properties and persons of [the] inhabitants there."[23]

A more thorough assertion of imperial sway and parliamentary power could hardly have been imagined. Knox's vague invocation of "jurisdiction" and his repeated emphasis on colonial "persons and property" were precisely the kind of thing that sent many English colonists of both the Caribbean and continental varieties into political hysterics. As a result, Knox was burned in effigy with his friend George Grenville and Lord Bute in both Boston and Savannah. Less than a year after reappointing their fellow planter to their colonial agency, the previously tractable Georgia Assembly fired him. He was the only agent to be dismissed for taking the wrong side in the controversy.

Franklin had, at first, a more private response to Knox's attack, though he seems to have appreciated immediately that the man had his number. With Knox's *The Claim of the Colonies*, Franklin renewed, for the first time in five years, his practice of writing marginalia in particularly important pamphlets on colonial matters. His handwritten responses form a digest of the themes he would bring out in private and public letters over the next several years.[24]

He did not deny that he had made the remark Knox quoted, comparing the supposed right of parliamentary taxation to a right to make American whites black. This racial metaphor had, after all, been part of

Franklin's rhetorical arsenal for years. (It is revealing that Knox depicted this rhetoric as a kind of signature of Franklin.) Instead Franklin corrected Knox's reading of Pennsylvania's charter. Parliament could tax, but only with the consent of the proprietor and Assembly. Parliamentary taxation in practice was "wicked," "unjust," a "Usurpation." Colonists were "subjects of the king" alone. Parliament had power only *"within the realm."* To Knox's claim that without parliamentary sovereignty the colonies did not, in fact, exist or prosper, however, Franklin scribbled furiously: "Highwaymen on Hounslow Heath have for Ages past exercised the same Jurisdiction over Subjects here [in England], but does that prove they had a right so to do?"[25]

If parliamentarians were making American whites black, they were acting like English outlaws. But the comparison to the thieves of Hounslow Heath is telling. Not everyone would have understood it the same way. A popular ballad celebrated the well-known highwaymen as Robin Hood–like heroes who victimized lawyers who took advantage of poor people's misfortunes, and who at the very least took to the highway out of necessity. By invoking Hounslow Heath in this particular negative way, Franklin identified himself with English gentlemen and cast the author Knox as a kind of provincial rogue who did not recognize law or rights in property.[26]

The successful repeal of the Stamp Act and the ascent of the Americans' hero, Pitt, to a lordship and the head of government in 1766 and 1767 raised the level of invective as not only constitutional but also partisan interests in England were now at stake. Franklin tried to keep alive the idea of colonists as gentlemen granted charter rights and under the authority of the king alone, but such arguments did not go far in England, where both parliamentary sovereignty and the king were associated with the remarkable midcentury rise of the empire. The victories of the Seven Years' War had, if anything, made imperial dominion a shared public thrill. Despite Pitt's triumph and the clout of merchants affected by American trade, Knox had his hand on the pulse of British public opinion more than Franklin did. It moved the erstwhile Briton Franklin to mock British political patriotism: "Every man in England seems to consider himself as a piece of Sovereign over America; seems to jostle himself into the Throne with the King, and talks of OUR *Subjects in the Colonies.*"[27] He thought about going home again.

Some of Franklin's English friends were promoting him for the new position of undersecretary of state in the newly created American department. The post would soon go, instead, to William Knox. In January 1768, though, after much wrangling, the Georgia Assembly decided to replace Knox as the colony's agent with Franklin himself. Now he had become a different kind of leader, an agent for multiple colonies. His first act as Georgia agent was to petition for the approval of the colony's new slave laws.

The irony was not lost on William Knox. He would devote parts of his next major pamphlets, written with Grenville, to attacking Franklin's "artful misrepresentations" of colonial demands in his testimony before Parliament. Knox was cutting his American losses, but he also held out the carrot of possible American elected positions in Parliament and talked of common trading privileges between Ireland and North America. And when invited, early in 1768, as an expert on the matter of colonial slavery, to give a lecture to the Society for the Propagation of the Gospel in Foreign Parts on the question of whether slaves should be evangelized—and if evangelized, someday freed—Knox brought together the colonial and slavery issues in a manner still more challenging to the views that Franklin promoted at this time.[28]

Knox defended slavery on the questionable though common ground that the enslaved were already slaves in Africa and so had been bought, not stolen. Colonists were participants in a preexisting market rather than its original or perpetuating cause. It would not be a good idea to teach slaves for life to read, Knox averred, for it would make them restless and bad workers. Yet neither of these facts justified treating Negroes as beasts of burden. They had to be taught the gospel without being taught to read, and the task, like imperial reform, had to be approached systematically, with a due awareness of the essential nature of the relationship in question.

Furthermore—and it is not hard to imagine Knox suppressing a smile—he observed that slavery existed in the colonies only by virtue of merely local laws. There was no British law regulating slavery; no wonder slaves had not been Christianized. It was too much to expect the planters to know how best to manage the institution. He went on, drawing out the implications of an imperial constitutionalism for slavery. If Parliament could tax the colonies, it could regulate slavery into a better existence—or into nonexistence!

What is shocking in retrospect is that Knox made not just a comparison but an explicit link between imperial subjection and the reform or abolition of slavery. Parliament could end slavery or support it for the simple reason that colonial slavery's legality had never even been officially determined. This was a problem Parliament ought to address. With tongue in cheek he suggested that Britain had "five hundred thousand of its subjects" waiting to find out if they had been "unlawfully made slaves."

Under the religious abolitionist assault, and with colonial protests firmly in mind, Knox's humor served his deadly serious contention that the answers to all dilemmas lay in imperial power. By the logic of an expansive empire of unequals who all had some but not equal rights, slavery looked much less like the racial caste status that Franklin assumed it to be. To Knox, colonial slavery, after all, was really "no more than a legal, perpetual servitude, or hereditary apprenticeship" that could and might indeed someday be ended by imperial decree. "The term slave having no legal significance in Great Britain, and being generally used for describing the subjects of the most despotic tyrants," Knox continued, in a stunning appropriation of the opposition's rhetoric, "it is commonly understood to denote, one who has no rights, his labor, property and life being at the discretion of his master. This definition of the term is far from being true in one respect to the Negroe slaves in the British colonies; their owners have no other than a legal property in them, and legal authority over them, and the same laws which make them slaves give them rights." Knox noted that no British patriot had yet taken up the cause of the empire's slaves. Perhaps this would be the historic role of the young patriot king.[29]

Was Knox being merely satirical? Perhaps only partly so. He had, five years earlier, floated the "whimsical" idea of seeding the newly acquired Florida and Louisiana territories with teenage Africans who would be educated in England for the purpose. Wherever his interventions register in terms of sympathy for Africans or for slavery, he—like his doppelgänger Franklin—certainly found African slavery good for thinking about the colonies. His talent for that, if nothing else, put him in Franklin's league in imperial debates and at loggerheads with his American rival. As the new undersecretary for the colonies, he solidified his position with Lord Hillsborough, the secretary, by answering John Dickinson's *Letters from a Farmer in Pennsylvania*, which Hillsborough believed to have been written by Franklin, in a book-length pamphlet.

How could the writer possibly believe that the Seven Years' War had not been conducted to protect the Americans? asked Knox. Why did the Americans throw themselves upon the altar of royal perogative, not trusting the king, Lords, and Commons together to be the people's representatives? The "artful misrepresentations of the colony advocates" had to be exposed as the selfish, ambitious, and partial designs they were.[30]

Franklin, meanwhile, received appointments as the colony agent for New Jersey and Massachusetts. Out of favor with the ministry, he hoped for royal beneficence. Giving up on the effort to extract a royal reorganization of government in the controversies over power and taxation in Pennsylvania, he looked to charter rights to solve the imperial controversy. The king emerged in Franklin's writings of the late 1760s as the true and only constitutional link between the home country and colonies. There was no point in even arguing about degrees of parliamentary sovereignty over the colonies, as he himself had done earlier in distinguishing internal from external taxation. Either Parliament could make all laws for the colonies, or none. He dispensed with the complex British notion of the King-in-Parliament as sovereign and instead insisted on colonial equality with other Britons vis-à-vis the king. Any other constitutional logic made the Americans something that by definition, he argued, could not exist: "subjects of subjects."

Britons, he recorded in the margins of other treatises, "are subjects themselves. They are not Sovereigns. They have no Subjects." This point had to be made, and made again, and soon. As Thomas Pownall, the other undersecretary for the American colonies and a friend of Franklin's, observed on the floor of Parliament, such definitions of British sovereignty over the colonies had deep implications. How would that sovereignty be limited? Surely it was limited somehow. When the debate reached this point, the rhetoric, as far as slavery was concerned, had come full circle. As an eminent historian of constitutional law in this period has observed, "slavery was an eighteenth century word describing the subjects of subjects."[31]

If discussions of taxation, sovereignty, and identity hadn't forced slavery into the center of the colonial controversy, a new group of players in Anglo-American politics would have done so. Slavery's opponents in England could not miss the opportunity to link—or contrast—their campaign with American bids for liberty. During the 1750s and early 1760s Pennsylvania Quakers like John Woolman and Anthony Benezet had made significant headway against slavery on the grounds that the institution was inconsistent with Christian principles; by the late 1760s, however, Benezet broadened the argument to embrace contemporary politics. At a time when many men inquired into ancient liberties at home, how could Britons remain insensitive to "tyrant custom" in the colonies? If Britons had natural rights, as colonists increasingly argued they did, were not Africans also "free by nature" as well as by God? Indeed, after the Society for the Propagation of the Gospel in Foreign Parts rebuffed Benezet's petition that they challenge the godliness of slavery and the slave trade, political and legal arguments against slavery looked more promising than religious ones.[32]

These arguments created real problems for would-be colonial patriots. Granville Sharp almost single-handedly launched British abolitionism by going to court for North American fugitive slaves. In his 1769 pamphlet entitled *A Representation of the Injustice and Dangerous Tendency of Tolerating Slavery; or of Admitting the Least Claim of Private Property in the Persons of Men, in England,* Sharp observed that "the pernicious practice of Slave-holding is become almost general in those parts," regardless of climate. "At New York, for instance, this infringement on civic and domestic liberty has become notorious and scandalous, notwithstanding that the political controversies of the inhabitants are stuffed with theatrical bombast and ranting expressions in praise of liberty." Sharp cited as evidence a copy of John Holt's *New-York Journal* for October 22, 1767, in which he found eight runaway and slave-for-sale ads. Noting that such ads had started to appear in London papers as well, Sharp deftly pointed out that the growth of the empire had brought slavery home to roost. "Natural born subjects"—people born not in Africa but in the colonies or England itself—might begin to be raised like livestock and sold. The North Americans sometimes even enslaved the native peoples, whose complexions hardly differed from those of some Britons. Race was hardly sufficient to explain the situation or to cordon off slavery. Colonial slavery could literally spell the end of English liberty.[33]

How did Franklin deal with the emergence of an antislavery that reflected so poorly on all white Americans and might, as a consequence, stymie their protests against taxes? During these years, it is generally said, Franklin experienced a kind of conversion to antislavery belief, even if he did not actually speak out publicly against the institution or join the movement. As we have seen, though, Franklin did not have to be converted by Quakers and French *philosophes*, let alone the energetic Sharp. He already believed slavery to be wrong, inefficient, and impolitic. What changed was not his beliefs but others' need to enlist or confront him.

These encounters always occupied highly charged ground, even before the politicization of colonial slavery, and even when conducted in private correspondence. In 1757 and 1758 Franklin helped the Associates of Dr. Bray—a spin-off of the Society for the Propagation of the Gospel in Foreign Parts, named after the founder and dedicated to educating black children in the colonies—choose school locations and teachers in North America, especially Philadelphia. The idea of black education was hardly a new or radical or controversial one, especially in the North and when performed under religious offices. Samuel Keimer had proposed it thirty years before.[34]

Yet Franklin chose to be careful nevertheless. He found that he had to be. For the first time, others ran with his seemingly pro-black words, and the first to do so was his wife. After he attended an Associates of Dr. Bray meeting in London, Deborah interpreted his actions as real enthusiasm for the project, which she may have shared. (Around this time she mounted the portrait of abolitionist Benjamin Lay on the wall of their Philadelphia home.) When she wrote him in 1759 after hearing seventeen African pupils examined publicly in church, she added that she planned to send Othello, one of the Franklins' slaves, to the school. Franklin, always eager to show his usefulness in behind-the-scenes public service, copied her testimony for the information of the London society. To Franklin's surprise and evident irritation, they promptly used the excerpt in their printed publicity. The Dr. Bray group had done a Franklin to Franklin. They went further. They promptly elected him a member and then, shortly thereafter, as their annual chairman.[35]

This projection and use of Franklin's name and reputation was precisely the opposite of Franklin's long-established style as a public servant, especially when it came to new ideas. Subsequently he did not attend many of the meetings and soon retreated into the task of helping with the Philadelphia school in particular. When he returned to Philadelphia in 1763, he visited the school and wrote back to his original contact, John Waring, that he had been "much pleas'd" by the students and had as a result revised upward his opinions of "the natural capacities of the black Race." In "Apprehension," "Memory," and "Docility" they seemed the equal of young white children. Yet Franklin still held back. "You will wonder perhaps that I should ever doubt it," he suggested, "and I will not undertake to justify all my Prejudices, nor to account for them."[36]

If Franklin was admitting he had been wrong in the past, or maintaining that he had freed himself of antiblack prejudice, why couldn't he describe his former views simply as "errata" corrected, in the printer's metaphor he would use in his autobiography and elsewhere? Instead he utilized the present tense, implying that he might well continue to rely on racial distinctions without looking too closely into the matter.

Yet these actions, and his past writings critical of slavery on economic grounds, had begun to gain him something of a reputation for advanced views—especially on the part of those who, like the Bray Associates, were very happy to enlist the most famous American on their side regardless of whether or not he was a true believer. Benezet, for one, may have relied upon a new family connection—his brother married a cousin of Deborah's in 1771—to approach Franklin for the first time as a prospective friend of antislavery. Two years later the tireless Quaker activist would write optimistically to Sharp about how he understood Franklin to have said that he would "act in concert with thee in the affair of slavery."[37]

If Franklin gained an antislavery reputation during the 1760s, in other words, it was not primarily because antislavery activists successfully awakened his conscience. It was because they cannily fudged the truth, sensing that Franklin could hardly risk correcting them publicly at a time when the Americans were beginning to be lambasted in the press as hypocritical slave-drivers. Benezet and Sharp, like Knox and Franklin, were political men as well as men of ideas. They knew as well as Franklin did that the slavery issue could no longer be addressed apart from the American issue.

Outside of his own library, Franklin kept his own counsel on the slavery issue during the late 1760s, years of renewed controversy over the Townshend duties and the American response of nonimportation. Nevertheless, the prominence of antislavery arguments, which derived strength from as well as contributed to anti-Americanism, led him in

1770 to confront the issue head-on for the first time in a fictionalized "Conversation between an ENGLISHMAN, a SCOTCHMAN, and an AMERICAN, on the Subject of SLAVERY."[38]

No one would have missed the political mission of a piece published to contest "the Many reflections being of late thrown out against the Americans, and particularly against our [London's] worthy Lord Mayor"—the absentee Jamaica planter William Beckford—"on Account of their keeping Slaves in their Country." The accusation of hypocrisy, of slaveholders complaining about tyranny, is right up front in the mouth of the Englishman, as is the latest antislavery offensive, *"Granville Sharpe's Book upon Slavery."* The American responds that it is indeed a good book, but that the hypocrisy lies with the English, since the larger effect of this attack on the Americans is "to render us odious, and encourage those who would oppress us, by representing us as unworthy of the Liberty we are now contending for."

The antislavery complaint against Americans, Franklin insists, is too "general," and consequently unjust, because the slavery in America is not general. New England has few slaves, mostly "Footmen or Housemaids"; the same is true for New York, New Jersey, and Pennsylvania. Even in the Chesapeake and the Carolinas, slavery is a vestige of privilege for the few, the "old rich" inhabitants. The real Americans—ninety-nine out of one hundred families—do not own a slave. Many "do every Thing in their Power to abolish it." Of the slaveholders, many are kind. What is more, the poor in England, far more than their counterparts in America, are regulated like slaves. England, in fact, began the slave trade, which continues only because "You bring the slaves to us, and tempt us to purchase them." Slavery, according to Franklin's American, is actually a good example of imperial presumption, arrogance, and inefficiency. Nothing else can explain the administration's penchant for disallowing colonists' attempts to discourage slave imports through their own taxation measures. In sum, England is to blame for slavery, and for an Englishman to denounce Americans as tyrants is like a thief blaming the buyer of the goods he fenced.

What is remarkable about this piece is Franklin's use of antislavery arguments against the British. When the Englishman cites the harshness of slave laws, Franklin's American responds by asserting that they are less harsh where there are fewer slaves, implying that such laws would never have existed if the colonists had been allowed to limit slave imports. He chides the abolitionist for sentimentalism concerning blacks:

"Perhaps you may imagine the Negroes to be a mild-tempered tractable kind of People. Some of them indeed are so. But the Majority are of a plotting Disposition, dark, sullen, malicious, revengeful, and cruel in the highest Degree . . . Indeed many of them, being mischievous Villains in their own Country, are sold off by their Princes by way of Punishment by Exile and Slavery, as you here ship off your Convicts." As in the "Observations" two decades earlier, Franklin undermined slavery and emphasized race in such a way as to escape any sense of responsibility for the institution, any ownership of its fruits, and any debts to its victims, who are depicted as criminals.

It was a useful syllogism, for it allowed Franklin to emphasize recent historical factors—that is, British power—rather than natural or biological factors in explaining colonial slavery. Where Sharp and others would single out slavery as a distinctive condition and a venal sin, Franklin emphasized the similarity of slavery to class relations in England. When the Scotsman in Franklin's "Conversation" objects that the Americans willingly buy both slaves and felons, the American retorts that with low prices, "you" (meaning Scottish merchants) "force upon us the Convicts as well as the Slaves." The American, transformed into the defender of all liberties, redefines slavery as all unfree, bought labor, accusing the English of founding their great empire on the slavery of soldiers and sailors who are also forced to cause the violent deaths of others.

It was certainly convenient for Franklin at this time to begin to depict England as an empire corrupted by its very rise. It was a strategy he would consistently work at for the next fifteen years, and it shaped much of his literary output during these decisive years of ideological combat. Was it logical or fair? Did it make contemporary sense?

The answer is a qualified yes. Franklin was both an American contesting British power and a participant in Britain's domestic politics during an already volatile political epoch, fanned by the post–Seven Years' War depression, objections to taxes, and debates over colonial liberties. The London press reported parliamentary debates at length for the first time. Audacious abuse of the king and lords surfaced with what seemed a shocking regularity. When the radical rogue John Wilkes, who had courted prison for his alleged libels of men in power, returned from exile, ran for Parliament, and won—only to be jailed, thrown out of office by the members of that body, and reelected in short order—opposition forces had a hero who championed traditional liberties against a corrupt court faction.

And Franklin had a useful foil. From early on, the Wilkite phenomenon had imperial resonances. When the Stamp Act had passed, it had been the Wilkites William Beckford and Rose Fuller, champions of the West India interest, who led the fight against it, and South Carolinians led the pack of American colonial assemblies offering tributes to Wilkes.[39] American and English domestic opposition converged in style and substance, around patriotic calls for parliamentary reform, doubts about the fairness of the tax-supported fiscal-military state, and condemnations of the king's ministers, beginning with the king's favorite Scotsman, Lord Bute.

Franklin, who had benefited from Bute's patronage, had little taste for Wilkite antiauthoritarianism and the alliance it may have portended between London crowds and an emerging urban middle class. He may have also wondered whether a movement with so narrow a definition of Englishmen—Wilkites regularly lambasted the Scots as placemen on the take—could really help Americans get their British due. He still wanted to persuade as broad a spectrum as possible that Americans deserved British rights, but he saw no need to offend ruling cliques. Besides, the Americans needed the friendship of the king, which required having friendly access to at least some of Whitehall's shifting inner circle. So Franklin went out of his way to stake out a more cautious position.

This proved no easy task. The striking resonances of Wilkite radicalism, American protest, and colonial slavery proved interesting, even irresistible, to some of the realm's foremost conservative writers and thinkers. Much as antislavery radicals like Franklin's British friends David Hartley, Richard Price, and Joseph Priestley began to see commonalities in the struggle to reform tyrannical institutions in England and abroad, these conservative thinkers saw in domestic rabble-rousing, American complaints, and slavery a set of similar, and inseparable, corruptions. When that sensibility found a political foothold in Britain's highest court, the results transformed the prospects of abolitionism and forced Franklin to still deeper confrontations with the problem of slavery.[40]

Beginning in 1767, Granville Sharp had brought successive lawsuits on behalf of runaway slaves in London. The cases by their very nature had imperial implications. Did colonial slave laws apply in England? What were the implications of English common law liberties for resident aliens who were slaves of colonists? Sharp argued that slavery was a colonial corruption that tainted British traditions of liberty. And in a 1772 case on behalf of the former Virginian James Somerset, his lawyers argued that no man could be a slave in England. The king could provide for slavery in the colonies, but Parliament never had. To remit Somerset to his master for sale would be to declare Virginia law supreme over Parliament in England itself.[41]

Sharp and Somerset won their case—setting off a wave of speculation about the beginning of the end of slavery in England. For all of Chief Justice Lord Mansfield's desire to limit the scope of the case to the rights of a man on English soil, the implications were clear enough. The highest jurist in the land had declared that there was something un-English about slavery, something unjust about the actions of American masters that the blackness of Africans could never justify. Antislavery gained an official imprimatur. More important, London's black community began to spread an optimistic interpretation of what would happen as a result.[42]

Within a few weeks Franklin published an anonymous response. In a passage usually pointed to as a key to the evolution of his antislavery conscience, he conceded the iniquities of the slave trade and supported the idea of gradual emancipation. He took details—and even the Quaker terminology of *thee* and *thou*—from Benezet's most recent letter to him. Still, he ended the response by placing the blame squarely on "Pharisaical Britain" for "setting free *a single Slave* that happens to land on thy coasts, while thy Merchants in all thy ports are encouraged by thy laws to continue a commerce whereby so many *hundreds of thousands* are dragged into a slavery that can scarce be said to end with their lives, since it is entailed on their posterity!"[43]

By the time of the decision Granville Sharp had agreed with Franklin to emphasize not American slaveholding difference but rather British imperial sin. During the remainder of the imperial controversy, in fact, Sharp went out of his way to suggest, as some New Englanders had begun to do, that American liberties and the cause of the Africans were, in the end, the same human or natural rights. Nevertheless, the Somerset case and its perhaps uncareful, mistaken, or simply opportunistic interpretation in the press had quite the opposite political effect. It underlined a different American identity: it separated American from English politics and law and institutionalized a sense of the former's stark injustice and inferiority.[44] There was no getting around it, for the existence of slavery in the colonies had everything to do with why Mansfield opened the Pandora's box of slavery and the law in the first place—and why American patriots like Franklin did their best to dodge the decision's potentially antislavery meanings.

Mansfield knew all about the problems of inequality for provincials. A Scotsman who spoke with an accent, he could not help but use such episodes as a further way to overcome his own provinciality. He became, over time and by degrees, a believer in the parliamentary settlement, a greater Britain, and the rule of law and custom. He had helped devise one compromise between Assembly and proprietor, but in 1764, as a key player in the Privy Council for plantation affairs, he had been disgusted by Franklin's machinations against the Penns. The Pennsylvanian, as he saw it, was trying to get around the charter and Parliament—using the king as a screen for provincial power, even independence. He even suggested that Franklin be displaced from the postmastership.

In 1766 Mansfield had emerged as the "arch defender of imperial constitutionalism" when he observed, in one of the most-often-quoted lines of the Stamp Act repeal debates, that the "colonists . . . are more emphatically subjects of Great Britain than those within the realm." Not only was the outstanding fact about Americans that they were outside "the realm," there was no difference, he insisted, between internal and external taxes. "Taxation without representation," to Mansfield, meant nothing, for taxation was a matter of sovereignty, and sovereignty remained indivisible, "whether such subjects have a right to vote or not."[45]

In this light, the Somerset case was about more than "one slave" or even slavery itself, and Franklin knew it. The case was about empire and nationality. Mansfield, a great jurist, had done what great jurists do in times of political and ideological stress: he simplified a political matter in terms of law. In expressing his concern about the consequences of emancipating slaves, he made it clear he was no abolitionist. Yet he took the plunge anyway because he saw American unlawfulness as a greater danger. If prominent Britons like Mansfield preferred to risk dealing a "deadly blow" to slavery in England rather than give up American inequality in the empire, Franklin had reason to be worried and ample excuse to be equally uncompromising.[46]

He also had, for the first time, a compelling reason to be publicly antislavery. He *had* to spin the slavery question Sharp's way, not Mansfield's, in order to take the issue out of anti-American hands. Slavery had to be seen as an example of British tyranny, not American provincialism and hypocrisy. As important was Franklin's need to deflect any sense of the priority or special timeliness of the slavery issue.

There were other possibilities besides Franklin's North American strategy of deflection, and to be sure some of them were worse for slaves. West Indians, with some encouragement from Mansfield, immediately began to argue for confirmation of colonial slavery's legality through a parliamentary statute. Samuel Estwick, the subagent for Barbados, stressed the royally granted charter rights of the African company, as well as the rights of colonists as Britons to retain their property. For Edward Long, the Jamaican writer and historian, the Somerset case proved the necessity for a racial justification for slavery. He got to work on it immediately and did not miss the chance to enlist Franklin's earlier writings.[47]

For Franklin, it was too late to stand on property rights or racism alone, not least because he did not think, as West Indian planters did, that slavery's survival was more important than colonial rights. After all, he had already criticized slavery and suggested that it mattered very little in the North American scheme of things and would matter even less if American privileges of self-government were restored. His portrait of a virtuous America rested on a sense of difference from West Indian planters.

There was also Knox's vision of a combined slavery and imperial reform, whereby the rules of empire would be rationalized and extended as far as possible. Slaves would be subjects, the Americans would be made secure in their property rights, and other ambiguities would be cleared up once and for all. Franklin's friend David Hartley linked these solutions explicitly in late 1775, proposing that "in exchange for having their fiscal autonomy restored, colonial assemblies would acknowledge Parliament's imperial sovereignty by 'admitt[ing] & register[ing] a new Declaratory Act' that would guarantee slaves throughout the empire a jury trial." But this was a last-ditch effort to prevent independence. Most metropolitan proposals to extend subjecthood to slaves went hand in hand with an unacceptable subjection of their masters. And Franklin was now an agent for Georgia as well as Massachusetts. He had tried to get local slave law ratified, not trumped, by the metropole.[48]

Franklin, in short, played both sides of the issue. His anonymous antislavery writings of the early 1770s responded to a political situation in which North Americans could hardly afford to defend slavery if they wanted to get a hearing for their theories of taxation and representation. Nor could they allow slavery reform to become a priority if their liberties were to be seen as a political imperative. Franklin's careful—and anonynmous—antislavery statements, then, must be considered as damage control, finesse, or "spin." Rather than leading the vanguard, Franklin scrambled to keep up with events like the Somerset decision and the growing tendency for all political players in England to use both the slavery and American issues to their advantage.

Privately, in letters, he assured antislavery advocates that he was with them in spirit. It may have eased his conscience to hear from Benezet in April 1773 that antislavery sentiment seemed to be spreading in America. He may well have believed that a consensus was building on slavery's evils, and it was only a matter of time before it could be addressed more forthrightly, but he kept such remarks carefully away from the public, displaying them mostly to antislavery men, whom he had good political reasons to mollify.[49]

This ambivalent stance appears most poignantly in an episode often construed to prove Franklin's true antislavery feelings. When the Boston slave Phillis Wheatley, already well known for her poetry, arrived in London seeking patrons for a volume of her poems—a project that the Massachusetts patriot printers resisted—Franklin obliged his Boston nephew Jonathan Williams, who knew the Wheatley family well, by paying a call and offering "any Services I could do her." Yet in the same letter he claimed that he was treated rudely by the young master of the house and had since "heard nothing of her." It is supposed (rather fancifully, for there is no evidence to the effect) that Franklin's rebuff by the much younger Nathaniel Wheatley came because the family suspected Franklin had come to offer the slave poet a liberal interpretation of the Somerset case and thus the prospect of freedom in England. Yet the older Wheatleys had set up the meeting in the first place, asking Jonathan Williams to mention Phillis, who was seeking patrons, to his famous uncle. Upon getting Franklin's letter a perplexed Williams chose to blame the Wheatleys.

Could they have changed their minds so quickly? It seems more likely, and more consistent given his other responses to the politics of slavery, that Franklin felt that one visit to the enslaved poet was dangerous enough. He chose to perceive or even invent a slight so that he would not in fact be responsible for any future services to Phillis, who had been supported by the Tory press in Boston but mostly ignored by Boston patriots eager to maintain the sympathy of the southern colonies at a time when Boston was out in the vanguard of colonial protest.[50]

Wheatley herself had endorsed the American resistance and, in a poem to the new secretary of state, Lord Dartmouth, tied her admiration for the colonial patriots to her sensitivity, as a slave, to matters of liberty. On the other hand, her observations on the hypocrisy of the patriot cause, in a letter to Mohegan preacher Samson Occom, appeared in a newspaper that opposed the resistance movement. She had the support of prominent whigs like John Hancock and royal government men like Thomas Hutchinson. In other words, she capitalized on both sympathy for and suspicion of the Massachusetts radicals. She would prove quite capable of making the most of Franklin's small gesture, proposing six years later to dedicate her second volume of poems to him, as if the most famous American had championed her art or her people. He had done neither; but why not try to make it seem as if he had when Franklin could hardly deny it publicly? As happened so often in the arena of slavery, slaves themselves relied on subtleties that their masters could barely perceive or admit.[51]

Franklin, though, was no ordinary master. By gesturing toward Wheatley yet keeping his distance, he ratified his vaguely antislavery credentials but resisted her sometime conflation of the patriot and African causes as well as her occasional criticism of patriots who sought to keep the slavery question off the agenda. He was no doubt glad he did so when English reviewers of her volume used it as another opportunity to condemn the hypocrisy of colonists like the Wheatleys for keeping such persons in bondage.

The situation encouraged Franklin, as well as Wheatley, to speak and write with a "double tongue." The gap between his public and private sentiments—or between what he said to different audiences—also reflected his long-standing desire, and talent, for bending situations with the artful and precise use of words. Contemporaries in England more and more often noticed his manipulative streak. His letters to Governor William Franklin were intercepted and read (by Knox, Franklin guessed). In them, and in dialogue with the radicals in power in Massachusetts, he seemed like a die-hard colonial rights man. Yet in England he continually insisted on American loyalty and willingness to compromise. He still served as postmaster general for North America—which meant he was a servant of both the colonies and the English government. Could he continue to be both things? His good image as a scientist and statesman spread, but they were increasingly hard to reconcile with political nicknames like "Dr. Doubleface."[52]

Matters came to a head for the American agent extraordinaire in precisely this period—between the Somerset decision and Wheatley's arrival in the summer of 1773. The drama began, ironically, at a seeming moment of triumph, when the intense lobbying of Franklin and his associates for their Ohio valley land grant finally brought Colonial Secretary Lord Hillsborough to make one anti-American stand too many. The secretary threatened to resign if the grant was approved, and his colleagues accepted the resignation. It looked as if Franklin had been behind the entire affair, forcing Hillsborough's hand. The successor in the colonial secretaryship, Lord Dartmouth, was known to be more sympathetic to the colonies. An optimistic Franklin approached Dartmouth in the fall with the latest petition from Massachusetts, which asserted the Assembly's right to pay the salary of the governor, Thomas Hutchinson.

For Dartmouth to even discuss a petition with Franklin was a concession, for Hillsborough had refused to acknowledge the Assembly's right (over that of the governor) to appoint him as agent. Dartmouth said that the petition would offend the king and Parliament and asked for a delay. Franklin, who had opposed the idea of a petition, reluctantly agreed. But what would he say to his constituents? Would they suspect him of being insufficiently warm to the cause? Or worse, as some in Massachusetts said openly, of being a double agent?[53]

Still miffed by the opening of his own letters, Franklin decided to placate the Massachusetts assembly by sending copies of private letters from several years before of Governor Hutchinson and former Governor Andrew Oliver to Grenville's right-hand man, Thomas Whatley. A friend to the American cause had apparently snatched them after Whatley died in 1772. These letters made it clear that Hutchinson had disdained his opponents and their arguments for liberty enough to ask the administration to crack down on them once and for all (a view not surprising given that his house had been destroyed, in a crowd action replete with symbolic and personal insults, in 1765). In forwarding them, Franklin went so far as to suggest that these very letters had "laid the foundation" of the colonial controversy.

Franklin knew very well that Hutchinson had been telling everyone who would listen that the colonial agent himself was behind the Massachusetts resistance. The governor had also refused to confirm Franklin's agency. Franklin also knew that Hutchinson had read his letters. (Actually, Franklin's letters may even have been what convinced Hutchinson that Franklin was a double-dealer—or at least that Franklin was truly a believer in colonial autonomy, a doctrine with which Hutchinson believed there could be no compromise.) The language he used to introduce the old Hutchinson and Oliver letters and sum up their meanings was exactly the sort of Boston rhetoric the radicals would have wanted to hear—and which he generally avoided in London. Particular gentlemen—seen as more dependable crown servants than he—had been "bartering away the Liberties of their native Country for Posts," and profiting from the ensuing controversy. They were the "Time-servers," the "Betrayers of Massachusetts," of "the Government they pretend to serve, and of the whole English Empire."[54]

Franklin in effect had turned the tables, offering up to Massachusetts another double agent. There was even a precedent for this sort of epistolary revelation to resolve a crisis. The exposure of Governor Francis Bernard's letters to Hillsborough had led to a demand for his recall in 1769; during the ensuing confrontation Bernard resigned. The game of exposé was, as Franklin would later maintain, fair play—if the rules were the same for both parties.

The problem was that they were not, any more than it was clear what "government" he or Hutchinson ought to serve, and Franklin knew it. He specifically asked Assembly Speaker Thomas Cushing, his most regular contact, not to publicize the illicitly procured letters. Cushing held on to them until the following June, when he galvanized the legislature by displaying them in a closed session. The effect was electric—and not easily contained to the chambers. Within weeks excerpts appeared in the papers, and still another round of petitions was on its way from Boston, calling for the removal of Hutchinson.

Attempting to mediate, Franklin had exacerbated a delicate situation. At first he tried to keep his role in the affair hidden. On the same day he wrote to his nephew about his visit to Phillis Wheatley, he also wrote to the Massachusetts Assembly urging unity and patience—and preparations for an intercolonial congress. To the British press he spoke rather differently, in anonymous calls for a return to the pre–Revenue Act status quo and for all private letters on American affairs to be opened up to public scrutiny on both sides of the ocean. He experimented with third-person allegorical voices in pieces like "Rules by Which a Great Empire may be Reduced to a Small One" and "An Edict by the King of Prussia" (declaring Englishmen to be his subjects). These were devastating, yet desperate, critiques of metropolitan power that bid, too late, to depersonalize matters after he himself had personalized them. He got attention but annoyed those in the ministry who were, after all, being compared to historical and imaginary tyrants. Mansfield had the grace to concede that Franklin's pieces were "very able and artful" but correctly predicted that they would only polarize things further.

Franklin's own role in the escalation of the controversy remained obscure during the summer and fall of 1773. Was he a messenger—or the maker of the message? Suddenly the spotlight moved in his direction. The fact that he had sent the Hutchinson and Oliver letters under cover of secrecy did not become known until after the brother of the late Thomas Whatley challenged and fought a duel with the chief suspect for the theft of the letters, their mutual friend John Temple. To head off a second fight to the death, Franklin admitted his role, in a newspaper piece widely read in England as a confession of guilt.[55]

In two weeks Franklin found himself called before the Privy Council's Committee on Plantation Affairs. Because they met ostensibly to discuss the Massachusetts petitions, he was ordered to prove the authenticity of the revealed Hutchinson letters. He accepted his right to get counsel and request a delay. The suspense mounted. Franklin's friends passed on rumors that the Privy Council hearing was to be the scene of a shaming ritual: he would be humiliated so that he could be dismissed from the postmastership, the Massachusetts petitions could be blamed on his faction and so ignored, and parliamentary sovereignty could be reaffirmed. News of the dumping of East India Company tea in Boston harbor arrived the day before the showdown in the long, narrow room known as the "cockpit."

Lord North and his allies turned to the solicitor general, Alexander Wedderburn, to present the case. They chose well. No one better understood the power or the practices of British patronage. Wedderburn had been so skilled at courtroom and literary invective that he had almost been disbarred in his native Scotland before he came to London. He was so good that, like Franklin's friend James Ralph before him, he was bought off with a pension—later upped to a peerage—to ensure his service to the Whigs. Before the three dozen lords on the committee, all seated at a long table, with the rest of the room filled with standing spectators, Wedderburn stood and thundered for more than an hour, banging his fist on the table several times for emphasis.[56]

What was at issue, he insisted, was the ability of the crown to even have a "standing servant" in the colonies. Franklin's "secret designs" made it necessary to "mark and brand" him as a subversive and a criminal. Wedderburn singled out Franklin, who had "forfeited the respect of societies and of men," for a kind of social death reserved in theory for British convicts—and slaves. As the life peers laughed and clapped, the solicitor drove the point home with two literary references. First he predicted that "men will watch him with a jealous eye; they will hide their papers from him, and lock up their escritoires [desks]. He will henceforth esteem it a libel to be called a *man of letters*; homo trium litterarum"— three words that in Latin suggested an anagram meaning "thief."

Second, argued the solicitor, Franklin had had the gall to admit his disgraceful actions without shame. "I can compare it," said Wedderburn, "only to Zanga in Dr. Young's *Revenge*," a Moorish slave bitter at being beaten by a kind master. "I ask, my Lords, whether the revengeful temper attributed by poetic fiction only, to the bloody African, is not surpassed by the coolness and apathy of the wily American?"[57]

A wily thief: a man of letters not to be trusted with letters. A well-treated captive who could not take the cuffs he deserved. Worse than an African: a bloody slave. In response Franklin remained as silent and "immovable" in his features as a slave accused. Only in 1783, after American independence, did testimony appear in the British press that on leaving the room he had paused to snarl at Wedderburn that he would make *his* master a "little king" for this treatment. The truth was less dramatic, yet deeper. The great imperial debate over taxation and representation had become a shouting match not only over who was acting like a slave-driver but also over who deserved to be considered British, and who could only be compared to slaves.

An initially mixed response to his humiliation encouraged Franklin to stay longer in London. During this interval he pulled out all the rhetorical stops to prove who were the genuine enslavers and who, by contrast, was being enslaved. In "An Open Letter to Lord North," the arrogant author, a "Friend to Military Government," insisted that the Americans "have degenerated to such a Degree that one born in Britain is equal to twenty Americans." After the soldiers did their easy work in suppressing the rebellion, the empire could employ "the Method made use of by the Planters in the West Indies . . . who appoint what they call a Negro Driver, who is appointed from among the slaves." Eventually, when "drained of their last shilling" by taxes, the colonists "should be sold to the best Bidder." In ventriloquized English voices, Americans were described as runaways, convicts, and chattel. Franklin took on the voice of a "FREEHOLDER OF OLD SARUM" (the ultimate rotten borough and a symbol of aristocratic corruption) to propose castration as "the most feasible Method of humbling our rebellious Vassals of North America," lest they "slip their Necks out of the Collar, and from being Slaves set up for Masters." Taxation itself became a form of human commodification in Franklin's June 1774 "Act for the More Effectual Keeping of the Colonies Dependent": every addition to American population, whether by immigration or birth, was to be taxed, as were grain exports.[58]

He had written of going home before the cockpit, but the role of lightning rod seemed to suit him. Like a man shocked, he could not let go so easily. So he stayed months longer, encouraged by attention from the opposition, including Pitt, who walked him in to hear the Lords debate the use of force against the colonies. On the floor Hillsborough said that there were men walking the streets of London who ought to be "in Newgate [prison], or at Tyburn." He meant Franklin. Meanwhile the ministry hunted for letters that would prove his treason. "If by some Accident the Troops and People of N[ew] E[ngland] should come to Blows I should probably be taken up" and jailed, he wrote to his old friend Joseph Galloway. Once again he identified with the fugitive. He had come full circle. It was time to go home.

In finally leaving England, Benjamin Franklin displayed his share of the craftiness for which American runaways were notorious. He did not in fact depart until a writ was issued for his appearance in a case brought by William Whatley, who accused him of theft of his brother's letters. According to Thomas Hutchinson, Franklin told people he would leave in two weeks—and promptly took the next boat a few days later.[59]

Probably the secrecy was not really necessary. Would Parliament have dared make a martyr of Franklin? An actual warrant for his arrest was not issued until he was known to have arrived safely in Philadelphia. A lucky sort of fugitive yet again, Franklin had decided, even before the fact, to publicize the notion of his narrow escape from the hands of tyranny. Somehow it felt right to make a run for it.

EIGHT

America the Free

One of the less-well-known facts about the Revolutionary War is that African Americans fought on both sides, primarily with their own freedom in mind. Perhaps even more obscure are the origins of this situation, and the partial origins of the war itself, in runaway slaves. Capitalizing on rumors of their emancipation, enslaved Africans took to their feet and in doing so forced the hands of British forces in Virginian and South Carolinian harbors. By the time the royal governor of Virginia, Lord Dunmore, issued his proclamation of freedom to all indentured servants and slaves who joined his majesty's troops, the threat of growing numbers of fugitive slaves had already helped shift these key southern colonies decisively toward support of independence and war.[1]

Informed contemporaries were hardly surprised. The role of slaves in the looming armed showdown was already being discussed when Franklin left England for Philadelphia in early 1775. William Knox proposed that any armed assault on the colonies should start in the South because slaves would revolt and bring a quick end to the conflict. Edmund Burke, a member of Parliament, colony agent of New York, and already a greatly respected writer on political affairs, proved more prophetic. In a three-hour speech in favor of reconciliation Burke maintained that the "spirit of liberty" among southern colonists derived from the "vast multitude of slaves" they held, a situation that made them "most proud and jealous of their freedom." Parliament had to back down, in effect, because the "haughtiness of domination" among slaveowning planters "fortifies" their sense of freedom "and renders it invincible."[2]

It had already been proposed, noted Burke, to "reduce" the Virginians and Carolinians "by declaring a general enfranchisement of their slaves." Here Burke sought to bring his innate and thoughtful conservatism to bear on the situation. Slaves were often attached to their masters; might not such masters arm their slaves against the empire? Moreover would not slaves "suspect the offer of freedom from that very nation which has sold them to their present masters? From that nation, one of whose causes of quarrel with those masters, is their refusal to deal any more in that inhumane traffic?" Like Franklin, Burke exaggerated the extent and the effects of colonial assemblies' attempts to tax or limit the slave trade, conflating the nonimportation movements, which did at times include the human commodity, with the patriot movement as a whole. He accepted, to a point, that American protests had antislavery implications, for it enabled him to reduce British policy to an image of extreme hypocrisy: a slave ship, "refused entry into the ports of Virginia or Carolina," whose captain would then simultaneously offer emancipation to loyal American blacks and "advertise his sale of [African] slaves."[3]

With friends like Burke, slaveowning Americans hardly needed enemies. Calling attention to such hypocrisies and blaming them on the British legitimated the debate over the rebellion's relationship to slavery and made it even more likely that British forces, and American slaves, would take matters into their own hands. The other brilliant conservative of the age, Dr. Samuel Johnson, foresaw this well in advance. He had long viewed the colonies and the wars for them as sources of corruption, and he identified English liberties as local, legally limited, precise, and the opposite of what one could expect in outlying countries acquired by theft. His disapproving acolyte James Boswell had heard him toast "to the next insurrection of the Negroes in the West Indies" and declare himself willing "to love all men, except an American." Even before 1769 he called Americans "a race of convicts" who taught slaves Christianity only to make them more docile.[4]

Johnson and Franklin had shared meals at William Strahan's house, but Franklin would dismiss Johnson as a "court pensioner" after he published *Taxation No Tyranny*, a devastating indictment of American arguments, in early 1775. Johnson homed in on the key problems with American claims: the indivisibility of British sovereignty, and the contradiction of claiming English rights through membership in the nation while also, at the same time, enlisting natural rights, which anyone anywhere—including slaves—could claim. There was something selfish, remarked Johnson, about "these lords of themselves, these kings of *Me*, these demigods of independence," constantly declaiming about their infringed-upon rights. In the "loud hurricane of Pennsylvanian eloquence," he wrote, referring directly to Franklin, "it has become very general practice to talk of 'slavery.'" If the American windbags could not be silenced, they could be conquered—without a battle—if and when British soldiers were turned out to free the real slaves. Then slaves, supplied with their own tools, could be transformed into the new, loyal colonists: "they may be more grateful and honest than their masters."

Johnson saved for near the end the famous lines that pinpointed American hypocrisy.

We are told, that the subjection of Americans may tend to the diminution of our own liberties: an event, which none but the most perspicacious of politicians are able to foresee. If slavery be thus fatally contagious, how is it that we hear the loudest yelps for liberty from the drivers of negroes?[5]

The image of slave-drivers yelping (like the chattel they whipped?) is even more devastating after the rarely noted preceding sentence and clause, which make clear that it is the opposition's equation of British and American freedoms that Johnson finds most outrageous. He detests it, he says, *because* of slavery. Slavery corrupts; it corrupts absolutely. The colonial relationship would always be an unequal one because slavery defined the colonies. Talk of raising up the slaves made the point as vividly as it could be made.

Franklin and the Americans poised for independence would have none if it. British calls to arm the slaves, and the first efforts to do so during the summer and fall of 1775, only proved British corruption and hypocrisy. This indeed was the Americans' worst nightmare come true. By July Franklin included "encouraging our blacks to rise and murder their masters" on the list of reasons he gave his British friends for why reconciliation was by then impossible. It was a "barbarous" kind of warfare.[6]

Franklin's eloquent outrage bore fruit in Jefferson's draft of the Declaration of Independence, which Franklin saw in manuscript and discussed with the author privately and in committee. A passage Congress edited out condemns slavery as a "cruel war" visited by the British upon another people, the Africans. It also depicts the royal recruitment of slaves as "paying off former crimes committed against the *liberties* of one people with crimes which he urges them to commit against the *lives* of another."

The language was pure Jefferson and the passion particularly Virginian, to be sure. Yet the casting of African slavery as further proof of British villainy is absolutely consistent with Franklin's influential and widely read writings of the past decade as well as with what he was saying in 1775 and 1776. So was the exaggerated boast that the colonies had tried to restrain the slave trade only to be frustrated by the king, who abused his veto power by "suppressing every legislative attempt to prohibit or restrain this execrable commerce." Franklin might have been more prudent, or allegorical in phrasing, but he evidently did not quarrel with its meaning. When he made marginal comments on Jefferson's draft, he left that paragraph just as it stood.[7]

Franklin's contribution to the Declaration's stance on slavery was more than inspiration for or support of the author. England's culpability for slavery in the Declaration reflected Franklin's evolving sense of an antislavery American identity that excluded slaves. That sense survived the famous deletion. The more ambiguous replacement for the excised paragraph—one that blames the king for having "instanced & excited domestic insurrections among us"—originated as an *addition* by Franklin to the manuscript Jefferson asked committee members to correct. In both Franklin's and Congress's final version, this charge begins a paragraph that—in language precisely like Franklin's in his letters of late 1775 and 1776—accuses the king of stirring up "the merciless Indian savages, whose known rule of warfare is an undistinguished destruction of all ages, sexes, & conditions of existence."[8] By allying slaves with Indians and (in the draft) treasonous Tories, Franklin and Jefferson insulated America from the Africans (as well as the Indians) who populated so much of the continent. Their very existence appears as British, not American. As domestic rebels against the rebellion, they are close, but distanced; *they are distanced because they are domestic.* Had slaves not been important, and threatening, they need not have been mentioned at all. But because they were, they had to be dealt with, if only by the act of writing them out of citizenship and denying their presence in the society and the polity.[9]

Franklin had developed this position during the debates of the Continental Congress in May 1776. When southern delegates asked that slaves not be included in the population count for taxation purposes under the proposed Articles of Confederation on the grounds that they, like New Englanders' sheep, were chattel, not people, Franklin replied that "slaves weaken rather than strengthen the State, and there is therefore some difference between them and sheep. Sheep will never make any Insurrections."[10] To make it up to the southerners, he then moved that the number of votes allotted per state in Congress be in proportion to population—including slaves. That motion did not pass. Nevertheless, in round one of the most important constitutional debates in American history, Franklin criticized slavery, only to compensate by empowering slaveholders by letting them be overrepresented. Slaves, who were otherwise spoken of as enemies, were to have a sort of representation, despite their not being members of the polity in any other sense, not even in the sense in which women and children were represented by male householders.[11] The government's powers to represent citizens and to tax them were to be linked, as patriot Whigs had long argued they should be, but now *through* slavery. Slaves were in but out: they were counted, but did not themselves count. The lesson would not be lost on southern slaveholders during the debates over the Constitution. With critics like Franklin, they hardly needed friends.

After he arrived in France in December 1776 as one of America's ministers seeking a treaty and alliance with Britain's great rival, Franklin continued to trumpet the barbarity of British enlistment of slaves.[12] Within a few months, however, he dropped the issue of Britain's liberation and mobilization of slaves from his rhetorical arsenal. He continued to depict the British as a man-commodifying nation. In a fake letter—written in French and widely reprinted in Europe—Franklin, in the voice of a Hessian Count de Schaumbergh, excitedly calculated the profits he earned for every one of his mercenaries killed on American battlefields.[13] But as Franklin realized that an alliance was likely and that support, especially financial, was of paramount concern, his emphasis shifted away from Britain's vices—which the French perhaps took for granted—and toward America's virtues.[14]

Franklin's largest task in France was to help the French think of America as a nation and as an investment in the future. It was in the French interest to do so, to be sure, after fighting a succession of wars with Great Britain and losing the last one so badly. Yet interest alone cannot account for what eventually, even tragically, amounted to French overspending on the American cause. Franklin's diplomacy in France was a battle for hearts and minds as well as for arms and dollars.[15] No one was in a better position to fight that battle, and it informed most of what he said and wrote for the next decade, perhaps especially with respect to slavery.

The French intelligentsia had long established America as a useful contrast to the old world and by the 1780s had begun a heated debate about the implications of the old world–new world contrast for both colonialism and for politics at home. Slavery occupied an important place in this debate. For the great naturalist Comte du Buffon and his followers, such as the Abbé Guillaume-Thomas-François Raynal, the new world, but especially the West Indies, was a theater of European decadence, a tropical death trap whose natives had been enslaved and extirpated so that greedy Spaniards and their followers could bring Africans to make impressive but ungodly profits. These very influential writers tended to have a condescending yet admiring view of "noble savages," extending that view toward white settlers in those northern regions perceived as less marked by conquest and slavery. Some of the same writers made their critiques of slavery into not-so-veiled attacks on absolute monarchy.[16]

Most of these French thinkers were especially well disposed toward Franklin, whose scientific renown had perhaps single-handedly disproven the speculation advanced by certain contenders that nothing truly good could come from the colonies, and that Europeans there would inevitably descend to a savage state. The issue of Franklin's virtues in relation to colonial vices had already been raised by David Hume in his 1762 letter to Franklin, but this itself may have been a reaction to the French interest in Franklin. Buffon himself looked to Franklin for a happy ending to the new world story: he had been the first to embrace Franklin's writings on electricity during the early 1750s, an event that if anything forced the hand of English men of science who had been in no rush to hand laurels to their mere suppliers of raw data across the ocean.[17]

When Franklin visited France in 1769 and conferred again with the physiocrats, he already had been cited by them as an authority on the rural idyll of mid-Atlantic America. With North America as a potential ally in 1776, such theories became political footballs—and Franklin a key player. Later critics of Franklin's diplomacy, such as the resolutely practical and somewhat Francophobic John Adams, missed this dimension of what Franklin was doing in France. Thomas Jefferson, who would soon enter the new world debate with his *Notes on the State of Virginia*, knew better. One of his favorite stories about Franklin concerned a dinner party Franklin held at his house in Passy. Among the French guests was Buffon's disciple the Abbé Raynal, who had written extensively about the failings of nature in America as demonstrated by the allegedly small sizes of American plants and animal species, including the natives.

"During the dinner," Jefferson recalled, Raynal "got on his favorite theory of the degeneracy of animals, and even of man, in America, and urged it with his usual eloquence." Franklin looked around and said, "Come, M[onsieur] l'Abbé, let us try this question by the fact before us. We are here one half Americans and one half French, and it happens that the Americans have placed themselves at one side of the table and our French friends on the other. Let both parties rise and we will see on which side nature has degenerated." The guests stood up. All the Americans at dinner were tall; the French were much shorter, "and the Abbé himself, was a mere shrimp." Franklin did not have to refute Raynal's well-known antislavery stance to change the story, the news, and the very subject, of the new world from Indian and African victimhood to "native" white American success.[18]

Upon arriving in December 1776, Franklin quickly appreciated how well known he was by all ranks of people in France, and he rightly realized that he could capitalize on the meeting of the minds he had been having with the physiocrats for more than a decade. The rural, egalitarian society they admired in contrast to feudalism and monarchy was with the American Revolution making a stand for rights on natural as well as historical grounds. Excitedly Franklin wrote back home to Samuel Cooper, " 'Tis a Common observation here that our Cause is the *Cause of all Mankind*; and that we are fighting for their liberty in defending our own." Within a few months these sentiments appeared in a widely translated position paper he wrote. "Every Man in America is employ'd. The greatest Number in cultivating their own Lands; the rest in handicrafts, Navigation and Commerce," Franklin asserted, implying that everyone worked for themselves or for wages. Americans lived simply; they could be trusted to repay debts, as they were still repaying their private debts to England (another exaggeration), even as that "old, corrupt, extravagant and profligate Nation" went into more debt to fight the war. America could even serve as the "asylum" of Europe, the refuge of the oppressed and "the Wealthy who love liberty."[19]

Slaves were nowhere to be seen in this vision, and Franklin did his best to keep it that way. The famous plain brown suit and fur hat he wore reinforced the message. Franklin's dressing down in France is rightly seen as a studied projection of rustic new world simplicity as imagined by the French.[20] It was also distinctively Quaker—and by implication, antislavery. By the 1760s the plain-dressing Quakers of the Philadelphia meeting were known all over the Western world as the first group to formally censure slaveowners.

The French loved the Quakers. Voltaire, no friend of religion, had portrayed their egalitarianism, rationalism, and simplicity as the antithesis of European aristocracies. On his earlier visit to France, Franklin discovered very quickly that he had been mistaken for a Quaker—after all, he was from Pennsylvania and had been allied with them politically. He did nothing to correct that impression—rather, on his return as ambassador he cultivated it. At the king's reception for the American ministers marking the establishment of the Franco-American alliance in March 1778, the other American ambassadors appeared in official court dress. Franklin wore his brown suit. The king's chamberlain had to be talked into letting the bareheaded Franklin, who at the last moment had discarded his wig, into the king's presence by the foreign minister, Comte de Vergennes, himself. Louis XVI did not miss a beat, and the crowd of aristocrats cheered, shouting, "The Apostle of Liberty, Citizen Franklin!"[21]

It is easy to see intimations of French revolutionary enthusiasm in such spectacles. Images of Franklin in a fur cap echoed the earlier cult of Jean-Jacques Rousseau, the writer who had sought to put all social relations on a natural basis. It is less obvious what Franklin was doing with respect to slavery, a matter of real concern for French intellectuals because of France's extensive holdings in the Caribbean. For them, African slavery was a new world corruption caused by old world appetites for luxuries like sugar and tobacco. Rousseau, not unlike Franklin, urged more natural consumption patterns and insisted on their moral and social benefits. Yet when Franklin the diplomat mimicked Rousseau, who had also worn a fur cap, he communicated a stance that his nation had by no means embraced.

In France, Franklin passed for a Quaker every bit as much as his old boss, Samuel Keimer, had fifty years before in Philadelphia. In the process Franklin passed as antislavery. The lessons in conspicuous non-consumption he learned from Keimer, his vegetarian antislavery "master" Thomas Tryon, and Benjamin Lay, as well as through his continued encounters with proponents of the French Enlightenment, helped Franklin appear more antislavery than he was, at a time and place when it was quite politic to do so. As with English and earlier colonial antislavery, the public position he took had more to do with politics and diplomacy than with belief.[22]

If any sea change toward antislavery occurred during Franklin's extended exposure to the French air, it was carried by a political wave and limited by a political undertow. For that position was a silent one at best. He allowed the French to think of him as antislavery and to think of his America as one that would quickly abolish slavery's remnants, as his friend the Marquis de Condorcet came to believe, and perhaps as he himself had come to believe.[23]

He had begun to lose touch with Philadelphia and home. After fifteen years of political existence abroad, the rhetoric of the Revolution may have begun to seem more real to him than its realities. He certainly urged his countrymen to avoid luxury and live up to the picture of republican simplicity he sought to embody on the world stage.[24] His increasingly passionate advocacy of worldwide free trade, which he argued would eliminate the need for prohibitive taxes and colonial wars, seemed to befit a generally antislavery stance. During the late 1770s he had the pleasure of seeing this ethos elaborated in Adam Smith's *The Wealth of Nations*. Franklin and Smith were part of an antimercantilist vanguard that depicted slavery as an old-fashioned institution, kept up artificially by policy, and likely to fade away in a more rational, free future.[25]

Even when his musings on privateering and Atlantic warfare veered, as they inevitably did, toward the sugar colonies (which some Europeans worried would become American satellites) and slavery, he regularly redirected the matter to a more general indictment of mercantilism. He cited without disputing, for example, Helvetius's observation that because of the enslaving wars fomented in Africa to support sugar cultivation in the Americas, sugar ought to be imagined as "spotted with human blood." Yet he trumped this quintessential French Enlightenment condemnation of slavery by adding, "If he had considered also the Blood of one another which the White Nations shed in fighting for those Islands he would have imagined his Sugar not as spotted only, but as thoroughly dyed red." Franklin's numbers were all wrong: it is hard to believe that someone with his commercial knowledge and demographic expertise did not know that far more Africans had died in the middle passage (not to mention the plantations) than Europeans in all the colonial wars combined. Yet while antislavery spokesmen described how consumption implicated so many people in the sins of slavery, Franklin redirected attention to the other, political iniquities of the colonial world.[26]

In the end, he played very carefully with antislavery to gain peace and favorable trading conditions—including access to the Caribbean islands—for the new nation. Whether he believed that North American slavery was being eliminated or not, in other words, it was extremely useful to say it was. Everything Franklin did in France reflected the need to depict America as virtuous, solvent, and united in all particulars. Like Smith, he was arguing against the mercantile system and the logic of suppressing American trade. He had little reason to emphasize the wealth slavery produced in the tobacco-, rice-, and sugar-producing regions, much less the roots of his beloved northern states' prosperity in the West Indies trade.[27]

The rural idyll Benjamin Franklin helped to spread in Europe during the war years created a certain problem: he was deluged by letters about the prospects for settlement in the United States. In September 1782 he wrote a generic response entitled *Information to Those Who Would Remove to America*. He liked the piece enough to print it on his own press at Passy in 1784. In it Franklin depicted the quintessential American as a freeholder who works for himself, with his own hands: "America is the Land of Labour." Wages paid to immigrants translated directly into their ownership of landed property, as "Multitudes of poor people from England, Ireland, Scotland and Germany, have by this means in a few Years become wealthy Farmers." The "commodity" of "high birth" was worth next to nothing in the United States: what mattered about a man was *"What can he DO?"* It was the very opposite of an old world order based on the aristocratic extraction of all agricultural profit. Only denizens of those old world regimes would believe the false reports then circulating that "the [American] Governments not only pay the Expence of personal Transportation, but give Lands gratis to Strangers, with Negroes to work for them, Utensils of Husbandry, and Stocks of Cattle."[28]

Where were the slaves, the multiracial unfree labor force, in Franklin's postrevolutionary vision? They were ventriloquized, in West Indian dialect, into commentators on the Americans' propensity to work. The Americans "are pleased with the Observation of a Negro, and frequently mention it," Franklin asserted.

> that *Boccarorra* (meaning the Whiteman) make de Blackman workee, make de Horse workee, make de Ox workee, make ebery ting workee; only de Hog. He de Hog, no workee; he eat, he drink, he walk about, he go to sleep when he please, *he libb like a Gentleman.* According to these Opinions of the Americans, one of them would think himself more oblig'd to a Genealogist, who could prove for him that his Ancestors & Relations for ten Generations had been Ploughmen, Smiths, Carpenters, Turners, Weavers, Tanners, or even Shoemakers, & consequently that they were useful members of Society; than if he could only prove that they were Gentlemen, doing nothing of Value, but living idly on the Labour of others, mere *fruges consumere nati*, and otherwise *good* for *nothing*, till be their Death, their estates like the Carcase of the Negro's Gentleman-Hog, come to be *cut up.*

Like his use of African American voices half a century before, Franklin's ventriloquism here repays close attention. The slave trickster tale embedded in his essay depicts whites as exceptional slave-drivers who become hoglike in the process. There is an unmistakable criticism of slavery here, voiced in an Afro-Caribbean accent that readers would have recognized instantly.

But who is being criticized? By implanting the black dialect story in a paragraph contrasting the hardy *North* American citizenry with a European aristocracy that derived its land and wealth from birth, Franklin compared new world slavery to old world tyranny, and the American yeomanry emerged as the antithesis of both. Some white people might be gentlemen-hogs—maybe in the West Indies, as in Europe—but not in our America. If some Americans were driving "de black man," that was less important than the value they so virtuously placed upon labor. The larger comparison of Europeans versus Americans distinguished the United States of America from the Americas, from the slave societies that the West Indian accent of the Negro tale-teller otherwise signaled. Americans were whites, but not true slave-drivers like the white Caribbeans. The way they drove "de Blackman" and other beasts of burden reflected only their own greater national industry rather than their historical, and continuing, debt to slavery.

Despite having a say, the slave in the story was neither a victim nor a moral victor. He was an alibi. In other words, Franklin's minstrelization did more than miss the point of the slave's tale. It actually appropriated the stories being told by new world slaves, and thus obscured their very different understanding of whose labor had made America and their different prediction of who, in the end, might justly find themselves under the knife and "cut up" into pieces.

In Franklin's French period, as in his years in England, this kind of appropriation of antislavery for the purpose of justifying America trumped antislavery itself. No one did it better than Franklin; maybe no one could. When confronted with actual slaves during the war years, Franklin did as he had done in Philadelphia. Their plight was not to interfere with the normal workings of property or the normal rules of war. Franklin's seizure of victimhood, of the very idea of enslaved innocence, on behalf of the United States pushed the dilemma of America's slaves off the table.

During the peace negotiations Franklin countered demands that loyalists be reimbursed for their property losses with resolutions from the state of Pennsylvania "that all losses of Negro or mulatto slaves or servants, who have been deluded and carried away," should be compensated. Even masters in counties that did not suffer British invasion but whose slaves had run away were due compensation. (This was the same Pennsylvania Franklin had just written about as if it contained no slaves.) Lord Shelburne, an old friend of Franklin's, later recalled having heard from his agent Richard Oswald that "Franklin threatened to sell the German prisoners [in America] unless the Negroes were restored or paid for." To Henry Laurens, the South Carolina patriot with his own doubts about the morality of slavery, Franklin mocked General Sir Guy

Carleton's claim that "honor" stood behind his promise to take loyalist blacks with him when he left America. The real reason Carleton insisted on taking them, Franklin surmised, was that if the slaves were returned to their masters, Britain could never again threaten America by encouraging slave revolt. For Franklin, runaway slaves were the equivalent of loyalist traitors and foreign mercenaries; masters were the patriots.[29]

As the American representative, Franklin had an investment in the prewar status quo that trumped even his advancing antislavery image. Perhaps more than ever, he simply could not admit the claims of slaves. That reality extended to his entire household at Passy, where he lived with his grandson and secretary, William Temple Franklin. It drew in Jonathan Williams Jr. as well, Franklin's other surrogate during this period, the grandnephew who as a merchant and logistician did so much to make Franklin's French mission work.

During the summer of 1780 William Robeson, an officer active in South Carolina's start-up navy, wrote to Temple Franklin asking for help recovering Jean Montague. His slave had escaped just before Robeson planned to sail from France. Robeson had bought Montague from another naval officer who lived in Passy, and he thought the young man would try to return to his former haunts. On July 22 Benjamin Franklin wrote to the head of the Paris police to help Robeson get the "authority" under French law to reclaim Montague.[30]

Three days later Jean Montague himself wrote an eloquent letter to Franklin looking for help getting out of one of Paris's most notorious dungeons, one so foul that the king ordered it demolished that very year. Whether from personal experience or more likely from the great man's antislavery reputation in France, Montague apparently believed that Franklin would take his side against his master—or at least that he could leverage Franklin's philanthropy against his master's anger and French law. (Robeson evidently had got his search complicated by going to the authorities. A 1777 edict forbade people of color from being imported into France; they were to be held in custody until shipped and resold in the West Indies.) In his letter from prison Montague carefully requested only to be remanded to his master, asking Franklin to pass on his apologies and consider his youth (he was about fifteen) as an excuse. Within a few weeks Montague returned to the service of Robeson, probably through Franklin's intervention.[31]

Eight months later, though, Robeson and Montague were captured en route to America by the British and returned to France, separately. At some point afterward Montague decided he had had enough of Robeson. He had been smuggled back to Passy, but refused, through Temple Franklin, to return to his master unless Robeson sent him money and guaranteed his future freedom. Captain Robeson admitted to the younger Franklin that he had promised to bring Montague to America and set him up as a barber (probably in Philadelphia, where a hairdresser who knew French fashions could do very well) and to free him after he earned his sale price. It is also likely that Montague's skills had influenced his original sale to Robeson. Montague's skills also account for why, soon after arriving in Passy, he had other offers, which he told Temple he was considering, for *"he was tired of being idle"*—a way of putting the matter that directly challenged the stereotype of laziness that he would have faced when he ran away or tried, again, to renegotiate. Temple reported to Robeson that "this Black Gentleman, who seems to have a great Opinion of his Importance, [is] not willing to be governed by me." But Montague nevertheless trusted the Franklins enough to come live in their household a few weeks later.[32]

Robeson, in response, claimed to be a "bountiful and kind" master. He wrote that Montague lacked "the Gratitude of a Savage," a claim that Temple may well have discounted, given the source. Temple's motives are hard to discern, but they probably included sympathy, curiosity, and the fact that Robeson owed him money. He wrote about the matter to his cousin Jonathan, who also had dealings with Robeson, after Robeson asked Temple, in one of these exchanges, to get Williams to cover the debt. He soon learned that his usually even-tempered cousin was also completely fed up with the captain, who had promised to repay his debts with the proceeds of lands it turned out he had never owned. The United States, and Franklin's mission, desperately needed even deadbeat mariners. Consequently it is striking how quickly both young men came to doubt Robeson, who continued to owe them money through a series of bad luck voyages.[33]

Nevertheless, thanks to the young Franklin's mediation Montague finally agreed to return to Robeson, and a grateful Robeson paid off his debt to Temple, at least. There matters stood until the spring of 1782, when, just as Robeson prepared to sail a ship owned and loaded by Jonathan Williams for Philadelphia, Montague took off for either Paris or Bordeaux. This time the runaway had robbed his master, or so said

Robeson—thus giving Williams, to whom Robeson owed a substantial debt, reason to be financially interested in Montague's recapture. Williams apparently took Robeson at his word about Montague despite the captain's known habits of prevarication. Williams asked his cousin Temple to try to recapture the "rogue and thief" as soon as possible. Temple must have succeeded, because Montague was on another of Williams's ships, the *Trio*, bound for Virginia with a hastily assembled crew in November 1782.[34]

Montague never went anywhere easily. The motley crew of the *Trio* conspired with two English prisoners aboard and mutinied, sailing the ship into an Irish port as a war prize. Williams had no doubt who was to blame. He wrote to the new prime minister, Lord Shelburne, that "from the Negro's known Wickedness & knowledge of two languages I believe him the principal Author of the Revolt."

Despite a great many reasons to doubt anything Robeson had ever said about Montague or anyone else, Williams chose to be especially outraged by the mutiny. He enlisted his uncle, who cast the matter as another example of English corruption and theft. Franklin also wrote to the prime minister, decrying how "the corrupting of Servants, & hiring them to betray the Trust reposed in them, & rob their Masters of the Property confided to them, by sharing the Plunder among them, was one of the most infamous Modes of making war against America adopted by the late Administration."[35]

His master's double-dealing had given Jean Montague some temporary leverage with Franklin and family.[36] In the end, though, Franklin and his nephew saw the enterprising barber, runaway, and mutineer as a dupe of the English, or at best as another example of how selfless patriots like themselves were taken advantage of by the Robesons of this world.

No Granville Sharp was needed, however, to see that whatever really happened aboard the *Trio*, Montague was trying to reverse the series of misfortunes that had befallen him after he had been sold to a slaveowning confidence man who happened also to be an American patriot. Even at the war's successful close, Benjamin Franklin and his America ran further away from the mirror image that Jean Montague and his fellow fugitives presented them.

NINE

The Long Arm of Benjamin Franklin

Having arrived in France with the look of a plain American farmer, did it seem strange to Benjamin Franklin to leave Passy nearly eight years later in the French royal litter? No one begrudged the nearly eighty-year-old philosopher the chance to take the load off his gouty feet. Nor did anyone snicker at his appropriation of all the cabin space for his party aboard his vessel for Philadelphia, a strategy that insulated him from the German redemptioners who had sold themselves for seven years in order to get passage to America. If these servants-to-be had read his widely translated essay on immigration, they would not have worried about what was in store for them, or minded any aloofness displayed by the world's most famous American.

Neither his wife, his business partners, nor his legions of friends had outlasted his diplomatic missions. Nor had any of the household slaves he had purchased: George, the last of them, who had been an essential part of the household since James Parker sold him to the Franklins as a debt payment, passed away in 1781. William Franklin, exchanged as a prisoner during the war, remained in England. Father and son met briefly in coastal Southampton, where the ship docked, for a business-like transfer of their respective English and American properties.[1]

Both grandsons remained with the elder Franklin. He had turned them into young men of the world, and now he designed for them respective kinds of American "independence." Temple had not begun that way. The new government denied Franklin's grandson (the son of a Tory governor) the diplomatic post for which Franklin had groomed him, despite his evident experience as Franklin's secretary; being a Franklin did not always pay off. The elder Franklin had tried to make all right by proposing a marriage, this time between Temple and the daughter of his intimate friend Madame Brillon, much as he had once tried to get William wedded to Will Strahan's daughter. In the meantime, Temple fathered an illegitimate child of his own before leaving France. Still, the patriarch had an idea: Temple Franklin would take up farming, "the most useful, the most independent, and therefore the noblest of employments," on his father's New Jersey lands, fulfilling at least one part of his grandfather's script for self-made men.[2]

Benjamin Franklin Bache, seventeen, had been apprenticed to Franklin's own printing press at Passy, which was taken apart and packed for the voyage home. His job would be to repeat the past—to prove that Franklins could still work with their hands as well as with their mouths and minds. Seeing Benny toil at the press—wondering if his Swiss and French secondary education, his finishing at the university in Philadelphia, or his very name might unfit him for business or artisanship—did Franklin shut out memories of Benny Mecom, the once-gifted-but-now-lost nephew who had liberated himself from his keepers as British troops overran New Jersey in '76 only to be never heard from again? Or did the younger namesake's hard work make it easier to forget Mecom, to forget the past? This time Franklin made no plans to send his printer protégé south to make his fortune. Philadelphia would do.[3]

His daughter and son-in-law, Sally and Richard Bache, could not have greeted the patriarch more enthusiastically. Richard got into a small boat and rode out to meet the incoming ship. Sally collapsed in tears in her garden at the news. They put the Market Street houses at his disposal. Sally must have worried what the father who had chided her for attending to finery during the war would say about her household management now that he was actually back in the house. Richard, who had not been the son-in-law of Franklin's choice, had made himself serviceable as a merchant and assistant postmaster during the war. He had listened, as Franklin's real son had not, to the colonial agent's repeated warnings not to depend on nepotism or political sinecures and to deal in cash business only.[4]

Franklin had lost years of salary when he lost his colonial agencies. But as he reported to those who doubted America's prospects, land values in Philadelphia had risen. He was worth far more now than when he had left. He planned a major addition onto the house in which he would live—work to commence as soon as labor prices abated. When it was finished later in 1786, the building would contain a sixteen-by-thirty-foot study and library, lined from floor to ceiling with Franklin's 4,200 books.[5]

He was elected president of the Executive Council (the equivalent of the governorship) by Pennsylvania's legislature—unanimously, he noted proudly—and on days when his ailments made it difficult for him to trudge the quarter-mile to the state house, he would order his own sedan chair, a simplified version of the one Louis XVI lent him. Benjamin Franklin had a right to expect all the help he could get—few if any had done as much to secure American independence. But rather than throw himself into matters of governance and rely on the muscles of domestic servants, Franklin made it a first order of business to invent several devices to render himself self-sufficient at home. A chair he designed swung over to become a stepladder. Another, more comfortable chair had a pedal attached to a fan overhead, so the sitter could cool himself. A special shoe-shaped tub enabled him to sit up and read while taking lengthy medicinal baths.[6]

Finally, he created a device "for taking down books from high shelves." He called it "the *Long Arm*." This "simple machine," a wooden pole with a somewhat pliable end piece, extended not only its inventor's arms but also his legs, since it made mounting a ladder unnecessary. In an essay describing the machine Franklin referred to its end pieces, which grasped the desired book, as "the Thumb" and "the Finger" and to the cord pulled taut by an operator as a "sinew."[7]

He enjoyed showing off the Long Arm as much as the second-story library and the books it contained. Here was the self-made, self-contained man nonpareil. The device was as symbolic as it was practical. One visitor watched him struggle with a plate-laden tome of natural history, brushing off offers of help. When another tried to help him heat some water over a fire, "[he] thanked me and replied he ever made it a point to wait upon himself and although he began to find himself infirm he was determined not to encrease his infirmities by giving way to them." The heated water, it turned out, "was to shave himself which Operation he performed without a Glass and with great Expedition." Asked if he ever "employed a Barber," Franklin answered "no and continued nearly in the following words: I think happiness does not consist so much in particular pieces of good fortune that perhaps accidentally fall to a Mans lot as to be able in his old age to do those little things which [if] he was unable to perform himself would be done by others with a sparing hand."[8]

Whose sparing, untrustworthy hand did he have in mind? The eighty-year-old showed a striking lack of trust in servants and children, even as he took on a new round of responsibilities and sought to keep his household, his books, and his body in good working order. The Long Arm solved the aging Franklin's problem of "giddiness" when reaching to grasp his distant books, but even more so it addressed the problem of success. The more books Franklin had, the more arm and leg he needed. The more power he had, the more he found himself potentially dependant on others.

In a series of lighthearted but revealing, even therapeutic, essays that Franklin wrote but did not publish, he personified those vulnerable, sometimes rebellious limbs. While still in France, he played with the popular image of gout as a parasite on the limb: the disease becomes the doctor, scolding and throwing bolts of pain at Franklin, the seeming master of the body who has failed to take care of his charge. After Franklin returned to America, however, this imagery of talking extremities took on more political resonances. The Left Hand, in a short piece of 1785, writes a petition objecting to its second-class, laboring status. The sense of crisis in these writings referred most directly to Franklin's bodily health, but also applied to the American body politic.[9]

By the mid-1780s America's own laboring hands, inspired by the revolutionary upheavals they helped foment, had begun to talk back, some of them in tax revolts, others in petitions against slavery. Pennsylvania had an especially intense "critical period," which some blamed on the new, seemingly more democratic state constitution of 1776. Both state and national constitutions were said to be in flux. The government operating under the Articles of Confederation came under attack for being unable to control its member states, which were too influenced by the selfish whims of ordinary, nonpropertied people. Artisans and other working people in Philadelphia had in fact taken an unprecedented interest in the framing of new political systems during the Revolution. Gentlemen responded by talking of themselves as innovative manipulators of political frameworks, as architects of political houses.[10]

European newspapers reported on the seeming disorder, some gleefully, others worriedly. The ramifications for American credit abroad concerned nationally minded statesmen like Franklin. He responded with letters to his British and European friends insisting that "America is in a most prosperous situation." To his French friend Louis-Guillaume Le Veillard he boasted that stories of American distress were as false as the published reports of his capture and enslavement at the hands of the pirates of Barbary. American workers were all employed and getting high wages, he reported (defining workers, of course, in a way that excluded those who did not receive any wages at all).[11] Everything would be fine if people continued to produce, to have confidence, to trust in progress.

The stability, unity, and independence of the nation that he seemed to personify remained Franklin's abiding focus during these active years. Controversy, however, again came to his door, in the form of an invitation to serve as a delegate to the Constitutional Convention that would meet in Philadelphia, and a request that he join an expanded Pennsylvania Society for Promoting the Abolition of Slavery and the Relief of Free Negroes Unlawfully Held in Bondage. He accepted both invitations during the spring of 1787, not imagining how soon and how much they would conflict.

Joining the Pennsylvania Abolition Society was a significant public act for Franklin, but not nearly as significant or clear in its meaning as it might at first seem. A desire to celebrate Franklin's apparently exceptional antislavery activism among the Founding Fathers has led some writers of late to combine an older view of a doddering Franklin sleeping through the Constitutional Convention debates, waking just long enough to offer an occasional sage counsel on the need for unity, with a newer but hardly consistent picture of an elder statesmen crusading, with sudden energy, against the blight of slavery. A similar confusion, also due to a desire for an embraceable Franklin, emerged at the time of the convention itself, as onlookers scratched their heads about Franklin's seeming inconsistencies. As always, he responded with his pen.

At the founding moment Franklin's truly remarkable activity lay in matters of state, in nation-making. In antislavery he remained cautious, even passive, to the point of getting manipulated into an appearance of hypocrisy during the public debate over the Constitution. No unambiguous antislavery moment would come until 1790, weeks before his death, after he had retired from both state and national politics and contemplated his historical reputation and legacy anew. The result was the emergence of the antislavery Franklin that we have come to remember and to associate with most of his political career.

Even into 1786 Franklin's published writings that touched upon slavery still expressed outrage at British—not American—hypocrisy. He lambasted postwar British attempts to get southern planters to repay their extensive prewar debts because, he said, their means of profit and thus repayment—their slaves—had been stolen by the British themselves. At the same time, in private conversations and letters to antislavery men, he sounded more and more convinced of slavery's inherent injustice as well as its supposed inefficiency and its political risks. Like many northerners after the Revolution, he seemed to take it for granted that the slave trade would end and, as a consequence, slavery, too. Pennsylvania had, in 1780, passed a gradual emancipation measure, and other northern states began to follow suit.[12]

Yet he still kept his few strong statements about the wrongs suffered by Africans for the ears of the already converted. When Josiah Wedgwood, the extremely successful English pottery manufacturer, sent him some of the famous abolitionist cameos showing a kneeling slave asking "Am I Not a Man and a Brother?" Franklin bragged of distributing the samples "among my Friends" and observing their sentimental reactions, but they apparently went only to antislavery friends. To Benjamin Rush—who had published a biting antislavery pamphlet a full fourteen years before—Franklin "spoke in high terms against negro Slavery" and took credit for having printed Benjamin Lay's writings. Identifying himself with the antislavery cause to some of the nation's most active antislavery advocates fit with his acceptance of membership in the Pennsylvania Abolition Society: they kept up his enlightened reputation—an image quite useful in certain circles, especially in Britain and France. In 1787 one French poet imagined Franklin returning to America via Cuba and Saint Domingue, where he sheds tears over the ravages of Spanish colonial slavery. In the poem's grand finale, George Washington erects a great temple of liberty, but the enemies of liberty—Pride and Avarice—bar blacks and Indians from entering, until Dr. Franklin decrees that liberty and black slavery are incompatible and pleads for the freedom of all slaves in America.[13]

His image, in short, had gotten far ahead of him, and his America. Franklin could hardly turn down the invitation from the Abolition Society when it came, more than six years after Pennsylvania had become the first state to pass a gradual emancipation statute. The invitation, and his subsequent nomination to serve as its president, were part of the society's explicit push for greater public exposure in 1787. The precise shape of its change in strategy, though, still lay on the horizon. Franklin was not part of those deliberations. Subsequently he rarely if ever attended the meetings of the society that reelected him president every year until his death. Their resolves were conveyed to him by the other officers, sometimes for his signature; he played a more active role when only he could, such as in writing other state governors about possible infractions of laws regulating the slave trade. Franklin became publicly and in a certain restricted sense actively antislavery, taking a stand beyond privately cheering on activists, precisely when antislavery became both respectable in Pennsylvania and all but necessary in order to keep up his, and America's, international image.[14]

The decentralized federal system of the 1780s made it possible for Franklin's Pennsylvanian and French personae to come together, with no specific or necessary implications for the rest of the young nation. He could be provincial and international at once because the nation-state remained in an infant stage. Indeed, in his public writings for an international audience Franklin enjoyed and encouraged the moment's heady mix of provincialism and cosmopolitanism by depicting Pennsylvania, with its reduced slave population and its emancipation statute, as America writ small. Thomas Jefferson, his fellow American abroad, had been doing something very similar with respect to Virginia. Like Franklin, Jefferson, while in France, wrote optimistic pieces designed to counter bad British press while developing a longer work. In *Notes on the State of Virginia*, Jefferson said unambiguously that slavery was an evil that he hoped would soon be eradicated—and with it the presence of blacks, who, he hypothesized, were racially inferior. They certainly hated whites for the injuries they had suffered, and for both reasons they could never be free Americans. Jefferson's Virginian logic of 1787, like that of 1776, did not differ much from Franklin's. When he owned up to the problem of slavery in the *Notes*, Jefferson was writing for the same international audience. He took care that his manuscript did not get a wide circulation in the United States, delaying American publication as long as he could.[15]

Antislavery proved less easy to spin in the national construction site of the Constitutional Convention. The movement for a stronger national government directly opposed the liberties the states had taken with commerce and law, inconsistencies that in some instances made a mockery of America's claims to be united states. The need for a stronger national government became all the more obvious to continentally thinking statesmen (many of them from Pennsylvania and Virginia) after the British Orders-in-Council of 1783 closed the British West Indies to American ships, making an effective, enforceable American trade policy more urgent.[16] The free-trade utopia that Franklin advocated, wherein Atlantic nations would no longer fight over rights to slave-grown profits, had turned out to be as yet a dream.

To be strong enough to arbitrate regional and national economic interests and to be approved by the member states, the new government had to be so devised as to not excessively favor particular interests. Two issues, then—the issue of economic power, and the issue of representation—practically guaranteed that the question of slavery would indirectly but decisively occupy the framers at the Constitutional Convention. Along with slavery's inseparability from economic and constitutional questions came the opportunity for the framers to do something about the institution while they were forming a national government.

The flowering of state legislation that marked the critical period between 1776 and 1787 included the first steps against slavery in the northern states, and the revival of the slave trade. The Continental Congress had intermittently moved against the slave trade and nearly banned slavery from the new northwestern territories. A consensus existed in many, perhaps most parts of the country that slavery was inconsistent with American revolutionary principles and ought to be consigned to the dustbin of history. On the other hand, many southerners and pockets of slaveholding northerners had good reason to believe that the Revolution had been fought to secure their rights to property—including their property in persons. The state-based autonomy they had fought for included the right to import still more slaves as they saw fit.

As a result, the document produced by the Constitutional Convention was a study in ambiguity. The proslavery and antislavery aspects of the Constitution have been debated down to our time, but the debate began soon after its publication. James Madison's equivocal defense of the protection offered by the Constitution to slavery in some of his *Federalist*

Papers reflected in part his own sense that the most basic compromises hammered out by the delegates on the shape of the legislative branches reflected not political wisdom but rather sectional economic disagreements with roots, ultimately, in slavery. In other words, these aspects of the Constitution epitomized the localism that Madison's nationalist position was designed to overcome. In the convention and during the subsequent public debate, there continued to be proslavery and antislavery agendas, as well as powerful impulses toward accommodation. In short, no outcome was certain.[17]

As the "oldest delegate," Franklin played a crucial symbolic role from the start. He was also the local governor and so "host" of the convention. He attended the proceedings daily throughout the summer of 1787 and followed his traditional habit of making his contributions to oral debate sparing, short, and careful. Some of his best-known interventions took the form of pleas for calmness and compromise. He embodied this ethos on the central questions of representation and slavery.

Early on Franklin strongly argued for a one-house legislature apportioned by population. As in 1776, when the Articles of Confederation were first debated, the various schemes proposed for representation in government based on numbers raised the question of whether slaves would be counted. There were two issues here: would the slave population be counted when the federal government taxed the states based on population? And would they be counted toward figuring the number of members of the federal Congress? The issues could not be separated, in part because of the contemporary republican understanding that representation in government was a right tied to citizenship, and thus to taxation. Madison, Franklin, and others believed that population was the best guide to true wealth and thus tax policy. Yet slaves were surely not citizens, and slaveholders and nonslaveholders wanted them counted for one purpose but not the other. Meanwhile, states with large populations argued with the less populous states over whether each would vote equally in the legislative branch or have seats according to population.

The soon-to-be-infamous "federal ratio," by which slaves would count for three-fifths of their numbers for the purposes both of taxation and apportionment of House seats, reemerged during the convention in a suggestion made by Franklin in a special committee. The compromise of a two-house legislature emerged from this committee's meetings. The upper house would represent states equally; the lower house, where all

money-related bills would originate, would be proportional to population, with three-fifths of slaves counted for both representation and
taxation. Other compromises would be made on slavery in the convention—most notably, the provision allowing the slave trade to be banned,
but not until January 1, 1808. This first compromise, however, made all
the others, and the Constitution itself, possible.[18]

Franklin's crucial part in it, and his choice to subordinate his antislavery principles (such as they might have been), becomes visible from
a close attention to timing. On July 2, 1787, Charles C. Pinckney of
South Carolina, staunch defender of his state's rights in slaves, endorsed
Franklin's calls for compromise on the representation question and proposed the formation of a "grand committee" responsible for coming up
with a plan. Franklin was then elected to the committee, which met over
dinner for the first time that night at his newly renovated house. They
met again on July 3, took a holiday on the fourth for Independence Day,
and came to the Convention's next session on the fifth with the famous
compromise.[19]

In urging compromise and making it happen, Franklin made an active decision to hush his own earlier objection to what other northerners
would soon call "slave representation." It was not a matter of omission
merely. On the very same day that Franklin invited the committee to dinner, Tench Coxe, as secretary of the Pennsylvania Abolition Society, delivered to him an antislavery petition that the society asked him, as its
president and a constitutional delegate, to present to the Convention.
The society did not know the state of the secret debates, and Franklin
kept his oath not to tell them. He declined to present the petition, suggesting that it be left to "lie over for the present," as Coxe quoted him as
having said.[20]

Perhaps Franklin thought the compromise struck the best that could
be done. His fellow society member (and fellow delegate) Coxe agreed
with him about the petition and argued in an anonymous essay that the
Constitution's temporary ban on legislating the slave trade was actually
an antislavery victory, for it guaranteed that the trade could be ended,
eventually, by federal decree. Coxe and Franklin voted together, unsuccessfully, to try to keep southern delegates from extending the slave
trade clause from 1800, another committee's original recommendation,
to 1808. But together they acquiesced in the compromise.

Other Pennsylvania delegates, such as James Wilson, Gouverneur

Morris, and John Dickinson, feared that their constituents would rail at the compromises on slavery, which they did. One newspaper essayist expressed disbelief that Franklin would "encourage and connive at slavery." A New Yorker called him plainly hypocritical. Critics also suggested that he was too old to know what he was doing. Franklin took up his pen to prove them wrong. *They* were old-fashioned. He compared antifederalist skeptics, who criticized the motives of the federalist leaders, to the "Ancient Jews" who doubted Moses' real intention to deliver *them* from slavery. And in a piece he did not publish, he lambasted one writer's attempt to tar the proratification government of Massachusetts by comparing its unpopular tax policies with its toleration of its citizens' participation in the slave trade. The "abominable African Trade, may deservedly be condemned," Franklin wrote, but the state had never encouraged it, and New England had always contained the fewest slaves. Regional comparisons that brought up slavery were unjust and impolitic at a time when "British Newswriters" continued to "Blacken America."[21]

For Franklin, slavery remained primarily a tool in the hands of shortsighted politicians and foreign enemies. His America could afford to compromise with a Deep South that was actually more isolated than ever before, lacking its Caribbean hubs, if not its northern trading partners, for the first time. As usual, a few called him out on his attempt to have things both ways, to be all things to all people. As usual, he used secrecy and anonymity to his advantage. Some things had changed, but more remained the same. Neither slavery nor the slavery question was to get in the way of American revolutionary nationalism. For Franklin as for the Founders more generally, silence sufficed where compromise failed.[22]

Precisely because the Constitution was ambiguous where it was not silent on slavery, opportunities remained to test the meanings of the antislavery upsurge, the implications of nationalist reform, the text of the new national charter, and ultimately the legacy of the Revolution itself.

During the fall of 1789 the Pennsylvania Abolition Society, along with several of its Quaker-led sister groups, decided to petition the first federal Congress for an end to the slave trade and for other legislation to discourage if not abolish slavery. An ailing Franklin continued to serve as president of the society and continued to claim to have played his small role in the vanguard by printing Ralph Sandiford and Benjamin Lay so many years before. But there is little evidence that he decided to be more "outspoken" or considered his presidency of the Abolition Society the "moral crusade" or "final public mission" that recent biographers have described.[23] After a hard fall in late 1788 he had been unable to attend many of the later sessions of the Pennsylvania Executive Council. When his term as president of that body ended, he began to refer to himself as retired, finally, from public duty.[24]

By 1790 the society's strategy combined gentlemanly, enlightened persuasion, Quaker witnessing, and a newly aggressive plan. The real energy belonged to the vice president and Quaker merchant James Pemberton, who greatly appreciated Franklin's symbolic value and understandably did not ask him for anything more than his signature on public resolutions soliciting contributions. When the society decided to petition the first federal Congress to do something about the slave trade, it was Pemberton who conveyed the document to Franklin for his signature, suggested the wording of Franklin's cover letter to the speaker of the House and president of the Senate, and later led the mostly Quaker members of the abolition societies as they converged on the House of Representatives in New York to watch the debates from the gallery.[25]

Perhaps because the society had been stymied by Coxe and Franklin in 1787, the petition delivered to Congress with Franklin's signature was the most radical of the three presented that term. It condemned not just the African slave trade but slavery itself as an "abomination of human nature," in the kind of natural rights language Franklin himself almost never used. It also argued that the powers granted to Congress under the Constitution to promote the general welfare did in fact give that body ways to discourage slavery outside of a direct ban. That understanding fit precisely with the society's belief that only legal means, pursued through existing channels, would end the blight on the new nation. Franklin's stature was part of that strategy, but it was not his own. He had already passed the sword, not fully realizing that his famous name had in fact become the sword.[26]

The gauntlet had been thrown. In the Senate, which also received the petition, South Carolinians seized the floor. Pierce Butler began with "a personal attack on Dr. Franklin." According to Butler, who had been a delegate, "the Doctor When Member of Convention had consented to the Federal Compact. Here he was in clearest Violation of it." William

Maclay, the Pennsylvania senator who recorded the debates in his diary, objected that Franklin "could not Strictly have the Acts of the Society charged to his personal Account,"[27] and expressed surprise that his fellow opponents of slavery, Rufus King and Gouverneur Morris, refused to stand up in favor of Franklin. The reasons were political and economic. Southerners, as the House debates would reveal, were being courted by Federalists in favor of Treasury secretary Alexander Hamilton's plan for federal funding of state debts. The petition actually interrupted consideration of Hamilton's report in Congress. President Washington and Vice President Adams agreed that the timing and character of the petition rendered it a nuisance, and it was buried in the Senate.

In the House, though, the antislavery movement had more sympathizers. The petition was presented by House Speaker Muhlenberg himself, and nascent opposition leader James Madison, who had just announced his opposition to the funding scheme, expressed some sympathy for ending the slave trade. These congressmen were not initially cowed by Carolina members' threats of civil war; nor did they feel shame when reminded that their southern colleagues had lost many slaves in the war and could hardly bring a slave to Philadelphia without him or her being enticed to run away. So it was in the House that a full debate ensued over receiving the antislavery petitions and sending them to committee.

Another debate followed a month later, when the committee reported. Here too Franklin's seeming hypocrisy quickly came under attack. Thomas Tucker said that Franklin "ought to have known the Constitution better." The criticism became "acrimonious" in March, after the committee reported with a watered-down endorsement of some of the petition's goals. "The firmness of [Franklin's] mind has been suspected," announced an exasperated Elias Boudinot, after William Loughton Smith argued that a Franklin still in his right mind could not possibly turn intolerant against slaveholders, whom God himself had rewarded with prosperity.[28]

Smith was not the only one to question whether Franklin could be taken seriously. His fellow filibusterer James Jackson of Georgia, who reminded the Congress that (as Franklin had long maintained) the British were to be blamed for slavery, insisted on the venerable

Franklin's senility as the only possible explanation for his seeming change of heart and policy. Jackson wanted to have his heroic Franklin and his proslavery American Revolution but could not have both—not with Franklin's name on the petition. In his effort to square the circle, he went far toward arguing that slavery was a positive good, not just an inherited evil.

This was something relatively new. It made the matter far less ambiguous, especially for Franklin, who no longer had to worry about political reverberations. When he read the debates in the newspapers, Franklin, struggling against pain medication and all too aware of his failing health as he tried to complete his autobiography, decided to respond, anonymously, in print.

Jackson's speech, he wrote, reminded him of the response of the imaginary Sidi Mehemet Ibrahim, a leading counsel of Algiers, in 1687, when a sect petitioned him against piracy and the enslavement of Christians. In an extended quotation from the "African," Franklin had Ibrahim rehearse the deep southern argument. Without slaves, the economy would collapse. Compensated emancipation was impractical, not to mention unjust to owners. Besides, "were they not Slaves in their own Countries?" Didn't the Europeans enslave, too, and weren't the captives better off in sunny north Africa, where they could catch the light of Islam? Everyone knew that, if freed, they would not work and were not wise enough to govern themselves. The Koran permitted slavery. Finally, abolishing it might produce a civil war.[29]

As satire, it was brilliant, vintage Franklin. The use of Algerian piracy and white slavery, on the upswing in these years, blackened the deep southerners and turned the spotlight on their religious pretensions.[30] In a real sense, Franklin had turned the South into the new Britain: greedy, hypocritical, set against liberty. In doing so he indeed proved Jackson right: this was not at all the Franklin that he had come to know and love.

The Sidi Mehemet Ibrahim essay was not reported to be Franklin's for a long time, but the House debate, published in the newspapers he did so much to advance, broadcast his name in conjunction with antislavery and the Quaker-dominated movement. Afterward abolitionists, black and white, happily claimed Franklin as an antislavery Founding Father. It was not in their interest to see him as anything less than an example of progress and enlightenment, or to notice that before his death Franklin had begun to write that script for them.[31]

The *Autobiography*, published in nearly complete form for the first time in 1818, preached the virtues of hard work and time management, virtues that early-nineteenth-century white northerners increasingly claimed for themselves. In the memoir, which became the most popular work of its kind in American history, Franklin escapes all traces of the legacy of slavery. The text makes no mention of slaves or of the institution. He did not tell the story of the Revolution, either.[32] His life remains unfinished, but not incoherent. He argues for the inescapability of self-regard, the gap between public image and private truths, and above all for the virtue, and necessity, of silence.

When Franklin died on April 17, 1790, his will, which he had signed in July 1788, distributed his goods and funds carefully to his extended family and surviving friends. He forgave all his relatives and former partners their debts to him, in the process reminding everyone who had come out ahead in life and in history. He left very little to his only surviving son, mocking the exile for losing his claim to "an estate he endeavored to deprive me of." Benny Franklin Bache got Franklin's stock in trade, the printing shop; William Temple Franklin got his manuscripts. The son-in-law who had turned out well enough, who had given him a printing namesake, earned his Ohio and Philadelphia lands, plus the houses on Market Street. Richard Bache's bond for more than £2,100, plus interest, the largest of all the personal debts, would be forgiven too, "requesting, in consideration thereof, he would immediately after my decease manumit and set free his negro man Bob."[33]

Franklin had freed his first slave. He got the credit. The younger generation remained in his debt.

RUN away from George Mumford, of Fisher's-Island, the 27th Instant, four Men Servants, a white Man and three Negroes, who hath taken a large two-Mast Boat, with a square Stern, and a large white Pine Canoe; the Boat's Timbers are chiefly red Cedar. The white Man named Joseph Heday, says he is a Native of Newark, in the Jerseys; a short well set Fellow, of a rudy Complection; his Cloathing when he went away was a red Whitney Great Coat, red and white flower'd Serge Jacket, a Swan-Skin strip'd ditto, lapell'd, a Pair of Leather Breeches, a Pair of Trowsers, old Shoes, &c. The Negroes are named Fortune, Venture, and Isaac; Fortune is a tall slim comely well spoken Fellow, had on a Kersey Great Coat, three Kersey Jackets, and Breeches of a dark Colour, a new Cloth colour'd Fly-Coat, with a red Lining, a blue Serge Jacket, with red Lining, a new Pair of Chocolate colour'd corded Drugget Breeches, a Pair of blue and white check'd Trowsers, two Pair of Shoes, one of them new, several Pair of Stockings, a Castor and a new Felt Hat. Venture had a Kersey dark colour'd Great Coat, three Kersey Jackets, two Pair of Breeches of the same, a new Cloth colour'd Fly-Coat, with red Shalloon Lining, a green Ratteen Jacket almost new, a crimson birded Stuff ditto, a Pair of large Oznabrigs Trowsers, a new Felt Hat, two Pair of Shoes, one Pair new, several Pair of Stockings; he is a very tall Fellow, 6 Feet 2 Inches high, thick square Shoulders, large bon'd, mark'd in the Face, or scar'd with a Knife in his own Country. Isaac is a Mustee, a short Fellow, seemingly clumsy and stiff in his Gate, bushy Head of Hair, sower Countenance, had on a Kersey Great Coat, Jacket and Breeches as aforesaid, a new Cloth colour'd Fly-Coat, with Lining, a Pair of Trowsers, of Guinea Cloth, a new Felt Hat, Shoes and Stockings as above. Stole and carried away with them, a Firkin of Butter, weighs about 60 Pound, two Cheeses weighs 64 Pounds, and Bread for the same.

Whoever takes up and secures said Run-aways, so that their Master may have them again, shall have TWENTY POUNDS, New-York Currency, Reward and all reasonable Charges paid, or equivalent for either of them; or secure the Boat, that the Owner may have her again, shall be well rewarded, by
28 .   GEORGE MUMFORD.

George Mumford's ad for Venture Smith and his fellow fugitives, *New York Gazette and Weekly Post Boy*, April 1, 1754. (Courtesy of the New-York Historical Society)

Epilogue: Debts, or the Claims
of Venture Smith

How would the American Revolution look if Charles Roberts or Jean Montague had told the story? If we knew as much about the lives and perspectives of Joseph, George, Bob, Peter, Jemima, King, Othello, or any of the Franklins' slaves and servants as we do about Franklin? Surely the story would be different. But is theirs *a different story* altogether?

The memoir of Venture Smith, the first former North American slave to publish one, suggests otherwise. Indeed, Elisha Niles, who shepherded Smith into print, called him "a Franklin and a Washington in a state of nature, or rather in a state of slavery."[1] While condescending, this introduction was meant also as a compliment to a self-made man. Smith in fact shows us precisely how the state of slavery shaped the contours of his life, even after he bought his freedom. In his hands, the state of slavery becomes a state of history in which whites as well as blacks lived.

The first third of Smith's *Narrative* covers his five years in his native country, the despoliation of his nation, the murder of his father, and the enslaving war "instigated by some white nation" that resulted in his forced journey to Africa's coast. The middle part describes his own middle passage on a Rhode Island vessel across the Atlantic, with a stop in Barbados. He avoided the West Indies death trap after being bought by a ship's mate named Robert Mumford "for four gallons of rum and a piece of calico, and [who] called [me] VENTURE, on account of his having purchased me with his own private venture." Mumford brought him to his family home on Fisher's Island, New York, the same piece of land Charles Roberts hoped to win twenty years later in the lottery of 1757.[2]

The Mumfords were the epitome of the mixed economy of the eighteenth-century coastal North. They farmed; they fished; they carded wool for home use; they sailed the Atlantic and the Caribbean Sea; and they traded in slaves. Three generations existed in one household, and it was generational tensions among the Mumfords that Smith emphasized because of how they put the eight-year-old slave at personal risk. The eldest Mumford patriarch demanded that Venture hand over the key to his venturesome seagoing son's trunk. Refusing, the young slave earned the "confidence" of his master but soon had trouble with Robert Mumford's teenage son, who gave him contradictory orders whenever he had the chance. Smith makes it clear that the honorable slave could not expect good treatment in a land of ventures, where fathers had questionable power and sons had questionable prospects. His labor was a weapon—his own and others'—in the battles among men.[3]

In 1754, at the age of twenty-six, Smith decided to join the white indentured servant Joseph Heday and two fellow slaves in a fantastic plan to sail all the way to "the Mississippi." This rebellion came to little, though, because Heday betrayed the others, absconding with the valuable clothes they had taken, which the master listed in great detail in an ad placed in James Parker's newspaper. During this episode Smith, though naïve about geography and perhaps still too willing to trust whites, displayed the brilliant awareness of the system that would make such a significant difference in his life. He himself successfully "advertised," probably with a one-sheet broadside, for the thief Heday's capture! When Heday was brought to them, Smith and his fellow fugitives decided to turn themselves in and Heday as well.[4]

In Smith's mind, his honesty and hard work—characteristics that made him legendary in his community in the years to come—should have been enough to secure the Mumfords' forgiveness. At the very least it should have been clear that Heday was the true rogue. Instead, he found himself sold away from his wife and infant daughter within the year. Thus began a series of removals, abuses, and negotiations throughout coastal Long Island and Connecticut, in which Smith tried again and again to hang on to the money he managed to make "by cleaning gentlemen's shoes and drawing boots, by catching musk-rats and minks, raising potatoes and carrots, &c. and by fishing in the night, and at odd spells." He got one master to buy his wife and daughter, only to get caught in violent disputes between his wife and mistress. By the time he was thirty-six, he "had already been sold three different times, made considerable money with seemingly nothing to derive from it, been cheated out of a large sum of money" by another master, who held it for him and then sold him away, "lost much by misfortunes," but managed to buy, with an "enormous sum," his own freedom.[5]

No close reader of Franklin and Smith can miss the echoes of each in the other's memoir. Reading Smith, it is difficult not to conclude, as did his editor, that there but for the grace of law, prejudice, and luck went Ben Franklin. Smith wore homespun and counted the cost of everything in a desperate and ultimately successful quest to buy his wife, his sons, his daughter, and some land with which to support them. His consciousness of the bottom line was almost a parody of Franklin's way to wealth, his rhetoric a weird echo of Franklin's play with the relationships between people and capital. When Smith's teenage son Solomon was enticed by an employer to go whaling and died aboard ship of scurvy, he "lost equal to seventy-five pounds" he had paid for him. When he purchased his pregnant wife for forty pounds in 1772, he saved "having another child to buy." There is something disturbing about Smith's absorption of the cash nexus in his society, as disturbing, perhaps, as his self-liberation is inspiring.[6]

That, however, was not his main message. What Smith emphasized, again and again, was not his own worries about money, nor even his adaptation of whites' pecuniary strategies, but how whites (and sadly, a few blacks with no other resources at their disposal) took advantage of his marginal status to steal the fruits of his labor. To Venture Smith, the American North was a society of sharpers, of confidence men—and race was the name of the game. This truth was epitomized for him in a favor he had agreed to do for a Native American boatman who sailed Long Island Sound, and Elisha Hart, a Saybrook, Connecticut, shipmaster who owned a barrel of molasses on board. With granddaughter in tow, Smith, at the request of the boatman, went to tell Hart of the boat's arrival after it docked. Meanwhile, at the wharf, the barrel fell overboard and sank. The Indian could not pay for it, so Hart took Smith to court, making him pay £10 damages, on the dubious presumption that he had taken possession of or responsibility for the shipment.

Afterward Hart "insultingly taunted me with my unmerited misfortune." Memories of Africa, in this context, gave Smith more than an identity. They gave him the means to criticize: "Such a proceeding as this, committed on a defenceless stranger, almost worn out in the hard service of the world, without any foundation in reason or justice, whatever it may be called in a christian land, would in my native country be branded as a crime equal to highway robbery. But Captain Hart was a *white gentleman*, and I a *poor African*, therefore it was *all right, and good enough for the black dog.*"[7]

The American relationships Smith describes and the American injustices he details are the essence of his claim. In this light to say only that Venture Smith has a different story to tell, a story somehow beyond the "central events" of revolutionary America, seems a cheat.[8] In every episode he narrates, Venture Smith makes it clear that he mastered his own destiny but created that life in relationship to others, white and black. He forced the hand of masters, getting himself into situations where he could negotiate opportunities to work on the side, making the cash that would free him and his family. He also faced unusual limits, however, different in extent but not always in kind from those faced by slaves, servants, and younger sons. He lamented, above all, the loss of his own sons, who could not, or would not, follow the path he laid out. His story is one of revolutions achieved but also of great pain and loss.

But it is not sufficient to recover Venture Smith as a black Benjamin Franklin. Understanding Benjamin Franklin requires us to see that he was a white Venture Smith: a runaway who made good but who never escaped the lessons painfully learned, or the bottom line. Franklin, it might be argued, was the rare runaway who got away. His antislavery, like that of the American Revolution, was a runaway's antislavery: compromised, and compromising.

What Smith had a stake in remembering, Franklin had reason to forget. That is why Smith finished his story, and perhaps why Franklin's has remained untold.

Notes

———

PREFACE: INHERITANCES, OR
SLAVERY AND THE FOUNDERS

1. John William Ward, "Benjamin Franklin: The Making of an American Character," *Red, White and Blue: Men, Books and Ideas in American Culture* (New York, 1969), 125–40; Verner W. Crane, *Benjamin Franklin: Englishman and American* (Baltimore, 1936), 72; H. W. Brands, *The First American: The Life and Times of Benjamin Franklin* (New York, 2000).

2. David Brion Davis, *The Problem of Slavery in Western Culture* (Ithaca, N.Y., 1966), 4; Winthrop D. Jordan, *White over Black: American Attitudes Toward the Negro, 1550–1812* (Chapel Hill, N.C., 1967); Bernard Bailyn, *The Ideological Origins of the American Revolution* (Cambridge, Mass., 1967), 232–46; Edmund S. Morgan, "Slavery and Freedom: The American Paradox," *Journal of American History* 59 (1972), 5–29; Morgan, *American Slavery, American Freedom: The Ordeal of Colonial Virginia* (New York, 1975); David Brion Davis, *The Problem of Slavery in the Age of Revolution, 1770–1823* (Ithaca, N.Y., 1975); Duncan J. MacLeod, *Slavery, Race, and the American Revolution* (Cambridge, Eng., 1974); MacLeod, "Toward Caste," and Davis, "American Slavery and the American Revolution," in Ira Berlin and Ronald Hoffman, eds., *Slavery and Freedom in the Age of the American Revolution* (Urbana, Ill., 1983), 217–36, 262–82; William W. Freehling, "The Founding Fathers, Conditional Antislavery, and the Nonradicalism of the American Revolution," in his *The Reintegration of American History: Slavery and the Civil War* (New York, 1994), 12–33.

3. Benjamin Quarles, *The Negro in the American Revolution* (Chapel Hill, N.C., 1961); Quarles, "The Revolutionary War as a Black Declaration of Independence," in Berlin and Hoffman, eds., *Slavery and Freedom*, 283–304; Sidney Kaplan and Emma Nogrady Kaplan, *The Black Presence in the Era of the American Revolution*, rev. ed. (Amherst, Mass., 1987); Gary B. Nash, *Race and Revolution* (Madison, Wisc., 1990); Sylvia Frey, *Water from the Rock: Black Resistance in a Revolutionary Age* (Princeton, N.J., 1991); Peter H. Wood, " 'Liberty is Sweet': African American Freedom Struggles in the Years before White Independence," in Alfred F. Young, ed., *Beyond the American Revolution: Explorations in the History of American Radicalism* (DeKalb, Ill., 1993), 149–84; Marcus Rediker, "A Motley Crew of Rebels: Sailors, Slaves, and the Coming of the American

Revolution," and Billy G. Smith, "Runaway Slaves in the Mid-Atlantic Region during the Revolutionary Era," in Ronald Hoffman and Peter J. Albert, eds., *The Transforming Hand of Revolution: Reconsidering the American Revolution as a Social Movement* (Charlottesville, Va., 1995), 155–98, 199–230; Ira Berlin, *Many Thousands Gone: The First Two Centuries of Slavery in North America* (Cambridge, Mass., 1998), 217–365; Robert Olwell, *Masters, Subjects, and Slaves: The Culture of Power in the South Carolina Lowcountry, 1740–1790* (Ithaca, N.Y., 1998); Patricia Bradley, *Slavery, Propaganda and the American Revolution* (Jackson, Miss., 1998); Woody Holton, *Forced Founders: Indians, Debtors, Slaves and the Making of the American Revolution in Virginia* (Chapel Hill, N.C., 1999); Graham Russell Hodges, *Root and Branch: African Americans in New York and East Jersey, 1613–1863* (Chapel Hill, N.C., 1999); Paul Finkelman, *Slavery and the Founding Fathers* (Armonk, N.Y., 1996); Francis Jennings, *The Creation of America: Through Revolution to Empire* (New York, 2001).

4. Gordon S. Wood, *The Radicalism of the American Revolution* (New York, 1991), 7; Stephen Ambrose, "Flawed Founders: To What Degree Do the Attitudes of Washington and Jefferson Toward Slavery Diminish their Achievements?" *Smithsonian* (November 2002), 126–33; Thomas G. West, *Vindicating the Founders: Race, Class, Sex, and Justice in the Origins of the United States* (Lanham, Md., 2002), 1–36.

5. The division of revolutionary effects on slavery from slavery's possible relationship to the Revolution also permits historians of slavery to keep their distance from political history, contributing to the limits of both fields of inquiry. For critiques of this tendency, see James Oakes, *Slavery and Freedom: An Interpretation of the Old South* (New York, 1990), xvii–xix, 209; Oakes, "Slaves Without Contexts," *Journal of the Early Republic* 19 (1999), 106; Freehling, *Reintegration of American History*, vii–xi, 253–74; Christopher L. Brown, "The Politics of Slavery," in David Armitage and Michael J. Braddick, eds., *The British Atlantic World, 1500–1800* (New York, 2002), 214–32. The conventional division of history into before and after the Revolution, as well as an analytical division of causes from effects, has also played an important role. Bailyn set a precedent when he shifted toward consequences precisely when discussing slavery. Bailyn, *Ideological Origins*, 232–46.

6. Joseph J. Ellis, *Founding Brothers: The Revolutionary Generation* (New York, 2000), 108–13; Finkelman, *Slavery and the Founding Fathers*, 147, 163, 201n10, 202n27; Mary Frances Berry, "Ashamed of George Washington?" *New York Times*, November 29, 1997.

7. On forgetting, see Michel-Rolph Trouillot, *Silencing the Past: Power and the Production of History* (Boston, 1995); Joanne Pope Melish, *Disowning Slavery: Gradual Emancipation and "Race" in New England, 1780–1860* (Ithaca, N.Y., 1998); Norman Klein, *The History of Forgetting: Los Angeles and the Erasure of Memory* (New York, 1996); Albert Memmi, *Racism*, trans. Steve Martinot (Minneapolis, Minn., 2000); Ernest Renan, "What Is a Nation?" [1882], in Homi Bhabha, ed., *Nation and Narration* (London, 1990), 8–22.

1. RUNAWAYS AND SELF-MADE MEN

1. *The Autobiography of Benjamin Franklin*, ed. Leonard W. Labaree et al. (New Haven, Conn., 1964), 68–70.

2. *Autobiography*, 70–77.

3. John Van Der Zee, *Bound Over: Indentured Servitude and American Conscience* (New York, 1985).

4. For an important exception, see William Moraley, *The Infortunate*, ed. Susan E. Klepp and Billy G. Smith (1743; repr., Philadelphia, 1992). Van Der Zee discusses Moraley and most of the other indentured servants who left extensive first-hand testimony in his eloquent but neglected study, *Bound Over*.

5. Billy G. Smith and Richard Wojtowicz, eds., *Blacks Who Stole Themselves: Advertisements for Runaways in the Pennsylvania Gazette, 1728–1790* (Philadelphia, 1989); Graham Russell Hodges and Alan Edward Brown, eds., *"Pretends to Be Free": Runaway Slave Advertisements from Colonial and Revolutionary New York and New Jersey* (New York, 1994); Daniel Meaders, *Dead or Alive: Fugitive Slaves and White Indentured Servants Before 1830* (New York, 1993); Meaders, ed., *Eighteenth-Century White Slaves: Fugitive Notices*, vol. 1, *Pennsylvania, 1729–1760* (Westport, Conn., 1993). See also Smith, "Runaway Slaves in the Mid-Atlantic Region during the Revolutionary Era," in Ronald Hoffman and Peter J. Albert, eds., *The Transforming Hand of Revolution: Reconsidering the American Revolution as a Social Movement* (Charlottesville, Va., 1995), 199–230; and my own "Reading the Runaways: Self-fashioning, Print Culture, and Confidence in Slavery in the Eighteenth-Century Mid-Atlantic," *William and Mary Quarterly*, 3rd ser., 56 (1999), 243–72.

6. *Pennsylvania Gazette*, May 9, 1751, in Smith and Wojtowicz, eds., *Blacks Who Stole Themselves*, 34.

7. *Pennsylvania Gazette*, March 5, 1745.

8. Hodges and Brown, eds., *"Pretends to Be Free,"* 56–57, 294; *Pennsylvania Gazette*, April 4, 1745; Smith and Wojtowicz, eds., *Blacks Who Stole Themselves*, 114; *Maryland Gazette*, September 6, 1749; Clement Price, ed., *Freedom Not Far Distant: A Documentary History of Afro-Americans in New Jersey* (Newark, N.J., 1980), 40–42.

9. Hodges and Brown, *"Pretends to Be Free,"* 16, 297; Smith and Wojtowicz, eds., *Blacks Who Stole Themselves*, 26, 124; *Pennsylvania Gazette*, September 11, 1740, November 2, 1749; Steven C. Bullock, "A Mumper Among the Gentle: Tom Bell, Colonial Confidence Man," *William and Mary Quarterly*, 3rd ser., 55 (1998), 231–58; Graham Russell Hodges, *Root and Branch: African Americans in New York and East Jersey, 1613–1863* (Chapel Hill, N.C., 1999); Mechal Sobel, *Teach Me Dreams: The Search for Self in Revolutionary America* (Princeton, N.J., 2000).

10. W. Jeffrey Bolster, *Black Jacks: African American Seamen in the Age of Sail* (Cambridge, Mass., 1997), 40–41; Ira Berlin, "From Creole to African: Atlantic Creoles and the Origins of African-American Society in Mainland North America," *William and Mary Quarterly*, 3rd ser., 53 (1996), 251–88.

11. *Pennsylvania Gazette*, February 10, 1744, January 24, 1749, November 1, 1753; *New-York Gazette*, February 1, 1768; *New-York Mercury*, September 2, 1754; *New-York Weekly Journal*, May 16, 1737; *New-York Gazette* [Weyman's], July 4, 1761; Hodges and Brown, eds., *"Pretends to Be Free,"* 94, 123–24, 146–47. For an elaboration of these and subsequent points see Waldstreicher, "Reading the Runaways," 254–61.

12. Smith and Wojtowicz, eds., *Blacks Who Stole Themselves*, 19, 24, 36, 62; Hodges and Brown, eds., *"Pretends to Be Free,"* xxx, 69, 120; *New-York Weekly Journal*, April 15, 1734; *Pennsylvania Gazette*, September 4, 1740, June 4, August 6, 1747.

13. Hodges and Brown, eds., *"Pretends to Be Free,"* 5, 14, 20, 29, 42, 228; Smith and Wojtowicz, eds., *Blacks Who Stole Themselves*, 40, 41–42, 65, 123–24, 129–30, 136; *New-York Weekly Journal*, August 26, 1734, January 19, 1736; Thelma Wills Foote, "Black Life in Colonial Manhattan" (Ph.D. diss., Harvard University, 1991), 249.

14. Hodges and Brown, eds., *"Pretends to Be Free,"* 47, 228; Smith and Wojtowicz, eds., *Blacks Who Stole Themselves*, 74–75.

15. Victor Hugo Paltsits, "John Holt—Printer and Postmaster," *Bulletin of the New York Public Library* 24 (1920), 483–99; Layton Barnes Murphy, "John Holt, Patriot, Printer and Publisher" (Ph.D. diss., University of Michigan, 1965), 2–3; Beverly McAnear, "James Parker versus John Holt," *Proceedings of the New Jersey Historical Society* 59 (1941), 77–78; Leola A. Walker, "Officials in the City Government of Colonial Williamsburg," *Virginia Magazine of History and Biography* 75 (1968), 38; Kevin J. Hayes, "John Holt," *American National Biography* (New York, 1999), 11:100–01.

16. George Fisher, a dealer in coffee and wine who penned his memoirs sometime later in the eighteenth century, remembered Holt as a remarkably unscrupulous businessman with no qualms about using his position to his advantage. Fisher tells an astounding tale of courtroom lies, arson, and outright theft, each of which turns on the presence of slaves. "Narrative of George Fisher," *William and Mary Quarterly*, 1st ser., 17 (1908), 147–58.

17. Samuel Davies to John Holt, March 2, 1751, Benjamin Rush Papers, Library Company of Philadelphia; McAnear, "Parker versus Holt."

18. *Connecticut Gazette*, July 2, 1757, October 7, 1758; *John Holt v. Charles Roberts*, shelf 24, New Haven County Court Files, Connecticut State Archives, Connecticut State Library.

19. *Holt v. Roberts*, vol. 5, p. 199, New Haven County Court Records, Connecticut State Library; *Samuel Avery v. John Holt*, Samuel Avery Papers, New York Public Library. The punishment of lengthening servitude was a distinctly colonial invention. Paul Craven and Douglas Hay, "The Criminalization of 'Free' Labour: Master and Servant in Comparative Perspective," in Paul Lovejoy and Nicholas Rogers, eds., *Unfree Labour in the Development of the Atlantic World* (London, 1994), 82–83.

20. *New York Gazette and Weekly Post Boy*, April 15, 1762; *Avery v. Holt*, Avery Papers.

21. *New York Gazette and Weekly Post Boy*, April 15, 29, May 6, 1762; *New-York Mercury*, March 29, April 19, 26, May 3, 10, 1762; *New-York Gazette* [Weyman's], April 1, 29, 1762. Holt moved his ad to the front page on May 6. It also appeared in the *Pennsylvania Gazette*.

22. James Parker to John Holt, various dates, New-York Historical Society; McAnear, "Parker versus Holt," 82–95, 198–212; *Avery v. Holt*, Avery Papers; Benjamin Franklin (hereafter BF) to Jared Ingersoll, December 19, 1763, James Parker to BF, June 6, 1766, in *The Papers of Benjamin Franklin*, ed. Leonard W. Labaree et al. (New Haven, Conn., 1959–) (hereafter *PBF*), 10:402–3, 11:416, 13:302–5; Parker to Ingersoll, April 6, 1767, June 1767, Papers Related to James Parker, Beinecke Rare Book and Manuscript Library, Yale University; Parker to Ingersoll, October 11, 1767, Jared Ingersoll Papers, New-Haven Colony Historical Society: Alan Dyer, *A Biography of James Parker, Colonial Printer* (Troy, N.Y., 1982), xi, 58–59, 69–70, 80, 95–110, 171n30.

23. James Lemon, *The Best Poor Man's Country: A Geographical Study of Early Southeastern Pennsylvania* (Baltimore, Md., 1972).

24. Edmund S. Morgan, *American Slavery, American Freedom: The Ordeal of Colonial Virginia* (New York, 1975); Philip D. Morgan, *Slave Counterpoint: Black and White Culture in the Eighteenth-Century Chesapeake and Lowcountry* (Chapel Hill, N.C., 1998); Berlin, *Many Thousands Gone: The First Two Centuries of Slavery in North America* (Cambridge, Mass., 1998).

25. Eric Williams, *Capitalism and Slavery* (1944; repr., New York, 1966); David Brion Davis, *The Problem of Slavery in Western Culture* (Ithaca, N.Y., 1966); Davis, *Slavery and Hu-*

man Progress (New York, 1984); Fernand Braudel, *Civilization and Capitalism 15th–18th Centuries*, vol. 2, *The Wheels of Commerce*, trans. Sian Reynolds (1979; New York, 1982), 272, 383; Robin Blackburn, *The Making of New World Slavery: From the Baroque to the Modern, 1492–1800* (London, 1996); Stanley Engerman, "The Atlantic Economy of the Eighteenth Century: Some Speculations on Economic Development in Britain, America, Africa and Elsewhere," *Journal of European Economic History* 24 (1995), 145; James Oakes, *The Ruling Race: A History of American Slaveholders* (New York, 1982); Oakes, *Slavery and Freedom: An Interpretation of the Old South* (New York, 1990); Joyce Chaplin, *An Anxious Pursuit: Agricultural Innovation and Modernity in the Lower South, 1730–1815* (Chapel Hill, N.C., 1993); Jeffrey Robert Young, *Domesticating Slavery: The Master Class in Georgia and South Carolina, 1670–1837* (Chapel Hill, N.C., 1999); Anne Norton, *Alternative Americas: A Reading of Antebellum Political Culture* (Chicago, 1986); Mark M. Smith, *Mastered by the Clock: Time, Slavery, and Freedom in the American South* (Chapel Hill, N.C., 1997).

26. John J. McCusker and Russell Menard, *The Economy of British North America* (Chapel Hill, N.C., 1985); Barbara L. Solow, "Capitalism and Slavery in the Exceedingly Long Run," in Solow and Stanley L. Engerman, eds., *British Capitalism and Caribbean Slavery: The Legacy of Eric Williams* (New York, 1987), 51–77; Solow, "Slavery and Colonization" and David Richardson, "Slavery, Trade, and Economic Growth in Eighteenth-Century New England," in Solow, ed., *Slavery and the Rise of the Atlantic System* (New York, 1991), 21–42, 237–64; David Eltis, "Slavery and Freedom in the Early Modern World," in Stanley L. Engerman, ed., *Terms of Labor: Slavery, Serfdom, and Free Labor* (Stanford, Calif., 1999), 25–49; Bernard Bailyn, "Slavery and Population Growth in Colonial New England," in Peter Temin, ed., *Engines of Enterprise: An Economic History of New England* (Cambridge, Mass., 2000), 253–60.

27. Arthur L. Jensen, *The Maritime Commerce of Colonial Philadelphia* (Madison, Wisc., 1963); Gary B. Nash, *The Urban Crucible: Social Change, Political Consciousness, and the Origins of the American Revolution* (Cambridge, Mass., 1979), 121; Edward G. Burrows and Mike Wallace, *Gotham: A History of New York City to 1898* (New York, 1999), 119–20, 126–28, 150, 170; Ian K. Steele, *The English Atlantic, 1675–1740: An Exploration of Communication and Community* (New York, 1986), 32–35, 53, 62, 68–76, 130; McCusker and Menard, *Economy of British North America*, 197–98; James G. Lydon, "Philadelphia's Commercial Expansion, 1720–1739," *Pennsylvania Magazine of History and Biography* 91 (1967), 401–18; Lemon, *Best Poor Man's Country*, 122, 219, 223; Nash, *Urban Crucible*, 120–21; T. H. Breen, "An Empire of Goods: The Anglicization of Colonial America, 1690–1776," *Journal of British Studies* 25 (1986), 467–99; Breen, " 'Baubles of Britain': The American and British Consumer Revolutions of the Eighteenth Century," *Past and Present* 119 (1988), 73–104; Cary Carson, Ronald Hoffman, and Peter J. Albert, eds., *Of Consuming Interests: The Style of Life in the Eighteenth Century* (Charlottesville, Va., 1994); Richard Bushman, *The Refinement of America: Persons, Houses, Cities* (New York, 1992); Jon Butler, *Becoming America: The Revolution Before 1776* (Cambridge, Mass., 2000), 137–84.

28. Darold D. Wax, "Negro Imports into Pennsylvania, 1720–1766," *Pennsylvania History* 72 (1965), 254–56; Jean R. Soderlund, "Black Importation and Migration into Southeastern Pennsylvania," *Proceedings of the American Philosophical Society* 133, no. 2 (June 1989), 145–53; Foote, "Black Life in Colonial Manhattan," 22–23, 41–43, 46–52; Berlin, *Many Thousands Gone*, 56–57.

29. Bernard Bailyn, *Voyagers to the West* (New York, 1986); Marilyn C. Baseler, *"Asylum for*

Mankind": America, 1607–1800 (Ithaca, N.Y., 1998); Aaron Spencer Fogelman, "From Slaves, Convicts and Servants to Free Passengers: The Transformation of Immigration in the Era of the American Revolution," *Journal of American History* 85 (1998), 43–76; Marianne S. Wokeck, *Trade in Strangers: The Beginnings of Mass Migration to North America* (Philadelphia, 2001).

30. Moraley, *Infortunate*, 93.

31. Sharon Salinger, *"To Serve Well and Faithfully": Labor and Indentured Servitude in Colonial Pennsylvania* (New York, 1987), 15, 71, 81; Darold D. Wax, "The Demand for Slave Labor in Colonial Pennsylvania," *Pennsylvania History* 34 (1967), 331–45; Wax, "Negro Import Duties in Colonial Pennsylvania," *Pennsylvania Magazine of History and Biography* 87 (1973), 26–44; James G. Lydon, "New York and the Slave Trade, 1700 to 1774," *William and Mary Quarterly*, 3rd ser., 35 (1978), 375–96; Gary B. Nash and Jean R. Soderlund, *Freedom by Degrees: Emancipation in Pennsylvania and Its Aftermath* (New York, 1990), 3–41; Christine Daniels, "Shadowlands: Freedom and Unfreedom in Anglo-America" (paper presented at the American Historical Association, Washington, D.C., January 1999); Jacqueline Jones, *American Work: Four Centuries of Black and White Labor* (New York, 1998), 125–68.

32. Christopher Hanes, "Turnover Cost and the Distribution of Slave Labor in Anglo-America," *Journal of Economic History* 56 (1996), 307–30; Steven Deyle, " 'By farr the most profitable trade': Slave Trading in British Colonial North America," *Slavery and Abolition* 12 (1989), 116–17; James A. Rawley, *The Transatlantic Slave Trade: A History* (New York, 1981), 385–418; Jean R. Soderlund, *Quakers and Slavery: A Divided Spirit* (Princeton, N.J., 1985), 54–86; A. J. Williams-Myers, "Hands That Picked No Cotton: An Exploratory Examination of African Slave Labor in the Colonial Economy of the Hudson River Valley to 1800," *Afro-Americans in New York Life and History* 11 (1987), 25–51; Foote, "Black Life in Colonial Manhattan," 23, 41–52; Edgar J. McManus, *Black Bondage in the North* (Syracuse, N.Y., 1973), 13–14, 47–51; Richard Shannon Moss, *Slavery on Long Island: A Study in Local Institutional and Early African-American Communal Life* (New York, 1993), 79–81, 97; Graham Russell Hodges, *Slavery and Freedom in the Rural North: Monmouth County, New Jersey, 1665–1865* (Madison, Wisc., 1997).

33. O. Nigel Bolland, "Proto-Proletarians? Slave Wages in the Americas," in Mary Turner, ed., *From Chattel Slaves to Wage Slaves: The Dynamics of Labour Bargaining in the Americas* (London, 1995), 123–47; John Bezís-Selfa, "Slavery and the Disciplining of Free Labor in the Colonial Mid-Atlantic Iron Industry," *Pennsylvania History* 64, suppl. (1997), 270–86; David Galenson, "Labor Market Behavior in Colonial America: Servitude, Slavery, and Free Labor," in Galenson, ed., *Markets in History: Economic Studies of the Past* (New York, 1989), 51–96; Galenson, "The Settlement and Growth of the Colonies: Population, Labor, and Economic Development," in Stanley L. Engerman and Robert E. Gallman, eds., *The Cambridge Economic History of the United States*, vol. 1, *The Colonial Era* (New York, 1996), 176, 207; Baseler, *"Asylum for Mankind."*

34. Robert J. Steinfeld, *The Invention of Free Labor: The Employment Relation in English and American Law and Culture, 1350–1870* (Chapel Hill, N.C., 1991), 107–16; Francis D. Pingeon, "Slavery in New Jersey on the Eve of Revolution," in William C. Wright, ed., *New Jersey in the American Revolution*, rev. ed. (Trenton, N.J., 1974), 58; McManus, *A History of Negro Slavery in New York* (Syracuse, N.Y., 1966), 32, 47–53; *New York Gazette and Weekly Post Boy*, September 13, 1764, February 21, March 7, April 25, May 31, June 13, November 28, 1765, May 3, 1766, August 28, 1770.

35. For the surprising mobility of slaves in the early plantation South, see Alex Bontemps, *The Punished Self: Surviving Slavery in the Colonial South* (Ithaca, N.Y., 2001), 178.

36. Christopher Hill, *Liberty Against the Law: Some Seventeenth-Century Controversies* (New York, 1996), 162; Nicholas Rogers, "Vagrancy, Impressment, and the Regulation of Labor in Eighteenth-Century Britain," *Slavery and Abolition* 15 (1994), 102–13; Marcus Rediker, "Good Hands, Stout Heart, and Fast Feet: The History and Culture of Working People in Early America," in Geoff Eley and William Hunt, eds., *Reviving the English Revolution: Reflections and Elaborations on the Work of Christopher Hill* (London, 1988), 236; Rediker, *Between the Devil and the Deep Blue Sea: Merchant Seamen, Pirates, and the Anglo-American Maritime World, 1700–1750* (New York, 1987); Peter Linebaugh, *The London Hanged: Crime and Civil Society in Eighteenth-Century England* (New York, 1992), 119–52, 169–70; Peter Linebaugh and Marcus Rediker, *The Many-Headed Hydra: Sailors, Slaves, Commoners, and the Hidden History of the Revolutionary Atlantic* (Boston, 2000); Kenneth Morgan, *Slavery, Colonialism, and the Atlantic World, 1660–1800* (Cambridge, Eng., 2000); Williams, *Capitalism and Slavery*; Solow, ed., *Slavery and the Rise of the Atlantic System*; Blackburn, *Making of New World Slavery*, 371–99, 509–80; David Eltis, *The Rise of African Slavery in the Americas* (New York, 2001), 258–80; Joseph E. Inikori, *Africans and the Industrial Revolution in England* (Cambridge, Eng., 2002).

37. Daniels, "Shadowlands"; Baseler, *"Asylum for Mankind,"* 99–102. See the examples from the narratives of indentured servants in Van Der Zee, *Bound Over*.

38. Moraley, *Infortunate*, 94; Winthrop D. Jordan, *White over Black: American Attitudes Toward the Negro, 1550–1812* (Chapel Hill, N.C., 1967); A. Leon Higginbotham Jr., *In the Matter of Color: Race and the Presumptions of the American Legal Process* (New York, 1978).

39. *Pennsylvania Gazette*, October 1 (prospectus), November 2, 1728; Smith and Wojtowicz, eds., *Blacks who Stole Themselves*; Meaders, ed., *Eighteenth-Century White Slaves*; Carl Van Doren, *Benjamin Franklin* (New York, 1938), 123, 129. For the number of ads, see the table in Waldstreicher, "Reading the Runaways," 250.

40. BF, "Accounts Posted or Ledger" [Ledgers A and B], Benjamin Franklin Papers, American Philosophical Society (hereafter APS), copy in Benjamin Franklin Collection, Yale University; *Pennsylvania Gazette*, September 12, 1732, June 20, 1734, October 2, 1735, September 8, 1738, August 9, 1739, September 4, December 4, 1740, September 3, 1741, January 6, July 22, December 2, 1742, December 6, 1745, September 4, 1746, May 7, 1747; *Pennsylvania Gazette*, May 3, 1733, May 22, 1734, June 12, 1740, in *PBF* 1:345, 378, 2:287; Waldstreicher, "Reading the Runaways," 268–72.

41. Jürgen Habermas, *The Structural Transformation of the Public Sphere*, trans. Thomas Berger and Frederick Lawrence (1962; Cambridge, Mass., 1989); Michael Warner, *The Letters of the Republic: Publication and the Public Sphere in Eighteenth-Century America* (Cambridge, Mass., 1990).

42. Claude-Anne Lopez and Eugenia W. Herbert, *The Private Franklin: The Man and His Family* (New York, 1975), 296–302, and more recently Lopez's "Franklin and Slavery: A Sea Change" in her *My Life with Benjamin Franklin* (New Haven, Conn., 2000), 196–205.

43. Nash and Soderlund, *Freedom by Degrees*, ix–xiv. In Franklin's will of 1757 two slaves, Peter and Jemima, were to be freed after his death, but he took Peter and another slave, King, to England with him that year. King ran away in 1760. Another slave, George,

served the family until his death in 1781. BF, Last Will and Testament [1757], in *PBF* 7:203; BF to Abiah Franklin, April 12, 1750, in *PBF* 3:474; BF to Deborah Franklin, February 19, 1758, June 27, 1760, in *PBF* 7:380 and 9:174; Deborah Franklin to BF, February 10, 1765, February 5–8, 1766, June 30, 1772, in *PBF* 12:45, 13:117–18, 19:192.

44. Nash and Soderlund carefully stated that Franklin only "probably acquired his first slaves in the late 1740s" but implied that his success in trade would in fact have made it unusual for him to not have owned any slaves earlier.

45. Bills from E. E. [H. S.] Warner and Charles Moore, vol. 66, folios 46a and 71a, Benjamin Franklin Papers, APS. Joseph Rose was the son of Aquila Rose, a highly respected printer and poet who had worked for Andrew Bradford and served as clerk of the assembly. In 1742 he would have been at least nineteen and possibly twenty-two years old. It seems surprising that Franklin would have held Joseph for eleven years or even longer. The hatter Moore may have assumed that Rose was still a servant. On the other hand, other scholars have stated that Rose was free, foreman of the shop, or even no longer present in Franklin's household by 1742. *Pennsylvania Gazette*, June 28, 1739, August 13, 1741; Joseph Rose to Jacob Taylor, November 11, 1741, *Pennsylvania Magazine of History and Biography* 3 (1879), 114–15; Joseph Rose, ed., *Poems on Several Occasions, by Aquila Rose* (Philadelphia, 1740); *PBF* 2:238–39n7; *Benjamin Franklin's Autobiography*, ed. J. A. Leo Lemay and P. M. Zall (New York, 1986), 54, 197; Van Doren, *Benjamin Franklin*, 125.

2. FATHERS, BROTHERS, AND MASTERS

1. *The Autobiography of Benjamin Franklin*, ed. Leonard W. Labaree et al. (New Haven, Conn., 1964), 43–56; Cynthia S. Jordan, *Second Stories: The Politics of Language, Form, and Gender in Early American Fictions* (Chapel Hill, N.C., 1989), 27–57.

2. *Autobiography*, 46–48; Genealogy, in *PBF* 1:l–liii.

3. *Autobiography*, 51; Arthur Bernon Tourtellot, *Benjamin Franklin: The Shaping of Genius* (New York, 1977), 42–46.

4. Genealogy, in *PBF* 1:lvi; Tourtellot, *Benjamin Franklin*, 34–35.

5. *Autobiography*, 49; *PBF* 1:3.

6. *Autobiography*, 54; William Temple Franklin, *Memoirs of the Life and Writings of Benjamin Franklin* (London, 1818), 1:447.

7. *Autobiography*, 52–53; "Verses From Benjamin Franklin (the Elder)," in *PBF* 1:3, 5; Carl Van Doren, *Jane Mecom: The Favorite Sister of Benjamin Franklin* (New York, 1950), 9.

8. *Autobiography*, 52–53. Tourtellot argues that young Franklin's lack of religiosity was the primary reason for the change, in *Benjamin Franklin*, 155–56.

9. Van Doren, *Jane Mecom*, 8; Marcus Rediker, *Between the Devil and the Deep Blue Sea: Merchant Seamen, Pirates, and the Anglo-American Maritime World, 1700–1750* (New York, 1987), 169–79.

10. Two brothers born after Josiah Jr., Ebenezer and Thomas, had died in 1703 and 1706, respectively. Genealogy, in *PBF* 1:lvi.

11. Genealogy, in *PBF*, 1:lvii, lix; *Autobiography*, 53, 57. On apprenticeship fees, see Lawrence William Towner, *A Good Master Well Served: Masters and Servants in Colonial Massachusetts, 1650–1750* (New York, 1998), 28.

12. *Autobiography*, 58–59.

13. Compare Rediker, *Between the Devil and the Deep Blue Sea*; Daniel Vickers and Vince Walsh, "Young Men and the Sea: The Sociology of Seafaring in Eighteenth-Century Salem, Massachusetts," *Social History* 24 (1999), 17–38.

14. Jacob Price, "Economic Function and the Growth of American Port Towns in the Eighteenth Century," *Perspectives in American History* 8 (1974), 143; Gary B. Nash, *The Urban Crucible: Social Change, Political Consciousness, and the Origins of the American Revolution* (Cambridge, Mass., 1979), 13, 54–57; Nian-Shen Huang, "Franklin's Father Josiah: Life of a Colonial Boston Tallow Chandler, 1657–1745," in *Transactions of the American Philosophical Society* 90, no. 3 (2001), 33–37; David Conroy, *In Public Houses: Drink and the Revolution of Authority in Colonial Massachusetts* (Chapel Hill, N.C., 1997). Boston's Long Wharf was built during the early 1710s. Phyllis Whitman Hunter, *Purchasing Identity in the Atlantic World: Massachusetts Merchants, 1690–1760* (Ithaca, N.Y., 2001), 1, 86.

15. Compare the figures in George H. Moore, *Notes on the History of Negro Slavery in Massachusetts* (New York, 1866), 50; Bridenbaugh, *Cities in the Wilderness: The First Century of Urban Life in America, 1625–1742* (New York, 1938), 249; Lorenzo J. Greene, *The Negro in Colonial New England* (1942; repr., New York, 1966), 80–81; Nash, *Urban Crucible*, 106–7; ·Robert E. Desrochers Jr., "Slave-for-Sale Advertisements and Slavery in Massachusetts, 1704–1781," *William and Mary Quarterly*, 3rd ser., 59 (July 2002), 623–64.

16. G. B. Warden, *Boston, 1689–1776* (Boston, 1970), 25–26; Miller, *New England Mind*, esp. bk. 3; Thomas Kidd, "From Puritan to Evangelical: Changing Culture in New England, 1690–1740" (Ph.D. diss., University of Notre Dame, 2001).

17. Huang, "Franklin's Father Josiah," 52–54, 73–75.

18. *Boston News-Letter*, June 15 and August 3, 1713; *New England Courant*, July 16, 1722; Van Doren, *Jane Mecom*, 13–14; Huang, "Franklin's Father Josiah," 67–72.

19. Lawrence Towner, " 'A Fondness for Freedom': Servant Protest in Puritan Society," *William and Mary Quarterly*, 3rd ser., 19 (1962), 201–19; Greene, *Negro in Colonial New England*.

20. Sidney Kaplan, "Introduction," Samuel Sewall, *The Selling of Joseph: A Memorial* (1700; repr., Boston, 1967); Ola Elizabeth Winslow, *Samuel Sewall of Boston* (New York, 1964), 70, 166; David Brion Davis, *The Problem of Slavery in Western Culture* (Ithaca, N.Y., 1966), 362–68; Lawrence W. Towner, "The Sewall-Saffin Dialogue on Slavery," *William and Mary Quarterly*, 3rd ser., 21 (1964), 40–52; Albert J. Von Frank, "John Saffin: Slavery and Racism in Colonial Massachusetts," *Early American Literature* 29 (1994), 254–72.

21. *Autobiography*, 58; Phyllis Franklin, *Show Thyself a Man: A Comparison of Benjamin Franklin and Cotton Mather* (The Hague, 1969), 44–45; Cotton Mather, *Bonifacius: An Essay Upon the Good*, ed. David R. Levin (Cambridge, Mass., 1966), 54; Mather, *Good Master*, 38, cited in Towner, " 'Fondness for Freedom,' " 210; Winthrop D. Jordan, *White over Black: American Attitudes Toward the Negro, 1550–1812* (Chapel Hill, N.C., 1967), 200–202; Richard Slotkin, "Narratives of Negro Crime in New England, 1675–1800," *American Quarterly* 25 (1973), 8–12. Writing to Mather's son in 1784, Franklin affected to have read an edition that was missing "several leaves"—a wry joke, or a Freudian slip, attesting to his selective reading of Mather. BF to Samuel Mather, May 12, 1784, in *Benjamin Franklin: Writings*, ed. J. A. Leo Lemay (New York, 1987), 1092.

22. *Diary of Cotton Mather, 1709–1724*, Massachusetts Historical Society *Collections*, 7th ser., vol. 8 (Boston, 1912), 139, 363, 446, 456, 467, 562; *Selected Letters of Cotton*

Mather, ed. Kenneth Silverman (Baton Rouge, La., 1971), 214–15; Silverman, *The Life and Times of Cotton Mather* (New York, 1984), 264. Onesimus eventually bought his freedom with funds sufficient to buy Mather another slave (and promised to add £5 more later). Towner, *Good Master Well Served*, 146–47.

23. On the Mathers and their quests for authority, see especially Miller, *From Colony to Province*; Robert Middlekauff, *The Mathers, Three Generations of Puritan Intellectuals* (New York, 1971); Darren M. Staloff, *The Making of an American Thinking Class: Intellectuals and Intelligentsia in Puritan Massachusetts* (New York, 1998).

24. Keith Arbour, "James Franklin: Apprentice, Artisan, Dissident and Teacher," *Papers of the Bibliographical Society of America* 94 (2000), 348–73; Jeffrey A. Smith, *Printers and Press Freedom: The Ideology of Early American Journalism* (New York, 1988), 97–106.

25. *Autobiography*, 58–60; *PBF* 1:6–7; Isaiah Thomas, *The History of Printing in America* (1810; repr., New York, 1970), 105–6.

26. Thomas C. Leonard, "Recovering 'Wretched Stuff' and the Franklins' Synergy," *New England Quarterly* 72 (1999), 444–55; Stephen Botein, " 'Meer Mechanics' and an Open Press: The Business and Political Strategies of Early American Printers," *Perspectives in American History* 9 (1975), 132–34; Sacvan Bercovitch, *The Puritan Origins of the American Self* (New Haven, Conn., 1975); David Paul Nord, "Teleology and the News: The Religious Roots of American Journalism, 1630–1730," *Journal of American History* 77 (1990), 9–38.

27. Mitchell Robert Breitwieser, *Cotton Mather and Benjamin Franklin: The Price of Representative Personality* (New York, 1984), 76–77; Daniel E. Williams, ed., *Pillars of Salt: An Anthology of Early American Criminal Narratives* (Madison, Wisc., 1993); Michael Warner, *The Letters of the Republic: Publication and the Public Sphere in Eighteenth Century America* (Cambridge, Mass., 1990), 24–26; Richard D. Brown, *Knowledge Is Power: The Diffusion of Information in Early America, 1700–1865* (New York, 1989); Staloff, *Making of an American Thinking Class*; J.C.D. Clark, *The Language of Liberty: Political Discourse and Social Dynamics in the Anglo-American World, 1660–1832* (New York, 1994); Leonard, "Recovering 'Wretched Stuff' and the Franklins' Synergy"; Perry Miller, *The New England Mind: The Seventeenth Century* (Boston, 1948), 170–71; Harry S. Stout, *The New England Soul: Preaching and Religious Culture in Early New England* (New York, 1986), 132.

28. *Autobiography*, 60.

29. Charles E. Clark, *The Public Prints: The Newspaper in Anglo-American Culture, 1665–1740* (New York, 1994), 104–14; Botein, " 'Meer Mechanics,' " 204; Thomas, *History of Printing in America*, 106.

30. Huang, "Franklin's Father Josiah," 75, 121.

31. John B. Blake, "The Inoculation Controversy in Boston: 1721–1722," *New England Quarterly* 25 (1952), 489–506; Ola Elizabeth Winslow, *A Destroying Angel: The Conquest of Smallpox in Colonial Boston* (Boston, 1974), 32–33; *New England Courant*, February 26, 1722; Maxine Van De Wetering, "A Reconsideration of the Inoculation Controversy," *New England Quarterly* 58 (1985), 46–67; Tourtellot, *Benjamin Franklin*, 233–74; Miller, *From Colony to Province*, 345–66; Miller, "Introduction," *The New England Courant. A Selection of Certain Issues Containing Writings of Benjamin Franklin Or Published By Him During his Brother's Imprisonment* (Boston, 1956), 6–9; Breitwieser, *Cotton Mather and Benjamin Franklin*, 119–22; Elizabeth Bancroft Schlesinger, "Cotton Mather and His Children," *William and Mary Quarterly*, 3rd ser., 10 (1953), 184; *Selected Letters of Mather*, ed. Silverman, 213–14.

32. Middlekauff, *The Mathers*, 356; *New England Courant*, August 14, 1721; *A Report of the Record Commissioners of the City of Boston Containing the Records of the Boston Selectmen, 1716 to 1736* (Boston, 1885), 9, 81–83.

33. Van De Wetering, "Reconsideration of the Inoculation Controversy"; William Douglass in *Boston News-Letter*, July 24, 1721, quoted in Tourtellot, *Benjamin Franklin*, 247; *Selected Letters of Mather*, ed. Silverman, 199; Douglass, *Inoculation of the Small Pox as Practiced in Boston* (Boston, 1722), 6–7.

34. *Boston Gazette*, July 31, 1721.

35. Warner, *Letters of the Republic*, 64–67. We would not know who authored many of the *Courant* pieces had not Franklin himself initialed a file he owned at some point. Worthington C. Ford, "Franklin's *New England Courant*," *Proceedings of the Massachusetts Historical Society* 57 (1941), 336–53.

36. *New England Courant*, August 7, 14, 21, 28, October 30, November 6, 13, 1721; T. H. Breen, *The Character of a Good Ruler: Puritan Political Ideas in New England, 1630–1730* (New Haven, Conn., 1970), 231–39; Richard L. Bushman, *King and People in Provincial Massachusetts* (Chapel Hill, N.C., 1985), 257–58; James Franklin, "On the Distress of the Town of Boston, occasioned by the small Pox," *New England Courant*, August 28, 1721; BF, "To 'Your Honour': Defense of James Franklin to Samuel Sewall," *New England Courant*, February 4, 1723, in BF, *Autobiography and Other Writings*, ed. Ormond Seavey (Oxford, Eng., 1993), 188–89; Miller, *From Colony to Province*, 334–45.

37. *New England Courant*, December 4, 1721, Feburary 5, 1722; *Boston Gazette*, January 29, 1722. See also Albert Furtwangler, "Franklin's Apprenticeship and *The Spectator*," *New England Quarterly* 52 (1979), 377–86. Tourtellot reprints most of these exchanges in *Benjamin Franklin*, 264–71.

38. *Autobiography*, 61–63.

39. *New England Courant*, April 2, 1722. Silence Dogood also mocks Cotton Mather's sermon "Silentarius" of September 1721. *Selected Letters of Mather*, ed. Silverman, 339.

40. Carol F. Karlsen, *The Devil in the Shape of a Woman* (New York, 1987); Elizabeth Reis, *Damned Women: Sinners and Witches in Puritan New England* (Ithaca, N.Y., 1998); Jane Kamensky, *Governing the Tongue: The Politics of Speech in Early New England* (New York, 1998).

41. *PBF* 1:9–14.

42. *PBF* 1:14–18; *Autobiography*, 68.

43. Ibid., 63, 68–69.

44. Franklin comes close to admitting as much a bit later, noting that despite his renewed beatings, his brother "was otherwise not an ill-natur'd Man: Perhaps I was too saucy and provoking." *Saucy*, of course, was a term often used for children, slaves, and servants in the eighteenth and early nineteenth century, and by employing it Franklin reveals the ambiguity of what in fact constituted tyranny or arbitrary power in such cases. *Autobiography*, 70. Richard L. Bushman has analyzed another passage in a similar light in "On the Uses of Psychology: Conflict and Conciliation in Benjamin Franklin," *History and Theory* 5 (1966), 230–34.

45. *New England Courant*, June 9, 18, 1722; John Bach McMaster, *Benjamin Franklin* (1893; repr., New York, 1980), 27, 32. Jeffrey A. Smith argues persuasively for Franklin's authorship of this first Janus piece, which is not usually attributed to Franklin. J. A. Leo Lemay, in attributing a later essay to Franklin, observes that the "rubs" Franklin claimed to have given the authorities during James's confinement did not appear that June, because Franklin "could hardly have reprinted this essay with pride," but this assumes a

kind of ethic of authorship, and lack of political motivation, not characteristic of Franklin or most writers for the Anglo-American press in the 1720s. That said, Franklin may have conflated the two episodes: he enlisted his pen on James's behalf both times. Smith, *Printers and Press Freedom*, 101–2, 204n15; J. A. Leo Lemay, *The Canon of Benjamin Franklin 1722–1776: New Attributions and Reconsiderations* (Newark, Del., 1986), 33. On the later Janus pieces, see *PBF* 1:48–50; Ralph Lerner, "Dr. Janus," in *Revolutions Revisited: Two Faces of the Politics of Enlightenment* (Chapel Hill, N.C., 1994), 3–17.

46. BF, Silence Dogood nos. 8, 9, in *PBF* 1:27–31; *Autobiography*, 69.

47. *New England Courant*, October 8, 29, November 5, December 10, 24, 1722, January 21, 1723; *PBF* 1:48–50.

48. Grantland S. Rice, *The Transformation of Authorship in America* (Chicago, 1997), 65–66; Albert Furtwangler, *American Silhouettes: Rhetorical Identities of the Founders* (New Haven, Conn., 1987), 15–34.

49. *New England Courant*, February 11, 1723; *PBF* 1:49–50; James Franklin, "A Caution to Batchellors," *New England Courant*, September 25, 1721; James Franklin, *The Life and Death of Old Father Janus, the Vile Author of the Late* Wicked *Courant. A Satyr* (Boston, 1726). For an argument that James Franklin was cowed into submission, see Clark, *Public Prints*, 138–39; for a contrary view see Smith, *Printers and Press Freedom*, 105–7.

50. Lerner, "Our Janus," 11.

51. *New England Courant*, July 15, 1723. J. A. Leo Lemay attributes the earlier April 15, 1723, piece, signed Timothy Wagstaff, to Franklin. See *Franklin: Writings*, ed. Lemay, 52–55, and Lemay, *Canon of Benjamin Franklin*, 38–39.

52. *New England Courant*, April 15, 29, June 17, July 8, November 24, 1724; *Boston News-Letter*, April 18, July 11, 1723; Greene, *Negro in Colonial New England*, 140; William D. Piersen, *Black Yankees: The Development of an Afro-American Subculture in Eighteenth-Century New England* (Amherst, Mass., 1988); Graham Russell Hodges, *Root and Branch: African Americans in New York and East Jersey, 1613–1863* (Chapel Hill, N.C., 1999), 69–99; Peter Linebaugh and Marcus Rediker, *The Many-Headed Hydra: Sailors, Slaves, Commoners, and the Hidden History of the Revolutionary Atlantic* (Boston, 2000), 174–210.

53. *Autobiography*, 70–71.

54. Ibid., 71; *New England Courant*, September 30, 1723; Cornelia Hughes Dayton, *Women Before the Bar: Gender, Law and Society in Connecticut, 1639–1789* (Chapel Hill, N.C., 1995).

55. *Selected Letters of Mather*, ed. Silverman, 199, 204, 340, 368; Silverman, *Life and Times of Cotton Mather*, 264; David Levin, *Cotton Mather: The Young Life of the Lord's Remembrancer, 1663–1703* (Cambridge, Mass., 1978), 296; George Lyman Kittredge, "Some Lost Works of Cotton Mather," *Proceedings of the Massachusetts Historical Society* 45 (1912), 429–31, 436–39; Mather, *Bonifacius*, 54.

56. BF to Samuel Mather, July 7, 1773, in *Franklin: Writings*, ed. Lemay, 881; Huang, "Father Josiah Franklin," 33. Other commentators, such as Carl Van Doren, place this visit to Mather in 1724, when Franklin returned to Boston; Van Doren, *Jane Mecom*, 22. But Franklin is quite specific in the letter to Samuel Mather that it was in 1723. He had gone over this chronology when writing the first part of the autobiography just two years before.

3. FRIENDS, SAVIORS, AND SLAVES

1. Stephen Botein, " 'Meer Mechanics' and an Open Press: The Business and Political Strategies of Early American Printers," *Perspectives in American History* 9 (1975), 127–225; Jeffrey A. Smith, *Printers and Press Freedom: The Ideology of Early American Journalism* (New York, 1988); Jürgen Habermas, *The Structural Transformation of the Public Sphere*, trans. Thomas Berger and Frederick Lawrence (Cambridge, Mass., 1989); Michael Warner, *The Letters of the Republic: Publication and the Public Sphere in Eighteenth-Century America* (Cambridge, Mass., 1990); Michael McKeon, *The Origins of the English Novel 1660–1740* (Baltimore, Md., 1987); J. Paul Hunter, *Before Novels: The Cultural Contexts of Eighteenth-Century English Fiction* (New York, 1990).

2. Warner, *Letters of the Republic*, 34–72; Ormond Seavey, *Becoming Benjamin Franklin: The Autobiography and the Life* (University Park, Pa., 1988); Grantland Rice, *The Transformation of Authorship in America* (Chicago, 1997); Peter Linebaugh, *The London Hanged: Crime and Civil Society in the Eighteenth Century* (London, 1992); Christopher Hill, *Liberty Against the Law: Some Seventeenth-Century Controversies* (New York, 1996); Daniel E. Williams, ed., *Pillars of Salt: An Anthology of Early American Criminal Narratives* (Madison, Wisc., 1993); Hunter, *Before Novels*; McKeon, *Origins of the English Novel*; Deidre Shauna Lynch, *The Economy of Character: Novels, Market Culture, and the Business of Inner Meaning* (Chicago, 1998); Srinivas Aravamudan, *Tropicopolitans: Colonialism and Agency, 1688–1804* (Durham, N.C., 1998).

3. Junto Commonplace Book, Ferdinand J. Dreer Collection, Historical Society of Pennsylvania.

4. David Freeman Hawke, *Franklin* (New York, 1976), 20.

5. Isaiah Thomas, *The History of Printing in America* (1810; repr., New York, 1970), 457–60; *The Autobiography of Benjamin Franklin*, ed. Leonard W. Labaree et al. (New Haven, Conn., 1964), 72–75.

6. *Autobiography*, 70–71; Thomas, *History of Printing*, 340–55; Douglas C. McMurtrie, *A History of Printing in the United States* (1932; repr., New York, 1969), 2:1–14; John Bach McMaster, *Benjamin Franklin* (1893; repr., New York, 1980), 37–39.

7. Anna Jannery DeArmond, *Andrew Bradford, Colonial Journalist* (Newark, Del., 1949), 14–15; and *Autobiography*, 76.

8. Ibid., 77–78.

9. Ibid., 78–79. Most Franklin scholars have simply repeated Franklin's judgment of Keimer, not recognizing the elements of competition, and even guilt, in Franklin's perspective. For example, the editors of *PBF* described Keimer as "[a] man of strange religious enthusiasms, inefficient, suspicious, unattractive, and pitiable." *PBF* 1:113n2. Douglas Anderson typically dismisses him as a "devious personality," forgetting that Franklin himself was described that way by even more extensive contemporary testimony. *The Radical Enlightenments of Benjamin Franklin* (Baltimore, Md., 1997), 77. This is an especially unfortunate remark since Keimer was part of the radical enlightenment that Anderson otherwise elucidates so well. Alfred Owen Aldridge came up with the most original and apt, if anachronistic, put-down when he described Keimer as "an eccentric intellectual with many of the traits of today's beatniks." *Benjamin Franklin: Philosopher and Man* (Philadelphia, 1965), 17. For more generous brief assessments, see McMaster, *Benjamin Franklin*, 46–48; Elizabeth Christine Cook, *Literary Influences in Colonial Newspapers* (New York, 1912), 60; Verner W. Crane, *Benjamin Franklin and a Rising*

People (Boston, 1954), 23; David S. Lovejoy, *Religious Enthusiasm in the New World: From Heresy to Revolution* (Cambridge, Mass., 1985), 171–72.

10. Samuel Keimer, *A Brand Pluck'd From the Burning: Exemplify'd in the Unparallel'd Case of Samuel Keimer* (London, 1718); C. Lennart Carlson, "Samuel Keimer: A Study in the Transition of English Culture to Colonial Pennsylvania," *Pennsylvania Magazine of History and Biography* 61 (1937), 357–63; Phyllis J. Guskin, " 'Not Originally Intended for the Press': Martha Fowke Sanson's Poems in the Barbados Gazette," *Eighteenth-Century Studies* 34 (2000), 63; Hillel Schwartz, *The French Prophets: The History of a Millenarian Group in Eighteenth-Century England* (Berkeley, Calif., 1980), 7–9, 95, 124, 322; Lovejoy, *Religious Enthusiasm in the New World*, 170; Clark Garrett, *Spirit Possession and Popular Religion: From the Camisards to the Shakers* (Baltimore, Md., 1987), 46–47.

11. Keimer, *Brand Pluck'd From the Burning*, 105, 124.

12. Carlson, "Samuel Keimer"; Samuel Keimer and Thomas Lawrence to Richard Hall, March 3, 1729, box 10, folder 44, Logan Papers, Historical Society of Pennsylvania; *American Weekly Mercury*, December 17, 1723, quoted in McMurtrie, *History of Printing*, 2:410n33; "To S.K.," *American Weekly Mercury*, January 18, 1726; Stephen Bloore, "Samuel Keimer: A Footnote to the Life of Franklin," *Pennsylvania Magazine of History and Biography* 54 (1930), 265–66; Samuel Keimer, ed., *Caribbeana. Containing Letters and Dissertations, Together with Poetical Essays, On Various Subjects and Occasions; Chiefly Wrote by Several Hands in the West-Indies, And Some of them to Gentlemen Residing There*, 2 vols. (London, 1741); Jack P. Greene, "Changing Identity in the British Caribbean: Barbados as a Case Study," in Nicholas Canny and Anthony Pagden, eds., *Colonial Identity in the Atlantic World, 1500–1800* (Princeton, N.J., 1987), 241; Thomas Krise, ed., *Caribbeana: An Anthology of English Literature of the West Indies, 1657–1777* (Chicago, 1999), 147–49; Bill Overton, "Introduction," *A Letter to My Love: Love Poems by Women First Published in the* Barbados Gazette (Newark, Del., 2001), 15–16; Keimer, "The Sorrowful Lamentation of Samuel Keimer, Printer of the Barbadoes Gazette," *Barbados Gazette*, May 4, 1734, in Thomas, *History of Printing*, 605–6; DeArmond, *Andrew Bradford*, 176.

13. Keimer, *A New Elegy On the much Lamented Death of the Ingenious and Well-Belov'd Aquila Rose* (Philadelphia, 1723); Joseph Rose, ed., *Poems on Several Occasions, by Aquila Rose* (Philadelphia, 1740).

14. DeArmond, *Andrew Bradford*, 25; Carl Van Doren, *Benjamin Franklin* (New York, 1938), 95; Chester E. Jorgensen, "A Brand Flung at Colonial Orthodoxy: Samuel Keimer's 'Universal Instructor in All Arts & Sciences,' " *Journalism Quarterly* 12 (1935), 272–77; Bernard Bailyn, *The Ideological Origins of the American Revolution* (Cambridge, Mass., 1967), 36, 43.

15. *Autobiography*, 79.

16. *Autobiography*, 79–81.

17. Ibid., 81–82. Franklin crossed out the phrase about his father saying he had already given James too much of his money. *Autobiography*, 82n3.

18. Ibid., 81–82.

19. William Breitenbach, "Religious Affections and Religious Affectations: Antinomianism and Hypocrisy in the Writings of Franklin and Edwards," in Barbara B. Oberg and Harry S. Stout, eds., *Benjamin Franklin, Jonathan Edwards, and the Representation of American Culture* (New York, 1993), 17; *Autobiography*, 83–86.

20. *Autobiography*, 86–87.

21. And indeed, Franklin soon tells us that Keimer himself failed to keep his part of the bargain, or act like a brother. He invited Franklin and two female friends to a break-the-fast of roast pig and "ate it all up before we came." *Autobiography*, 87–88, 89.

22. Thomas Tryon, *The Way to Health, Long Life, and Happiness*, 2nd ed. (London, 1691), 367, 368–82; Tryon, *The Planter's Speech to His Neighbors & Country-Men of Pennsylvania, East and West Jersey* (London, 1684), 41–73; Tryon, *Friendly Advice to the Gentlemen-Planters of the East and West Indies. In Three Parts* (London, 1684); Tryon, *Tryon's Letters, Upon Several Occasions* (London, 1700), 183–85, 198–200; David Brion Davis, *The Problem of Slavery in Western Culture* (Ithaca, N.Y., 1966), 371–74; Wylie Sypher, *Guinea's Captive Kings: British Antislavery Literature of the Eighteenth Century* (Chapel Hill, N.C., 1942), 67–68; Dickson D. Bruce Jr., *The Origins of African American Literature, 1680–1815* (Charlottesville, Va., 2001), 22–25, 73, 100.

23. *Autobiography*, 93–95, 296; *American Weekly Mercury*, July 26, 1733.

24. *Autobiography*, 95–96.

25. Ibid., 98–99; Robert W. Kenny, "James Ralph: An Eighteenth-Century Philadelphian in Grub Street," *Pennsylvania Magazine of History and Biography* 64 (1940), 218–42, quoted at 232; Smith, *Printers and Press Freedom*, 27–28; James Ralph, *The Touch-Stone; or, Historical, Critical, Political, Moral, Philosophical and Theological Essays upon the Reigning Diversions of the Town* (London, 1728), xiv; Philip Stevick, "Introduction," *The Case of Authors by Profession or Trade (1758) Together with The Champion (1739–1740) by James Ralph* (Gainesville, Fla., 1966), vi–x.

26. *Autobiography*, 95–96; John M. Murrin, "Anglicizing an American Colony: The Transformation of Provincial Massachusetts" (Ph.D. diss., Yale University, 1966); Phyllis Whitman Hunter, *Purchasing Identity in the Atlantic World: Massachusetts Merchants, 1690–1760* (Ithaca, N.Y., 2001). In later years Franklin remembered Sloane seeking him out, but his first surviving letter reveals that it was quite the other way around: Franklin sought out Sloane, like a salesman, selling not only his goods but himself as worthy of being sought out. Franklin to Sir Hans Sloane, June 2, 1725, in *PBF* 1:54; *Autobiography*, 98n1.

27. William Wollaston, *The Religion of Nature Delineated*, 6th ed. (London, 1738), 7; BF, *A Dissertation on Liberty and Necessity, Pleasure and Pain* (London, 1725), in *PBF* 1:61, 67; Kerry S. Walters, *Benjamin Franklin and His Gods* (Urbana, Ill., 1999), 45–57.

28. Anderson, *Radical Enlightenments*, 44, 49–50; Aldridge, *Benjamin Franklin*, 21–22; *Autobiography*, 96–97.

29. Crane, *Benjamin Franklin and a Rising People*, 16; *Autobiography*, 103–5.

30. There is no question that he took his new mercantile apprenticeship very seriously: his remaining manuscripts from 1725–27 show the effects of much practice in rendering accounts and balances. Ledger fragment, 1725, vol. 46, folder 26, Benjamin Franklin Papers, APS; Benjamin Franklin Commonplace Book, Dreer Collection, Historical Society of Pennsylvania. For the importance of Denham's example, see Frederick W. Tolles, *Meeting House and Counting House: The Quaker Merchants of Colonial Philadelphia, 1682–1763* (1948; repr., New York, 1963), 248–49; Hugh Dawson, "Fathers and Sons: Franklin's 'Memoir' as Myth and Literature," *Early American Literature* 14 (1980), 269–92; Seavey, *Becoming Benjamin Franklin*, 136–37, 139–40.

31. *Autobiography*, 107; Francis Jennings, *Benjamin Franklin, Politician* (New York, 1996), 31, citing Van Doren, *Franklin*, 70; BF, "Plan of Conduct," in *PBF*, 1:99–100; BF, "Journal of a Voyage," in *PBF* 1:91; and H. W. Brands, *The First American: The Life and Times of Benjamin Franklin* (New York, 2000), 78.

32. BF, "Articles of Belief and Acts of Religion," in *PBF* 1:102–9. This depiction of Franklin's religious development mediates the accounts of Alfred Owen Aldridge, *Benjamin Franklin and Nature's God* (Durham, N.C., 1967); Anderson, *Radical Enlightenments*, 64–74; and Walters, *Benjamin Franklin and His Gods*, 1–15, 67–95.

33. BF, "Epitaph," in *PBF* 1:111; Warner, *Letters of the Republic*, 73–74; Larzer Ziff, *Writing in the New Nation: Prose, Print and Politics in the Early United States* (New Haven, Conn., 1992), 83–106; Lewis P. Simpson, "The Printer as a Man of Letters: Franklin and the Symbolism of the Third Realm," in J. A. Leo Lemay, ed., *The Oldest Revolutionary: Essays on Benjamin Franklin* (Philadelphia, 1976), 3–20.

34. *Autobiography*, 107–8.

35. Thomas, *History of Printing*, 1:364–65; Bloore, "Samuel Keimer," 267–68; *Pennsylvania Gazette*, November 10, 1729.

36. *Autobiography*, 108–11.

37. Ibid., 111–12, 114–15.

38. *Autobiography*, 120n6; *Pennsylvania Gazette* (advertisement), October 1, 1728; Hawke, *Franklin*, 33–34; Cook, *Literary Influences in Colonial Newspapers*, 60–61; DeArmond, *Andrew Bradford*, 241; McMaster, *Franklin*, 48–49; Van Doren, *Franklin*, 95; Jorgensen, "Brand Flung at Colonial Orthodoxy," 272–77; Charles R. Hildeburn, *A Century of Printing: The Issues of the Press in Pennsylvania, 1685–1784*, 1:63, 65, 67–69, 71, 74–75, 80, 82, 85, 88, 94. Franklin himself actually thought enough of Chambers's *Cyclopedia* to order the fifth edition six years after it was published. BF to William Strahan, May 17, 1749, in *PBF* 3:379.

39. Jorgensen, "Brand Flung at Colonial Orthodoxy"; BF, *Busy-Body* No. 3, in *PBF* 1:121; "An Answer to the BUSY-BODY," *Pennsylvania Gazette*, January 13, 1729. Some have assumed that Keimer did not read the abortion article before printing it (see for example Hawke, *Franklin*, 34). Keimer deserves somewhat more credit than that. The article said nothing about the intentional termination of pregnancy; only Franklin's two fictional outraged readers, Martha Careful and Celia Shortface, contended that it had. *Pennsylvania Gazette*, November 21, 1728; *PBF* 1:112–13.

40. DeArmond, *Andrew Bradford*, 44.

41. *PBF* 1:139n5, 157; *Pennsylvania Gazette*, July 18, 1729; Bloore, "Samuel Keimer," 272; *Autobiography*, 120, 126.

42. *Autobiography*, 128; BF to Sarah Davenport, June 1730, in *PBF* 1:171.

43. BF, "On the Providence of God in the Goodness of the World," in *PBF* 1:264–69. J. A. Leo Lemay dates this piece at 1730; see *Benjamin Franklin: Writings* (New York, 1987), 163–68. Junto Commonplace Book, Ferdinand J. Dreer Collection.

44. *Franklin: Writings*, ed. Lemay, 145–51; Alfred Owen Aldridge, "Franklin and the Ghostly Drummer of Tedworth," *William and Mary Quarterly*, 3rd ser., 7 (1950), 559–67; J. A. Leo Lemay, *The Canon of Benjamin Franklin* (Newark, Del., 1986), 42–46; *Pennsylvania Gazette*, July 30, 1730, in *PBF* 1:187; BF, "Apology for Printers," *Pennsylvania Gazette*, June 10, 1731, in *PBF* 1:194–99. See also BF, "Witch Trial at Mount Holly," *Pennsylvania Gazette*, October 22, 1730, in *PBF* 1:182–83.

45. Merton A. Christensen, "Franklin on the Hemphill Trial: Deism Versus Presbyterian Orthodoxy," *William and Mary Quarterly*, 3rd ser., 10 (1953), 422–40; Aldridge, *Benjamin Franklin and Nature's God*, 86–98; Melvin H. Buxbaum, *Benjamin Franklin and the Zealous Presbyterians* (University Park, Pa., 1975), 93–115; Anderson, *Radical Enlightenments*, 79–85; Bryan F. LeBeau, *Jonathan Dickinson and the Formative Years of*

American Presbyterianism (Lexington, Ky., 1997), 45–63; BF, "Dialogue Between Two Presbyterians," *Pennsylvania Gazette*, April 10, 1735, in *PBF*, 2:27; BF, *Some Observations on the Proceedings Against the Rev. Mr. Hemphill; with a Vindication of his Sermons* (Philadelphia, 1735), in *PBF* 2:37–65; BF, *A Letter to a Friend in the Country . . .* (Philadelphia, 1735), in *PBF* 2:66–67, 71, 84. Andrews, in his charge against Hemphill, had accused him of representing church doctrine as "only for tyrants to impose and slaves to obey." Quoted in LeBeau, *Jonathan Dickinson*, 49.

46. Ralph Sandiford, *A Brief Examination of the Practice of the Times* (Philadelphia, 1729); *Pennsylvania Gazette*, December 22, January 26, 1731; Roberts Vaux, *Memoirs of the Lives of Benjamin Lay and Ralph Sandiford* (Philadelphia, 1815), 59–73; Thomas E. Drake, *Quakers and Slavery in America* (New Haven, Conn., 1950), 39–40; Davis, *Problem of Slavery in Western Culture*, 320–31.

47. Sandiford, *Brief Examination*, 9, 13, 17–20, 22, 24–25, 38, 41. He sent thirty-six copies of Sandiford to James Franklin in Newport. Ledger A and B, APS.

48. Benjamin Lay, *All Slave-keepers That Keep the Innocent in Bondage* (Philadelphia, 1737), 106; Vaux, *Memoirs of the Lives*, 17, 20, 24, 32; Drake, *Quakers and Slavery*, 43–44.

49. Ledger A and B, 174, Ledger D, 89, Benjamin Franklin Papers, APS; *Pennsylvania Gazette*, August 10, 1738; *Pennsylvania Gazette*, March 25, 1742, in *PBF* 2:357; Vaux, *Memoirs of the Lives*, 28, 32; Davis, *Problem of Slavery in Western Culture*, 321–24; Drake, *Quakers and Slavery*, 43–46; Jean R. Soderlund, *Quakers and Slavery: A Divided Spirit* (Princeton, N.J., 1985), 16.

50. *Pennsylvania Gazette*, August 10, November 2, 1738; Ledger D, Benjamin Franklin Papers, APS; BF to Deborah Franklin, June 10, 1758 in *PBF* 8:92; Susan Rather, "Benjamin West's Professional Endgame and the Historical Conundrum of William Williams," *William and Mary Quarterly*, 3rd ser., 59 (2002), 826.

51. *Pennsylvania Gazette*, March 25, 1742; Vaux, *Memoirs of the Lives*, 48.

52. Sydney James, *A People Among Peoples: Quaker Benevolence in Eighteenth-Century America* (Cambridge, Mass., 1963), 124.

53. *Pennsylvania Gazette*, December 29, 1730, July 8, 1731, in *PBF* 1:189, 217.

4. PEOPLE AND CAPITAL

1. Charles Baudelaire, "Further Notes on Edgar Poe" [1856] in *The Painter of Modern Life and Other Essays* (New York, 1964), 101; D. H. Lawrence, *Studies in Classic American Literature* (1923; repr., New York, 1951), 19–31; Max Weber, *The Protestant Ethic and the Spirit of Capitalism*, trans. Talcott Parsons (New York, 1930), 48–55, 65, 71, 124, 180; William Carlos Williams, *In the American Grain* (1925; repr. New York, 1938), 153–57.

2. *The Autobiography of Benjamin Franklin*, ed. Leonard W. Labaree et al. (New Haven, Conn., 1964), 149.

3. *Pennsylvania Gazette*, August 2, 1736, in *PBF*, 2:159.

4. Michael Zuckerman, "The Selling of the Self: Franklin to Barnum," *Almost Chosen People* (Berkeley, Calif., 1993). For more or less ironic takes on the compatibility of Franklinian republicanism with putatively liberal self-interest, see Mitchell Robert Breitwieser, *Cotton Mather and Benjamin Franklin: The Price of Representative Personality* (New York, 1984); R. Jackson Wilson, *Figures of Speech: American Writers and the Literary Marketplace* (New York, 1989), 21–65; Michael Warner, *The Letters of the Republic:*

Publication and the Public Sphere in Eighteenth-Century America (Cambridge, Mass., 1990), 34–72; Larzer Ziff, *Writing in the New Nation: Prose, Print and Politics in the Early United States* (New Haven, Conn., 1992), 83–106; Albert H. Wurth, "The Franklin Persona: The Virtue of Practicality and the Practicality of Virtue," and Michael Zuckerman, "Doing Good While Doing Well: Benevolence and Self-Interest in Franklin's Autobiography," in J. A. Leo Lemay, ed., *Reappraising Benjamin Franklin* (Newark, Del., 1993), 76–101, 441–51.

5. Paul W. Conner, *Poor Richard's Politicks: Benjamin Franklin and His New American Order* (New York, 1965); Warner, *Letters of the Republic*; Jeffrey A. Smith, *Printers and Press Freedom: The Ideology of Early American Journalism* (New York, 1988); Charles E. Clark, *The Public Prints: The Newspaper in Anglo-American Culture, 1665–1740* (New York, 1994).

6. *Autobiography*, 126.

7. "Multilateral" and "invisible" transactions of this sort were more important than is sometimes realized for the eighteenth century. Counting them or not counting them greatly affects the data upon which economic historians rely to measure the importance of various aspects of trade. Interestingly, labor historians have been noticing the same phenomenon with respect to the mix of slavery, servitude, and wage labor during this period. Kenneth Morgan, *Slavery, Atlantic Trade, and the British Economy, 1660–1800* (Cambridge, Eng., 2000), 23; O. Nigel Bolland, "Proto-Proletarians? Slave Wages in the Americas," in Mary Turner, ed., *From Chattel Slaves to Wage Slaves: The Dynamics of Labour Bargaining in the Americas* (London, 1995), 123–47; John Bezís-Selfa, "Slavery and the Disciplining of Free Labor in the Colonial Mid-Atlantic Iron Industry," *Pennsylvania History* 64, supp. (1997), 270–86.

8. *PBF*, 1:348, 378–79, 2:232; Ledger A and B, Benjamin Franklin Papers, APS; George Simpson Eddy, *Account Books Kept by Benjamin Franklin* (New York, 1928), 47; George Edward Moranda, "Financial Aspects of Benjamin Franklin's Printing House" (M.A. thesis, University of Wisconsin, 1964); Norma Summers, "Benjamin Franklin—Printing Entrepreneur" (Ph.D. thesis, University of Alabama, 1979).

9. Ledger A and B, June 4, 1731, July 2, October 6, 1732, November 7, 1734, September 20, 1739, BF Journal, (1730–40), 35–36, Ledger D (1739–1747), 49, Benjamin Franklin Papers, APS; *Pennsylvania Gazette*, December 5, 1734, October 27, 1737, January 1, 1741, April 22, 29, 1742. During a 1748 reckoning of the profits of the printing house, Franklin maintained that most ads were paid for in cash. Moranda, "Financial Aspects," 15.

10. *Pennsylvania Gazette*, October 17, 1734, October 6, 1737, May 17, August 9, 1739, March 3, 1747; Fernand Braudel, *Afterthoughts on Material Civilization and Capitalism* (Baltimore, Md., 1977), 53–61; Immanuel Wallerstein, *Historical Capitalism; with Capitalist Civilization* (London, 1995), 29–39.

11. *Pennsylvania Gazette*, March 1, 1748. Recent literature suggests that the regions and sectors most integrated into the Atlantic economy were the most likely to rely at least in part on slave labor, and that even a relatively small influx of slaves could have a large impact on the labor market. Numbers of imports and census figures rose and fell according to many factors of supply and demand, including imperial wars and occasional decisions to tax imports in the wake of slave unrest, but the larger pattern before 1760 is one of rising numbers, even if per capita figures do not reflect a linear rise. Darold D. Wax, "Negro Imports into Pennsylvania, 1720–66," *Pennsylvania History* 32 (1965), 254–66; Wax, "The

Demand for Slave Labor in Colonial Pennsylvania," *Pennsylvania History* 34 (1967), 331–45; James G. Lydon, "Philadelphia's Commercial Expansion, 1720–1739," *Pennsylvania Magazine of History and Biography* 91 (1967), 401–18; Gary B. Nash, "Slaves and Slaveowners in Colonial Philadelphia," *William and Mary Quarterly*, 3rd ser., 30 (1973), 223–56; Lydon, "New York and the Slave Trade, 1700 to 1774," *William and Mary Quarterly*, 3rd ser., 35 (1978), 375–96; Jean R. Soderlund, *Quakers and Slavery: A Divided Spirit* (Princeton, N.J., 1985), 54–65; Soderlund, "Black Importation and Migration into Southeastern Pennsylvania, 1682–1810," *Proceedings of the American Philosophical Society* 133, no. 2 (1989), 145–53; Cathy D. Matson, *Merchants and Empire: Trading in Colonial New York* (Baltimore, Md., 1998), 202–5; David Galenson, "Labor Market Behavior in Colonial America: Servitude, Slavery and Free Labor," in Galenson, ed., *Markets in History: Economic Studies of the Past* (New York, 1989), 51–96; Galenson, "The Settlement and Growth of the Colonies: Population, Labor, and Economic Development," and Daniel Vickers, "The Northern Colonies: Economy and Society, 1600–1775," in Stanley L. Engerman and Robert E. Gallman, eds., *The Cambridge Economic History of the United States*, vol. 1, *The Colonial Era* (New York, 1996), 176–77, 229–37; Bezís-Selfa, "Slavery and the Disciplining of Free Labor"; Christine Daniels, "Shadowlands: Freedom and Unfreedom in Anglo-America" (paper presented at the American Historical Association, Washington, D.C., January 1999); Jacqueline Jones, *American Work: Four Centuries of Black and White Labor* (New York, 1998), 111–42; Marilyn C. Baseler, *"Asylum for Mankind": America, 1607–1800* (Ithaca, N.Y., 1998), 74–119; Lawrence William Towner, *A Good Master Well Served: Masters and Servants in Colonial Massachusetts, 1620–1750* (New York, 1998), 83, 88, 112–13; Joanne Pope Melish, *Disowning Slavery: Gradual Emancipation and "Race" in New England, 1780–1860* (Ithaca, N.Y., 1998), 11–40; Mary M. Schweitzer, *Custom and Contract: Household, Government, and the Economy in Colonial Pennsylvania* (New York, 1987), 21–56.

12. Bills of E. E. [H. S.] Warner and Charles Moore, vol. 66, folios 46A and 71A, Benjamin Franklin Papers, APS.

13. Moranda, "Financial Aspects," 10.

14. BF, Articles of Agreement with Thomas Whitemarsh, Articles of Agreement with Louis Timothée, in *PBF* 1:339–41; Ledgers A and B, November 7, 1734, Benjamin Franklin Papers, APS; Eddy, *Account Books*, 15; Ralph D. Frasca, "From Apprentice to Journeyman to Partner: Benjamin Franklin's Workers and the Growth of the Early American Printing Trade," *Pennsylvania Magazine of History and Biography* 114 (1990), 241–47; *Pennsylvania Gazette*, March 1, 1748.

15. Hannah Benner Roach, "Benjamin Franklin Slept Here," *Pennsylvania Magazine of History and Biography* 84 (1960), 141–42. In 1732 the ledger shows him owing Franklin from one to eight pounds. Moranda, "Financial Aspects," 77–78.

16. Shop Book, March 1736, Ledgers A and B, August 22, 1730, January 7, 1732, March 2, 1733, Benjamin Franklin Papers, APS; *Autobiography*, 108, 294; BF to Hugh Roberts, September 16, 1758, in *PBF* 8:158–59.

17. *Autobiography*, 117; Alfred Owen Aldridge, *Benjamin Franklin: Philosopher and Man* (Philadelphia, 1965), 40–42; The Junto Commonplace Book, Ferdinand J. Dreer Collection, Historical Society of Pennsylvania. Both literary and social historians generally depict Franklin as a champion of all artisans' interests versus those of merchants and professional men. See for example Bruce Ingraham Granger, *Benjamin Franklin: An*

American Man of Letters (Ithaca, N.Y., 1964), 40; Ronald Schultz, *The Republic of Labor: Philadelphia Artisans and the Politics of Class, 1720–1830* (New York, 1993), 25. For the importance of artisan slaveholding in other areas of the North during the late eighteenth century, see Shane White, *Somewhat More Independent: The End of Slavery in New York City, 1770–1810* (Athens, Ga., 1991), 10–22; Tina H. Sheller, "Freemen, Servants, and Slaves: Artisans and the Class Structure of the Revolutionary Baltimore Town," in Howard B. Rock, Paul A. Gilje, and Robert Asher, eds., *American Artisans: Crafting Social Identity, 1750–1850* (Baltimore, Md., 1995), 25–29.

18. BF, "Observations on Reading History" [1731], "Doctrine to be Preached" [1731], in *PBF* 1:192–93, 213; "Lying Shopkeepers" and "On Simplicity" in *Benjamin Franklin: Writings*, ed. J. A. Leo Lemay (New York, 1987), 158–61, 181–84.

19. BF, "On Conversation," "Petition to the Pennsylvania Assembly Regarding Fairs," in *PBF* 1:177–81, 211–12; Braudel, *Afterthoughts on Material Civilization and Capitalism*, 23–26; Peter Burke, *Popular Culture in Early Modern Europe* (New York, 1978); Peter Stallybrass and Allon White, *The Politics and Poetics of Transgression* (Ithaca, N.Y., 1986), chap. 1; Jean-Christophe Agnew, *Worlds Apart: The Market and the Theater in Anglo-American Thought* (New York, 1986); John Mullan and Christopher Reid, "Introduction," *Eighteenth-Century Popular Culture: A Selection* (Oxford, Eng., 2000), 4, 16.

20. *Pennsylvania Gazette*, November 18, 1731; Draft of Petition, Junto Commonplace Book, Dreer Collection; *PBF* 1:211–12. J. A. Leo Lemay established Franklin's authorship of the *Gazette* piece in *The Canon of Benjamin Franklin* (Newark, Del., 1986), 57.

21. Erin Mackie, *Market à la Mode: Fashion, Commodity, and Gender in* The Tatler *and* The Spectator (Baltimore, Md., 1997); Stallybrass and White, *Politics and Poetics of Transgression*, chap. 2; Albert Furtwangler, *American Silhouettes: Rhetorical Identities of the Founders* (New Haven, Conn., 1987), 15–34.

22. *PBF* 1:278–79, 348, 2:131–32, 236–37, 454; BF, "Thieving and Pilfering," Junto Commonplace Book, Dreer Collection. For the rise in such crime during the 1730s, see Douglas Greenberg, *Crime and Law Enforcement in the Colony of New York* (Ithaca, N.Y., 1974), 136; Kenneth Scott, *Counterfeiting in Colonial America* (New York, 1957).

23. Daniel E. Williams, ed., *Pillars of Salt: An Anthology of Early American Criminal Narratives* (Madison, Wisc., 1993); David Paul Nord, "Teleology and News: The Religious Roots of American Journalism, 1630–1730," *Journal of American History* 77 (1990), 9–38; Daniel A. Cohen, *Pillars of Salt, Monuments of Grace: New England Crime Literature and the Origins of American Popular Culture* (New York, 1993); Karen Halttunen, *Murder Most Foul: The Killer and the American Gothic Imagination* (Cambridge, Mass., 1998); Andrew Delbanco, *The Death of Satan* (New York, 1995). Because none of these fine works consider eighteenth-century newspapers (as opposed to pamphlets), they do not evaluate the role that Franklin and his contemporaries played in the secularization of crime reports.

24. *Pennsylvania Gazette*, December 23, 1729, January 13, 20, 1730, in *Franklin: Writings*, ed. Lemay, 138–42; Michael Meranze, *Laboratories of Virtue: Punishment, Revolution and Authority in Philadelphia, 1760–1835* (Chapel Hill, N.C., 1996).

25. BF, *Poor Richard's Almanack*, 1733 and 1734, in *PBF* 1:288, 311, 349. On the issue of women's fashion, see Mackie, *Market à la Mode*; Laura Brown, *Ends of Empire: Women and Ideology in Early Eighteenth-Century English Literature* (Ithaca, N.Y., 1993).

26. *Pennsylvania Gazette*, August 23, 1733; *Franklin: Writings*, ed. Lemay, 218–20. Lemay made a convincing case for attribution to Franklin in *Canon of Benjamin Franklin*,

78–79. Franklin's partner reprinted this essay in the *South Carolina Gazette* in March 1735. Alex Bontemps, *The Punished Self: Surviving Slavery in the Colonial South* (Ithaca, N.Y., 2001), 143.

27. For these developments in England, see James Thompson, *Models of Value: Eighteenth-Century Political Economy and the Novel* (Durham, N.C., 1996); Deidre Shauna Lynch, *The Economy of Character: Novels, Market Culture, and the Business of Inner Meaning* (Chicago, 1998), 1–79.

28. Braudel, *Capitalism and Material Life*; Joyce Appleby, *Economic Thought and Ideology in Seventeenth-Century England* (Princeton, N.J., 1978); Colin Nicholson, *Writing and the Rise of Finance: Capital Satires of the Eighteenth Century* (New York, 1994); Thompson, *Models of Value*; Patrick Brantlinger, *Fictions of State: Culture and Credit in Britain, 1694–1994* (Ithaca, N.Y., 1994), 48–87; Margaret Ellen Newell, *From Dependency to Independence: Economic Revolution in Colonial New England* (Ithaca, N.Y., 1998), 111–213.

29. T. H. Breen, *The Character of a Good Ruler: Puritan Political Ideas in New England, 1630–1730* (New Haven, Conn., 1970), 261–69; G. B. Warden, *Boston, 1689–1776* (Boston, 1970), chaps. 4–5; Newell, *From Dependency to Independence*.

30. *PBF* 1:144, 146–47.

31. *PBF* 1:153–56; Carl Van Doren, *Benjamin Franklin* (New York, 1938), 102.

32. Karl Marx, *On America and the Civil War*, ed. Saul K. Padover (New York, 1972), 18–19; Marx, *Capital*, trans. Ben Fowkes (New York, 1977), 1:142n18; Lewis J. Carey, *Franklin's Economic Views* (New York, 1928), 16–44; Schultz, *Republic of Labor*, 25.

33. *PBF* 1:217; Ronald Clark, *Benjamin Franklin: A Biography* (New York, 1983), 54. I thank John Bezís-Selfa for his observations on coined labor, personal communication. Quantifiers in the Anglo-American world were generally on the side of capitalist agriculture, against champions of traditional privileges and a subsistence economy. Appleby, *Economic Thought and Ideology*, 242–79; E. P. Thompson, *Customs in Common: Studies in Traditional Popular Culture* (New York, 1991); Simon Shaffer, "A Social History of Plausibility: Country, City, and Calculation in Augustan Britain," in Adrian Wilson, ed., *Rethinking Social History: English Society and Its Interpretation, 1750–1820* (Manchester, Eng., 1993), 144–45; Mary Poovey, *A History of the Modern Fact* (Chicago, 1998), 120–37; Charlotte Sussman, *Consuming Anxieties: Consumer Protest, Gender, and British Slavery, 1713–1833* (Stanford, Calif., 2000), 49–80; C. B. Macpherson, *The Political Theory of Possessive Individualism: Hobbes to Locke* (New York, 1962); George Caffentzis, *Clipped Coins, Abused Words, and Civil Government: John Locke's Philosophy of Money* (New York, 1989); Constantine George Caffentzis, *Exciting the Industry of Mankind: George Berkeley's Philosophy of Money* (Dordrecht, Netherlands, 2001), 134.

34. BF, "Celia Single," "On Censure or Backbiting," "Alice Addertongue," *Franklin: Writings*, ed. Lemay, 188–90, 192–96, 196–200; *Autobiography*, 124–25; Breitwieser, *Cotton Mather and Benjamin Franklin*, 215–16; Rice, *Transformation of Authorship in America*, 45–69; Jennifer Jordan Baker, "Benjamin Franklin's Autobiography and the Credibility of Personality," *Early American Literature* 35 (2000), 274–93; Newell, *From Dependency to Independence*, 166; Timothy Hall and T. H. Breen, "Structuring Provincial Imagination: The Rhetoric and Experience of Social Change in Eighteenth-Century New England," *American Historical Review* 103 (1998), 1411–38; Bruce H. Mann, *Neighbors and Strangers: Law and Community in Colonial Connecticut* (Chapel Hill, N.C., 1987), 12–42.

35. A scholarly debate concerns how seriously Franklin meant the almanacs; it often focuses on the question of whether the 1748 compendium of the maxims in *The Way to Wealth* reflects a changing sensibility on Franklin's part, or is an ironic refutation of all of Poor Richard's advice over the years. Generally, there is agreement that the portrait of a mendacious ethos drawn by Weber and D. H. Lawrence is overdrawn. My interpretation attempts to do justice to the countervailing themes and irony in the almanacs while still insisting not only that it adds up to an important moment in the rise of capitalist culture but also that the form and substance of the almanacs intelligently and self-consciously (not derivatively or accidentally) refracts both the historic changes of the moment and events in Franklin's life. For the most recent assertion of a grand design and an ambitious interpretation of its relation to Franklin's biography, see Douglas Anderson, *The Radical Enlightenments of Benjamin Franklin* (Baltimore, Md., 1997), 91–109. For the idea of *The Way to Wealth* as not quite serious, or as a departure, see Granger, *Benjamin Franklin*, 53–59; John F. Ross, "The Character of Poor Richard: Its Source and Alteration," in Esmond Wright, ed., *Benjamin Franklin: A Portrait* (New York, 1970), 27–40; James A. Sappenfield, *A Sweet Instruction: Franklin's Journalism as a Literary Apprenticeship* (Carbondale, Ill., 1973), 121–78; Cameron C. Nickels, "Franklin's Poor Richard's Almanacs: 'The Habit of His Labors,' " in J. A. Leo Lemay, ed., *The Oldest Revolutionary* (Philadelphia, 1976), 85–88; Wright, *Franklin of Philadelphia*, 55. For a stress on Franklin's populism that admits its exclusions, see William Pencak, "Politics and Ideology in Poor Richard's Almanack," *Pennsylvania Magazine of History and Biography* 116 (1992), 183–211.

36. *PBF* 1:293, 311; Benjamin Franklin, *Poor Richard: The Almanacks for the Years 1733–1758* (New York, 1976), 2–3, 14, 25–26, 297–98. The Leeds hoax also echoed one perpetrated by Jonathan Swift. Ross, "Character of Poor Richard."

37. Roy Porter, *The Creation of the Modern World: The Untold Story of the British Enlightenment* (New York, 2000), 151.

38. Van Doren, *Franklin*, 73, 105, 107; Aldridge, *Benjamin Franklin*, 64; *Autobiography*, 126–27, 284; Anna Jannery DeArmond, *Andrew Bradford, Colonial Journalist* (Newark, Del., 1949), 14–15. The two men actually remained friends; Godfrey was later a member of the American Philosophical Society. BF to Cadwallader Colden, April 5, 1744, in *PBF* 2:406.

39. *Autobiography*, 128–29, 296; Sheila Skemp, *William Franklin: Son of a Patriot, Servant of a King* (New York, 1990), 4–5; J. A. Leo Lemay, "Essay Review: Recent Franklin Scholarship, with a Note on Franklin's Sedan Chair," *Pennsylvania Magazine of History and Biography* 126 (2002), 336–37.

40. BF, "Celia Single," "Anthony Afterwit," "Alice Addertongue," in *PBF* 1:240–48; J. A. Leo Lemay, "Benjamin Franklin," in Everett Emerson, ed., *Major Writers of Early American Literature* (Madison, Wisc., 1972), 205–43; Gary E. Baker, "He That Would Thrive Must Ask His Wife: Franklin's Anthony Afterwit Letter," *Pennsylvania Magazine of History and Biography* 109 (1985), 27–42. Baker ties the Godfrey fiasco to Anthony Afterwit, but to my knowledge scholars have not previously made the connection to *Poor Richard's Almanack*.

41. BF, *Poor Richard*, 4–11, 15–16, 20, 28, 32, 40; *Franklin: Writings*, ed. Lemay, 320–22, 305–8. For Franklin's reliance on women and his sensitivity about the relationship between women and money see especially Jan Lewis, "Sex and the Married Man: Benjamin Franklin's Families," in Larry Tise, ed., *Benjamin Franklin and Women* (University Park, Pa., 2000), 67–82.

42. *Autobiography*, 129, 145; BF, Shop Book, 1735–39, Benjamin Franklin Papers, APS; *PBF* 1:332, 2:127.
43. Bill of E. E. [H. S.] Warner, Benjamin Franklin Papers, APS; Claude-Anne Lopez and Eugenia W. Herbert, *The Private Franklin: The Man and His Family* (New York: 1975), 30–33.
44. Bridget Hill, *Women, Work, and Sexual Politics in Eighteenth-Century England* (Oxford, 1989), 24, 49; Naomi Tadmor, "The Concept of Household and Family in Eighteenth-Century England," *Past and Present* 151 (1996), 111–40; Jeanne Boydston, "The Woman Who Wasn't There: Women's Market Labor and the Transition to Capitalism in the United States," *Journal of the Early Republic* 16 (1996), 183–206; Melish, *Disowning Slavery*, 14–23; Richard L. Bushman, "The Place of the Eighteenth Century in American Agricultural History," in Michael V. Kennedy and William G. Shade, eds., *The World Turned Upside Down: The State of Eighteenth-Century American Studies at the Beginning of the Twenty-First Century* (Bethlehem, Pa., 2001), 40–77; Jan Lewis, " 'Of Every Age Sex and Condition': The Representation of Women in the Constitution," *Journal of the Early Republic* 15 (1995), 359–87.
45. Van Doren, *Franklin*, 132; *PBF* 1:198–99; Steven C. Bullock, *Revolutionary Brotherhood: Freemasonry and the Transformation of the American Social Order, 1730–1840* (Chapel Hill, N.C., 1996), 50–52, 66–68.
46. *PBF* 2:200–202; DeArmond, *Andrew Bradford*, 137–38.
47. Ruth Lapham Butler, *Doctor Franklin, Postmaster General* (Garden City, N.Y., 1928), 32–33; Alexander Spotswood to BF, October 12, 1739, in *PBF* 2:235–36; DeArmond, *Andrew Bradford*, 84–118; Smith, *Printers and Press Freedom*, 114.
48. DeArmond, *Andrew Bradford*, 101–7, 223–27; *PBF* 2:263–64, 268; Sappenfield, *Sweet Instruction*, 107.
49. *PBF* 2:265–69, 271–81; DeArmond, *Andrew Bradford*, 228–33; Sappenfield, *Sweet Instruction*, 98.
50. *PBF* 2:304–5.

5. CHILDREN AND COLONIES

1. *General Magazine, and Historical Chronicle, for all the British Plantations in America* 1 (1741), in *PBF* 2:302–4.
2. John M. Murrin, "Anglicizing an American Colony: The Transformation of Provincial Massachusetts" (Ph.D. diss., Yale University, 1966); Ian K. Steele, *The English Atlantic 1675–1740: An Exploration of Communication and Community* (New York, 1986); Cary Carson, ed., *Of Consuming Interests: The Style of Life in the Eighteenth Century* (Charlottesville, Va., 1992); Jon Butler, *Becoming America: The Revolution Before 1776* (Cambridge, Mass., 2000); Jack P. Greene, *Peripheries and Center: Constitutional Development in the Extended Polities of the British Empire and the United States, 1607–1788* (1986; repr., New York, 1990); Francis Jennings, *Benjamin Franklin, Politician* (New York, 1996).
3. BF, *Poor Richard's Almanack . . . 1741*, in *PBF* 2:292, 292n3.
4. Richard Pares, *Yankees and Creoles: The Trade Between North America and the West Indies Before the American Revolution* (London, 1956), 31, 51–56; Joshua Gee, *The Trade and Navigation of Great-Britain Considered* (London, 1729), 23–24, 26, 62, 99; John Oldmixon, *The British Empire in America*, 2 vols. (1741; repr., New York, 1969), 1:xxviii; "The Case of Pennsylvania and New Jersey" [n.d.], vol. 56i, folder 6, Benjamin Franklin

Papers, APS; Lawrence Henry Gipson, *The British Empire Before the American Revolution*, vol. 3, *The British Isles and the American Colonies: The Northern Plantations, 1748–1754* (Caldwell, Id., and New York, 1937–70), 287; Steele, *The English Atlantic*, 222–23, 246–47; David Armitage, *The Ideological Origins of the British Empire* (New York, 2000), 170–73, 180–82.

5. Theodore Thayer, *Pennsylvania Politics and the Growth of Democracy, 1740–1776* (Harrisburg, Pa., 1953), 12–13; *PBF* 2:289n7.

6. Herbert L. Osgood, *The American Colonies in the Eighteenth Century*, 4 vols. (New York, 1924), 4:58–61; Robert L. D. Davidson, *War Comes to Quaker Pennsylvania, 1682–1756* (New York, 1957), 28–33; Cheesman Herrick, *White Servitude in Colonial Pennsylvania* (Philadelphia, 1926), 233–49; *Colonial Records of Pennsylvania* (Harrisburg, 1851–53), 4:427–68.

7. *Pennsylvania Gazette*, April 22, 1742; Davidson, *War Comes to Quaker Pennsylvania*, 157–58; Alan Rogers, *Empire and Liberty: American Resistance to British Authority, 1755–1763* (Berkeley, 1974), 42–44; BF, "Militia Act," Pennsylvania Assembly to Governor, in *PBF* 6:272, 396–400. None of this prevented the Pennsylvanians from buying nineteen slaves brought in by privateers, "several of the Men Stout able bodied Seamen," as plunder of war. *Pennsylvania Gazette*, December 5, 1745.

8. BF to Cadwallader Colden, October 1, 1747, in *PBF* 3:179; "A Proclamation," *New York Weekly Post Boy*, May 4, 1747; *New York Gazette and Weekly Post Boy*, March 10, 1755; "A Letter from a Country Man in the Jerseys, to the Printers," *New York Gazette and Weekly Post Boy*, February 23, 1756; Sheila Skemp, *William Franklin: Son of a Patriot, Servant of a King* (New York, 1990), 10.

9. Carl Van Doren, *Benjamin Franklin* (New York, 1938), 138.

10. Ibid.; *PBF* 2:380; BF to Samuel Johnson, August 23, 1750, in *PBF* 4:42; Harry S. Stout, *The Divine Dramatist* (Grand Rapids, Mich., 1991); Frank Lambert, *Pedlar in Divinity* (Princeton, 1994); David S. Shields, *Oracles of Empire: Poetry, Politics and Commerce in British America, 1690–1750* (Chicago, 1990).

11. John Clyde Oswald, *Benjamin Franklin, Printer* (New York, 1917), 139; Marion Reynolds King, "One Link in the First Newspaper Chain: *The South Carolina Gazette*," *Journalism Quarterly* 9 (1932), 257–68; Van Doren, *Franklin*, 116–22; Ian M. G. Quimby, "Apprenticeship in Colonial Philadelphia" (M.A. thesis, University of Delaware, 1963), 85–86; Ward L. Miner, *William Goddard, Newspaperman* (Durham, N.C., 1962), 3–4, 6; BF, Articles of Agreement with James Parker, February 21, 1742, in *PBF* 2:341–45; BF, Agreement with Samuel Holland, in *PBF* 4:506–8. For a stress on the liberating aspects of the partnerships for the other printers, see Ralph D. Frasca, "From Apprentice to Journeyman to Partner: Benjamin Franklin's Workers and the Growth of the Early American Printing Trade," *Pennsylvania Magazine of History and Biography* 114 (1990), 229–48. My own interpretation turns on a different understanding of the difficulties of the printing trade, for which see Stephen Botein, "Meer Mechanics and an Open Press: The Business and Political Strategies of Early American Printers," *Perspectives in American History* 9 (1975), 127–225; Jeffrey A. Smith, *Printers and Press Freedom: The Ideology of Early American Journalism* (New York, 1988); Jeffrey L. Pasley, *The Tyranny of Printers: Newspaper Politics in the Early American Republic* (Charlottesville, Va., 2001), 24–47.

12. BF to Deborah Franklin, n.d., in *PBF* 5:463; William Daniell to BF, June 23, 1754, in *PBF* 5:355; William Weyman to Deborah Franklin, January 26, 1756, in *PBF* 6:374;

George Simpson Eddy, *Account Books Kept by Benjamin Franklin: Ledger "D,"* *1739–1747* (New York, 1928), 19 and passim; Ledger D, Benjamin Franklin Papers, APS; BF, Memorandum to send paper to Timothy and Daniel, n.d., vol. 66, folder 68A, Benjamin Franklin Papers, APS; Claude-Anne Lopez and Eugenia W. Herbert, *The Private Franklin: The Man and His Family* (New York, 1975), 31.

13. *Autobiography*, 181; Peter Timothy to BF, June 14, 1754, June 8, 1755, in *PBF* 5:341–43, 6:68–69; Hennig Cohen, *The South Carolina Gazette, 1732–1775* (Columbia, S.C., 1953), 6.

14. BF to William Strahan, July 10, 1743, in *PBF* 2:383–84; Robert Hurd Kany, "David Hall: Printing Partner of Benjamin Franklin" (Ph.D. diss., Pennsylvania State University, 1963).

15. William Strahan to David Hall, March 9, June 22, August 23, 1745, David Hall Papers, APS; BF to Strahan, July 4, September 18, 1744, February 12, November 12, 1745, in *PBF* 2:409, 416–18, 3:14, 46; editorial note, in *PBF* 3:263; BF to Strahan, November 28, 1747, October 19, 1748, in *PBF* 3:213, 323.

16. J. A. Cochrane, *Dr. Johnson's Printer: The Life of William Strahan* (London, 1964), 62; Kany, "David Hall," 96–97; BF to William Strahan, June 1, July 29, 1747, October 19, 1748, October 27, November 27, 1753, in *PBF* 3:140, 165, 4:321–23, 5:82–83, 120–21.

17. By the time Strahan was finally ready to sue him for an unpaid shipment of books, Read had managed to alienate Franklin, his cousin by marriage, by trying to wrest away his clerkship of the Assembly. J. Bennett Nolan, *Printer Strahan's Book Account: A Colonial Controversy* (Reading, Pa., 1939); Kany, "David Hall," 69, 90–91, 97; BF to William Strahan, April 29, 1749, in *PBF* 3:377; David Hall to Strahan, August 7, 1754, May 1, 1755, June 16, 1756, July 4, September 13, 1757, Strahan to Hall, February 13, May 25, 1751, November 9, 1754, March 3, 1755, March 13, September 11, 1756, July 11, 1758, March 24, 1759, June 29, July 16, 1763, David Hall Letterbooks, David Hall Papers, APS; Strahan to Hall, July 27, 1751, August 26, 1752, *Pennsylvania Magazine of History and Biography* 60 (1936), 460–61, 465–66. Like Peter Timothy and David Hall, James Parker named a son, Samuel Franklin Parker, after Franklin.

18. BF to William Strahan, September 25, 1746, January 4, June 1, 1747, October 19, 1748, June 2, 1750, June 28, 1751, October 7, 1755, in *PBF* 3:73, 108, 140, 322–23, 479–80, 4:142, 6:220; Strahan to David Hall, March 5, 1745, David Hall Papers, APS. For the Sally Franklin–Billy Strahan Jr. liaison, which became all too real for Sally, see Lopez and Herbert, *Private Franklin*, 76–77; Larry E. Tise, "Liberty and the Rights of Women: Sarah Franklin's Declaration of Independence," and Jan Lewis, "Sex and the Married Man: Benjamin Franklin's Families," in Tise, ed., *Benjamin Franklin and Women* (University Park, Pa., 2000), 45, 47, 79; BF to Strahan, March 30, 1764, in *PBF* 11:149.

19. *Autobiography*, 169, 282; *PBF* 2:154n2; Bill from Alexander Annand, 1738, in *PBF*, 2:388, 388n4; James Franklin: Indenture of Apprenticeship, in *PBF* 2:261–63; Skemp, *William Franklin*, 8–9; Lopez and Herbert, *Private Franklin*, 109.

20. James Franklin Indenture, in *PBF* 2:262; Alfred Owen Aldridge, *Benjamin Franklin: Philosopher and Man* (Philadelphia, 1965), 84; BF to Jane Mecom, June 1748, in *PBF* 3:303–4; BF to William Strahan, October 27, 1753, in *PBF* 5:82; Lopez and Herbert, *Private Franklin*, 11n.

21. Lopez and Herbert, *Private Franklin*, 60–61; "Extracts from the Diary of Daniel Fisher, 1755," *Pennsylvania Magazine of History and Biography* 60 (1936), 276–77; Aldridge, *Benjamin Franklin*, 84–85; *PBF* 5:187n6. For styles of parenting during the age of high

infant mortality and large families, see Philippe Ariès, *Centuries of Childhood* (New York, 1962).

22. *PBF* 3:89n4–5; Skemp, *William Franklin*, 9–10; David Freeman Hawke, *Franklin* (New York, 1976), 75; BF to John Franklin, April 2, 1747, in *PBF* 3:119; Sheila Skemp, *Benjamin and William Franklin: Father and Son, Patriot and Loyalist* (New York, 1994), 15; Philip Greven, *The Protestant Temperament* (New York, 1977); Jay Fliegelman, *Prodigals and Pilgrims: The American Revolution Against Patriarchal Authority, 1750–1800* (New York, 1982); John Gillis, *A World of Their Own Making: Myth, Ritual, and the Quest for Family Values* (New York, 1996); Gillian Brown, *The Consent of the Governed: The Lockean Legacy in Early American Culture* (Cambridge, Mass., 2001).

23. BF to Cadwallader Colden, September 29, 1748, to Peter Collinson, October 18, 1748, to Abiah Franklin, September 7, 1749, April 12, 1750, to William Strahan, October 23, 1749, June 2, December 6, 1750, February 4, 1751, in *PBF* 3:218, 320, 389, 394, 474–75, 479, 4:78, 114; *Autobiography*, 231; Lopez and Herbert, *Private Franklin*, 61–62; Van Doren, *Franklin*, 211–12.

24. BF to Edward and Jane Mecom, in *PBF* 2:448; Carl Van Doren, *Jane Mecom* (New York, 1950), 24–25, 28–29.

25. This guess about Newport's identity, which the *PBF* editors were unable to discover, is based on the fact that adult white men were usually referred to by a full name or by a title if they were not well-known intimates, and that slaves often had generic names of that sort. BF to Jane Mecom, June 1748, in *PBF* 3:301.

26. BF to Jane Mecom, June 1748, in *PBF* 3:303–4.

27. Ibid., 304; BF to Jane Mecom, September 20, 1750, in *PBF* 3:64.

28. BF to Edward and Jane Mecom, September 14, 1752, in *PBF* 3:355–57.

29. BF to Edward and Jane Mecom, November 20, 1752, in *PBF* 4:385.

30. Aldridge, *Benjamin Franklin*, 110; H. W. Brands, *The First American: The Life and Times of Benjamin Franklin* (New York, 2000), 242; Van Doren, *Jane Mecom*, 10–13, 28; Benjamin Mecom to Deborah Franklin, September 21, 1754, vol. 1, folio 29, Benjamin Franklin Papers, APS; Lopez and Herbert, *Private Franklin*, 111.

31. BF to William Strahan, May 9, 1753, April 18, 1754, November 27, 1755, in *PBF* 4:487, 5:264, 6:277–78; Van Doren, *Jane Mecom*, 39; Isaiah Thomas, *The History of Printing in America* (1810; repr., New York, 1970), 141–42.

32. BF to William Strahan, November 27, 1755, in *PBF* 6:277; BF to Jane Mecom, June 28, 1756, in *PBF* 6:463–64.

33. BF to Jane Mecom, June 28, July 12, December 30, 1756, to William Strahan, July 2, 27, December 31, 1756, in *PBF* 6:463–65, 467, 470, 477, 7:68–69; BF, Bond with Benjamin Mecom, December 27, 1756, vol. 66, folio 9, Benjamin Franklin Papers, APS; BF, *Poor Richard Improved . . . 1757*, in *PBF* 7:86.

34. *PBF* 7:196n3, 329–30; BF and Deborah Franklin to Jane Mecom, May 21, 1757, in *PBF* 7:216; Wilberforce Eames, "The Antigua Press of Benjamin Mecom, 1748–1765," *Proceedings of the American Antiquarian Society* 38 (1928), 334; Van Doren, *Jane Mecom*, 55–57; Lopez and Herbert, *Private Franklin*, 111–12; *New England Magazine*, in *PBF* 8:123; BF to Jane Mecom, May 30, 1757, in *PBF* 7:222–23; Benjamin Mecom to Deborah Franklin, Feburary 9, 1761 in William Duane, ed., *Letters to Benjamin Franklin from His Family and Friends, 1751–1796* (New York, 1859), 184–85.

35. BF, *Plain Truth: or, Serious Considerations On the Present State of the City of Philadelphia, and Province of Pennsylvania, By a Tradesman of Philadelphia* (Philadelphia, 1747), in *PBF* 3:198–99, 202–4. Franklin had used somewhat similar language com-

menting on the controversy between Governor Burnet and the Massachusetts Assembly in 1729: *PBF* 1:161.

36. For a contrary view, suggesting that Franklin was aware of the dangerous implications and actually playing with them merely to induce assimilation, see Douglas Anderson, *The Radical Enlightenments of Benjamin Franklin* (Baltimore, Md., 1997), 159, 194. Anderson is right that Franklin was not a xenophobic racist. He was, rather, a political one; and it is very much in the spirit of Anderson's appreciation of Franklin's pragmatism to insist that strategic racism is important. For views closer to my own, see Paul W. Conner, *Poor Richard's Politicks: Benjamin Franklin and His New American Order* (New York, 1965), 69–79; Timothy Shannon, *Indians and Colonists at the Crossroads of Empire* (Ithaca, N.Y., 1998), 98–101.

37. BF to Abiah Franklin, April 12, 1750, in *PBF* 3:474.

38. *PBF* 3:474n8.

39. BF, "Observations on the Increase of Mankind," in *PBF* 4:225–34; *Reasons Against the Making and Manufacture of Bar-Iron in America* (n.p., 1750), Broadsides Collection, New-York Historical Society; Gipson, *British Empire in the Age of the American Revolution*, 3:206–25.

40. Eighteen years later Franklin altered the phrase "every slave being by nature a thief" to "every slave being by the nature of slavery a thief," a change that has encouraged the *PBF* editors, and subsequent scholars, to stress his rethinking of the matter and a final, or ultimate, stance against racism as well as against slavery. *PBF* 4:229, 19:113n1.

41. For the report of the treaty, see James Parker's *New York Gazette and Weekly Post Boy*, May 27, 1751.

42. David Brion Davis, *The Problem of Slavery in Western Culture* (Ithaca, N.Y., 1966), 150–51.

43. BF, *Poor Richard's Almanack . . . for 1752*, in *PBF* 4:247–53, quoted at 253.

44. David Hume, "Of National Characters" [1748], "Of Money" [1752], *Political Essays*, ed. Knud Haakonsen (Cambridge, Eng., 1994), 86, 123; Roy Porter, *The Creation of the Modern World: The Untold Story of the British Enlightenment* (New York, 2000), 200; Van Doren, *Franklin*, 290; Davis, *Problem of Slavery in Western Culture*, 485.

45. Verner W. Crane, *Benjamin Franklin—Englishman and American* (Baltimore, Md., 1936); Gerald Stourzh, *Benjamin Franklin and American Foreign Policy*, 2nd ed. (Chicago, 1969), 33–112; Ormond Seavey, "Benjamin Franklin as Imperialist and Provincial," in Gianfranca Balestra and Luigi Sanpietro, eds., *Benjamin Franklin: An American Genius* (Rome, 1993), 19–37; Esmond Wright, " 'The Fine and Noble China Vase, the British Empire': Benjamin Franklin's 'Love-Hate' View of England," *Pennsylvania Magazine of History and Biography* 111 (1987), 435–64; Gordon S. Wood, "Not So Poor Richard," *New York Review of Books* 43 (June 6, 1996), 47–51; T. H. Breen, "Ideology and Nationalism on the Eve of the American Revolution: Revisions Once More in Need of Revising," *Journal of American History* 84 (1997), 13–39; Stephen Conway, "From Fellow-Nationals to Foreigners: British Perceptions of the Americans, circa 1739–1783," *William and Mary Quarterly*, 3rd ser., 59 (2002), 65–100.

46. BF to James Parker, March 20, 1751, in *PBF* 4:120–21; Pennsylvania Committee Report on Paper Currency, August 1752, in *PBF* 4:327–28, 348–50. Franklin's fascination with demographics at this time can also be seen in *Poor Richard's Almanack* for 1751: *PBF* 4:97–99; Alfred Owen Aldridge, "Franklin as Demographer," *Journal of Economic History* 9 (1949), 25–44.

47. *New York Gazette and Weekly Post Boy*, July 29, 1751, November 20, 1752; *Pennsylvania*

Gazette, April 11, May 9, 1751, in *Benjamin Franklin: Writings*, ed. J. A. Leo Lemay (New York, 1987), 357–61; Kany, "David Hall," 94–95; Roxann Wheeler, *The Complexion of Race: Categories of Difference in Eighteenth-Century British Culture* (University Park, Pa., 2000), 1–48.

48. Karen Severud Cook, "Benjamin Franklin and the Snake that Would not Die," *British Library Journal* 22 (1996), 95; Edwin Wolf II, "Benjamin Franklin's Stamp Act Cartoon," *Proceedings of the American Philosophical Society* 99 (1955), 398; Albert Mathews, "The Snake Device," *Publications of the Colonial Society of Massachusetts* 11 (1906–7), 407–52.

49. Jack P. Greene, "An Uneasy Connection: An Analysis of the Preconditions of the American Revolution," in Stephen G. Kurtz and James H. Hutson, eds., *Essays on the American Revolution* (New York, 1973), 32–80; James Henretta, *"Salutary Neglect": Colonial Administration under the Duke of Newcastle* (Princeton, 1972), 317–19, 332–33; Greene, *Peripheries and Center*, 18, 48–53; Greven, *Protestant Temperament*; Peter N. Miller, *Defining the Common Good: Empire, Religion, and Philosophy in Eighteenth-Century Britain* (Cambridge, Eng., 1994), 159–213.

50. BF to Peter Collinson, November 27, 1753, May 28, 1754, to Thomas Darling and Nathan Whitney, November 25, 1754, to Collinson, May 9, 1753, in *PBF* 4:486, 5:160, 332, 441. On the Albany Congress and its meanings, see Shannon, *Indians and Colonists*; Fred Anderson, *Crucible of War: The Seven Years' War and the Fate of Empire in British North America, 1754–1766* (New York, 1999); Jennings, *Benjamin Franklin, Politician*.

51. BF to William Shirley, December 12, 1754, in *PBF* 5:441, 447; compare BF, "Dialogue Between X Y and Z," *Pennsylvania Gazette*, December 18, 1755, in *PBF*, 6:299.

52. BF to Shirley, December 24, 1754, in *PBF* 5:451; BF, "A Plan for Settling Two Western Colonies" [1754], in *PBF* 5:458.

53. *PBF* 6:397–99.

54. BF to Sir Everard Faulkener, July 27, 1756, in *PBF* 6:472–75. Franklin later negotiated with the authorities for payment of masters whose servants were taken into service. BF to Lord Loudon, May 21, 1757, to Isaac Norris, May 30, 1757, in *PBF* 7:214–15, 224–26; Herrick, *White Servitude in Pennsylvania*, 249.

55. For the continuing significance of the servant-slave enlistment issue, see BF to Pennsylvania Assembly Committee, June 10, 1758, to Joseph Galloway, April 29, 1759, Richard Jackson to BF, April 24, 1758, Isaac Norris to BF, April 29, 1758, January 15, 1759, BF to Assembly, May 13, 1758, Charles Thomson to BF, May 14, 1758, in *PBF* 8:90, 311–12, 27, 56, 227, 66, 78–79.

56. *PBF* 7:174, 199; Nash and Soderlund, *Freedom by Degrees*, x–xi.

6. PRINTERS, AGENTS, AND BLACKENED MEN

1. *The Autobiography of Benjamin Franklin*, ed. Leonard W. Labaree et al. (New Haven, Conn., 1964), 213–14. For the darker side of Franklin's relationship with Morris, and Morris's politics, see Robert Middlekauff, *Benjamin Franklin and His Enemies* (Berkeley, Calif., 1996), 46–47, 59–62; Francis Jennings, *Benjamin Franklin, Politician* (New York, 1996), 94, 100–3, 111, 123–37. Eight years later Franklin objected that his enemies had accused him of being an "opponent of his majesty's Service . . . I think they might as justly have accus'd me of being a Blackamore." BF to Henry Bouquet, August 16, 1764, in *PBF* 11:318.

2. Winthrop D. Jordan, *White over Black: American Attitudes Toward the Negro, 1550–1812* (Chapel Hill, N.C., 1967); Kathleen M. Brown, *Good Wives, Nasty Wenches, and Anxious Patriarchs: Gender, Race and Power in Colonial Virginia* (Chapel Hill, N.C., 1996); Kirsten Fischer, *Suspect Relations: Sex, Race and Resistance in Colonial North Carolina* (Ithaca, N.Y., 2002), 1–12, 131–58.

3. Fred Anderson, *Crucible of War: The Seven Years' War and the Fate of Empire in British North America, 1754–1766* (New York, 1998); Jennings, *Benjamin Franklin, Politician*; Alan Rogers, *Empire and Liberty: American Resistance to British Authority, 1755–1763* (Berkeley, Calif., 1974); John Brewer, *The Sinews of Power: War, Money, and the English State, 1688–1783* (London, 1989); Linda Colley, *Britons: Forging the Nation, 1707–1837* (New Haven, Conn., 1992), 85–145; Peter N. Miller, *Defining the Common Good: Empire, Religion, and Philosophy in Eighteenth-Century Britain* (Cambridge, Eng., 1994); Eliga H. Gould, *The Persistence of Empire: British Political Culture in the Era of the American Revolution* (Chapel Hill, N.C., 1999); Theodore Draper, *A Struggle for Power: The American Revolution* (New York, 1995).

4. John Brewer, *Party Ideology and Popular Politics at the Accession of George III* (Cambridge, Eng., 1976); George Rudé, *Wilkes and Liberty* (London, 1965); Colley, *Britons*; Nicholas Rogers, *Whigs and Cities* (London, 1989); Frank O'Gorman, "Eighteenth-Century England as an Ancien Regime," in Stephen Taylor et al., eds., *Hanoverian Britain and Empire: Essays in Memory of Philip Lawson* (Woodbridge, Eng., 1998), 30–31; Pauline Maier, *From Resistance to Revolution: Colonial Radicals and the Development of American Opposition to Britain, 1763–1776* (New York, 1972), 77–112, 161–97; David Waldstreicher, "Rites of Rebellion, Rites of Assent: Celebrations, Print Culture and the Origins of American Nationalism," *Journal of American History* 82 (1995), 34–61.

5. Lawrence Stone and Jeanne C. Fawtier Stone, *An Open Elite? England, 1554–1880* (New York, 1984); John Brewer, "The Commercialization of Politics," in Neil McKendrick, John Brewer, and J. H. Plumb, *The Birth of a Consumer Society* (Bloomington, Ind., 1982), 197–262; Dror Wahrman, "The English Problem of Identity in the American Revolution," *American Historical Review* 106 (2001), 1236–62; Don Herzog, *Policing the Minds of the Lower Orders* (Princeton, N.J., 1999); Colley, *Britons*; Gerald Newman, *The Rise of English Nationalism, 1730–1790* (New York, 1987).

6. On struggles for identity in the late colonial and revolutionary eras, see Jack P. Greene, "Search for Identity: An Interpretation of the Meaning of Selected Patterns of Social Response in Eighteenth-Century America" and "Changing Identity in the British West Indies in the Early Modern Era: Barbados as a Case Study," in *Imperatives, Behaviors, and Identities: Essays in Early American Cultural History* (Charlottesville, Va., 1992), 13–67, 143–73; Michael Zuckerman, "Identity in British America: Unease in Eden," in Nicholas Canny and Anthony Pagden, eds., *Colonial Identity in the Atlantic World, 1500–1800* (Princeton, N.J., 1987), 115–57.

7. Jack P. Greene, "All Men Are Created Equal: Some Reflections on the Character of the American Revolution," in *Imperatives, Behaviors, and Identities*, 264; Edmund S. Morgan, *American Slavery, American Freedom: The Ordeal of Colonial Virginia* (New York, 1975).

8. Jennings, *Benjamin Franklin, Politician*, 38; Allan Tully, *Forming American Politics: Ideals, Interests and Institutions in Colonial New York and Pennsylvania* (Baltimore, Md., 1994), 84, 266; Pennsylvania Assembly Reply to Governor Morris, May 17, August 19,

September 29, 1755, in *PBF* 6:49, 161–62, 202–3. Jennings argues that the latter resolves were drafted by Franklin; internal evidence, in the similarity to other writings, suggests that he is right. *Benjamin Franklin, Politician*, 117, 215n36.

9. Proposed Reply to Governor, November 25, 1755, Pennsylvania Assembly Committee's
Report on the Governor's Instructions, September 23, 1756, in *PBF* 6:264–65, 518.

10. BF to Isaac Norris, January 14, 1758, to Joseph Galloway, April 7, 1759, in *PBF*
7:361–62, 360n8, 362n6, 8:310–11.

11. David T. Morgan, *The Devious Dr. Franklin, Colonial Agent: Benjamin Franklin's Years in
London* (Macon, Ga., 1996), 27–29, 33–35, 56–57; Alfred Owen Aldridge, *Benjamin
Franklin: Philosopher and Man* (Philadelphia, 1965), 145–48; Jennings, *Benjamin
Franklin, Politician*, 49–58, 81–93, 138–45; James H. Merrell, *Into the American Woods:
Negotiators on the Pennsylvania Frontier* (New York, 1999), 36; Middlekauff, *Benjamin
Franklin and His Enemies*, 43–76; Verner W. Crane, *Benjamin Franklin and a Rising
People* (Boston, 1954), 79, 84; David Freeman Hawke, *Franklin* (New York, 1976), 173,
177, 181; William Franklin to the Printer of *The Citizen*, September 1757, in *PBF*
7:255–63; *PBF* 7:291–2n1.

12. BF to Isaac Norris, September 16, 1758, January 19, 1759, to Israel Pemberton, March 19,
1759, in *PBF* 8:157–58, 235–36, 299–300, to Ann Penn [1760], to Edward Pennington,
May 9, 1761, January 9, 1762, in *PBF* 9:260–62, 315–17, 10:6; Morgan, *Devious Dr.
Franklin*, 64; David Martin Luebke, *His Majesty's Rebels: Communities, Factions, and
Rural Revolt in the Black Forest, 1725–1745* (Ithaca, N.Y., 1997); Hawke, *Franklin*, 93;
Esmond Wright, *Franklin of Philadelphia* (Cambridge, Mass., 1986), 149; James H. Hut-
son, *Pennsylvania Politics, 1746–1770: The Movement for Royal Government and Its Con-
sequences* (Princeton, N.J., 1972); Jennings, *Benjamin Franklin, Politician*, 148ff.

13. Jennings, *Benjamin Franklin, Politician*, 91; *PBF* 7:192; Hutson, *Pennsylvania Politics*,
144–45; Sheila Skemp, *William Franklin: Son of a Patriot, Servant of a King* (New York,
1990), 15; Hawke, *Franklin*, 190–93.

14. Skemp, *William Franklin*, 62; Ronald Clark, *Benjamin Franklin: A Biography* (New York,
1983), 169; R. C. Simmons, "Colonial Patronage: Two Letters from William Franklin to
the Earl of Bute, 1762," *William and Mary Quarterly*, 3rd ser., 59 (2002), 123–34; Merrill Jensen, *The Founding of a Nation: A History of the American Revolution, 1763–1776*
(New York, 1968), 39; William Strahan to David Hall, November 30, 1764, David
Hall Papers, APS; William Franklin, Receipt to R. Stone, October 12, 1764, vol. 66,
folder 119c, Benjamin Franklin Papers, APS; BF to Deborah Franklin, April 6, 1766,
PBF 13:234.

15. BF to Deborah Franklin, January 21, 1758, William Franklin to BF, September 3, 1758,
to John Morgan, August 16, 1762, in *PBF* 7:369, 8:132, 10:146; Claude-Anne Lopez and
Eugenia W. Herbert, *The Private Franklin: The Man and His Family* (New York, 1975),
93–94. William Strahan saw to the child's care. William Franklin expressed guarded interest in the Barbados governorship when it opened up in 1766. William Franklin to BF,
in *PBF* 8:336.

16. For an early intimation, circulated on both sides of the water, see "London," *New York
Gazette and Weekly Post Boy*, January 19, 1756; Draper, *Struggle for Power*, 19.

17. BF to Lord Kames, January 1760, BF, *The Interest of Great Britain Considered*, in *PBF*
9:5–7, 78–79, 95–96.

18. BF, Commission to James Parker, April 22, 1757, in *PBF* 7:192–94; Ruth Lapham Butler, *Doctor Franklin, Postmaster General* (Garden City, N.Y., 1928), 69, 81; Morgan, *Devi-*

ous Dr. Franklin, 72; Parker to Jared Ingersoll, March 11, 1768, box 2, folder 5, Ingersoll Papers, New-Haven Colony Historical Society; Winifred Reynolds Reid, "Beginnings of Printing in New Haven," *Papers in Honor of Andrew Keogh* (New Haven, Conn., 1938), 75–80; Beverly McAnear, "James Parker versus William Weyman," *Proceedings of the New Jersey Historical Society* 59 (1941), 1–23; McAnear, "James Parker versus John Holt," *Proceedings of the New Jersey Historical Society* 59 (1941), 78; Alan Dyer, *A Biography of James Parker, Colonial Printer* (Troy, N.Y., 1982).

19. Isaiah Thomas, *The History of Printing in America* (1810; repr., New York, 1970), 294–96; Dyer, *James Parker,* 54–58, McAnear, "Parker versus Holt," 77–80; Layton Barnes Murphy, "John Holt, Patriot Printer and Publisher" (Ph.D. diss., University of Michigan, 1965), 2–10; Kevin J. Hayes, "John Holt," *American National Biography* (New York, 1999), 11:100–101.

20. *Samuel Avery v. John Holt,* Samuel Avery Papers, New York Public Library; McAnear, "Parker versus Holt," 81–82; Dyer, *James Parker,* 58–59.

21. James Parker, *An Appeal to the Publick of New-York* (Woodbridge, N.J., 1759), broadside, Library Company of Philadelphia; Dyer, *James Parker,* 61–75; *New York Gazette and Weekly Post Boy,* February 12, 19, September 17, 1759; Parker to John Holt, September 20, 1758, June 19, 1760, July 6, 1762, Parker MSS, New-York Historical Society. When Parker dunned Holt because he had received only £80 of the partnership money, Holt threatened—in print—to start his own paper. *New York Gazette,* April 29, 1762.

22. Dyer, *James Parker,* 69–71, 75–76; James Parker, *A Letter to a Gentleman in the City of New York* (New York, 1759); Mack Thompson, "Massachusetts and New York Stamp Acts," *William and Mary Quarterly,* 3rd ser., 26 (1969), 253–58.

23. Indeed, seven years earlier Parker had lured a prospective partner to Woodbridge with the promise of free help from his newly inherited slaves.

24. Parker, *Letter to a Gentleman;* Ian K. Steele, *The English Atlantic, 1690–1740: An Exploration of Communication and Community* (New York, 1986). For Parker's Franklinian free press ethic, see Jeffrey A. Smith, *Printers and Press Freedom: The Ideology of Early American Journalism* (New York, 1988), 18, 126–31. Parker mentioned his desire to start a paper mill in *Letter to a Gentleman,* 2, in the course of complaining that Irish printers were getting bounties for such efforts.

25. BF to Jared Ingersoll, December 19, 1763, in *PBF* 10:402–3; *New York Gazette,* April 1, 15, 1762; Dyer, *James Parker,* 79; McAnear, "Parker versus Holt," 83–85; Parker to Hamilton and Balfour, January 3, 1766, vol. 47, folder 31, Benjamin Franklin Papers, APS; J. Bennett Nolan, *Benjamin Franklin in Scotland and Ireland* (Philadelphia, 1938).

26. Anthony Todd to BF and John Foxcroft, March 12, August 13, 1763, BF to Anthony Todd, April 14, June 10, 1763, in *PBF* 10:221, 251–54, 276–83, 323; Butler, *Doctor Franklin, Postmaster General,* 82ff.

27. Benjamin Franklin Memorandum Book, November 1762, April 6, 1763, Reel 1, Benjamin Franklin Account Books, APS; editorial note on Parker-Franklin accounts, in *PBF* 10:261–64; BF, Bond with James Parker, November 15, 1763, vol. 66, folder 10, Benjamin Franklin Papers, APS; Butler, *Doctor Franklin, Postmaster General,* 129–31; Parker to BF, October 27, 1764, in *PBF* 11:413, 416.

28. BF to William Dunlap, April 4, 1757, Deborah Franklin to BF, June 10, 1758, Dunlap to BF and John Foxcroft, October 1764, BF and Foxcroft to Dunlap, October 1764, Parker to BF, November 23, 1764, January 22, 1765, Dunlap to BF, February 1, 1766, in *PBF* 7:169, 8:93, 11:419–23, 469, 12:24, 13:84–87.

29. BF to Jane Mecom, May 16, 30, 1757, September 16, November 11, 1758, January 9, 1760, in *PBF* 7:216, 221–22, 8:152, 173, 9:19; Wilberforce Eames, "The Antigua Press of Benjamin Mecom," *Proceedings of the American Antiquarian Society* 38 (1928), 328, 334; Lopez and Herbert, *The Private Franklin*, 111–12; Carl Van Doren, *Jane Mecom* (New York, 1950), 54–56, 64, 66.

30. James Parker to Jared Ingersoll, April 11, 1764, box 2, folder U, Ingersoll Papers, New-Haven Colony Historical Society; BF to Jane Mecom, November 11, 1762, June 19, 1763, to William Strahan, June 2, 1763, in *PBF* 10:153, 263, 292; Van Doren, *Jane Mecom*, 68; Alfred Lawrence Lorenz, *Hugh Gaine: A Colonial Printer-Editor's Odyssey to Loyalism* (Carbondale, Ill., 1972), 27, 30; William Strahan to David Hall, February 26, July 15, 1761, July 16, 1763, David Hall Papers, APS; *New York Pacquet*, July 11, 1763. Only two of the seven issues of the *Pacquet* survive: the latter issue at the New York Public Library, and one other at the New-York Historical Society.

31. Mecom, *To the PUBLICK. New-Haven, June 18, 1764*, broadside, Beinecke Library, Yale University; BF to William Strahan, June 25, 1764, James Parker to BF, January 22, March 22, 1765, in *PBF* 11:241, 12:24, 88.

32. Benjamin Mecom, *To the Public of Connecticut* (New Haven, Conn., 1765), broadside, Beinecke Library, Yale University; *Connecticut Gazette*, July 5, 12, September 20, 1765.

33. *Connecticut Gazette*, September 13, 20, 1765.

34. BF, *A Narrative of the Late Massacres* (Philadelphia, 1764), in *PBF* 11:53, 55, 61–62, 66; *PBF* 11:366n8. Scholars debate where Franklin's anti-anti-Indian writings of this period stand with respect to regnant racism. I agree with those who find the antiracism rather muted and ineffectual: he mainly used antiracism for other ends and wound up affirming the unquestioned reality of racial differences, if in a kinder, gentler key. For similar conclusions, see Carla Mulford, "*Caritas* and Capital: Franklin's *Narrative of the Late Massacres*," in J. A. Leo Lemay, ed., *Reappraising Benjamin Franklin* (Newark, Del., 1993), 347–58; Jennings, *Benjamin Franklin, Politician*.

35. *Pennsylvania Journal*, September 27, 1764, in *PBF* 11:375; BF, "Preface," *The Speech of Joseph Galloway, Esq.* (Philadelphia, 1764), in *PBF* 11:292, 299; *To the Freeholders and Other Electors for the City and County of Philadelphia* (Philadelphia, 1764), in *PBF* 11:378; Clark, *Benjamin Franklin*, 177; *The Scribbler. Being a Letter from a Gentleman in Town* (Philadelphia, 1764), in *PBF* 11:387–89; Tully, *Forming American Politics*, 184–86; Jennings, *Benjamin Franklin, Politician*, 169–71; J. Philip Gleason, "A Scurrilous Colonial Election and Franklin's Reputation," *William and Mary Quarterly*, 3rd ser., 18 (1961), 68–84.

36. *What Is Sauce for the Goose* (Philadelphia, 1764), in *PBF* 11:380–84; Lopez and Herbert, *Private Franklin*, 117–19; Middlekauff, *Benjamin Franklin and His Enemies*, 97; Edward Raymond Turner, *The Negro in Pennsylvania: Slavery—Servitude—Freedom, 1639–1861* (1911; repr., New York, 1969), 31n43.

37. Patricia U. Bonomi, *The Cornbury Scandals: The Politics of Reputation in British America* (New York, 1999); Annette Gordon-Reed, *Thomas Jefferson and Sally Hemings: An American Controversy* (Charlottesville, Va., 1997), 59–77.

38. BF, "Scheme for Supplying the Colonies with a Paper Currency," *PBF* 12:53–60; BF, "Concerning Sweets," *Poor Richard's Almanack . . . for 1765*, in *PBF* 12:9; BF to David Hall, February 14, June 8, August 9, 1765, Hall to BF, June 20, 1765, in *PBF* 12:65–66, 171–72, 188–89, 233; William Strahan to Hall, July 8, August 19, 1765, Hall to Strahan, September 19, December 16, 1765, David Hall Papers, APS; Verner W. Crane, "Ben-

jamin Franklin and the Stamp Act," *Publications of the Colonial Society of Massachusetts* 32 (1934), 56–77; Crane, *Benjamin Franklin and a Rising People*, 102–15; Edmund S. Morgan and Helen M. Morgan, *The Stamp Act Crisis: Prologue to Revolution* (1953; repr., New York, 1962), 307–11; Edmund S. Morgan, *Benjamin Franklin* (New Haven, Conn., 2002), 149–65; Anderson, *Crucible of War*, 644–46.

39. BF to John Hughes, August 9, 1765, Hughes to BF, September 8–17, Thomas Wharton to BF, October 5, 1765, Deborah Franklin to BF, October 9, 1765, Samuel Wharton to BF, October 13, 1765, in *PBF* 12:234–35, 263–66, 290–91, 301, 301n4, 315–16; Joseph Galloway to BF, June 7, 16, 1766, in *PBF* 13:295, 317; Hutson, *Pennsylvania Politics*, 192–207; Lopez and Herbert, *Private Franklin*, 124–29; Arthur M. Schlesinger, *Prelude to Independence: The Newspaper War on Britain, 1764–1776* (1957; repr., Boston, 1980), 74, 81–82; Benjamin H. Newcomb, *Franklin and Galloway: A Political Partnership* (New Haven, Conn., 1972), 142, 147; Lawrence Henry Gipson, *Jared Ingersoll* (New Haven, Conn., 1920), 145–46; Morgan and Morgan, *Stamp Act Crisis*, 280–324.

40. *Connecticut Gazette*, September 27, October 11, 1765, January 31, 1766; Grand Jurors of New Haven to Jared Ingersoll, April 13, 1766, Gen MSS, vol. 251, Papers Related to James Parker, Beinecke Library, Yale University. Ingersoll himself received the indictment as justice of the peace. It is unclear how it was acted upon.

41. David Hall to BF, September 6, October 14, 1765, March 11, 1766, BF to Hall, September 14, 1765, in *PBF* 12:255–59, 267–68, 319–20, 13:193; Smith, *Printers and Press Freedom*, 136–37; Skemp, *William Franklin*, 67–69; Robert Hurd Kany, "David Hall: Printing Partner of Benjamin Franklin" (Ph.D. diss., Pennsylvania State University, 1963), 148–49, 160; "James Parker: Final Report on the Franklin and Hall Account," in *PBF* 13:87–99.

42. BF to David Hall, February 24, 1766, Hall to BF, July 12, 1766, BF, "Observations on Mr. Parker's State of the Account," in *PBF* 13:110–16, 176, 331–32; Morgan, *Devious Dr. Franklin*, 111, 118; William Franklin to BF, November 13, 1766, in *PBF* 13:499–501; Ward L. Miner, *William Goddard, Newspaperman* (Durham, N.C., 1962), 62–73.

43. Kany, "David Hall," iv, 163–66, 207–19, 246; David Hall to BF, January 27, 1767, BF to Hall, April 14, 1767, *PBF* 14:18–19, 126–28; Hall to William Strahan, April 30, June 12, September 21, 1767, David Hall Papers, APS. Franklin preferred to blame Parker and Hall for not crediting him funds for the copyright of the *Pennsylvania Gazette* or *Poor Richard's Almanack*—matters that had never been raised in their original agreement.

44. Victor Hugo Paltsits, "John Holt—Printer and Postmaster," *Bulletin of the New York Public Library* 24 (1920), 483–99; Hayes, "John Holt," 11:100–101; McAnear, "Parker versus Holt," 88–90, 198–212; Miner, *William Goddard*, 50–51; Cadwallader Colden to BF, October 1, 1765, in *PBF* 12:287–88; James Parker, *An Humble Address to the PUBLICK. New York, May 30, 1766* (this is a broadside on which Parker wrote, "Suppressed on Mr. Holt's engaging to settle in 2 Months tho' I doubt his compliance then"), APS; Smith, *Printers and Press Freedom*, 37, 138; Dyer, *James Parker*, 89–104.

45. *New York Gazette and Weekly Post Boy*, May 8, 29, July 17, 1766; James Parker to BF, May 6, June 11, 1766, May 23, 1767, in *PBF* 13:263–64, 302, 14:169; McAnear, "Parker versus Holt"; Clifford K. Shipton and James E. Mooney, eds., *National Index of American Imprints through 1800* (Barre, Mass., 1969), 1:285.

46. Schlesinger, *Prelude to Independence*, 68; Stephen Botein, "Printers and the American Revolution," in Bernard Bailyn and John B. Hench, eds., *The Press and the American Revolution* (Worcester, Mass., 1980), 28–31.

47. John Holt to Jared Ingersoll, November 3, December 17, 1767, April 14, May 9, 10, 19, June 20, 1768, box 2, folder F, Ingersoll Papers, New-Haven Colony Historical Society; John Holt account with Ingersoll, 1759–67, Parker to Ingersoll, April 6, 1767, Papers Related to James Parker, Beinecke Library; Parker to Ingersoll, October 11, 1767, March 11, 1768, box 2, folder V, Ingersoll Papers.

48. James Parker to BF, March 22, April 25, August 8, December 20, 1765, February 11, June 11, July 1, 15, September 11, October 11, November 11, December 15, 1766, April 5, May 2, 23, June 13, October 1, 1767, April 18, 1768, in *PBF* 12:88–90, 111–12, 227–32, 407–10, 13:109–10, 301–12, 325–27, 342, 410–13, 454–58, 491–94, 525–28, 14:98, 146, 169, 186, 266, 15:101; Parker to Deborah Franklin, December 8, 12, 22, 1766, vol. 48, folders 98–100, Benjamin Franklin Papers, APS; Parker to Ezra Stiles, January 8, 1767, Ezra Stiles Papers, Beinecke Library; Parker to Ingersoll, March 16, April 6, June 1767, Beinecke Library; Parker to Ingersoll, October 11, 1767, March 11, December 29, 1768, Ingersoll Papers.

49. James Parker to BF, January 4, February 3, March 27, May 6, June 11, July 1, July 15, August 28, September 11, October 25, December 15, 1766, February 23, June 15, October 24, December 24, 1767, January 21, April 18, 1768, Joseph Chew to BF, January 24, 1766, February 23, 1767, in *PBF* 13:14–15, 108, 158–60, 204, 265, 307, 310–11, 327, 344, 395, 411–12, 474–75, 517, 14:60–61, 187, 296, 347–48, 15:28, 102; Parker to Ingersoll, February 12, 1767, box 2, folder U, Ingersoll Papers.

50. *Connecticut Gazette*, February 28, November 14, 1767, February 19, 1768; Parker to BF, December 24, 1767, *PBF* 14:347–48.

51. Deborah Franklin to BF, January 21–22, May 20–23, 1768, BF to Deborah Franklin, December 12, 1768, William Franklin to BF, January 2, 1769, James Parker to BF, March 29, 1769, in *PBF* 15:24–25, 137–38, 292, 16:5–6, 76–77; Parker to Deborah Franklin, March 8, 1769, vol. 48, folder 106, Benjamin Franklin Papers, APS; Van Doren, *Jane Mecom*, 87, 90–91, 97; *Philadelphia, Sept. 11, 1770. SIR*, broadside, John William Wallace Ancient Records of Philadelphia Collection, Historical Society of Pennsylvania.

52. Charles Wetherell, " 'For These or Such Like Reasons': John Holt's Attack on Benjamin Franklin," *Proceedings of the American Antiquarian Society* 88 (1978), 251–75; Victor Hugo Paltsits, "John Holt," *Dictionary of National Biography* (New York, 1929), 9:181. The tombstone at St. Paul's, which is partly broken, was apparently carved to look exactly the same as the memorial cards Elizabeth Hunter Holt printed and distributed, which are described in Thomas, *History of Printing*, 475–76.

53. Account with Elizabeth Mecom, Estate of Benjamin Franklin, Gratz MSS, Historical Society of Pennsylvania; Eames, "Antigua Press of Benjamin Mecom"; Van Doren, *Jane Mecom*, 130, 132–33; Lopez and Herbert, *Private Franklin*, 218.

7. AMERICA THE ENSLAVED

1. BF, *Poor Richard Improved . . . for the Year of our Lord 1765* (Philadelphia, 1764), in *PBF* 12:4–9; BF to Richard Jackson, January 16, 1764, to Peter Collinson, April 30, 1764, in *PBF* 11:18–20, 181.

2. *Considerations Upon the Act of Parliament* (Boston, 1764), in Bernard Bailyn, ed., *Pamphlets of the American Revolution, 1750–1776* (Cambridge, Mass., 1965), 1:368–69, 372.

3. Stephen Hopkins, "An Essay on the Trade of the Northern Colonies," *Newport Mer-*

cury, February 6, 13, 1764, in Merrill Jensen, ed., *Tracts of the American Revolution, 1763–1776* (Indianapolis, Ind., 1967), 5, 9–11; Donald L. Robinson, *Slavery and the Structure of American Politics, 1765–1820* (New York, 1971), 58–61.

4. James Otis, *The Rights of the British Colonies Asserted and Proved* (Boston, 1764), in Bailyn, ed., *Pamphlets of the American Revolution*, 1:435–36, 439–40.

5. Bernard Bailyn, *The Ideological Origins of the American Revolution* (Cambridge, Mass., 1967), 232–46; Bailyn, "The Central Themes of the American Revolution," in Stephen G. Kurtz and James H. Hutson, eds., *Essays on the American Revolution* (New York, 1973), 28–30; Gordon S. Wood, *The Radicalism of the American Revolution* (New York, 1992), 7, 186–87.

6. David Brion Davis, *The Problem of Slavery in Western Culture* (Ithaca, N.Y., 1966), 440–42; Davis, *The Problem of Slavery in the Age of Revolution, 1770–1823* (Ithaca, N.Y., 1975), 86, 119; Christopher L. Brown, "The Politics of Slavery," in David Armitage and Michael J. Braddick, eds., *The British Atlantic World, 1500–1800* (New York, 2002), 227.

7. Agnes M. Whitson, "The Outlook of the Continental Colonies on the British West Indies, 1760–1775," *Political Science Quarterly* 45 (1930), 56–86; Wylie Sypher, *Guinea's Captive Kings: British Antislavery Literature of the Eighteenth Century* (Chapel Hill, N.C., 1942); Eric Williams, *Capitalism and Slavery* (Chapel Hill, N.C., 1944), 117–20; Andrew Jackson O'Shaughnessy, *An Empire Divided: The American Revolution and the British Caribbean* (Philadelphia, 2000), 15–17, 26, 62–67; Kathleen Wilson, *The Island Race: Englishness, Empire and Gender in the Eighteenth Century* (New York, 2002); Nuala Zahedieh, "Economy," in Armitage and Braddick, eds., *British Atlantic World*, 58.

8. Stephen Hopkins, *The Rights of Colonies Examined and Proved* (Newport, 1764), in Jensen, ed., *Tracts of the American Revolution*, 43; Robinson, *Slavery and the Structure of American Politics*, 60. As Hopkins's definition of slavery—highlighting not just political rights but also power and property—suggests, just because the colonists could talk about slavery without meaning the racial slavery of Africans does not mean that the issues were wholly different and can be treated as separate. The separation was as much a goal in a political minefield as it was an already achieved reality. Compare F. Nwabueze Okoye, "Chattel Slavery as the Nightmare of the American Revolutionaries," *William and Mary Quarterly*, 3rd ser., 37 (1980), 3–28, with John Philip Reid, *The Concept of Liberty in the Age of the American Revolution* (Chicago, 1988), 38–48, and Barry Alan Shain, *The Myth of American Individualism: The Protestant Origins of American Political Thought* (Princeton, N.J., 1994), 289–319. For another interpretation of the origins of the "slavery" metaphor that stresses the "discovery of inequality" and "fear of exclusion" by colonists (but not property or labor), see T. H. Breen, "Ideology and Nationalism on the Eve of the American Revolution: Revisions *Once More* in Need of Revising," *Journal of American History* 84 (1997), 13–39. For an account that ties the slavery issue to the rhetorical exigencies of the colonial protest, seeing the slavery issue as "a lever promoting revolutionary action," see Patricia Bradley, *Slavery, Propaganda, and the American Revolution* (Jackson, Miss., 1998), xii. See also Edmund S. Morgan, "Slavery and Freedom: The American Paradox," *Journal of American History* 59 (1972), 5–29; David R. Roediger, *The Wages of Whiteness: Race and the Making of the American Working Class* (New York, 1991), 27–33.

9. Fred Anderson, *Crucible of War: The Seven Years' War and the Fate of Empire in British North America, 1754–1766* (New York, 1999), 521; Jack P. Greene, *The Intellectual Con-*

struction of America: Exceptionalism and Identity from 1492 to 1800 (Chapel Hill, N.C., 1993); Greene, "Empire and Identity from the Glorious Revolution to the American Revolution," in P. J. Marshall, ed., *The Oxford History of the British Empire*, vol. 2, *The Eighteenth Century* (New York, 1998), 208–30; Michael J. Rozbicki, "The Curse of Provincialism: Negative Perceptions of Colonial American Plantation Gentry," *Journal of Southern History* 63 (1997), 727–52; Stephen Conway, "From Fellow-Nationals to Foreigners: British Perceptions of the Americans, circa 1739–1783," *William and Mary Quarterly*, 3rd ser., 59 (2002), 65–100.

10. Robin Blackburn has recently made a similar observation in a review, "The Bourgeois Revolutionary," *Nation*, August 4–11, 2003, 33–34.

11. David Hume to BF, May 10, 1762, in *PBF* 10:81–82; David Hume, "Of National Characters" [1748], "Of Money" [1752], in Hume, *Political Essays*, ed. Knud Haakonsen (Cambridge, Eng., 1994), 86, 123; Eric Richards, "Scotland and the Uses of the Atlantic Empire," in Bernard Bailyn and Philip D. Morgan, eds., *Strangers Within the Realm: Cultural Margins of the First British Empire* (Chapel Hill, N.C., 1991), 85, 90; Michael A. Bellesiles, "Creating Empires," *Journal of British Studies* 40 (2001), 185–86; Alfred Owen Aldridge, "Franklin as Demographer," *Journal of Economic History* 9 (1949), 38–39; Roy Porter, *The Creation of the Modern World: The Untold Story of the British Enlightenment* (New York, 2000), 200; Anthony Pagden, *Lords of All the World: Ideologies of Empire in Spain, Britain and France, c. 1500–1800* (New Haven, Conn., 1995), 169.

12. BF to David Hume, May 19, 1762, in *PBF* 10:83–84.

13. BF to Richard Jackson, February 11, 1764, to Peter Collinson, April 30, in *PBF* 11:76, 181–83.

14. BF to Cadwalader Evans, in *PBF* 15:52–53; to Lord Kames, February 26, 1769, in *PBF* 16:47; BF, "Positions to Be Examined," in *PBF*, 16:109. For Franklin's evolution toward physiocracy, see Lewis J. Carey, *Franklin's Economic Views* (New York, 1928), 134–67; Paul W. Conner, *Poor Richard's Politicks: Benjamin Franklin and His New American Order* (New York, 1965), 217; Cecil B. Currey, *Road to Revolution: Benjamin Franklin in England, 1765–1775*, 2nd ed. (Gloucester, Mass., 1978), 89; Tracy Mott and George W. Zinke, "Benjamin Franklin's Economic Thought: A Twentieth Century Appraisal," in Melvin H. Buxbaum, ed., *Critical Essays on Benjamin Franklin* (Boston, 1987), 111–27. Franklin would shortly become the darling of the French physiocrats—landed aristocrats who were thinking about the economics of agriculture and its taxation for their own reasons. Elizabeth Fox-Genovese, *The Origins of Physiocracy: Economic Revolution and Social Order in Eighteenth-Century France* (Ithaca, N.Y., 1976), 19–28.

15. BF to Richard Jackson, September 29, 1764, to William Franklin, November 9, 1765, in *PBF* 11:359, 12:363; *Examination of Dr. Franklin, before an August Assembly, relating to the repeal of the Stamp Act* (Philadelphia, 1766), in *PBF* 13:129–59; Carl Van Doren, *Benjamin Franklin* (New York, 1938), 336–54; Anderson, *Crucible of War*, 707.

16. BF, "Scheme for Supplying the Colonies with a Paper Currency" [1765], "The Legal Tender of Paper Money in America" [1767], "Remarks and Facts Related to American Paper Money" [1767], in *PBF* 12:47–60, 14:33–39, 73; BF, "Magna Britannia," in *PBF* 13:66–72; BF to David Hall, February 24, 1766, to Deborah Franklin, February 27, 1766, in *PBF* 13:170, 176; Edwin Wolf, "Benjamin Franklin's Stamp Act Cartoon," *Proceedings of the American Philosophical Society* 99 (1954), 388–96; Olson, *Emblems of American Community*, 103–9; Michael G. Kammen, *A Rope of Sand: The Colonial Agents and the American Revolution* (Ithaca, N.Y., 1968), 119–20.

17. *PBF* 12:407.
18. BF to Hugh Roberts, February 28, 1766, in *PBF* 13:178; BF, "A Virginian," "Pacificus Secondus," "Fragments of a Pamphlet," " 'N.N.': First reply to Vindex Patriae," in *PBF* 12:253, 414, 13:5–6, 79; Kevin J. Hayes, "The Board of Trade's 'Cruel Sarcasm': A Neglected Franklin Source," *Early American Literature* 28 (1993), 171–76. For the importance of the gratitude theme, see Fred J. Hinkhouse, *The Preliminaries of the American Revolution as Seen in the English Press, 1763–1776* (New York, 1926), 71–72.
19. R. C. Simmons and Peter D. G. Thomas, eds., *Proceedings and Debates of the British Parliaments Respecting North America 1754–1783* (Millwood, N.Y., 1982–   ), 2:86, 88–89; *PBF* 13:7–8, 45–48. These essays are reprinted in *Benjamin Franklin: Writings*, ed. J. A. Leo Lemay (New York, 1987), 568–69, 574–78.
20. Brown, "Politics of Slavery"; Brown, "Empire Without Slaves: British Concepts of Emancipation in the Age of the American Revolution," *William and Mary Quarterly*, 3rd ser., 56 (1999), 273–306.
21. Leland J. Bellot, *William Knox: The Life and Thought of an Eighteenth-Century Imperialist* (Austin, Tex., 1977), 14–15, 32–34.
22. Bellot, *William Knox*, 48–55; Kammen, *Rope of Sand*, 28n35; Betty Wood, *Slavery in Colonial Georgia, 1730–1775* (Athens, Ga., 1984), 138, 235n20.
23. William Knox, "Memorandum to the Earl of Shelburne" [1763], in Howard H. Peckham, ed., *Sources of American Independence: Selected Manuscripts from the Collections of the William L. Clements Library* (Chicago, 1978), 1:148; Knox, *The Claim of the Colonies to an Exemption from Internal Taxes Imposed by Authority of Parliament, Examined: In a Letter from a Gentleman in London, to a Friend in America* (London, 1765), 2, 5–6, 13, 22.
24. P.D.G. Thomas, *British Politics and the Stamp Act Crisis: The First Phase of the American Revolution, 1763–1767* (Oxford, Eng., 1975), 29, 34; Simmons and Thomas, eds., *Proceedings and Debates*, 2:7–8; William Knox, *A Letter from a Gentleman in London, to Another in the Country* (London, 1765), 9, 12; Bellot, *William Knox*, 75; Verner W. Crane, "Franklin's Marginalia, and the Lost 'Treatise' on Empire," *Papers of the Michigan Academy of Arts, Science and Letters* 42 (1957), 163–76.
25. Knox, *Claim of the Colonies*, New York Public Library copy, 5–6, 9, 13.
26. Peter Linebaugh, *The London Hanged: Crime and Civil Society in Eighteenth-Century England* (London, 1992), 184–218; Christopher Hill, *Liberty Against the Law: Some Seventeenth-Century Controversies* (New York, 1996), 129–30. As Linebaugh observes, "these communities of woodland and commons that surrounded London are analogous to the colonial frontier zones, the forests and mountains to which servants, slaves, and runaways fled" (189). Franklin was playing with a kind of pun, for the Scottish and Irish outlanders who had supposedly perfected highway robbery were often known as "the blacks" for their practices of disguise and affinity for the night.
27. BF to Lord Kames, February 25, 1767, in *PBF* 14:67.
28. David T. Morgan, *The Devious Dr. Franklin, Colonial Agent: Benjamin Franklin's Years in London* (Macon, Ga., 1996), 126–28, 156; *PBF* 15:94–97; Philip Lawson, "George Grenville and America: The Years of Opposition, 1765 to 1770," *William and Mary Quarterly*, 3rd ser., 37 (1980), 364; William Knox, *The Present State of the Nation* (London, 1768), 19–20, 80–81; Knox, *The Controversy Between Great Britain and Her Colonies Reviewed* (London, 1769), 3–4, 105, 111–12, 133, 206–7; Edward Bancroft, *Remarks on the Review of the Controversy Between Great Britain and the Colonies* (London,

1769), 109; William Knox, *Extra Official State Papers. Addressed to the Right Honorable Lord Rawdon* (Dublin, 1789), 2:30–31.

29. William Knox, *Three Tracts Respecting the Conversion and Instruction of the Free Indians and Negro Slaves in the Colonies* (London, 1768), 19–20, 22–25, 27, 31–33. A later, substantially different edition, in which Knox identified himself as the author, appeared in 1789 and is discussed in Leland J. Bellot, "Evangelicals and the Defense of Slavery in Britain's Old Colonial Empire," *Journal of Southern History* 37 (1974), 19–40. Brown calls attention to the significance of Knox's definition of African slaves as British subjects in "Empire Without Slaves," 284–85, 303.

30. Knox, "Memorandum," 157; Knox, *Controversy*, 67, 105, 111–12, 133, 206–7; *Benjamin Franklin's Letters to the Press, 1757–1775*, ed. Verner W. Crane (Chapel Hill, N.C., 1950), 75; *True and Constitutional Means for Putting an End to the Disputes Between Great-Britain and the American Colonies* (London, 1769); see also Franklin's Marginalia in *PBF* 16:288–94.

31. Morgan, *Devious Dr. Franklin*, 148–51; Currey, *Road to Revolution*, 175–77; BF to William Franklin, March 13, 1768, in *PBF* 15:75–76; BF, Marginalia, in *PBF* 13:215; BF, "Subjects of Subjects," in *PBF* 15:36–38; BF, Marginalia on Various Pamphlets, in *PBF* 16:323–24, 17:321, 324, 334, 346–47, 385, 388; Simmons and Thomas, eds., *Proceedings and Debates*, 2:485; John Philip Reid, *Constitutional History of the American Revolution: The Authority of Law* (Madison, Wisc. 1993), 77–78. On the conflicting views of sovereignty generally, see H. T. Dickinson, "Britain's Imperial Sovereignty: The Ideological Case Against the American Colonists," in Dickinson, ed., *Britain and the American Revolution* (London, 1998), 64–87.

32. Anthony Benezet, *Observations on the Inslaving, Importing, and Purchasing of Negroes* (Germantown, Pa., 1760); Anthony Benezet, *A Caution to Great Britain and her Colonies*, in *A Short Representation of the Calamitous State of the Enslaved Negroes in the British Dominions* (London, 1767), 3; Davis, *Problem of Slavery in Western Culture*, 330–31, 483–93; Davis, *Problem of Slavery in the Age of Revolution*, 375.

33. Granville Sharp, *A Representation of the Dangerous Tendency* (London, 1769), 81–85, 91–93.

34. Robert T. Sidwell, " 'An Odd Fish'—Samuel Keimer and a Footnote to American Educational History," *History of Education Quarterly* 6 (1966), 16–30.

35. Edgar Legare Pennington, "Thomas Bray's Associates and Their Work Among the Negroes," *Proceedings of the American Antiquarian Society* 48 (1938), 311–403; John C. Van Horne, ed., *Religious Philanthropy and Colonial Slavery: The American Correspondence of the Associates of Dr. Bray, 1717–1777* (Urbana, Ill., 1985), 152; Deborah Franklin to BF, August 9, 1759, BF to Deborah Franklin, June 27, 1760, in *PBF* 8:425, 9:174; Richard Shelling, "Benjamin Franklin and the Dr. Bray Associates," *Pennsylvania Magazine of History and Biography* (1939), 285–87; David Freeman Hawke, *Franklin* (New York, 1976), 301–2; Jennifer Read Fry, " 'Extraordinary Freedom and Great Humility': A Reinterpretation of Deborah Franklin," *Pennsylvania Magazine of History and Biography* 127 (2003), 188. I follow Hawke and Fry in seeing Deborah as showing initiative beyond what Franklin intended. For examples of the gradual enlightenment approach to Franklin and slavery that tend to ascribe both transparency and originality to Franklin's antiracist remark in the letter to Waring, see John C. Van Horne, "Collective Benevolence and the Common Good in Franklin's Philanthropy" in J. A. Leo Lemay, ed., *Reappraising Benjamin Franklin* (Newark, Del., 1993), 433–37; editorial note, *PBF*

19:112–13; I. Bernard Cohen, *Science and the Founding Fathers* (New York, 1995), 190–93.

36. BF to John Waring, December 17, 1763, to Francis Hopkinson, December 16, 1767, January 24, 1768, in *PBF* 10:395–96, 14:339–40, 15:30.

37. George S. Brookes, *Friend Anthony Benezet* (Philadelphia, 1937), 294; Anthony Benezet to BF, April 27, 1772, in *PBF* 19:113–17; Benezet to Granville Sharp, April 1773, in Roberts Vaux, *Memoirs of the Life of Anthony Benezet* (York, Eng., 1817), 47. BF called Daniel Benezet "cousin" in a letter to Deborah Franklin, May 1, 1771, in *PBF* 18:90, 90n8.

38. *PBF* 17:37–44; Conner, *Poor Richards' Politicks*, 81–83.

39. John Brewer, *Party Ideology and Popular Politics at the Accession of George III* (Cambridge, Eng., 1976); John Derry, *English Politics and the American Revolution* (London, 1976); Bernard Donoghue, *British Politics and the American Revolution: The Path to War, 1773–1775* (London, 1964), 89; Lawrence Henry Gipson, *The British Empire Before the American Revolution*, vol. 11, *The Triumphant Empire: The Rumbling of the Coming Storm, 1766–1770* (Caldwell, Id., and New York, 1936–70), 191–222, 561; Jensen, *Founding of a Nation*, 316–19; Pauline Maier, *From Resistance to Revolution: Colonial Radicals and the Development of American Opposition to Britain, 1763–1776* (New York, 1972).

40. Davis, *Problem of Slavery in the Age of Revolution*, 375; Nicholas Hudson, " 'Britons Never Will be Slaves': National Myth, Conservatism, and the Beginnings of British Antislavery," *Eighteenth-Century Studies* 34 (2001), 559–76; Colin Bonwick, *English Radicals and the American Revolution* (Chapel Hill, N.C., 1977); Jerome Reich, *British Friends of the American Revolution* (Armonk, N.Y., 1998), 129, 168.

41. A. Leon Higginbotham Jr., *In the Matter of Color: Race and the Presumptions of the American Legal Process, the Colonial Period* (New York, 1978), 334–38; James Walvin, *Black Ivory: A History of British Slavery* (London, 1994), 13–16; Gretchen Gerzina, *Black London: Life Before Emancipation* (New Brunswick, N.J., 1995), 1–2, 19, 90–132; Prince Hoare, *Memoirs of Granville Sharp* (London, 1820), 70, 75–77, 119–20; Mark S. Weiner, "New Biographical Evidence on *Somerset's* Case," *Slavery and Abolition* 23 (2002), 122–24.

42. Davis, *Problem of Slavery in the Age of Revolution*, 473–89; Seymour Drescher, *Capitalism and Antislavery: British Mobilization in Comparative Perspective* (New York: 1987), 40, 47; William R. Cotter, "The Somerset Case and the Abolition of Slavery in England," *History* 79 (1994), 31–56.

43. BF, "The Sommersett case and the Slave Trade," in *PBF* 19:188–89; *Franklin's Letters to the Press*, ed. Crane, 221–23; Conner, *Poor Richard's Politicks*, 83–84.

44. Anthony Benezet to Granville Sharp, May 14, 1772, in Roger Bruns, ed., *Am I Not a Man and a Brother?: The Antislavery Crusade of Revolutionary America, 1689–1789* (New York, 1980), 195; Granville Sharp, *An Essay Upon Slavery, Proving from Scripture Its Inconsistency with Humanity and Religion* (Burlington, N.J., 1773), vi, viii–ix; Hoare, *Memoirs of Granville Sharp*, 120–21; E. P. Lascelles, *Granville Sharp and the Freedom of Slaves in England* (London, 1928), 37–38; Davis, *Problem of Slavery in the Age of Revolution*, 395–96. Bradley, *Slavery, Propaganda, and the American Revolution*, 81, notes Sharp and Franklin's different responses and argues that Massachusetts patriots tamped down news of the decision because of their desire to keep the patriot movement together.

45. Edmund Heward, *Lord Mansfield* (Chichester, Eng., 1979); Lord Mansfield, *The Thistle; A*

Dispassionate Examination of the Prejudice of Englishmen in General to the Scottish Nation (London, 1747), 14–15; William S. Hanna, *Benjamin Franklin and Pennsylvania Politics* (Stanford, 1964), 141; John Philip Reid, *Constitutional History of the American Revolution: The Authority to Tax* (Madison, Wisc., 1987), 265; Simmons and Thomas, eds., *Proceedings and Debates*, 2:130; Lawrence Henry Gipson, *The Coming of the Revolution, 1763–1775* (New York, 1954), 113–14; Robert W. Tucker and David C. Hendrickson, *The Fall of the First British Empire: Origins of the War for Independence* (Baltimore, Md., 1982), 167–68.

46. Higginbotham, *In the Matter of Color*, 351; Gerzina, *Black London*, 128; Drescher, *Capitalism and Antislavery*, 39.

47. Davis, *Problem of Slavery in the Age of Revolution*, 376, 480; Samuel Estwick, *Considerations on the Negroe Cause Commonly So Called, Addressed to the Right Honourable Lord Mansfield* (London, 1772); Davis, *Problem of Slavery in Western Culture*, 461.

48. Eliga Gould, "Zones of Law, Zones of Violence: The Legal Geography of the British Atlantic, circa 1772," *William and Mary Quarterly*, 3rd ser., 60 (2003), 505–6; Brown, "Empire Without Slaves." The letter Gould cites, G.B. to BF, November 14, 1775, is in the Public Records Office, London, and is not reproduced in *PBF*.

49. BF to Anthony Benezet, February 10, 1773, to Richard Woodward, April 10, 1773, Benjamin Rush to BF, May 1, 1773, BF to Rush, July 14, 1773, in *PBF* 20:41, 155–56, 193–94n3–4, 314.

50. Franklin artfully and characteristically blamed the situation on himself for not calling first on the "master" Wheatley.

51. BF to Jonathan Williams Sr., July 7, 1773, Williams to BF, October 17, 1773, in *PBF* 20:291–92, 445; Wheatley to David Wooster, October 18, 1773, in John C. Shields, ed., *The Collected Works of Phillis Wheatley* (New York, 1993), 169–70; David Grimsted, "Anglo-American Racism and Phyllis Wheatley's 'Sable Veil,' 'Length'ned Chain,' and 'Knitted Heart,' " in Ronald Hoffman and Peter J. Albert, eds., *Women in the Age of the American Revolution* (Charlottesville, Va., 1989), 338–40, 405–6; Betsy Erkkila, "Phyllis Wheatley and the Black American Revolution," in Frank Shuffleton, ed., *A Mixed Race: Ethnicity in Early America* (New York, 1993), 228–38; Kristin Wilcox, "The Body into Print: Marketing Phyllis Wheatley," *American Literature* 71 (1998), 1–29; Dickson D. Bruce Jr., *The Origins of African American Literature, 1680–1815* (Charlottesville, Va., 2001), 42–50; Bradley, *Slavery, Propaganda, and the American Revolution*, 103–6.

   Larry E. Tise and the editors of *PBF* agree on Franklin's encouragement of Wheatley. Tise explicitly says that the Wheatleys rushed Phillis back to America to avoid her liberation at the hands of Franklin and other abolitionists. But why Nathanael Wheatley would have chosen to take his worries out on Franklin is unclear. After all, it was Granville Sharp who strolled around the Tower of London with Phillis Wheatley. There is another possibility: that Nathanael Wheatley did insult Franklin because of his own (Tory) politics, perhaps not knowing that his parents had valued what Franklin could possibly do in procuring literary patronage. *PBF* 20:292n3; Tise, *The American Counterrevolution: A Retreat from Liberty, 1783–1800* (Mechanicsburg, Pa., 1999), 91–92; Tise, "Principal Women in the Life of Benjamin Franklin," in Tise, ed., *Benjamin Franklin and Women* (University Park, Pa., 2000), xxv.

52. Erkkila, "Phyllis Wheatley," 231; BF to William Franklin, December 2, 1772, in *PBF* 19:417; Van Doren, *Franklin*, 446; Aldridge, *Benjamin Franklin*, 209.

53. This account draws on Van Doren, *Franklin*, 441–45; Headnotes, *PBF* 19:217, 399–409;

Jensen, *Founding of a Nation*, 419–20; Tucker and Hendrickson, *Fall of the First British Empire*, 309n.

54. Verner W. Crane, *Benjamin Franklin and a Rising People* (Boston, 1954), 135–36; Van Doren, *Franklin*, 450; Jack M. Sosin, *Agents and Merchants: British Colonial Policy and the Origins of the American Revolution* (Lincoln, Nebr., 1965), 156–59; H. W. Brands, *The First American: The Life and Times of Benjamin Franklin* (New York, 2000), 452–54; Robert Blair St. George, *Conversing by Signs: Poetics of Implication in Colonial New England Culture* (Chapel Hill, N.C., 1998), 263–66, 283–93; Bernard Bailyn, *The Ordeal of Thomas Hutchinson* (Cambridge, Mass., 1974); Reid, *Constitutional History of the American Revolution: Authority of Law*, 91–93; Thomas Cushing to BF, June 25, 1773, *PBF* 20:243–44; BF to Cushing, December 2, 1772, *PBF* 19:411–12.

55. BF to Thomas Cushing and BF to Massachusetts House of Representatives, July 7, 1773, in *PBF* 20:271–76, 279–86; BF, "An Infallible Method to Restore Peace and Harmony," "On the Hutchinson Letters," "Rules by Which a Great Empire May Be Reduced to a Small One," "An Edict by the King of Prussia," "Franklin's Public Statement about the Hutchinson Letters," in *PBF* 20:380–81, 389–99, 413–18, 516n1, 517–18; Edmund S. Morgan, *Benjamin Franklin* (New Haven, Conn., 2002), 179–80; Van Doren, *Franklin*, 456.

56. Van Doren, *Franklin*, 464; Aldridge, *Benjamin Franklin*, 234–35; Hawke, *Franklin*, 325–26; Catherine Drinker Bowen, *The Most Dangerous Man in America: Scenes from the Life of Benjamin Franklin* (Boston, 1974), 237.

57. BF, "The Final Hearing Before the Privy Council Committee on Plantation Affairs," in *PBF* 21:43–44, 48–49; BF to Thomas Cushing, February 15–19, 1774, in *PBF* 21:92; Van Doren, *Franklin*, 470–774; Hawke, *Franklin*, 326; Jack P. Greene, "The Alienation of Benjamin Franklin, British American," in *Understanding the American Revolution: Issues and Actors* (Charlottesville, Va., 1992), 247–49; Edward Young, *The Revenge: A Tragedy, As Written By E. Young, LLD* (London, 1777). Franklin himself was familiar enough with Young's works to quote one of his satires of 1725 in the *Autobiography*. *The Autobiography of Benjamin Franklin*, ed. Leonard W. Labaree et al. (New Haven, Conn., 1964), 99.

58. Hinkhouse, *Preliminaries of the American Revolution*, 159n1; Donoghue, *British Politics and the American Revolution*, 32, 47; BF, "An Open Letter to Lord North" [1774], "A Method of Humbling Rebellious American Vassals" [1774], "An Imaginary Speech" [1775], "Fragments of Two Letters to the Press" [1774–75], "Notes on Britain's Intention to Enslave America" [1774–75], in *PBF* 21:183–86, 221–22, 485, 605, 608; *Franklin: Writings*, ed. Lemay, 719–22.

59. BF to Joseph Galloway, October 12, 1774, in *PBF* 21:334; Claude-Anne Lopez and Eugenia W. Herbert, *The Private Franklin: The Man and His Family* (New Haven, Conn., 1975), 195; Aldridge, *Benjamin Franklin*, 242; Ronald Clark, *Benjamin Franklin: A Biography* (New York, 1983), 251–53, 268; *The Diary and Letters of His Excellency Thomas Hutchinson, Esq.*, ed. Peter Orlando Hutchinson (1884–86; repr., New York, 1971), 2:238, 420–21; Van Doren, *Franklin*, 521. The *PBF* editors take a reasonably agnostic view, suggesting that Whatley's chancery suit "may even have been a reason why he left England when he did." *PBF* 21:14.

8. AMERICA THE FREE

1. Benjamin Quarles, *The Negro in the American Revolution* (Chapel Hill, N.C., 1961); Quarles, "The Revolutionary War as a Black Declaration of Independence," in Ira Berlin and Ronald Hoffman, eds., *Slavery and Freedom in the Age of the American Revolution* (Urbana, Ill., 1983), 283–301; Sylvia Frey, *Water from the Rock: Black Resistance in a Revolutionary Age* (Princeton, N.J., 1991); Woody Holton, " 'Rebel Against Rebel': Enslaved Virginians and the Coming of the American Revolution," *Virginia Magazine of History and Biography* 105 (1997), 157–92; Robert Olwell, *Masters, Subjects, and Slaves: The Culture of Power in the South Carolina Lowcountry, 1740–1790* (Ithaca, N.Y., 1998).

2. Donald L. Robinson, *Slavery and the Structure of American Politics, 1765–1820* (New York, 1971), 101, 110; S. C. Lomas, "The Manuscripts of Captain Howard Vincente Knox," in Historical Manuscripts Commission, *Report on Manuscripts in Various Collections* 6 (Dublin, 1909), 259, 289; R. C. Simmons and Peter D. G. Thomas, eds., *Proceedings and Debates of the British Parliaments Respecting North America 1754–1783* (Millwood, N.Y., 1982–   ), 5:607.

3. Simmons and Thomas, eds., *Proceedings and Debates*, 5:612.

4. Peter N. Miller, *Defining the Common Good: Empire, Religion and Philosophy in Eighteenth-Century Britain* (Cambridge, Eng., 1994), 218; James J. Sack, *From Jacobite to Conservative: Reaction and Orthodoxy in Britain, c.1760–1832* (New York, 1993), 161, 165; James G. Basker, "Multicultural Perspectives: Johnson, Race and Gender," in Philip Smallwood, ed., *Johnson Re-Visioned: Looking Before and After* (Lewisburg, Pa., 2001), 69; James Boswell, *Life of Johnson*, ed. R. W. Chapman, rev. ed. (New York, 1980), 374, 591, 876.

5. Samuel Johnson, *Taxation No Tyranny*, 3rd ed. (London, 1775), 36, 79, 85, 89. The original page proofs closed with a paragraph that referred directly to "Dr. Franklin's rule of progression" (in "Observations on the Increase of Mankind") predicting the demographic rise of the colonies over the mother country. Donald Greene, ed., *Samuel Johnson: Political Writings* (New Haven, Conn., 1977), 444, 455n; Robert DeMaria Jr., *The Life of Samuel Johnson: A Critical Biography* (Cambridge, Mass., 1993), 255–56. Other scholars have maintained that Johnson replied directly to Franklin in *Taxation No Tyranny*. Helen Louise McGuffie, "Dr. Johnson and the Little Dogs: The Reaction of the London Press to *Taxation No Tyranny*," in Donovan H. Bond and W. Reynolds McLeod, eds., *Newsletters to Newspapers: Eighteenth-Century Journalism* (Morgantown, W.V., 1977), 196; Neill R. Joy, "Politics and Culture: The Dr. Franklin—Dr. Johnson Connection, with an Analogue," *Prospects* 23 (1998), 60–81.

6. Hugh Williamson, *The Plea of the Colonies, On the Charges Brought Against Them by Lord M—d, and Others* (London, 1775), 33–34; BF to Jonathan Shipley, July 7, September 13, 1775, to David Hartley, September 12, 1775, in *PBF* 22:97, 196, 200.

7. Draft of the Declaration of Independence with Congress's changes, in *The Papers of Thomas Jefferson*, ed. Julian P. Boyd et al. (Princeton, N.J., 1950–   ), 1:315–19; Julian P. Boyd, *The Declaration of Independence: Evolution of the Text* (Washington, D.C., 1999), document 5 (Library of Congress). Quarles observes that the ban on slave importation was part of the larger nonimportation movement: *Negro in the American Revolution*, 41; see also W.E.B. Du Bois, *The Suppression of the African Slave Trade* (1896; repr., Baton Rouge, La., 1969), 41–48.

Historians differ on Franklin's influence on the Declaration; he did make some handwritten corrections on a draft, but they are not extensive, leaving most to assume a minimal role. He was well occupied during late June and early July. Jefferson later insisted that Adams and Franklin contributed only a few minor handwritten corrections. On the other hand, by the time he made those remarks, as Pauline Maier observes, Jefferson was trying to make sure he got full credit for his masterpiece. My interpretation rests not primarily on Franklin's edits (though for an important one see below) but rather on the similarities of Jefferson's rhetoric to what Franklin had been developing for a long time. Carl Becker, though, argued more than eighty years ago that Jefferson incorporated changes suggested verbally by Adams and Franklin in earlier meetings, before the "rough draft" was submitted to the committee. Becker, *The Declaration of Independence: A Study in the History of Political Ideas* (1922; repr., New York, 1933), 152–53.

The antislavery passage has troubled commentators since Becker, who generally agree that it made little sense and have debated whether its antislavery, its blame of the king for slavery, or its outrage about armed slaves is most hypocritical or inconsistent or just infelicitous. Highlights of this body of scholarship include Becker, *Declaration of Independence*, 172–77; David Hawke, *A Transaction of Free Men* (New York, 1964), 157–58; Garry Wills, *Inventing America: Jefferson's Declaration of Independence* (New York, 1978), 172–75; Joseph E. Ellis, *American Sphinx: The Character of Thomas Jefferson* (New York, 1996), 51–52; Pauline Maier, *American Scripture: Making the Declaration of Independence* (New York, 1997), 146–47. I am suggesting, by contrast, that its inclusion reflected the ideology of the moment so memorably expressed by Franklin, however contradictory (as ideologies generally are).

8. Jefferson's Rough Draft, document 5 in Boyd, *Declaration of Independence*, 70; also at the Library of Congress website, www.loc.gov/exhibits/treasures/trt001.html. Most scholars have credited to Franklin only the small emendations Jefferson marked with a plus sign or "x" *and* "Dr. Franklin's hand" or "Dr. Franklin." These appear to be in Franklin's hand. There are two other longer ones on the same page with the plus sign only, but Jefferson did not write Franklin's name. I conclude that Jefferson was not being consistent or specific about which changes were Franklin's language and which actually in Franklin's hand. The larger ones appear to be Jefferson's hand and have been assumed to be Jefferson's in origin; but then why the mark? I conclude that Jefferson wanted to credit Franklin but could not write his name because he had already committed to doing that only when the handwriting was Franklin's. This would be consistent with his practice in the rest of the document, where there are other emendations in his hand without any special mark.

Franklin later used the phrase "excites domestic insurrections among their servants" in the same manner in the first edition of the fake "Supplement to the Boston Independent Chronicle," an anti-British propaganda piece, in April 1782. *The Writings of Benjamin Franklin*, ed. Albert Henry Smyth (New York, 1906), 8:445. For the "domestic insurrections" passage, see Sidney Kaplan, "The Domestic Insurrections of the Declaration of Independence," *Journal of Negro History* 62 (1976), 243–55.

When Franklin suggested or made the addition, there was still another "he has" accusation against the king, after this one and before the culminating attack. Deleted later by Congress, it covered the other antinationals, the loyalists, "fellow citizens" whose "treasonable insurrections" have been enticed by the prospects of looting patriot property. Thus Franklin's version of these culminating accusations would have begun with the slaves, moved on to the Indians, then to the Tories, and then returned to the Black-British alliance. It is possible, though, that Franklin intended his "instanced & excited domestic insurrections among us" as a replacement for the entire "he has waged cruel war" slavery paragraph. No documentary evidence exists, but Franklin did urge Jefferson to accept the committee of the whole's revisions as a more concise, and quite sufficient, version. In his memoir Jefferson would stress the role of both the Deep South and northerners like Franklin who "also I believe felt a little tender under those censures; for tho' their people have very few slaves themselves yet they have been pretty considerable carriers of them to others." *Jefferson: Writings*, ed. Merrill Peterson (New York, 1984), 18.

The possibility that Franklin urged the excision of the slavery paragraph has been broadcast widely in the otherwise wonderful musical play *1776*. The authors may have picked it up from the invented dinner party dialogue in Cornel Lengyel, *Four Days in July: The Story Behind the Declaration of Independence* (Garden City, N.Y., 1958), 175, 247–48. Peter Stone and Sherman Edwards, *1776: A Musical Play* (New York, 1970), 116–17, 124.

9. For the "close distancing" of working people through the construction of such categories, see Robert John Ackermann, *Heterogeneities: Race, Gender, Class, Nation, State* (Amherst, Mass., 1996), 19–20; Patrick Wolfe, "Land, Labor, and Difference: Elementary Structures of Race," *American Historical Review* 106 (2001), 867, 880; Albert Memmi, *Racism*, trans. Steve Martinot (Minneapolis, Minn., 1996), 67–70, 139.

10. *PBF* 22:536–38. For the definition of Africans as an enemy nation by Jefferson, see Peter S. Onuf, *Jefferson's Empire: The Language of American Nationhood* (Charlottesville, Va., 2000), 147–88.

11. Jan Lewis, " 'Of Every Age Sex and Condition': The Representation of Women in the Constitution," *Journal of the Early Republic* 15 (1995), 359–88.

12. Franklin and the other commissioners also stressed the "great Danger" of a British victory should they be able to launch an invasion against the southern colonies. BF to Lord Howe, July 20, 1776, in *PBF* 22:519; American Commissioners to Vergennes, "Memoir on the State of the Former Colonies" (before January 5, 1777), February 1, 1777, BF to Jan Ingenhousz, February 12, 1777, in *PBF* 23:118, 261, 310; Quarles, *Negro in the American Revolution*, 114.

13. BF, "The Sale of the Hessians," in *Benjamin Franklin: Writings*, ed. J. A. Leo Lemay (New York, 1987), 917–19; David Schoenbrun, *Triumph in Paris: The Exploits of Benjamin Franklin* (New York, 1976), 158. I follow Lemay in thinking this piece is by Franklin, though other scholars note that there is no positive evidence that he wrote it. *PBF* 22:480–84.

14. The edition of Franklin's writings published in 1779 avoided slavery, omitting the 1770 "Conversation About Slavery." *Benjamin Franklin's Letters to the Press, 1757–1775*, ed. Verner W. Crane (Chapel Hill, N.C., 1950), 186. Franklin and the Marquis de Lafayette did propose to include Dunmore's proclamation and slaves plundering masters in a series of prints "to illustrate British Cruelties" in a children's book, but the project never came off. *PBF* 29:591–92; BF to David Hartley, February 2, 1780, in *PBF* 31:439; BF to William Hidgson, in *PBF* 32:557.

15. Edmund S. Morgan, *Benjamin Franklin* (New Haven, Conn., 2002), 251; Bernard Bailyn, "Realism and Idealism in American Diplomacy: Franklin in Paris, Couronné Par La Liberté," in *To Begin the World Anew: The Genius and Ambiguities of the American Founders* (New York, 2003), 60–99; Jonathan R. Dull, "France and the American Revolution Seen as a Tragedy," in Ronald Hoffman and Peter J. Albert, eds., *Diplomacy*

and Revolution: The Franco-American Alliance of 1778 (Charlottesville, Va., 1981), 73–106.

16. Durand Ecchevaria, *Mirage in the West: The French Image of American Society to 1815* (Princeton, N.J., 1957); Alfred Owen Aldridge, *Franklin and His French Contemporaries* (New York, 1957), 28–29; Antonello Gerbi, *The Dispute of the New World: The History of a Polemic, 1750–1900*, rev. ed., trans. Jeremy Moyle (Pittsburgh, 1973); Peter Gay, *The Enlightenment: An Interpretation*, vol. 2, *The Science of Freedom* (New York, 1969), 414–15, 555–56; David Brion Davis, *The Problem of Slavery in Western Culture* (Ithaca, N.Y., 1966), 12–17, 411–21; Anthony Pagden, *Lords of All the World: Ideologies of Empire in Britain, Spain, and France, c.1500–c.1800* (New Haven, Conn., 1995), 3–4, 163–72; Sue Peabody, *"There Are No Slaves in France": The Political Culture of Race and Slavery in the Ancien Regime* (New York, 1996), 9, 96–97.

17. I. Bernard Cohen, *Science and the Founding Fathers* (New York, 1995), 171–88; Tom Tucker, *Bolt of Fate: Benjamin Franklin and His Electric Kite Experiment* (New York, 2003), 110–23, 177–80; Thomas P. Slaughter, *The Natures of John and William Bartram* (New York, 1996).

18. Thomas Jefferson to Richard Walsh, December 4, 1818, in *The Complete Thomas Jefferson*, ed. Saul K. Padover (New York, 1943), 894; Jefferson, *Notes on the State of Virginia with Related Documents*, ed. David Waldstreicher (Boston, 2002).

19. BF to Samuel Cooper, May 1, 1777, to John Winthrop, May 1, 1777, to Jonathan Williams, May 27, 1777, "Comparison of Great Britain and America as to Credit, in 1777," in *PBF* 24:7, 9, 90, 509–14.

20. Claude-Anne Lopez, *Mon Cher Papa: Franklin and the Ladies of Paris* (New Haven, Conn., 1966), 15–16, 131, 195; Ronald Clark, *Benjamin Franklin: A Biography* (New York, 1983), 313–15; R. Jackson Wilson, *Figures of Speech: American Writers and the Literary Marketplace* (New York, 1989), 21–23.

21. Schoenbrun, *Triumph in Paris*, 95, 182–83; Carl Van Doren, *Benjamin Franklin* (New York, 1939), 569–70; Simon Schama, *Citizens: A Chronicle of the French Revolution* (New York, 1989), 42–44; Daniel Roche, *France in the Enlightenment* (Cambridge, Mass., 1998), 590; Robert Darnton, "The Craze for America: Condorcet and Brissot," *George Washington's False Teeth: An Unconventional Guide to the Eighteenth Century* (New York, 2003), 119–36; Joan B. Landes, *Women and the Public Sphere in the Age of the French Revolution* (Ithaca, N.Y., 1988), 73–74. This impression carried back to America. When the New Englander Manasseh Cutler visited Philadelphia in 1787, he reported in his diary that Franklin wore "a plain Quaker dress." Alfred Owen Aldridge, *Benjamin Franklin: Philosopher and Man* (Philadelphia, 1965), 394.

22. For a different view, see Claude-Anne Lopez, "Franklin and Slavery: A Sea Change," in *My Life with Benjamin Franklin* (New Haven, Conn., 2002), 196–205.

23. Jack P. Greene, *The Intellectual Construction of America: Exceptionalism and Identity from 1492 to 1800* (Chapel Hill, N.C., 1993), 154–56.

24. Barbara B. Oberg, "Introduction," in *PBF* 30:lxiii–lxiv; BF to John Jay, October 4–28, 1779, in *PBF* 30:471; BF to Stephen Hills et al., March 11, 1779, in *PBF* 29:96; Drew McCoy, "Benjamin Franklin's Vision of a Republican Political Economy for America," *William and Mary Quarterly*, 3rd ser., 35 (1978), 605–28.

25. William E. Juhnke, "Benjamin Franklin's View of the Negro and Slavery," *Pennsylvania History* 41 (1974), 383; *PBF* 36:336; see the works cited above, 280n14, and David Waldstreicher, "Capitalism, Slavery and Benjamin Franklin's American Revolution," in

Cathy D. Matson, ed., *The Early American Economy: New Directions* (University Park, Pa., forthcoming).

26. Phillip Gibbes, Minutes of a Conversation with Franklin, January 5, 1778, in *PBF* 25:423; BF, "Thoughts on the West India Trade" [c.1781], vol. 49, folder 14, Benjamin Franklin Papers, APS; BF to Benjamin Vaughan, with "Thoughts on Privateering" and "Thoughts Concerning the Sugar Colonies," July 10, 1782, in *PBF* 37 (forthcoming); BF to Richard Oswald, January 14, 1783, in *Franklin: Writings*, ed. Smyth, 9:4–6; BF to David Le Roy, "Maritime Observations," in *Franklin: Writings*, ed. Smyth, 9:404–5.

27. Eric Williams, *Capitalism and Slavery* (Chapel Hill, N.C., 1944), 107, 120; Greene, *Intellectual Construction of America*, 109; Michael Perelman, *The Invention of Capitalism: Classical Political Economy and the Secret History of Primitive Accumulation* (Durham, N.C., 2000), 237–47, 254–79; Richard B. Sheridan, *Sugar and Slavery: An Economic History of the British West Indies* (Essex, Eng., 1974), 5–11; David Brion Davis, *The Problem of Slavery in the Age of Revolution, 1770–1823* (Ithaca, N.Y., 1975), 351–54; Seymour Drescher, *The Mighty Experiment: Free Labor versus Slavery in British Emancipation* (New York, 2002), 19–33, 247n41; Waldstreicher, "Capitalism, Slavery, and Benjamin Franklin's American Revolution."

28. *Franklin: Writings*, ed. Lemay, 976–77; Richard B. Morris, *The Forging of the Union, 1781–87* (New York, 1987), 9; Ormond Seavey, "Benjamin Franklin as Imperialist and Provincial," in Gianfranca Balestra and Luigi Sanpietro, eds., *Benjamin Franklin: An American Genius* (Rome, 1993), 30–31. A contemporary who knew Franklin's politics and writings very well responded at length on the occasion of Franklin's death and insisted that immigration to America actually produced "white Negroes." *Memoirs of the late Dr. Benjamin Franklin: With a Review of his Pamphlet, Entitled "Information to those who would wish to remove to AMERICA"* (London, 1790), 68.

29. BF to Richard Oswald, November 26, 1782, in *Writings of Franklin*, ed. Smyth, 8:621, 623, 626; Morris, *Forging of the Union*, 5–6; Richard B. Morris, *The Peacemakers: The Great Powers and American Independence* (New York, 1965), 535n156; BF to Henry Laurens, July 6, 1783, in *Writings of Franklin*, ed. Smyth, 9:58. The linkage of loyalist and slave masters' claims remained unresolved and continued to trouble Anglo-American diplomacy for more than a decade.

30. Editors' note, BF to Jean-Charles-Pierre Lenoir, July 22, 1780, in *PBF* 33:96–97; Jonathan Williams Jr. to Hebre and St. Clement, May 18, 1782, Jonathan Williams Letterbook, Benjamin Franklin Collection, Yale University.

31. Jean Montague to BF, July 25, 1780, in *PBF* 33:121–22; Peabody, *"There Are No Slaves in France,"* 106.

32. William Temple Franklin to William Robeson, September 3, 8, 1781, in *PBF* 35:435, 456. When John and Sarah Jay's slave Abigail ran away from Passy, William Temple Franklin dealt with the police. Benjamin Franklin advised ignoring her for fifteen or twenty days. Daniel C. Littlefield, "John Jay, the Revolutionary Generation, and Slavery," *New York History* (2000), 129; compare the harsher conclusion in Lopez and Herbert, *Private Franklin*, 300.

33. William Robeson to BF, January 22, 1781, in *PBF* 34:298; Robeson to BF, August 9, 1781, William Temple Franklin to Jonathan Williams Jr., August 25, 1781, Robeson to William Temple Franklin, September 11, 15, 1781, in *PBF* 35:347–48, 407, 407n2, 464–65, 489.

34. Robeson had lied to Williams about money and about trying to smuggle his French mis-

tress and daughter aboard the ship, something that horrified the recently betrothed Williams, who knew of Robeson's wife and family in North Carolina. Jonathan Williams Jr. to BF, March 9, 1782, in *PBF* 36:676–77; Jonathan Williams Jr. to Hebre and St. Clement, May 18, 1782, Robert Mumford to William Temple Franklin, May 18, Jonathan Williams to William Temple Franklin, June 4, Jonathan Williams to Bache and Shee, December 22, 1782, Jonathan Williams Letterbook, Benjamin Franklin Collection, Yale University. I am more than usually indebted to Kate Ohno of the Benjamin Franklin Papers, who was kind enough to call my attention to the Montague affair and supply these documents before they appeared in print with her careful annotation in the recently published volumes of *PBF*.

35. *Morning Herald and Daily Advertiser*, January 3, 1783; Jonathan Williams to Lord Shelburne, January 9, 1783, BF to Shelburne, January 15, 1783, Jonathan Williams Letterbook.

36. Montague, who spoke French and English, may not have been of much use to the wigless, passably bilingual Franklin (though it is easy to imagine him coiffing the dandyish Temple).

9. THE LONG ARM OF BENJAMIN FRANKLIN

1. Sheila Skemp, *William Franklin: Son of a Patriot, Servant of a King* (New York, 1990), 224, 270; Alfred Owen Aldridge, *Benjamin Franklin: Philosopher and Man* (Philadelphia, 1965), 384.

2. BF to Jonathan Shipley, February 24, 1786, in *The Writings of Benjamin Franklin*, ed. Albert Henry Smyth (New York, 1906), 9:490–91.

3. Claude-Anne Lopez and Eugenia W. Herbert, *The Private Franklin: The Man and His Family* (New York, 1975), 266, 272–75, 286.

4. Ibid., 194, 222–23, 282.

5. Edmund S. Morgan, *Benjamin Franklin* (New Haven, Conn., 2002), 301; BF to Ferdinand Grand, January 29, to Jane Mecom, May 30, 1787, in *Writings of Franklin*, ed. Smyth, 9:482, 590.

6. Aldridge, *Benjamin Franklin*, 384–85; Murphy D. Smith, *Due Reverrence: Antiques in the Possession of the American Philosophical Society*, American Philosophical Society *Memoirs*, vol. 203 (1997), fig. 8b; J. A. Leo Lemay, "Essay Review: Recent Franklin Scholarship, with a Note on Franklin's Sedan Chair," *Pennsylvania Magazine of History and Biography* 126 (2002), 338–40; William Parker Cutler and Julia Perkins Cutler, eds., *The Life Journals and Correspondence of Rev. Manasseh Cutler, LL.D.* (Cincinnati, Oh., 1888), 2:234; Carl Van Doren, *Benjamin Franklin* (New York, 1938), 736, 741.

7. BF, "Description of an Instrument for Taking Down Books from High Shelves," in *Writings of Franklin*, ed. Smyth, 9:483–85. For further reflections on the meaning of this invention and Franklin's veritable obsession with limbs more generally, see David Waldstreicher, "The Long Arm of Benjamin Franklin," in Katherine Ott, David Serlin, and Stephen Mihm, eds., *Artificial Parts, Practical Lives: Modern Histories of Prosthetics* (New York, 2002), 300–326.

8. Cutler and Cutler, eds., *Rev. Manasseh Cutler*, 1:269–70; Catharine Van Cortlandt Mathews, *Andrew Ellicott: His Life and Lessons* (New York, 1908), 50–51.

9. BF, "Dialogue Between the Gout and Dr. Franklin," "The Handsome and Deformed Leg," "Petition of the Left Hand," in *Benjamin Franklin: Writings*, ed. J. A. Leo Lemay (New

York, 1987), 943–52, 1115–16; Roy Porter and G. S. Rousseau, *Gout: The Patrician Malady* (New Haven, Conn., 1998).

10. Merrill Jensen, *The New Nation: A History of the United States During the Confederation, 1781–1789* (New York, 1950); Eric Foner, *Tom Paine and Revolutionary America* (New York, 1976); Allan Kulikoff, "The American Revolution, Capitalism, and the Formation of the Yeoman Classes," in Alfred F. Young, ed., *Beyond the American Revolution: Explorations in the History of American Radicalism* (DeKalb, Ill., 1993), 80–119; Laura Rigal, *The American Manufactory: Art, Labor, and the World of Things in the Early Republic* (Princeton, N.J., 1998), 3–54.

11. BF to David Hartley, October 27, 1785, to Ferdinand Grand, January 29, March 5, 1786, to M. Le Veillard, March 16, 1786, to Charles Biddle, November 2, 1786, in *Writings of Franklin*, ed. Smyth, 9:472, 482, 493, 495–96, 548; M. LeVeillard to BF, October 9, 1785 in *The Works of Benjamin Franklin*, ed. John Bigelow (New York, 1904), 8:206; Ronald Clark, *Benjamin Franklin: A Biography* (New York, 1983), 404.

12. Arthur Zilversmit, *The First Emancipation: The Abolition of Slavery in the North* (Chicago, 1967), 124–37; David Brion Davis, *The Problem of Slavery in the Age of Revolution, 1770–1823* (Ithaca, N.Y., 1975), 285–326; Gary B. Nash, *Race and Revolution* (Madison, Wisc., 1990), 19, 112–14; Gary B. Nash and Jean B. Soderlund, *Freedom by Degrees: Emancipation in Pennsylvania and Its Aftermath* (New York, 1990), 74–136.

13. BF, "The Retort Courteous," in *Franklin: Writings*, ed. Lemay, 1122–30; Josiah Wedgwood to BF, February 29, 1788, vol. 36, folder 28, Benjamin Franklin Papers, APS; BF to Josiah Wedgwood, May 15, 1788, in Roger Bruns, ed., *Am I Not a Man and a Brother?: The Antislavery Crusade of Revolutionary America, 1689–1789* (New York, 1980), vi; "Extract from the Papers of Dr. Benjamin Rush," *Pennsylvania Magazine of History and Biography* 29 (1905), 25; BF to James Pemberton, May 2, 1788, Reel 2, Manuscripts vol. 1, Papers of the Pennsylvania Abolition Society, Historical Society of Pennsylvania (hereafter PAS Papers); Alfred Owen Aldridge, *Franklin and His French Contemporaries* (New York, 1957), 139–41.

14. Reel 1, Minutes 1787–1916, PAS Papers; BF to James Pemberton, May 2, 1788, John Langdon to BF, May 6, 1788, BF to James Pemberton, August 21, 1788, Reel 2, PAS Papers; Tench Coxe to BF, June 9, 1787, May 29, 1788, n.d., 1788, vol. 35, folder 75, vol. 36, folder 55, vol. 40, folder 213, James Pemberton to BF, May 2, 1788, vol. 36, folder 47, Benjamin Franklin Papers, APS; Wayne D. Eberly, "The Pennsylvania Abolition Society, 1775–1830" (Ph.D. diss., Pennsylvania State University, 1973), 28–29, 203. Some scholars assert a more active role for Franklin in the drafting of a "Plan for Improving the Condition of Free Blacks," but the Plan, routinely ascribed to Franklin, does not survive in his hand. See the manuscript and broadside versions of "Plan," PAS Papers; Lewis J. Carey, *Franklin's Economic Views* (New York, 1928), 89–91; and the works cited in note 24 below.

15. Thomas Jefferson, *Notes on the State of Virginia with Related Documents*, ed. David Waldstreicher (Boston, 2002), 18–20, 63–66, 125–29, 175–81, 195–96. On the strengths and weaknesses of American nationalism in the decade after independence, compare John M. Murrin, "A Roof without Walls: The Dilemma of American National Identity," in Richard Beeman et al., eds., *Beyond Confederation: Origins of the Constitution and American National Identity* (Chapel Hill, N.C., 1987), 333–47; David Waldstreicher, *In the Midst of Perpetual Fetes: The Making of American Nationalism, 1776–1820* (Chapel Hill, N.C., 1997), 17–84.

16. The Orders-in-Council were authored by Franklin's old nemesis William Knox, who had lost his Georgia lands, though not his slaves, in the war. Historical Manuscripts Commission, *Report on Manuscripts in Various Collections* (Dublin, 1909), 6:192, 196; Leland J. Bellot, *William Knox: The Life and Thought of an Eighteenth-Century Imperialist* (Austin, Tex., 1977), 193; Richard B. Morris, *The Forging of the Union, 1781–1789* (New York, 1987), 139.

17. Bernard Bailyn, ed., *The Debate over the Constitution*, 2 vols. (New York, 1993), 1:100, 111–12, 153, 318–21, 395, 829–31, 2:20–21, 25, 152, 196–201, 453, 706–8; Max Farrand, *The Records of the Federal Convention of 1787*, rev. ed., 4 vols. (New Haven, Conn., 1966); James H. Hutson, ed., *Supplement to Max Farrand's The Records of the Federal Convention of 1787* (New Haven, Conn., 1987); John P. Kaminski, ed., *A Necessary Evil?: Slavery and the Debate over the Constitution* (Madison, Wisc., 1995); Staughton Lynd, *Class, Conflict, Slavery, and the United States Constitution: Ten Essays* (Indianapolis, Ind., 1967), 153–215; Howard A. Ohline, "Republicanism and Slavery: Origins of the Three-Fifths Clause in the United States Constitution," *William and Mary Quarterly*, 3rd ser., 28 (1971), 563–84; Donald Robinson, *Slavery in the Structure of American Politics, 1765–1820* (New York, 1971), 131–247; William M. Wiecek, *The Sources of Antislavery Constitutionalism in America, 1760–1848* (Ithaca, N.Y., 1977), 62–83; Paul Finkelman, "Making a Covenant with Death: Slavery in the Constitutional Convention," in Beeman et al., eds., *Beyond Confederation*, 188–225; Wiecek, "The Witch at the Christening: Slavery and the Constitution's Origins," in Leonard Levy and Dennis J. Mahoney, eds., *The Framing and Ratification of the Constitution* (New York, 1987), 167–84; Jack N. Rakove, *Original Meanings: Politics and Ideas in the Making of the Constitution* (New York, 1996), esp. 72–74, 85–88; Don E. Fehrenbacher, *The Slaveholding Republic: An Account of the United States Government's Relations to Slavery* (New York, 2001), 15–48.

18. BF, "Speech in the Constitutional Convention; on the Proportion of Representation and Votes," in *Writings of Franklin*, ed. Smyth, 9:595–96; Van Doren, *Franklin*, 745–49; Barbara B. Oberg, " 'Plain, insinuating, persuasive': Benjamin Franklin's Final Speech to the Constitutional Convention of 1787," in J. A. Leo Lemay, ed., *Reappraising Benjamin Franklin* (Newark, Del., 1993), 175–92; Paul Finkelman, "The Pennsylvania Delegation and the Peculiar Institution: The Two Faces of the Keystone State," *Pennsylvania Magazine of History and Biography* 112 (1988), 70–71; William G. Carr, *The Oldest Delegate: Franklin in the Constitutional Convention* (Newark, Del., 1990), 20.

19. Farrand, ed., *Records of the Federal Convention*, 1:520–1, 526, 2:12–13; Carr, *Oldest Delegate*, 102–5; Finkelman, "Making a Covenant with Death," 201.

20. Tench Coxe to James Madison, March 31, 1790, in Farrand, ed., *Records of the Federal Convention*, 3:361; Morris, *Forging of the Union*, 183; Carr, *Oldest Delegate*, 102–3; Kaminski, ed., *Necessary Evil*, 42.

21. Hutson, ed., *Supplement to Max Farrand's Records*, 158; Robinson, *Slavery in the Structure of American Politics*, 188, 197–98; Kaminski, ed., *Necessary Evil*, 119, 131; BF, "A Comparison of the Conduct of the Ancient Jews and of the Anti-Federalists of the United States of America," *Franklin: Writings*, ed. Lemay, 1144–48; BF, "To the Printer of the Evening Herald," in *Writings of Franklin*, ed. Smyth, 9:627–28. Coxe actually argued both sides of the debate over the Constitution's meanings for slavery in anonymous essays, telling southerners it secured the institution and Pennsylvanians that it had been put on the road to extinction. James Wilson did something very similar, depicting the clause as ensuring that Congress would have the power to eliminate slavery. Howard A.

Ohline, "Slavery, Economics, and Congressional Politics, 1790," *Journal of Southern History* 46 (1980), 338; Paul Finkelman, "The Problem of Slavery in the Age of Federalism," in Doron Ben-Atar and Barbara B. Oberg, eds., *Federalists Reconsidered* (Charlottesville, Va., 1998), 140.

22. An eloquent account of the founders' silence appears in Joseph J. Ellis, *Founding Brothers: The Revolutionary Generation* (New York, 2000), 81–119, though he pushes to an extreme the recent trend to make an antislavery exception of Franklin and conflates the 1787 PAS petition, which he implies Franklin supported, with the 1790 petition (discussed below). I do not think Franklin was being inconsistent, for he had been making the same choices all along. The evidence might support a slightly different interpretation, though: that Franklin at first agreed that the Constitution was the time and place to present such a petition, but changed his mind later when confronted with southern intransigence and the prospect of the Convention's failure. In that case, the Convention would appear very similar to the Declaration of Independence committee with an almost identical role for Franklin.

23. William E. Juhnke, "Benjamin Franklin's Views of the Negro and Slavery," *Pennsylvania History* 41 (1974), 386–88; H. W. Brands, *The First American: The Life and Times of Benjamin Franklin* (New York, 2001), 703–4; Stephen A. Schwartz, "Dr. Franklin's Plan," *Smithsonian* 33, no. 3 (June 2001), 123; Walter Isaacson, *Benjamin Franklin: A Life* (New York, 2003), 463; see also *The Real Benjamin Franklin*, a documentary produced by the Discovery Channel and shown, since 2000, at the Franklin Court site of Independence Hall National Park (courtesy of Karie Diethorn); and the "Abolitionist" section of *Benjamin Franklin*, a documentary aired on PBS in 2002, written by Ronald Blumer and sponsored by Twin Cities Public Television, and the accompanying website: www.pbs.org/benfranklin/13_citizen_abolitionist.html. Edmund S. Morgan more carefully argues that Franklin "lost no time in joining others" to petition the new government against slavery, which is literally true, but only because during the two and a half years between his squelching of the 1787 petition and the presentation of the 1790 petition on the floor of the House, there was no other body except the soon-to-be-defunct Continental Congress to which to present a petition. In the meantime, the slave trade revived, as Spain opened its colonies to free trade in slaves and the southern economy began to experience a rebound. Morgan, *Benjamin Franklin* (New Haven, Conn., 2002), 312.

24. BF to John Wright, November 4, 1789, in *Writings of Franklin*, ed. Smyth, 10:62–63; Brands, *First American*, 702. Brands, like many, assumes that Franklin wrote the resolves and petitions of the PAS that went out under his name, even though the prose is far from Franklinesque to say the least. Eberly implies that Franklin did not author the resolves, two of which Lemay includes in the Library of America edition of Franklin's writings. The PAS minutes do not credit an author, but Franklin seems far too distant from the active leadership to have done the drafting. "Address to the Public From the Pennsylvania Society for Promoting the Abolition of Slavery, & the Relief of Free Negroes Unlawfully Held in Bondage" [November 9, 1789] in *Works of Franklin*, ed. Bigelow, 12:157–59, also in *Writings of Franklin*, ed. Smyth, 9:66–68; BF, "Plan for Improving the Condition of Free Blacks," in *Writings of Franklin*, ed. Smyth, 10:127–29; Eberly, "Pennsylvania Abolition Society," 39, 203; *Franklin: Writings*, ed. Lemay, 1154–56.

25. James Pemberton to BF, February 5, 1790, vol. 36, folder 194, Benjamin Franklin Papers, APS; *Writings of Franklin*, ed. Smyth, 10:86. For the PAS's strategy, compare William C. diGiacomantonio, " 'For the Gratification of a Volunteering Society': Antislav-

ery and Pressure Group Politics in the First Federal Congess," *Journal of the Early Republic* 15 (1995), 169–97: and Richard S. Newman, *The Transformation of American Abolitionism: Fighting Slavery in the Early Republic* (Chapel Hill, N.C., 2002), 16–38.

26. Newman, *Transformation of American Abolitionism*, 16, 39, 41.

27. Kenneth R. Bowling and Helen E. Veit, eds., *Documentary History of the First Federal Congress of the United States of America, March 4, 1789–March 3, 1791*, vol. 9, *The Diary of William Maclay and Other Notes on Senate Debates* (Baltimore, Md., 1988), 202–3; James Madison to Tench Coxe, March 28, 1790, in Robert A. Rutland et al., eds., *The Papers of James Madison* (Charlottesville, Va., 1981), 13:128; Ohline, "Slavery, Economics, and Congressional Politics, 1790," 343–44.

28. Linda Grant DePauw, ed., *Documentary History of the First Federal Congress* (Baltimore, Md., 1977), 3:295, 334–41; Bowling and Veit, eds., *Documentary History*, 12:270, 287, 302, 313, 725, 808–9, 813, 825; Joseph Gales, ed., *The Debates and Proceedings in the Congress of the United States* (Washington, D.C., 1834), 2:1202, 1471; diGiacomantonio, "Antislavery and Pressure Group Politics," 176–77; Richard S. Newman, "Prelude to the Gag Rule: Southern Reactions to Antislavery Petitions in the First Federal Congress," *Journal of the Early Republic* 16 (1996), 571–99; Ellis, *Founding Brothers*, 112.

29. Philadelphia *Federal Gazette*, March 25, 1790; "Sidi Mehemet Ibrahim on the Slave Trade," in *Franklin: Writings*, ed. Lemay, 1157–59.

30. A brief analysis in this context is provided by Robert Allison, *The Crescent Obscured: The United States and the Muslim World, 1776–1815* (New York, 1993), 103–6.

31. "From the NEW-YORK DAILY ADVERTISER," "From a late New-York Paper," *Federal Gazette*, March 26, 1790; "FRANKLIN," *Aurora* (Philadelphia), December 15, 1820, quoted in Matthew Mason, "The Battle of the Slaveholding Liberators: Great Britain, the United States, and Slavery in the Early Nineteenth Century," *William and Mary Quarterly*, 3rd ser., 59 (2002), 685–86n81; *Dr. Franklin an Abolitionist* (Boston, 1835), Broadsides Collection, Historical Society of Pennsylvania; William Lee Miller, *Arguing About Slavery: The Great Battle in the United States Congress* (New York, 1996), 280; Paul Goodman, *Of One Blood: The Abolitionists and the Origins of Racial Equality* (Berkeley, 1999), 141; George Livermore, *An Historical Research Respecting the Opinions of the Founders on Negroes as Slaves, as Citizens, and as Soldiers*, 4th ed. (Boston, 1863), 35–41; "Benjamin Franklin and Freedom," *Journal of Negro History* 4 (1919) 41–50; W.E.B. Du Bois, *The Story of Benjamin Franklin* (Vienna, 1956).

32. Christopher Looby, *Voicing America: Language, Literary Form, and the Origins of the United States* (Chicago, 1996), 99, 124–31.

33. "Franklin's Last Will and Testament" in *Works of Franklin*, ed. Bigelow, 12:203–5. Bob had been in the family since at least 1770. Franklin's sister Jane, an occasional visitor, mentioned him in a letter to Sally Franklin Bache, asking, "Does George bob & [Jack?] Do any beter, & how Does the Little molato Behave to his master." Jane Mecom to Deborah Franklin, before August 1770, in *The Letters of Benjamin Franklin and Jane Mecom*, ed. Carl Van Doren (Philadelphia, 1950), 120.

EPILOGUE

1. "Preface," *A Narrative of the Life and Adventures of Venture, a Native of Africa: But resident above sixty years in the United States of America. RELATED BY HIMSELF* (New London, Conn., 1798), repr. in Vincent Carretta, ed., *Unchained Voices: An Anthology of*

Black Authors in the English-Speaking World of the 18th Century (Lexington, Ky., 1996), 369; "Traditions of Venture! Known as Venture Smith, Compiled by H. M. Selden" [1897], in Arna Bontemps, ed., *Five Black Lives* (Middletown, Conn., 1971), 26.

2. Smith, *Narrative*, 374–75. Robert R. Desrochers Jr., " 'Not Fade Away': The Narrative of Venture Smith, an African American in the Early Republic," *Journal of American History* 84 (1997), 40–66.

3. Smith, *Narrative*, 375–76; *New York Gazette and Weekly Post Boy*, July 7, 1755; Desrochers, " 'Not Fade Away,' " 58n35.

4. Smith, *Narrative*, 375–77; *New York Gazette and Weekly Post Boy*, April 1, 1754. This ad is also reprinted in Graham Russell Hodges and Alan Edward Brown, *"Pretends to Be Free": Runaway Slave Advertisements from Colonial and Revolutionary New York and New Jersey* (New York, 1994), 49–50. The existence of the ad and its closeness to what Smith says can be taken to document the whole. It adds to Desrochers's documentation of other accurate references to Africa the fact that Venture had been "mark'd in the Face, or scar'd with a Knife in his own Country."

5. Smith, *Narrative*, 377–81, 384; Selden, comp., "Traditions of Venture!," 27–29.

6. Ibid., 381–84; William L. Andrews, *To Tell a Free Story: The First Century of Afro-American Autobiography, 1760–1865* (Urbana, Ill., 1989), 51–53, 59–60; Philip Gould, *Barbaric Traffic: Commerce and Antislavery in the Eighteenth-Century Atlantic World* (Cambridge, Mass., 2003), 144–50.

7. Smith, *Narrative*, 384.

8. Compare Desrochers, " 'Not Fade Away,' " with Joseph J. Ellis, *Founding Brothers: The Revolutionary Generation* (New York, 2000), 12–13, who cites Desrochers's article on Smith as a new kind of history that recovers "lost voices" but misses the "center of the national story."

Acknowledgments

———•═•═•———

After giving Ben Franklin such a hard time for underrating his reliance on others, I have all the more reason to acknowledge the debts I have incurred.

It all began at Bennington College, when my early American history students read the runaway ads Billy G. Smith and Richard Wojtowicz collected in *Blacks Who Stole Themselves* alongside Franklin's *Autobiography*. I thank the members of that class, especially Lise Johnson, for seeing the drama in those documents and for their doubts about tales told by great men.

Mechal Sobel, Fredrika Teute, Ronald Hoffman, the Omohundro Institute of Early American History and Culture, and the University of Haifa provided me with the opportunity to write about the runaway ads, as well as suggestions that have guided me since. In Haifa P. Gabrielle Foreman gripped me by the intellectual collar and informed me that I was really writing a book about Benjamin Franklin. Stunned, I denied it, but later her prophecy worked on me.

Colleagues at Yale and Notre Dame heard other early versions: I especially thank the African American Studies Colloquium at Yale and the McNeil Center for Early American Studies for their incisive and appreciative responses at an early stage. Audiences at Rutgers, Brandeis, Columbia, and UCLA asked especially helpful questions. For comments on papers, I thank sympaticos John Bezís-Selfa, Chris Brown, Steve Bullock, Elizabeth Dillon, Peter Hinks, Graham Hodges, Shan Holt, Matt Jacobson, Cathy Matson, Joanne Melish, Robert Johnston, Rip Lhamon, Phil Morgan, Kate Ohno, Robert Perkinson, Jonathan Prude, David Serlin, Shane White, and Kariann Yokota.

Fellowships from the Gilder Lehrman Institute of American History, the University of Notre Dame, and the American Philosophical Society aided the research immeasurably. A year at the Center for Scholars and Writers of the New York Public Library made it possible to write in a concentrated and timely fashion.

Everyone who writes about Franklin stands on the shoulders of the editors of the Papers of Benjamin Franklin at Yale University, past and present. Claude-Anne Lopez plowed so much of the ground I cover in her own books and in many volumes of the Papers. Kate Ohno's sleuthing, her generosity with references, her encouragement, and her friendship have enriched not only this project but my life for a decade now. Barbara Oberg, by now too an old friend, tolerated my interruptions of her staff, wrote letters on my behalf, and on one occasion subtly let me know when I was being dogmatic and when interesting. Jonathan Dull and Ellen Cohn answered novice questions with good humor and indeed educated me every time we spoke about Franklin. These gifted editors welcomed me to the world of Franklin scholarship long before I knew I'd become a true "friend of Franklin" by writing about him. So did Roy Goodman of the American Philosophical Society. Friend of all friends of Franklin, Roy made Franklin seem fun. More recently, as we strolled through Independence Hall Park, he demonstrated his Franklinian ability to move people—and get a laugh or two in the process—by stopping Dr. Franklin himself, aka impersonator Ralph Archbold, to inform him of my discovery of a document suggesting that he'd held slaves in the early 1730s. Archbold's bemused stare over his glasses put the fear of Franklin in me. Thanks too to Robert S. Cox, king of manuscripts at the APS and a great conversationalist, for helping to make several trips to Philadelphia remarkably efficient, despite all the time we spent talking about Franklin, the universe, and everything.

As Franklin knew all too well, father figures can never be adequately thanked. Maybe that's why God created not only religion but also footnotes. Mine refer to no one as often as David Brion Davis. When I returned to Yale as faculty, David treated me, a former student, as a colleague. In ways I only now begin to perceive, this made it possible for me to walk more deliberately in his footsteps. Now that I am a father as well as a professor, it is a lesson I intend to study.

Alfred F. Young, one of the intellectual grandfathers of this project, provided invaluable advice at several points along the way, plus characteristically wise readings of draft chapters. The incomparable Mike Zuckerman refused to be easily convinced, explained at great length why, let me try his patience again, invited me to his salon, and explained still another time. Shane White, an honorary New Yorker, has been an indispensable fellow traveler. Steve Bullock, a genteel sort, shared notes on confidence men and won't mind if I make free with his name.

Near the finish line, John Bezís-Selfa, Jill Lepore, and Thomas P. Slaughter read most of the manuscript and provided sage editorial advice. At Hill and Wang, Lauren Osborne helped shape the book from the start. Thomas LeBien melded the virtues of entrepreneurship and good old-fashioned, rigorous editing. Franklin would be proud—but I have a still better compliment, one of my best, for Thomas: he belongs on Union Square.

Speaking of New York, Jacqueline Robinson heard most of the ideas first and foretold the kind of story it had to become. She understood everything, but that was only the beginning. Most of all I thank her for running away with my heart—and with me.

Index

abolitionists, 18, 81, 191, 193, 198, 230; *see also* antislavery movement

"Act for the More Effectual Keeping of the Colonies Dependent" (Franklin), 208

Adam (slave), 35

Adams, John, 216, 237

Adams, John Quincy, xi

Adams, Matthew, 37

Addison, Joseph, 41, 44, 45, 95

advertisements, 22–25; in Boston newspapers, 34, 39; for Franklin's shop, 24–25; in *Pennsylvania Gazette*, 7, 19, 24–25, 90–91, 113, 114; revenue of, 24; of slave trade, 24–25, 90, 91; taxation of, 166; *see also* runaways, advertisements for

Advice to a Young Tradesman (Franklin), 107

Africa: enslavement in, 190, 197, 218–19; *see also* slavery; slave trade

African Americans, *see* blacks; slavery; slaves

Akan (Coromantee) people, 40

Albany Congress of 1754, 142

Algerian piracy, 238

All Slave-keepers That Keep the Innocent in Bondage (Lay), 81

almanacs, 102–103, 112, 169; English anti-astrological, 102–103; of Godfreys, 104, 105; *see also Poor Richard's Almanack*

American Magazine, or a Monthly View of the Political State of the British Colonies, 113–14

American Philosophical Society, 120

American Revolution, 18, 145, 155, 180, 210–24, 225, 238, 241; antislavery movement linked to, 177, 181; Benny Mecom's death in, 131, 172, 226; critical period in, 228–29, 232; Franco-American alliance in, 217; Hessian mercenaries in, 214, 221; loyalist blacks in, 210–13, 214, 221–22; peace negotiations of, 221; *see also* Constitutional Convention

Americanus essay, 140–41

American Weekly Mercury, 58–59, 79, 113–14; *Busybody* series in, 75; postal delivery of, 112; religious issues in, 78

Amistad case, xi

Andrews, Jedediah, 79

Anglicanism (Church of England), 34, 36, 38, 41, 48, 63, 75

Anthony (runaway slave), 9

Anthony Afterwit essay, 106

antiastrology, 102–103

Antigua, 116, 121, 130; Benny Mecom in, 130–33; deaths in, 130, 131

Antigua Gazette, 131

antislavery movement, x–xiii, 18, 57, 117, 175–82, 186, 190, 192–204, 211; American Revolution as linked to, 177, 181; arguments of, 9, 176–77, 193, 195–98; Congress petitioned by, 235–38; foundational, x; Franklin's conversion to, 25, 181–82, 193–98, 199–204, 214, 217,